Secrets of Computer Espionage: Tactics and Countermeasures

Joel McNamara

WILEY

Wiley Publishing, Inc.

Secrets of Computer Espionage: Tactics and Countermeasures

Published by
Wiley Publishing, Inc.
10475 Crosspoint Boulevard
Indianapolis, IN 46256
www.wiley.com

Secrets of Computer Espionage:
Tactics and Countermeasures

About the Author

Joel McNamara has over 20 years of experience in the computer industry. Since 1995 he has consulted on computer security and privacy issues. He maintains the Complete Unofficial TEMPEST Information Page (a Web site devoted to demystifying classified government surveillance technology), wrote the popular open-source privacy tool *Private Idaho* (an easy-to-use front-end for PGP and anonymous remailers), and is credited with developing one of the first Microsoft macro viruses and then publicizing the security risks. In his spare time Joel competes in ultramarathons and other endurance sports, and volunteers as an EMT on a disaster medical assistance team.

Credits

ACQUISITIONS EDITOR
Katie Feltman

PROJECT EDITOR
Mark Enochs

TECHNICAL EDITOR
Russell Shumway

COPY EDITOR
Nancy Sixsmith

EDITORIAL MANAGER
Mary Beth Wakefield

VICE PRESIDENT & EXECUTIVE GROUP PUBLISHER
Richard Swadley

VICE PRESIDENT AND EXECUTIVE PUBLISHER
Bob Ipsen

EXECUTIVE EDITOR
Carol Long

EXECUTIVE EDITORIAL DIRECTOR
Mary Bednarek

PROJECT COORDINATOR
Dale White

GRAPHICS AND PRODUCTION SPECIALISTS
Beth Brooks
Stephanie D. Jumper
Heather Pope

QUALITY CONTROL TECHNICIAN
John Tyler Connoley
John Greenough

PERMISSIONS EDITOR
Laura Moss

MEDIA DEVELOPMENT SPECIALIST
Travis Silvers

ILLUSTRATOR
Karl Brandt

PROOFREADING AND INDEXING
TECHBOOKS Production Services

Acknowledgments

To all the folks at Wiley, especially my acquisitions editor Katie Feltman and project editor Mark Enochs, thank you for your time and patience in shepherding a new author through his first book. And to Nancy Sixsmith, my copy editor, and Russ Shumway, my technical editor, thank you for your eagle eyes and insights.

I'm very much in debt to my friend Jeff Madden, who has been trying to get me to write a book for a long time. Thanks for your encouragement and volunteering to play unofficial literary agent and publishing industry advisor for me.

Thanks to my wife Darcy for all of your support over the years, and especially during the last six all-consuming months when I was working on this project.

And finally, I likely would never have written this book if it weren't for my father Doug, who started my interest in espionage pretty darn young by taking me to my first James Bond movie when I was six.

Contents at a Glance

Acknowledgments vii

Introduction. xvii

Chapter 1   Spies 1
Chapter 2   Spying and the Law 25
Chapter 3   Black Bag Jobs 47
Chapter 4   Breaching the System 67
Chapter 5   Searching for Evidence 95
Chapter 6   Unprotecting Data 135
Chapter 7   Copying Data 163
Chapter 8   Snooping with Keyloggers 177
Chapter 9   Spying with Trojan Horses 205
Chapter 10   Network Eavesdropping 227
Chapter 11   802.11b Wireless Network Eavesdropping 259
Chapter 12   Spying on Electronic Devices 289
Chapter 13   Advanced Computer Espionage 313

Appendix A: What's on the Web Site. 341

Index. 343

Contents

Acknowledgments vii

Introduction xvii

Chapter 1   **Spies** 1
Getting to Know Spies 1
What Spies Are After and Who They Are 2
    Business Spies — Economic Espionage 4
    Bosses — Employee Monitoring 6
    Cops — Law Enforcement Investigations 7
    Private Eyes and Consultants — Private Investigations 9
    Spooks — Government-Sponsored Intelligence Gathering 11
    Criminals — Ill-Gotten Gains 14
    Whistleblowers — For the Public Good 15
    Friends and Family — with Friends like These 16
Determining Your Level of Paranoia 18
Risk Analysis 101 20
    Five-Step Risk Analysis 21
Summary 24

Chapter 2   **Spying and the Law** 25
Laws that Relate to Spying 25
    Omnibus Crime Control and Safe Streets Act of 1968
      (Title III — Wiretap Act) 26
    Foreign Intelligence Surveillance Act of 1978 27
    Electronic Communications Privacy Act of 1986 29
    Computer Fraud and Abuse Act of 1986 32
    Economic Espionage Act of 1996 34
    State Laws 34
Implications of the USA Patriot Act of 2001 35
    Wiretap and Stored Communications Access Acts 36
    Foreign Intelligence Surveillance Act 36
    Computer Fraud and Abuse Act 37
    Other Provisions 39
    State Laws 39
The Realities of Enforcement 39
Civil versus Criminal Court 41
Bosses and Employees — Legal Spying 42
Legal Issues with Family Members 43
Summary 45

Chapter 3   Black Bag Jobs 47
              A Look Inside the Black Bag 47
                  Physical and Network Black Bag Jobs 48
                  Planned and Opportunistic Black Bag Jobs 49
              Spy Tactics 50
                  Spy Games 50
                  Inside a Government Black Bag Job 51
              Exploiting the Vulnerabilities 55
                  Researching and Planning the Operation 55
                  Gaining Entry 57
                  Documenting the Scene 60
              Countermeasures 62
                  Physical Security 63
                  Security Policies 64
              Summary 66
Chapter 4   Breaching the System 67
              Spy Tactics 67
                  Exploiting the Vulnerabilities 68
                  System-Breaching Tools 83
              Countermeasures 89
                  Security Settings 89
                  Effective Passwords 93
                  Encryption 93
              Summary 94
Chapter 5   Searching for Evidence 95
              Legal Spying 95
                  How Computer Cops Work 95
                  Seizure 98
                  Forensic Duplication 100
                  Examination 101
              Spy Tactics 102
                  Exploiting the Vulnerabilities 102
                  Evidence-Gathering Tools 117
              Countermeasures 122
                  Encryption 122
                  Steganography 127
                  File Wipers 130
                  Evidence-Eliminating Software 133
              Summary 133
Chapter 6   Unprotecting Data 135
              Spy Tactics 135
                  Exploiting Vulnerabilities 136
                  Cracking Tools 146

Countermeasures 153
  Strong Encryption 153
  Password Policies 154
  Password Lists 156
  Password Alternatives 157
  Summary 161

Chapter 7   **Copying Data** 163
Spy Tactics 163
  Use Available Resources 164
  Use Compression Tools 164
  Consider Other Data 164
  Understand What's Involved in Copying Data 164
Storage Media to Target 165
  Floppy Disks 166
  CD-R/CD-RWs 166
  DVDs 168
  ZIP Disks 169
  Memory Storage Devices 169
  Hard Drives 171
  Tape Backup Systems 174
Alternate Methods of Copying Data 174
  Transferring Data Over a Network 174
  Digital Cameras 175
  Summary 176

Chapter 8   **Snooping with Keyloggers** 177
An Introduction to Keyloggers 177
Spy Tactics 178
  Exploiting the Vulnerabilities 179
  Keylogger Tools 186
Countermeasures 191
  Viewing Installed Programs 191
  Examining Startup Programs 191
  Examining Running Processes 193
  Monitoring File Writes 195
  Removing Visual Basic Runtimes 196
  Searching for Strings 196
  Using Personal Firewalls 196
  Using File Integrity and Registry Checkers 196
  Using Keylogger-Detection Software 197
  Using Sniffers 198
  Detecting Hardware Keyloggers 199
  Exploiting Keylogger Passwords 200
  Using Linux 200
  Watching for Unusual Crashes 201
  Removing Keyloggers 202
  Summary 202

Chapter 9   Spying with Trojan Horses 205
             Spy Tactics 205
                 Exploiting the Vulnerabilities 206
                 Trojan Horse Tools 216
             Countermeasures 221
                 Network Defenses................................. 221
                 Using Registry Monitors and File-Integrity Checkers 222
                 Using Antivirus Software 223
                 Using Trojan Detection Software 223
                 Removing Trojan Horses 224
                 Using Non-Microsoft Software 224
             Summary 225
Chapter 10   Network Eavesdropping 227
             Introduction to Network Spying 227
                 Types of Network Attacks 227
                 Network Attack Origin Points 228
                 Information Compromised During Network Attacks 229
                 Broadband Risks 230
             Spy Tactics 232
                 Exploiting the Vulnerabilities 232
                 Network-Information and -Eavesdropping Tools 242
             Countermeasures 246
                 Applying Operating System and Application Updates 246
                 Using Intrusion Detection Systems 246
                 Using Firewalls 247
                 Running a Virtual Private Network 250
                 Monitoring Network Connections 251
                 Using Sniffers 251
                 Using Port and Vulnerability Scanners 252
                 Encrypting Your E-Mail 253
                 Encrypting Your Instant Messages 253
                 Using Secure Protocols 254
                 Don't Trust "Strange" Computers and Networks 254
                 Hardening Windows File Sharing 254
                 Using Secure Web E-Mail 255
                 Using Anonymous Remailers 255
                 Using Web Proxies 256
             Summary 257
Chapter 11   802.11b Wireless Network Eavesdropping 259
             An Introduction to Wireless Networks 259
                 History of the Wireless Network 259
             Spy Tactics 260
                 Exploiting the Vulnerabilities 261
                 Wireless-Network-Eavesdropping Tools 266

Countermeasures 284
    Audit Your Own Network 284
    Position Antennas Correctly 284
    Detect Wireless Discovery Tools 285
    Fool Discovery Tools 285
    Enable WEP 286
    Change WEP Keys Regularly 286
    Authenticate MAC Addresses 286
    Rename the SSID 286
    Disable Broadcast SSID 287
    Change the Default AP Password 287
    Use Static IP Addresses versus DHCP 287
    Locate APs Outside Firewalls 287
    Use VPNs 287
    Don't Rely on Distance as Security 288
    Turn Off the AP 288
Summary 288

Chapter 12   Spying on Electronic Devices 289
Office Devices 289
    Fax Machines 289
    Shredders 292
Communication Devices 294
    Telephones 294
    Cellular Phones 299
    Answering Machines and Voice-Mail 303
    Pagers 305
Consumer Electronics 307
    PDAs 307
    Digital Cameras 309
    GPS Units 309
    Video Game Consoles 310
    MP3 Players 311
    Television Digital Recorders 311
Summary 311

Chapter 13   Advanced Computer Espionage 313
TEMPEST — Electromagnetic Eavesdropping 313
    Emanation Monitoring: Fact or Fiction? 314
    EMSEC Countermeasures 318
Optical TEMPEST — LEDs and Reflected Light 319
HIJACK and NONSTOP 319
ECHELON — Global Surveillance 320
    How ECHELON Works 321
    ECHELON Controversy and Countermeasures 322

Carnivore/DCS-1000 325
   An Overview of Carnivore 325
   Carnivore Controversy and Countermeasures 326
Magic Lantern 327
Modified Applications and Operating System Components ... 329
Intelligence-Gathering Viruses and Worms 332
   Viruses and Worms 333
   Countermeasures 336
Surveillance Cameras 336
   Webcams 337
   Commercial Surveillance Cameras 339
Summary 340

Appendix A: What's on the Web Site 341

Index 343

Introduction

"Information is the oxygen of the modern age. It seeps through the walls topped by barbed wire, it wafts across the electrified borders."
— Ronald Reagan

What This Book Is About

What Ronald Reagan (the "Great Communicator") didn't mention is that sometimes information is also highly sought after, and people will go to great lengths to get it.

Maybe you don't have anything to hide, but nosy co-workers, family-member snoops, malicious crackers, corporate spies, law enforcement officers, system auditors, private investigators, and jealous boyfriends or girlfriends still might be interested in what's on your computer. And if you do have something to hide, what happens if they find out about it?

You don't need CIA training or an NSA-sized budget to conduct computer espionage. A quick search on the Internet will turn up hundreds of available and affordable programs, with complete instructions, which can turn the average person into a digital James Bond, and these tools are being used daily to legally and illegally spy on computer users.

It's really hard to say how much computer espionage takes place on a day-to-day basis (if someone ever tries to give you a hard number, take it with a healthy dose of skepticism because it's just a guess). The media do a pretty good job of reporting on high-profile espionage cases, but the only reason we know about these incidents is because someone got caught. It's also difficult to gauge how much spying is going on because in many circumstances businesses and government agencies don't go out of their way to publicize successful or failed eavesdropping attempts due to negative public relations. (Stockholders aren't too happy and confident when they learn that someone breached corporate security and gained access to research and development information for future products.)

Although we don't know how much computer spying is actually taking place, there are some known data points that can help us better understand the potential scope:

✓ Computers are increasingly used to store sensitive and confidential data (whether it is of a personal, business, or government nature). This information is faster and easier to copy compared with other nonelectronic storage media such as paper.

✓ There are numerous operating-system and application vulnerabilities and many easy-to-use software tools that are designed to exploit the vulnerabilities.

✓ Over the past several years an increasing number of computers are connected to the Internet, increasing their attack potential from remote locations.

✓ In many publicized cases, it's been shown that the greatest risks come from insiders. External attacks, although more publicized and worried about, are less likely than someone on the inside compromising your computer, whether in a home or corporate setting.

When you start thinking about these things, you begin to realize there is some serious potential for someone to engage in a modernized version of what's been called the second oldest profession. The risk increases with the large amount of cracking and spying information and tools that are readily available on the Internet, which makes it very easy for anyone to become an amateur computer spy. (Indeed, the risks from amateurs may even be greater because there are more of them, and an amateur can often do as much damage as a professional can on a computer that hasn't been properly secured.)

This book discusses the tools and techniques that both amateur and professional spies use to compromise data, as well as countermeasures for defeating them. Crackers commonly use some of these techniques, particularly the ones involving networks, but a number of espionage attacks rely on having physical access to a computer. (Many books on computer security gloss over such methods, stating only that if an opponent has physical access to your computer, the game is over. To me, this generalization is too broad. It's important to know how a computer can be compromised in case someone has access to it. Knowing this will help you better prepare to defend your computer against physical attacks.)

Most of the time, this book focuses on Microsoft Windows systems (because Windows currently has a dominant market share and is what most people use). However, there are a number of general concepts and techniques that apply to just about any computer system, so if you're using Linux, OpenBSD, or Mac OS, you'll still find this book useful.

Who This Book Is for

This book is for anyone who's concerned that someone might be spying or possibly wants to spy on his or her computer. This ranges from individual PC users to system administrators responsible for enterprise security.

If your job involves gathering evidence from computers (in a sense, a legal form of espionage), and you're a law enforcement officer, system administrator, or forensic examiner, you'll also find this book is a practical addition to your library.

You don't need to have a top-secret clearance or a strong background in cryptography or computer security to read this book. Both technical and nontechnical readers will find useful information that helps them better understand espionage risks and how to defend their computers from all sorts of different types of spies.

How This Book Is Organized

Most of the chapters in the book are divided into two sections: "Spy Tactics" and "Countermeasures." "Spy Tactics" describes the vulnerabilities, exploits, tools, and techniques for compromising data. For example in the "Spy Tactics" section of Chapter 4, "Breaching the System," you'll learn about how a spy bypasses BIOS passwords and Windows logon authentication.

In many of these sections, you'll be asked to assume the role of a spy who is interested in covertly accessing some type of information. This isn't meant to be a tutorial for electronic eavesdroppers, but to simply get yourself in the mindset of someone interested in gaining unauthorized access to your data. Thinking like a spy who is determined to steal sensitive data is a powerful way of figuring out what you need to do to shore up your defensive measures.

That brings us to the "Countermeasures" section, in which you'll learn about practical tools and methods for defeating spy techniques and tools. As an example, you'll learn about using strong passwords, Windows security settings, and other ways to keep data safe from a spy attempting to breach your system in the "Countermeasures" section of Chapter 4.

The book contains a number of sidebars (like the one below) with real stories about spies, tactics they employ, vulnerabilities they seek to exploit, and countermeasures you can implement to protect your system from them. The sidebars are written to inform, educate, and entertain. There are also a large number of Web site links listed throughout the book for tools and more detailed information sources.

Countermeasures: OODA Loop

John Boyd was a United States Air Force fighter pilot during the Korean War. Boyd wondered why almost any time the Americans engaged in aerial combat with the Chinese, they prevailed. Compared with the F-86s the U.S. pilots were flying, the Russian-designed MiG-15s were both faster and more maneuverable. Although pilot skill and training obviously made a difference, there was some other factor at play that accounted for the 10:1 American victory ratio.

Although from a performance standpoint the MiGs could out-turn and out-climb the F-86s, the American planes had a larger canopy bubble that gave pilots a better view of their surroundings. Additionally, the controls on the F-86 made it more nimble. Because of these two factors, Boyd hypothesized that a good pilot in an F-86 could observe more effectively and decide and act more quickly than a pilot of equivalent skill flying a MiG-15.

This observation helped Boyd develop a concept known as the OODA or Boyd Loop. OODA stands for Observe, Orient, Decide, and Act. Whenever someone is in a state where he needs to make a decision, he unconsciously goes through an OODA cycle. First, he observes the situation, he orients himself to it, makes a decision based on past experience, and finally acts.

Boyd postulated that in circumstances of conflict, if you could speed up your own OODA loop while slowing down the opponent's loop, you would prevail. The interesting thing with OODA loops is after a step is interrupted, the cycle resets. For example, if you interrupt an opponent's cycle after he's made a decision but before he acts, he will start all over again with observing the present situation.

(Boyd went on to help develop the F-16 fighter, and his philosophies on tactics and strategy are incorporated into current Army and Marine maneuver warfare doctrines, as well as business theory. He's regarded as one of the 20th century's most brilliant military strategists. You can learn more about Boyd by visiting www.belisarius.com.)

This book is designed to help speed up your own OODA loop when it comes to dealing with computer espionage. At the very least it will help you better orient yourself to possible threats, and if you discover that you're the victim of computer spying, you might consider using variations of some of the countermeasures to get inside your opponent's OODA loop in an attempt to turn things to your advantage.

Icon boxes appear in the text throughout the book to indicate important or especially helpful items. Here's a list of the icon boxes and their functions:

This icon box provides additional or critical information and technical data on the current topic.

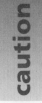

This icon box points out useful techniques and helpful hints to avoid pitfalls.

This handy icon box points you to a place where you can find more information about a particular topic.

A Few Caveats

Before starting to read this book, please keep these few caveats in mind:

- ✓ **Links.** URLs, links, Web pages, or whatever you like to call them that are mentioned were current when the book went to press. If you've used the Web at all, you know that links can unfortunately be temporary. If a link doesn't work, there should be enough information in a paragraph to select bits of text to plug into Google (or whatever your favorite search engine is) to find what you're looking for. There's also a companion Web site that goes with the book that provides current links and saves you from typing in long URLs. It's at www.wiley.com/compbooks/mcnamara.

- ✓ **Prices.** Throughout the book, there are many sections that discuss tools, and I try to list prices for different pieces of hardware and software (I happen to be pretty frugal and like free or cheap effective tools, so you'll see a bias there). Most books don't mention prices, which is something I find rather annoying, especially when I get all excited about some cool product and then find out the price and realize there's no way it's going to fit into a departmental or personal budget. Although I realize that costs fluctuate and there will be a several-month lag between when I finish this book and when it appears in print, the prices should at least give you a ballpark idea of how much something is going to cost. Prices reflect suggested retail costs as of the beginning of 2003.

✓ **Tool sources.** A number of the tools listed in the book are available in what some consider the more unsavory neighborhoods of the Internet. If you download a tool from a cracker Web site or even one of the more reputable security sites, always take a few simple precautions. Be sure you're running current antivirus and anti-Trojan horse software, and test the tool on a noncritical computer (preferably running a personal firewall) to make sure it doesn't do anything malicious.

✓ **Legal.** Throughout the book, especially in Chapter 2, "Spying and the Law," you'll find general discussions of various legal topics. However, I'm not a lawyer, and I don't play one on TV. If you have specific questions about laws and penalties, always seek qualified legal counsel.

Chapter 1

Spies

"I could have been a devastating spy, I think, but I didn't want to be a devastating spy. I wanted to get a little money and to get out of it."
— Robert Hanssen, FBI agent and convicted Soviet spy

Getting to Know Spies

Computer spies typically don't wear trench coats. They don't dress in tight black clothes and hang upside down from trapeze wires over your keyboard. They probably aren't named Boris and don't speak with heavy Slavic accents. Most of them aren't even hackers or crackers, and likely wouldn't know the difference between a rootkit and root beer. If computer spies don't match the popular media's perceptions, just who are they?

As with most avocations, computer espionage is divided into the amateurs and the professionals.

Amateurs are casual spies. Although they may have very good reasons for snooping, their livelihood doesn't depend on it. These spies have a bit more experience with computers than the average user. That doesn't mean they're extremely technical; it means only that they have taken the time to learn about various technologies that can be used for computer eavesdropping and then applied that knowledge for espionage purposes. Learning about spying tools and then acquiring them is only a point and click away with an Internet connection. When you think about these types of spies, don't picture Tom Cruise or Sandra Bullock. Instead think of your boss, coworker, spouse, children, or the neighbor next door.

Professional spies tend to have more technical experience than the amateurs. One aspect or another of the professionals' jobs is to spy on people. This spying can be legal, as in the case of a law enforcement officer collecting intelligence for a child pornography criminal case, or illegal, in the case of a spy hired to obtain trade secrets from a corporation's network. Although these spies use some of the same tools and technologies that the amateurs use, they have a deeper understanding of the technology as well as access to more advanced and sophisticated eavesdropping tools. As with amateurs, you usually can't tell a professional spy by his or her appearance. Consider Aldrich Ames or Robert Hanssen: white, middle-class, average-looking CIA and FBI insiders who successfully spied for the Russians but blended in with society for years. Again, professional computer spies don't match the popular media's romanticized versions of espionage reality — although perhaps one or two might have a partner in crime named Natasha.

There are two reasons why it's important to have insights into the different types of spies:

✓ **To understand the technical capabilities and limitations of a potential adversary.** This is obvious because you want to make sure that your own security measures can withstand a spy's attempt to breach them.

✓ **So you can put yourself in the spy's shoes.** Throughout this book, there are sections that present spying tactics, specifically regarding how people spy on computers. In most of these sections, you're asked to put on the spy's trench coat so you can better assess your own security; to fully protect yourself, however, you need to know not only the tools and the techniques, but also the mindset of a spy. Popular culture has the saying, "What would _____ (Jesus, Gandhi; fill in your favorite wise role model) do?" When you review your security, you need to ask, "What would Corporate Spy (or whichever type of spy may be a threat) do?"

The famous Chinese military strategist Sun Tzu said, "If you know the enemy and know yourself, you need not fear the result of a hundred battles. If you know yourself but not the enemy, for every victory gained you will also suffer a defeat. If you know neither the enemy nor yourself, you will succumb in every battle."

Throughout this chapter, the concepts of knowing the enemy, knowing yourself, and knowing both the enemy and yourself are applied to computer spying.

What Spies Are After and Who They Are

Let's start with knowing the enemy. Computer espionage is about the purposeful discovery of information or evidence. If you use a dictionary definition (in this case, the _American Heritage Dictionary of the English Language, Fourth Edition_), information is "knowledge of specific events or situations that has been gathered or received by communication, intelligence, or news." Evidence, on the other hand, is "a thing or things helpful in forming a conclusion or judgment." An industrial spy may be looking for secret information on a Microsoft project manager's laptop that specifically relates to the company's future and hush-hush Longhorn operating system. A wife who suspects her husband of having an online affair may be looking for evidence in e-mail messages in an attempt to confirm her suspicions. Depending on what the information is, it could evolve into evidence. For example, a phone number stored in a PDA address book could belong to a known drug dealer and become supporting evidence for a criminal case.

Remember that spying is a purposeful activity. Although the suspicious wife may have stumbled across evidence that her husband was cheating because he accidentally left an Instant Messenger window open on the family computer, that's not spying. She wasn't actively seeking the information.

The types of information and evidence gathered can be very targeted or generalized, depending on what the spy is trying to accomplish. Perhaps he is looking only for financial information that relates to an upcoming merger and will be content with snooping through spreadsheet files with accounting information. On the other hand, a government intelligence agency may examine the entire contents of a hard drive that belonged to a terrorist, seeking not only evidence, but any information that may relate to future terrorist attacks.

In addition to information and evidence, there are two other important concepts in computer espionage: The activity is typically unauthorized and unknown. In most cases, you aren't going to give explicit or implicit permission to have someone snoop through your computer. Exceptions might be in the workplace in which employee monitoring takes place or when you tell the friendly police officer that you don't have anything to hide, you don't need a lawyer, and certainly he can look at your computer. Also in some types of law enforcement investigations you won't have a say if a court has granted permission to a police agency to spy on your computer because of suspected illegal activities on your part. Remember that *unauthorized* doesn't necessarily mean *illegal*. Although breaking into a computer network to steal trade secrets clearly violates a number of laws, placing a keylogger on your son's computer without his permission to see if he talks to his friends about doing drugs would not be illegal, though it may be unethical to some people.

The second element of computer spying is that if you're the target, you don't know it's taking place until perhaps after the fact. Unlike clothing manufacturers, eavesdroppers don't go around leaving tags on computers that read "Snooped on by Spy #39." Sometimes, spies do leave tracks, but they usually aren't that obvious. Whoever is spying doesn't want you to know they are looking for information or evidence. Exceptions would be a publicized employee-monitoring program or the government's ECHELON data surveillance system (discussed later in this chapter), which is known about — much to the chagrin of those running the program.

ECHELON is an example of the government's frequent "cult of secrecy" attitude. Although the existence of ECHELON has been exposed, the government steadfastly refuses to acknowledge its existence. For more on ECHELON and other data surveillance systems, turn to Chapter 13.

So far, this discussion has all been about what spies are generally after, but we still haven't answered Sun Tzu's question of knowing who the enemy is. This is important because it gives us insights into their motivations and methods. Thinking like the bad guys is a valuable exercise in helping you protect yourself from them.

In general, spies can be lumped into seven different categories:

✓ Business spies

✓ Bosses

✓ Cops

✓ Private eyes and consultants

✓ Spooks

✓ Criminals

✓ Whistleblowers

✓ Friends and family

Let's take a quick look into the world of each type of these spies to better understand who they are and what they are after.

Business Spies — Economic Espionage

Economic espionage is a large, yet often ignored problem. Trade publications and organizations and the news media have been warning businesses about the dangers of economic espionage, formerly called industrial espionage, since the 1980s. The warnings seem to have fallen on deaf ears.

Consider these key points of a study released in 2002 by the American Society for Industrial Security, U.S. Chamber of Commerce, and PricewaterhouseCoopers, a survey of Fortune 1000 corporations and 600 small to mid-sized U.S. companies:

- ✓ Forty percent of the companies that responded to the survey reported having episodes of known or suspected loss of proprietary data. (Cutting away the jargon, that means someone on the inside or outside spied on them and stole company information.)

- ✓ Proprietary information and intellectual property losses accounted for between $53 billion and $59 billion.

- ✓ Economic spies are looking for information; they most commonly target research and development, customer lists and related data, and financial data.

- ✓ Despite the potential impact of possibly successful attacks, only 55 percent of the responding companies said their management was concerned about information loss and were taking precautions to prevent it. The implication of this is a significant number of managers underestimate or don't understand the risks and costs of data theft.

Companies suffering economic espionage attacks don't just suffer simple financial losses. They also have to contend with eroded competitive advantages, legal fees in the case of litigation, and diminished stockholder and public trust if an attack is publicized (which many are not publicizing for this reason alone).

Business spying isn't confined just to large corporations, either. Smaller companies, from mom-and-pop retailers to light manufacturers that operate at thinner margins without the cash reserves of a larger corporation, may actually suffer more significant damage from economic espionage.

Former employees, domestic and foreign competitors, and on-site contractors are the usual perpetrators of economic spying. (It's worth noting that economic espionage is very different from competitive intelligence. Competitive or business intelligence is practiced by using legal and open source methods. Economic espionage is where illegal means are used to obtain information. Granted, at times there can be gray areas, but most business intelligence professionals adhere to a fairly strict set of ethics.)

For more information on the differences between legitimate competitive intelligence and illegal espionage, visit the Society of Competitive Intelligence Professionals Web site at www.scip.org.

Although movies and TV shows portray corporate spies as shadowy mercenaries who cleverly break into super-secure locations, the reality is that insiders who have access to unsecured information are responsible for most economic espionage. Current or former employees with greed or revenge as motivation are much more of a threat than professional spies hired by a competitor.

Spies: Niku versus Business Engine

In August of 2002, several dozen FBI agents raided the offices of Business Engine, a Silicon Valley software company specializing in Web-based collaboration tools. The raid was prompted when competitor Niku Corporation discovered in its server logs that someone with an IP address that mapped back to Business Engine had used Niku passwords to access the company's network more than 6,000 times. More than 1,000 documents had been downloaded during the intrusions, including information about upcoming features, lists of potential customers, pricing, and sales call schedules. Subsequent investigations revealed that since October 2001, outsiders had logged onto the internal Niku network, using up to 15 different accounts and passwords to access proprietary documents.

As of late September 2002, the once-thriving Niku was on the brink of being delisted by NASDAQ because of its low stock value. It doesn't take a Harvard MBA to speculate that an extensive economic espionage campaign could have contributed to Niku's ill fortunes.

Niku has filed suit against Business Engine, and it will be interesting to watch the details of this case emerge.

The problem isn't confined only to lower-level employees. Jose Ignacio Lopez, the head of purchasing for General Motors, abruptly resigned in 1993 and took a job with Volkswagen. GM later accused Lopez of masterminding the theft of more than 20 boxes of research, sales, and marketing documents. Included were blueprints for an assembly plant GM hoped would displace VW's dominance in emerging small-car markets. In 1997, the case ended when VW admitted no wrongdoing, but settled the civil suit by paying GM $100 million and offering to buy $1 billion of GM parts over the next seven years. German prosecutors eventually dropped industrial espionage charges against Lopez, but ordered him to donate a quarter of a million dollars to charity.

Outsider attacks still occur though, and are either committed by an employee or agent of a competitor. Outside attacks typically fall into two categories:

✓ **Opportunistic attack.** A competitor may casually see if information may be easily accessible, akin to twisting a doorknob to see whether it's locked. Information is stolen if there's not much of a risk of discovery or involves little effort. An example of this attack is a spy using a port scanner or vulnerability-assessment tool to see if there are any holes he can exploit to enter a corporate network. If exploitable vulnerabilities are discovered, a targeted attack may be launched.

✓ **Targeted attack.** A targeted attack is a serious attempt to steal information. The spy has a specific goal and employs a variety of techniques to get what he wants. When the monetary stakes are high, a large amount of money and resources may be committed to a spying operation.

Because computers are used to store all sorts of corporate information, they present a prime target for business spies. Networks, laptops, desktop PCs, and PDAs are all vulnerable to attack.

The technical skills that business spies have range from eavesdroppers with minimal skills, such as copying a confidential file to a floppy disk, to skilled technicians who can easily bypass a firewall to access a corporate database.

There are strict penalties for economic espionage in the United States. Turn to Chapter 2 for details.

Bosses — Employee Monitoring

Employee monitoring in the United States is growing rapidly. In the American Management Association's (AMA) 2001 survey on Workplace Monitoring & Surveillance, 77.7 percent of major U.S. companies stated that they recorded and reviewed employee on-the-job communications and activities. This amount is double what the AMA reported in its first monitoring report released in 1997.

If you work for someone else, there's a good chance the boss is spying on you. That means your e-mail, Web surfing, instant messaging, and hard drives could all be under scrutiny. Employee privacy really doesn't contribute to the bottom line and in fact may detract from it. Employers are interested in finding evidence that you aren't being productive or are somehow violating company policy.

How can companies get away with this?

When you're dealing with a government entity, you have a series of constitutional rights that protect your privacy. When it comes to private businesses and the workplace, however, these rights don't apply. Because your time is being paid for by an employer and the computer equipment you're using belongs to the company, you shouldn't have any expectation of privacy when it comes to your computer activities.

Anytime an employer has a compelling interest in what you do at work because of legal, productivity, performance, or security reasons, he or she can monitor your computer, as well as your telephone, coffee breaks, and just about anything else short of using the company restrooms.

Monitoring is either accomplished at the server, where administrators can view logs or examine exchanged electronic messages, or at the desktop PC, where keyboard-monitoring software can be installed.

Keyloggers are discussed in detail in Chapter 8.

Typically, the corporate IT staff or an outside consultant is responsible for implementing the monitoring program and will be fairly technically skilled. Consider that if you try to defeat an employee-monitoring program, you might end up calling attention to yourself and presenting a personal challenge to a bored system administrator to see what you're up to.

Spies: Justified Snooping

Employee monitoring, whether by using video cameras, recording phone calls, or monitoring computers, is big in corporate America.

A driving factor for this is that a number of local, state, and federal court decisions have ruled that employers are responsible for employee wrongdoing while they are at work. Companies use this as one rationale for implementing employee-monitoring programs. Employers can also justify workplace monitoring as part of reducing legal liability.

There have been a number of high-profile monitoring cases. In 1995, a subsidiary of Chevron was sued for sexual harassment over an e-mail that circulated through the company entitled "25 Reasons Why Beer Is Better Than Women." The case was settled out of court for $2.2 million, and Chevron now monitors employee e-mail. In July 2000, Dow Chemical fired 50 employees and disciplined 200 others for accessing online pornography. In October 1999, 40 employees at Xerox were fired for surfing forbidden Web sites (Xerox monitors Web usage of all of its more than 90,000 employees worldwide).

Whether employees like it or not, employee monitoring has become a commonly used management tool.

Despite the rather Orwellian overtones of employee monitoring, most responsible companies will at least be upfront about it. Monitoring programs should be publicized in employee handbooks, employment agreements, and computer banners. Letting employees know that a monitoring program is in place in most cases is a better deterrent against bad behavior than being sneaky.

The coming years will likely bring legislation at the state level that increases workplace privacy, but for now it's important to realize that while at work, your electronic on-the-job privacy can be invaded at your employer's discretion. While there are countermeasures you can take against snooping bosses, the best option is to simply keep your personal life separate from the computer activities of your day job.

Cops — Law Enforcement Investigations

Aside from employee monitoring, another form of legitimate spying is performed by law enforcement. While most cops would never consider themselves spies or think they'd be involved in espionage, it's all a matter of semantics. Intelligence activities, surveillance, and investigations are all much more socially acceptable terms for spying.

Cops are primarily interested in finding evidence that you've committed some crime. From a computer standpoint, evidence may be collected before or after you've been charged with the crime.

If you're under investigation, your network activity might be monitored (including e-mail, instant messaging, and Web browsing), and under certain circumstances, officers might gain physical access to your computer to look at its contents or place monitoring hardware or software on it.

If you've been charged with a crime, almost certainly your computer will be seized and will undergo forensic examination. In this examination, a technician searches through your hard drive and any other storage media to find any evidence that may relate to this specific crime or possibly other crimes.

Computer forensics, the process of gathering evidence from computers, is discussed at length in Chapter 5.

When it comes to computer spying, police officers need to follow a very strict set of rules and guidelines. The Constitution gives citizens a number of rights that protect them from unreasonable government intrusion, whether they are criminals or not. For law enforcement investigations, this protection requires getting a court order or search warrant from a judge before the computer surveillance activities can begin.

Following the terrorist attacks of September 11, 2001, however, Congress has recently granted broader investigative powers to law enforcement agencies.

Expanded powers under the USA Patriot Act (USAPA) as they relate to computer spying are discussed in Chapter 2.

Despite having to follow strict legal rules for evidence collection, individual law enforcement officers have abused their power in the past, whether by design or accident, and stepped outside the law. An example is a secret internal FBI memo that was leaked in October 2002 that described "mistakes," such as intercepting innocent citizen's e-mail, recording the wrong phone conversations, illegally videotaping suspects, and performing unauthorized searches. Although most of the time law enforcement agencies abide by set rules of engagement, don't be surprised if sometimes they don't.

How competent a cop will be at computer spying varies tremendously. Generally, law enforcement is completely understaffed when it comes to technicians who have the skills and knowledge to effectively collect and analyze electronic evidence. Most cops aren't that savvy when it comes to computers, and the minority that are savvy are overburdened with large caseloads where electronic evidence is involved. Police agencies tend to hire from within and then send officers outside to get the training they need to perform their new job duties. Because of higher-paying positions in private industry and the differences in police and high-tech culture, very few skilled computer industry people who would be excellent at evidence gathering are attracted to law enforcement.

As a general rule of thumb, the larger the police agency, the greater the chance of having a technical specialist available to deal with computers. Federal law enforcement agencies such as the FBI and Secret Service have the most highly trained personnel, but again, their skills vary on an individual basis.

Busted: Good Cop, Bad Cop?

During the summer of 2000, the FBI was investigating a series of e-commerce site computer break-ins in which credit card information was being stolen. The trail pointed to crackers in Russia.

FBI Special Agent Michael Schuler had a good idea who the suspects were and designed an elaborate sting operation to catch the perpetrators. In November 2000, Vasily Gorshkov and Alexey Ivanov came to the United States to interview for jobs with a Seattle computer security company called Invita. Invita employees asked the pair to demonstrate their skills. In the process, they logged on to their own computers in Chelyabinsk, Russia. Instead of getting stock options, the two Russians found themselves in the stockade. Invita was a fake company set up by the FBI, and the interviewers were all FBI agents.

Gorshkov and Ivanov didn't know it, but the FBI had installed a sniffer on the computer they used to access the computers in Russia. Immediately after they were arrested, Schuler used the sniffed accounts and passwords to log on to the suspect's computers and download 250GB of evidence that would link the two men to the computer break-ins and credit card fraud.

Schuler received accolades for being the first FBI agent to electronically "utilize the technique of extra-territorial seizure." However, no search warrant was ever issued before the data was downloaded (one was issued after the fact), and no one from the FBI ever talked to Russian law enforcement. Gorshkov's attorney argued these points and the fact that Russian laws had been violated, but the judge ruled that Russian law did not apply to the agents' actions.

Nearly two years later, in August 2002, the FSB, Russia's Federal Security Service, accused Schuler of unauthorized access to computers in Russia and began criminal proceedings against him. The issue will likely be resolved diplomatically, but Schuler probably won't be planning any vacations to Eastern Europe in the near future.

As a postscript, Gorshkov was sentenced in October of 2002 to three years in prison and ordered to pay restitution of $690,000. Ivanov pleaded guilty to a number of charges in August 2002. As of mid-March 2003, he has yet to be sentenced.

Private Eyes and Consultants — Private Investigations

Other types of spies, who may be legally or illegally electronically eavesdropping on you, are private investigators and technical consultants. These specialists find evidence that relates to criminal or civil matters, and it may be used by businesses, law enforcement, or individuals. Private eyes have formal investigative backgrounds, usually gained from dealing with a variety of different types of cases. Consultants tend to have specific technical areas of specialization, particularly in computer networks and forensics.

PRIVATE EYES

Although the stereotype of Sam Spade gumshoes in trench coats is etched into American culture, private eyes have changed with the times and are increasingly engaging in computer-related investigations.

Private eyes have long been involved in audio and video surveillance activities, and it's a natural progression for them to start becoming involved in computer surveillance. Traditional private investigators often come from law enforcement and likely have limited computer skills. Generally, the average private investigator has some technical computer skills but will likely employ easy-to-use and common spying tools. However, a new generation of PIs that have grown up around computers will be much more skilled than their fathers and grandfathers.

Spies: Garbage Gate

In 2000, database giant Oracle hired detectives from Investigative Group International (IGI) to investigate and research two organizations: the Independent Institute and the Association for Competitive Technology (ACT). (IGI is staffed with a number of former FBI agents and gained some notoriety for being retained by President Bill Clinton to investigate matters related to Paula Jones and Monica Lewinsky.) This happened while the Microsoft antitrust investigation was underway, and both the nonprofit organizations, which were strong supporters of Microsoft, were reputed to have financial ties to the Redmond, Washington company.

During the summer, a woman identifying herself as private investigator Blanca Lopez offered janitors $700 in cash to go through ACT's office trash. Lopez had gained access to the locked building by using a cardkey that belonged to Robert Waters, a private investigator associated with IGI, who had rented an office in the same executive suite as ACT under the name of Upstream Technologies.

When the story broke, Washington D.C. police said there was no Blanca Lopez registered as a private investigator in the city. Investigative journalists questioned whether Upstream was a front company, whose only purpose was to provide a cover for being in the same building as ACT. Larry Elison, Oracle CEO, admitted hiring IGI, justifying that it was important to expose Microsoft, but he carefully sidestepped the trash issue stating, "I'm prepared to ship our garbage to Redmond, and they can go through it."

Basically what appears to have happened was Oracle believed ACT and the Independent Institute, both promoting themselves as independent advocacy groups, were actually front organizations for Microsoft, charged with influencing public opinion to favor Microsoft during its antitrust trial. Someone tipped off the *Wall Street Journal* after the cash-for-trash incident, and journalists there were able to piece together the Oracle and IGI relationship. Oracle maintained that IGI informed the company that they would only use 100-percent legal investigative techniques. The incident caught the attention of the national media for a week or two and then faded into obscurity.

> ## Countermeasures: Big 5 Forensics
>
> Don't always think of technical consultants as individual, freelancing geeks with a penchant for computer security. Computer forensics is starting to become a hot commodity these days, and large corporations are cashing in on the demand.
>
> For example, accounting giant Deloitte & Touche maintains a Boston-area facility dubbed the "War Room." The laboratory has more than half a million dollars of sophisticated computer hardware used for client computer investigations. Technicians can recover damaged hard drives and sift through bytes looking for incriminating evidence. The technicians have dealt with everything from white-collar crime to investigations relating to homicide.
>
> Handling around 250 cases a year, business is booming.

Although as a general rule, private eyes don't tend to have the technical skills that other types of spies may have, one skill many excel at is social engineering. Called "pretext" in the PI and law enforcement business, social engineering is conning and sweet-talking information out of someone. Taking advantage of human nature can be just as damaging as the most sophisticated technical attack.

CONSULTANTS

Businesses and law enforcement are increasingly realizing that when it comes to network intrusions and electronic evidence gathering, they may not internally have the necessary experience or skills to be effective. The computer security consulting industry has grown tremendously over the past several years in response to an increasing number of computer attacks as well as media hype.

Highly skilled technical consultants are being used to find spies and plug holes to prevent them from stealing information, and the consultants are also being used to conduct forensic examinations of computers. Typically, consultants have computer science or similar degrees and various industry certifications.

Of course the skills required to catch a spy can also be used for espionage itself. Although most private investigators and consultants are ethical and abide by the laws that protect you from electronic spying, there are always a few exceptions who operate outside the law to earn their paychecks. Unethical consultants have the potential to be some of the most difficult spies to detect because of their skills and insider knowledge.

Spooks — Government-Sponsored Intelligence Gathering

When you say the word "spy," most people think of bona fide, card-carrying, cloak-and-dagger government agents. In the spy business, they're known as spooks, and the spooks that practice what has been called the world's second oldest profession, at the behest of a government, are typically pretty good at what they do.

In most cases, spying is pretty boring, tedious work. Forget James Bond or even Austin Powers for that matter. Spying is about collecting both open source and classified information, trying to put the many pieces of a puzzle together to make a guess at what's happening and then perhaps how to affect change for a government's benefit.

Traditionally, countries' intelligence agencies have been pitted against each other trying to ferret out political and military secrets, and although that is still the case, intelligence agencies all over the world have been scrambling to find new ways to justify their existence with the end of the Cold War. Across the board, the two new missions are economic intelligence and, more recently, the fight against terrorism (which has received a great deal more emphasis).

Intelligence-gathering operations are either specifically targeted or more generalized in approach (for example, seeking specific information about a certain type of missile versus gathering general data on an entire missile defense system). If an intelligence agency is interested in information you have, time will be spent researching your vulnerabilities and how best to covertly obtain the information.

Programs such as ECHELON take more of a vacuum cleaner approach. E-mail and electronic communications that travel over the Internet are collected in bulk, stored, and then analyzed for key words of interest. Also, since ECHELON is a cooperative data-sharing program, the need for probable cause and warrants is circumvented when, say, Australia collects data that relates to a United States citizen and then passes it on to a U.S. intelligence agency.

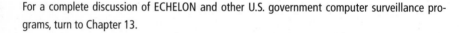

x-ref

For a complete discussion of ECHELON and other U.S. government computer surveillance programs, turn to Chapter 13.

If a government intelligence agency ever does take an interest in you or your company, prepare for the possibility of having a large number of resources (skilled technicians, hardware, and spies) used against you.

DOMESTIC

The Intelligence Community is a group of 13 government agencies and organizations that carry out the intelligence activities of the United States government. Agencies that spy or counterspy include the Department of State, Department of Energy, Department of the Treasury, Federal Bureau of Investigation, National Reconnaissance Office, National Imagery and Mapping Agency, Marine Corps Intelligence, Air Force Intelligence, Navy Intelligence, Army Intelligence, National Security Agency, Defense Intelligence Agency, and Central Intelligence Agency.

Up until the mid-1970s, the CIA and other members of the Intelligence Community illegally spied on Americans. Despite being statutorily prohibited from doing so, the CIA kept tabs on thousands of citizens with Operation CHAOS, a program originally designed to gather intelligence on Vietnam War protestors, student activists, and black nationalists. The Church Commission (a Senate investigative panel chaired by Senator Frank Church of Idaho) revealed many of these abuses, and domestic surveillance of Americans was greatly curtailed. However, with the September 11, 2001 terrorist attacks and passage of the USA Patriot Act, discussed in detail in Chapter 2, the Intelligence Community now has more powers to conduct espionage activities against citizens. Whether the loss of personal rights provides more security or the Intelligence Community's increased power allows it to unjustly abuse private citizens, as in the past, remains to be seen.

The Church Commission hearings were extremely broad in scope; assassination attempts of foreign leaders, overthrowing governments, illegal FBI and CIA domestic surveillance. For more information see *Inside the CIA — Revealing the Secrets of the World's Most Powerful Spy Agency*, by Ronald Kessler.

Although the CIA and NSA have stated that they don't perform economic espionage, anyone even slightly clued into the intelligence business knows that they do. In 1995, shortly after the CIA Director said the agency didn't engage in business espionage to benefit American corporations, five CIA agents were expelled from France for doing just that. There are allegations that the NSA intercepted faxes and telephone calls from foreign businesses to give Boeing and Raytheon a competitive advantage during high-stakes bidding.

American intelligence agencies excel when it comes to surveillance technology. They are very good at intercepting and collecting information, particularly when it's digital. This is one of the reasons the Al Qaeda terrorist network is using old-fashioned, nonelectronic communications methods in addition to high-tech e-mail and satellite phones.

FOREIGN

It's in the best interest of a nation if its businesses have an advantage over foreign competitors. Countries such as China, South Korea, France, and Israel have known this for a long time and have successfully used their intelligence services to covertly gather economic information that can be passed on to large corporations within their borders. They're not as prudish as the U.S. in trying to deny it, either.

Spies: Project RAHAB

Since the mid-1990s, rumors have swirled around the computer underground and security communities about German government-sanctioned crackers involved in an operation codenamed RAHAB.

RAHAB refers to the name of a Biblical prostitute and spy (commonly known as Rahab the Harlot). According to various sources, around 1987 a group within the German Federal Intelligence Service (the Bundesnachrichtendienst, or BND) started a covert operation designed to penetrate networks and databases and steal technical and economic information. Supposedly the project broke into computers in Russia, the United States, Japan, France, Italy, and the United Kingdom. Some of its accomplishments included compromising DuPont's corporate networks as well as cracking the banking industry's SWIFT secure transaction protocol (which meant the cracker could eavesdrop on financial transactions or create bogus transactions to shift money from one account to another).

Very little substantiated public source information exists about Project RAHAB, but if the few tidbits are true, it presents an interesting glimpse at foreign state-sponsored espionage during a period when large corporations increasingly started to use computers.

The American Society of Industrial Security conducts occasional surveys of economic and industrial espionage incidents experienced by U.S. businesses. In a 1998 survey, foreign countries perceived as key threats (in order of highest threat) included China, Japan, France, the United Kingdom, Canada, Mexico, Russia, Germany, South Korea, and Israel.

During the Cold War, there were clear distinctions between friends and enemies. Today, the situation isn't as apparent. The majority of countries engaged in economic espionage against the United States are our political allies. For example, there are reports of the French intelligence service bugging first- and business-class seats on Air France jets to eavesdrop on private conversations and snooping through laptops left in hotel rooms by American business visitors.

If your business activities take you abroad or if you come in contact with foreign nationals who take an interest in your company and products, give some thought to the potential of economic espionage.

Criminals — Ill-Gotten Gains

Although any spy that breaks a law is a criminal, "criminal spies" tend to be opportunistic data thieves. They conduct computer espionage, seeking information that helps them make an illegal profit or create some personal gain. Criminals fall into two categories: crackers and members of organized crime.

CRACKERS

Crackers are people who illegally break into computers. (I use the word "cracker" instead of the more widely used "hacker," which is an old-school complimentary term for someone who is technically clever and skilled, but doesn't necessarily break any laws.) Crackers are usually interested in financial information, particularly credit card numbers, and accounts and passwords that will allow them to break into other systems. They also may be malicious and erase files or publicize confidential information. Crackers range from "script-kiddies" (people with minimal technical skills who use automated tools and scripts to remotely break into computers) to more experienced, to unscrupulous Internet service provider administrators, to skilled professionals who understand the intricacies of operating systems and network protocols. There tend to be more script-kiddies than pros out there, and it's fairly easy to thwart the kiddies' attempts at spying.

ORGANIZED CRIME

Although you never see anyone on *The Sopranos* involved with computer espionage, organized crime has seen the future and it is digital. Computers offer all sorts of ways to illegally make money, and eavesdropping is one of them. Organized crime is mostly interested in financial and personal identity data that can be used for fraud and information that can be used in helping to plan other crimes — computer-related or not. Organized crime is in many ways like law enforcement in terms of adopting technology. Most old-school criminals won't be that technically skilled, but as new generations replace the old, the potential for more computer espionage perpetrated by organized crime increases. The one exception to the old-fashioned goodfellas is the drug cartels, which have been using skilled technicians and state-of-the-art technology for years, both to protect their own infrastructure and spy on their opposition.

Spies: Computer Spying, Colombian Style

The Colombian drug cartels have spent billions of dollars on building sophisticated computer infrastructures. In 1994, Colombian police raided a condominium complex in Cali. They found a $1.5 million IBM AS400 mainframe computer with half a dozen monitors connected to it. Dubbed the "Santacruz computer" after Cali Cartel frontman Jose Santacruz Londono, the machine was shipped to the United States for analysis. Reports on what technicians found on the computer are classified, but information has leaked out through the years.

The computer had a database of residential and office phone numbers of U.S. diplomats and agents (both known and suspected U.S. law enforcement, intelligence, and military operatives) based in Colombia. In addition, the phone company was supplying the Cartel with complete records of all telephone calls in the form of the originating and destination phone numbers. The Cartel's intelligence arm then used custom-designed software to cross-reference the phone company records against their own list of suspected law enforcement, military, and intelligence officials or agents to find out the phone numbers that these officials were calling or the phone numbers that were used to place calls to the officials. These phone numbers were then correlated back to addresses and names, giving the Cartel a list of people who were possibly informing on them.

Law enforcement officials haven't said what happened to the informers that the Santacruz computer found, but considering the Cartel's penchant for violence, it seems reasonable to believe suspected informants were tortured to reveal information or killed outright. There are no public sources that estimate the potential loss of life that resulted from the Cartel's computer operation.

Whistleblowers — For the Public Good

Another type of spy, generally considered benevolent (depending on whom he is spying on) is the whistleblower who exposes corruption and unsafe practices for the public good. Of course, whistleblowers wouldn't exist without the media, who give them a chance to tell their story, and sometimes engage in independent, investigative whistleblowing of their own.

Whistleblowers are typically insiders who have access to evidence of some wrongdoing. They might also be journalists working on a story. Whistleblowers often have above-average technical (Internet and computer-related) skills, which they use to their advantage in exposing wrongs. With the advent of the Internet, whistleblowers have an easy way to pass their knowledge along and yet remain anonymous. Through temporary e-mail accounts and anonymous remailers, a spy can reveal information to a third-party source without much fear of discovery. Embarrassing and damning company e-mail and instant-messaging logs are being exposed on the Internet with a greater frequency.

If you work for a company such as Enron, you may have potential whistleblower spies in your midst — which might not be a bad thing.

Spies: Cryptome.org

John Young is a New York architect who strongly believes in personal privacy and exposes the secrets of those who invade the privacy of others. He runs the cryptome.org Web site, a clearinghouse of esoteric information related to intelligence agencies, government, privacy, cryptography, surveillance, and freedom.

Since 1996, Young has collected a remarkable amount of whistleblowing information from anonymous sources. This information includes lists that blew the cover of foreign intelligence agents; a customer list from a surveillance hardware company with names of government, military, and law enforcement employees; copies of disreputable monitoring software; and various open and closed source government documents.

Cryptome.org has gained an international reputation for publicizing tantalizing details for those who study espionage. In addition to privacy advocates, spy buffs, and investigative reporters, various intelligence agency *bots* (automated software robots that collect data) frequently visit the site, downloading new information for government analysts to study in an attempt to find leaks or discover pieces in some larger intelligence puzzle.

Friends and Family — with Friends like These . . .

Although spying is usually thought of in a business or government context, the reality is that the home computer is probably the most vulnerable when it comes to espionage. However, the threat is not from crackers who break in through broadband connections, but rather from family and friends.

Maybe they suspect you of doing something wrong and are looking for evidence. Maybe they are just curious about what's on your computer and are nosing around for information. As computers have become integrated into our lives, they can cast a light onto parts of our personal lives we want to keep private.

For the most part, friends and family generally have the lowest amount of technical skills compared to other spies, and they typically rely on browsing through file directories and using easy-to-install-and-run commercial and free software.

Keyloggers are probably the biggest threat when it comes to family spying. These surveillance tools are discussed in detail in Chapter 8.

ROOMMATES

The number of roommates and boarders in the United States is on the rise. In the past, it just used to be college roommates, but now because of tight economic times, 20- and 30-something-year-old couples that have purchased their first home are increasingly taking in boarders to help offset

---

Busted: Best Friends?

Nicholas J. Suchyta, 19, shared an apartment in Bay City, Michigan with a 19-year-old woman. The female roommate said she and Nicholas had been best friends since grade school.

In January 2002, acquaintances of the woman told her they had seen live video of her on the Internet having sex with her 18-year-old boyfriend in Suchyta's apartment. The woman searched through Suchyta's computers and found nude pictures of her. She then complained to the police who found a hidden Web camera attached to her computer and four files of the teens having sex.

In May 2002, Suchyta was arraigned on two counts of installing eavesdropping devices and two counts of divulging information from eavesdropping devices. He had previously been in trouble for alleged cracking activities while employed by a local school district. In that case, Suchyta and his parents sued the school for defamation of character, invasion of privacy, intentional infliction of emotional distress, and gross negligence, as a result of Suchyta being branded a "hacker."

The case is scheduled to go to trial in late April 2003. If Suchyta is convicted, he faces up to two years in prison as well as a fine.

---

costs. Whether you have a school dorm roommate or are sharing a house or apartment with someone, an unsecured computer is a tempting target for snooping.

SIGNIFICANT OTHERS

Trust seems to be passe these days. Jealous boyfriends, girlfriends, husbands, and wives are heading to their current and former significant others' computers in an attempt to find evidence of real or virtual unfaithfulness.

Maybe it has something to do with the relatively anonymous and easy way that electronic relationships can be found and maintained through e-mail, instant messaging, and chat rooms, or perhaps the media is encouraging interest and experimentation with lurid coverage of online affairs and cyber-sex. Or possibly all of those advertisements on Web sites for spy software designed to catch your spouse electronically cheating gives people doubts about their relationships. Whatever the reason, "significant other" computer spying is turning into a booming business.

PARENTS

When the Internet first started to become popular, parents were concerned about keeping their children away from adult-oriented Web sites. Now in addition to Web sites, kids have access to chat rooms, instant messaging, and personal e-mail accounts. Media hype about the dangers of the Internet has caused some parents to take an active interest in spying on their children's computer activities. Web-filtering software now includes features that monitor chatting and e-mail, and keyloggers are advertised to help parents discover what their children are up to while online.

Busted: 'Til Keyboards Do Us Part

In 2001, Steven Paul Brown separated from his wife Patricia, but the separation wasn't amicable. Brown installed a commercial keylogger program called eBlaster on his former wife's computer. The program recorded her e-mail, Web surfing, and online chatting and then e-mailed a copy of her activities to Brown. Brown made the mistake of mentioning the contents of an e-mail exchange between his former wife and a friend. His wife became suspicious, and the Michigan Attorney General's High Tech Crime Unit investigated.

Brown was charged with installing an eavesdropping device, eavesdropping, using a computer to commit a crime, and having unauthorized computer access (all felony offenses). He faces penalties of up to five years in prison and fines of up to $19,000.

CHILDREN

A significant portion of the adult population isn't very savvy when it comes to computers. Although they can perform common tasks such as using a word processor, sending e-mail, and surfing the Web, they've never had to develop more esoteric skills, especially those that are security-related. On the other hand, their children have grown up on the Internet, many collecting a remarkable set of technical skills that go way beyond those of their parents'.

Kids actually pose a significant threat as junior spies—spy tools are discussed in e-mail and chat rooms and then readily downloaded from cracker Web sites. A savvy 12-year-old can easily install a keylogger on the family computer and eavesdrop on whatever Mom, Dad, brother, and sister are up to. Privacy involving financial transactions, connections to work computers, e-mail, and Web surfing can easily be compromised.

Determining Your Level of Paranoia

Sun Tzu said that to prevail in battle, you need to know yourself. So the question is, with all of these potential spies at work, at home, and seemingly everywhere you look, just how paranoid should you be?

Part of the answer is to know yourself (or in the case of a business, your organization). Here's a quick test that might help. There's no time limit, so give the questions some thought.

- ✓ Can you tell the difference between a credible probable threat to your computer or network versus an unfounded possible one? If you're big into black helicopters, U.N. takeovers, and unfounded government conspiracies, answer no.

- ✓ Can you put on a spy's cloak and use his dagger to try to poke holes in your computer system? Thinking like a bad guy is important for understanding your weaknesses. You'll be asked to do this throughout this book.

✓ Are you willing to put policies in place to ensure your computer's security? Security policies are extremely important, but they go beyond the scope of this book, which focuses on espionage tactics and countermeasures.

✓ Will you follow the policies you created? If you think security policies are a waste of time or too much of a burden to follow, answer no.

✓ Are you the type of person that's willing to put up with a little inconvenience for increased security? The general rule of thumb is that as any type of security increases, convenience and usability typically decrease.

If you answered yes to all of the questions, you're not paranoid, but simply prepared and can reduce your chances of being spied on.

If you answered yes to most of the questions, examine the questions you answered no to. There might be a few issues holding you back from being entirely effective in preventing computer espionage.

If you didn't answer yes very often and someone is planning on spying on you, he could be very successful. If you're concerned about this, it might be time to bring in some outside help.

Protecting yourself from computer spying is somewhere between blissful ignorance and wearing a tinfoil hat to keep the radio waves out of your brain. You need to find the right balance.

Risk: Color Codes

Colonel Jeff Cooper, a prominent firearms instructor, developed a widely used color code for awareness and preparedness based on his experience in the Marines. (Recently, the U.S. Government has implemented a similar color code for homeland defense purposes.) Cooper breaks his system into the following four colors:

✓ **Condition White.** This is a complete lack of awareness of any possible threats or information that might lead you to believe there is a threat. Most people go through their lives in this condition.

✓ **Condition Yellow.** This is relaxed awareness, much like you have when you're driving defensively. You're aware of your environment and things that seem out of place. Code yellow awareness shouldn't be that taxing, and with training you should be able to be in this state during your waking hours.

✓ **Condition Orange.** This is an awareness of a potential threat that makes your antenna go up and starts you planning on options for dealing with the threat.

✓ **Condition Red.** This is when you identify a real, specific threat and then take control of the situation.

Although the color code is primarily designed for self-defense, it is equally applicable to a mindset for preventing computer spying. Are you willing to move to a Condition Yellow state with your computer and then be ready to escalate to higher levels if need be?

Risk Analysis 101

At the start of this chapter, Sun Tzu said, "If you know the enemy and know yourself, you need not fear the result of a hundred battles." That's what risk analysis is all about. It quite simply involves identifying the most probable threats, analyzing the vulnerabilities, and determining what countermeasures should be put in place.

Before continuing, it's important to have a good understanding of these three key terms:

- ✓ **Threat.** A threat is something that poses danger. Throughout this book, spies are the key threats as they present a danger of compromising information on computers.

- ✓ **Vulnerability.** A vulnerability is a condition that causes something to be susceptible to attack. Spies look for weaknesses in security, or vulnerabilities, to exploit. For example, a spy may exploit a known buffer-overflow vulnerability in a Web server to gain access to files on a corporate network.

- ✓ **Countermeasure.** A countermeasure is an action taken to offset another. Quite simply, countermeasures prevent exploits. An example of a countermeasure is installing a vendor's patch to prevent a Web server buffer-overflow attack.

Let's go through an imaginary risk-analysis example.

Your Aunt Sara had a prize-winning chocolate cake recipe that was the envy of everyone in the county. With her final breath, she gave you the recipe and told you to never reveal the ingredients to anyone. You've kept the recipe on your hard drive ever since, and despite bribes and threats you've never shared it with anyone.

Is it possible that government spies are interested in your Aunt Sara's recipe? Because anything is possible, does that mean you should withdraw your life savings, hire armed guards, install a retina scanner on your PC, and shield your office to prevent stray electromagnetic emanations from being intercepted by men in black vans with TEMPEST intercept equipment?

Although it's possible that there's a rogue CIA agent with a sweet tooth that heard about Aunt Sara's cake, it's not very probable. So scratch off a government-sponsored intelligence operation as a threat, and because now that you don't have to worry about all the sophisticated tools and methods associated with state-sponsored espionage, you can fire the armed guards and return the retina scanner and TEMPEST shielding. (Of course, everything might change if Aunt Sara's real name was Natasha, and she had this funny little tattoo on her arm with a sword and shield and tiny little letters underneath that spelled out KGB.)

A more realistic threat comes from your sister-in-law Christina, who's been after the recipe for years. Christina and her family show up every year for Thanksgiving and Christmas, and when her kids get bored, you send them off to your office to play computer games. Little Billy is especially good with computers, and over dinner you get into long discussions with him about various Microsoft security holes. You've never really trusted Christina after the nasty incident involving Aunt Sara's silverware. So now what's the threat, what are the vulnerabilities, and how should you respond?

If you thought Billy's mom might put him up to snooping through your computer to see if he can find the prize-winning cake recipe, you've identified a probable threat. You know Billy is a whiz when it comes to Microsoft operating systems, so you've cleverly put the games on the Windows XP machine while the recipe is safely encrypted with Blowfish on a Linux laptop, which is locked in your bedroom desk drawer. You've identified the vulnerability and came up with several countermeasures. (This book is full of espionage vulnerabilities and countermeasures.)

There are all sorts of methodologies for performing risk analysis. Some use mathematical models, assigning numeric values to different types of and duration of risk. Statistical probabilities can be derived that rank the potential of different types of risk so you can make better decisions about protecting yourself from different threats.

Five-Step Risk Analysis

Lots of time can be spent discussing risk analysis, but because this book is primarily about computer spying, here's a quick, five-step model to help you perform a simple yet effective computer espionage risk analysis.

Let's discuss each of the steps and then apply them to two fictional organizations with different situations:

✓ e4bics Corporation, a high-tech startup developing a Voice over Internet Protocol (VoIP)

✓ No More Violence, a nonprofit support organization for battered women

DETERMINE WHAT YOU HAVE

To start out, what's on your computer that has value? This information is either stored on a computer's hard drive (or some other storage medium) or is transferred between computers if you're using the Internet or a local area network (LAN). Although some economists would argue that you could assign a monetary value to everything, value doesn't necessarily equal cash in this case. Although the information could have a tangible value (such as a credit card number or trade secret), it also might not. Perhaps it is some bit of evidence that if discovered could send you to prison or destroy your relationship with someone.

✓ e4bics Corporation has just completed work on a new communications server designed for voice-centric and multimedia technology. The proprietary software and hardware dramatically beat all of the competition in terms of performance and pricing. The official marketing rollout is planned for six months from now, but industry rumors have been circulating about the product. Any information that has to do with product R&D, marketing, and sales is valuable for obvious reasons.

✓ In an attempt to streamline its operations, No More Violence has started to use a computer database to track women that the organization is supporting. Part of the organization's mission is to find temporary safe places for domestic-violence victims to live. The database contains women's names, addresses, and other personal information. All of this data is extremely sensitive and thus valuable in a nonmonetary way.

LIST WHO MIGHT WANT IT

Now, consider who might want whatever it is you think has value. The first part of this chapter contains a rather long laundry list of people who typically spy, so you should have some ideas about the usual suspects. Remember to categorize your adversaries as probable rather than possible, so you can focus your energy on exploits that are *likely* to happen and not ones that merely *could* happen. Keep your imagination in check and your paranoia well founded.

✓ In e4bics' case, any number of large or small competitors would love to have the inside scoop on their newly developed technology. This includes companies both inside and outside the United States. The company's executives have recently been approached by representatives from several large competitors asking to partner on future projects, but the nondisclosure agreements seem pretty one-sided in favor of the competitors.

✓ Some of the women that No More Violence supports have violent former partners who currently have restraining orders filed against them. With a pattern of continued abuse and harassment, a number of these men want to find their former wives and girlfriends.

DECIDE HOW BAD THEY WANT IT AND HOW MIGHT THEY GET IT

Let's say the adversaries you've identified know or suspect that valuable information resides on your computer. How bad might they want it, and how might they try to get it? When answering this question, consider the security measures you already have in place, and how effective they will be in stopping or slowing down an adversary. Also, remember to keep suspected attacks probable, not possible. Although it's worthwhile to spend some time brainstorming all sorts of creative attack possibilities, time is a finite commodity, and it's a better investment to first focus on the probable.

✓ Because e4bics' new product could have a significant impact on the industry, the company is quite concerned about economic espionage. J.D., the company's chief engineer, formerly specialized in penetration-testing work for the Air Force and has a long list of ways a competitor could try to get e4bics' trade secrets, including dumpster diving, social engineering, breaking into the offices after hours, or trying to enter through some hole in the networks.

✓ One of the women that No More Violence helped is named Sue and is a network administrator with a background in security. In talking with the organization's office manager, Sue mentioned that someone could break in and steal the database files or the entire computer. Because the Windows XP desktop is connected to the Internet through a cable modem, a spy could try to remotely break in and access the database. The office manager knows that one of the women's former husbands has a burglary conviction and another's former boyfriend used to crack e-commerce Web sites for fun. The database is running on Microsoft Access, and is protected using the program's built-in encryption. Sue points out Access's weak encryption and tells about her personal experience of discovering the lost password for a protected database in a matter of seconds using a free cracking program.

SPECULATE ABOUT WHAT HAPPENS IF THEY GET IT

Imagine the worst-case scenario. Your adversary manages to get the information on your computer. What are the probable implications and consequences? Try to be as detail-oriented with this question as possible, looking at the present and into the future.

✓ In e4bic's case, the impact of having proprietary information compromised depends on just what it is. If sales data were stolen, competitors could target accounts that the company is in the process of developing. If marketing plans are revealed, a competitor could develop a counterstrategy. If a competitor gained access to e4bics' R&D crown jewels, the company's planned competitive edge could be weakened if not entirely crippled. As a small startup, the company and all of the employee's livelihoods could be at stake.

✓ The worst-case scenario for No More Violence is relatively simple. If the database with the women's names and addresses fell into the wrong hands, it could put the safety and perhaps the lives of the organization's clients in jeopardy at any point after the information was compromised.

DETERMINE HOW YOU SHOULD PROTECT IT AND WHAT THE COST IS

You've now identified what you have that is valuable, who might want it, how bad they might want it, how they may try to get it, and what happens if they succeed. The final step is to factor all of this together to create a plan that will protect that item of value.

Because you probably don't have an infinite budget to spend, you need to make some conscious decisions about the levels of security you'll use to protect the information. Don't think only in terms of how much a security product costs. Remember that there is a negative correlation between security and usability. As security levels increase, it becomes more difficult for users to perform their everyday job duties, which can incur another cost to the company—namely, a slowdown in efficient, quantitative output.

✓ J.D. knows that there's a lot riding on keeping his e4bics's information safe. He first performed a risk analysis and identified vulnerabilities a spy could exploit. He then came up with a planned series of countermeasures to plug the vulnerabilities. Finally, he developed a strict security policy that addressed both computer and physical security issues. The CEO and investors understood the importance of information security and approved J.D.'s security budget and plan. (In real life, you'll have much more of a challenge convincing the suits that the threat of espionage is real and measures should be taken to prevent it, but because this is a hypothetical case, let's have a happy ending.)

✓ After discussions with a friendly police officer and Sue, the No More Violence office manager planned to beef up physical security by installing both new locks and a monitored security system. A NAT router (NAT stands for Network Address Translation; it provides transparent access to the rest of the IP network, usually the Internet, through one gateway computer) was purchased to protect the computer from Internet intruders, and current security patches were applied to the Windows operating system. Finally, the popular and secure Pretty Good Privacy, also known as PGP, strong encryption utility was used to protect the database. No More Violence doesn't have a very large budget and its staff doesn't have many technical skills, so all of the security measures were affordable, as well as fairly unobtrusive so as not to discourage their use.

Summary

You now should have a better idea of who your enemy (a spy) is, whether you have the right stuff to take him or her on, and how to go about assessing the risk of computer espionage.

Throughout the rest of this book, you will be exposed to a number of tactics that spies use to compromise data. When you read about these spy tactics, pretend you're a spy, and see how effective some of these attacks would be on you, your business, or your organization. Always consider whether an attack is probable or possible, though. All the espionage tactics described are possible, but your own personal situation will make them either more or less likely.

As new vulnerabilities are discovered on a daily basis, with some taking a long time to percolate into public view, it's impossible to create a perfectly secure computer. There's an old saying in the security industry that the only way to absolutely secure a computer is to cut all the cables, fill it with cement, and then bury it. Then it still might not even be secure.

Your job should be to minimize the risk of computer espionage as much as possible. You can't be 100 percent certain that you can keep a spy from accessing information or evidence, but you can make his job as difficult as possible. Hopefully, the cost in time and effort will cause him to look elsewhere for other targets.

Chapter 2

Spying and the Law

"I fought the law, and the law won."
— The Crickets, Bobby Fuller, and other more famous bands

Laws that Relate to Spying

Aside from computer-spying tactics and countermeasures, there's also a legal side to consider. This chapter presents an overview of some key laws and how they relate to computer eavesdropping. Some of the material might seem pretty dry compared to learning about how to spy on computers (and more importantly, how to stop the eavesdroppers), but this legal information is important to understand for several reasons:

✓ If you believe that you've been victimized by computer espionage, whether on a personal or business level, you should contact a law enforcement agency, which will work with a prosecutor to determine whether there's a criminal case and how to go about dealing with it. Having a basic understanding of laws that relate to spying, particularly those associated with computer crime, will give you a leg up when working with a district attorney (or a private attorney retained for civil lawsuits).

✓ If you think law enforcement is conducting computer surveillance on you, for real or imagined reasons, it's useful to understand the laws that define their "rules of engagement." That may help you vindicate yourself if it turns out you're being illegally spied upon.

✓ If you're in law enforcement, obviously you need to know the correct way to go about setting up a computer surveillance operation. Judges don't look too favorably on cops who don't play by the rules, and cops don't like to see bad guys go free because a mistake was made regarding legal procedure.

✓ If you're a spy or have aspirations of being one, heads-up; if you get caught, there are some serious laws in place that could cost you significant amounts of money and time behind bars. If you opt for a life of crime, now might be a good time to line up a defense attorney who has experience with some of the statutes discussed, just in case your eavesdropping plans are discovered.

To quote a popular USENET newsgroup acronym, IANAL (I am not a lawyer), and this chapter doesn't constitute legal advice. If you get involved with computer spying at any level, whether as a victim or perpetrator, seek legal counsel. That could be your corporate counsel, a district attorney if you're a cop, or a private lawyer (you're not going to find too many lawyers in the Yellow Pages who advertise that espionage is one of their specialties, but you should look for someone who is knowledgeable about computer technology and trade secrets).

With this in mind, let's look at some of the main laws that prohibit elements of computer espionage and how they are applied to spies that get caught.

Omnibus Crime Control and Safe Streets Act of 1968 (Title III — Wiretap Act)

What does a crime bill enacted in the pre-PC days of 1968 that promotes safe streets have to do with computer espionage? After the assassinations of Robert Kennedy and Martin Luther King, Jr., the Safe Streets Act was a "get tough on crime" bill intended to keep firearms out of the hands of those deemed unfit to possess them because of age, criminal background, or mental incompetency. Buried in the Act (in Title III to be precise) is a section that has to do with wiretapping. It's commonly known as Title III or the Wiretap Act, or officially Title 18 of the United States Code (U.S.C.), Sections 2510–2521.

Wiretap means to place a concealed listening or recording device on a communications line; back then it almost exclusively meant telephones. Title III grants authority to law enforcement agencies to use wiretaps and sets the standards for when they do. The act also puts restrictions on anyone who performs electronic eavesdropping. Prior to the passage of the law, anyone could wiretap, and there were no laws to criminalize illegal eavesdropping.

In a 1967 case, Katz vs. the U.S., the Supreme Court ruled that FBI use of electronic devices to listen to and record telephone conversations without a warrant violated unreasonable search-and-seizure provisions established by the Fourth Amendment. This case provided the Court with an opportunity to state general criteria for allowable government surveillance, which formed the foundation of Title III.

A major point of Title III was to recognize that the privacy of citizens is endangered without a clear policy on wiretaps, but that "organized criminals make extensive use of wire and oral communications in their criminal activities." The act provides for intercepting these transmissions while safeguarding citizens' rights.

Title III spells out in great detail just what wiretaps can be used for. For example, the FBI can't legally wiretap you for an unpaid parking ticket. According to the original act, a wiretap could be used only for serious crimes such as bribery, kidnapping, robbery, murder, counterfeiting, fraud, narcotics, or conspiracy. (However, since Title III came into being, the number of suspected offenses for which wiretapping is allowed has gone from 26 to more than 100, among them dangerous offenses such as making false statements on student-loan applications.)

There is a check-and-balance system in place, so law enforcement agencies can't run around wiretapping whomever they want. A judge has to issue a wiretap order before legal eavesdropping can be started. Wiretaps must always be used as a last resort, and it has to be demonstrated to a judge that all alternatives have been exhausted during the investigation. The law enforcement agency also has to demonstrate that there's probable cause. This means there must be other compelling evidence that justifies to the judge that wiretapping a suspect is warranted. In other words, law enforcement can't simply go on fishing expeditions by asking for the court to approve a wiretap.

Although wiretaps originally applied to telephones, they now also apply to electronic communications. For example, if the police are investigating you, a wiretap order must be granted for them to intercept your e-mail. It also means if you're a spy and secretly use a sniffer to illegally obtain information from a network, you're guilty of violating federal wiretap statutes.

Tools of the Trade: Pen Registers and Trap-and-Trace Devices

Long before the Internet came into being, law enforcement started using *pen registers* and *trap-and-trace* devices on telephone lines. A pen register is a surveillance device that captures phone numbers dialed on outgoing calls. A trap-and-trace device identifies incoming phone numbers (a caller ID box fits the criteria of a trap-and-trace device). Neither devices monitor the actual conversation, only the origin and destination phone numbers.

Although the technology originally applied to telephones, pen register and trap-and-trace statutes now apply to communications conducted over the Internet (this was formalized with the passage of the USA Patriot Act). In the case of computer eavesdropping, special software attached to a router would collect information such as e-mail headers (except the subject line), source and destination IP addresses and ports, and Web page URLs. Essentially anything that is "transactional" (doesn't contain "content") is fair game.

Pen registers and trap-and-trace devices require a court order, but they don't require law enforcement to demonstrate that there is probable cause, as wiretap orders require, which makes them easier for cops to employ.

The pen register and trap-and-trace statutes can be viewed here: www.law.cornell.edu/uscode/18/3121.html.

Title III violations are a felony and subject up to a maximum of five years in prison and a fine of up to $10,000.

For a detailed discussion of the Department of Justice's views on Title III and computer investigations, see www.usdoj.gov/criminal/cybercrime/usamarch2001_2.htm.

Foreign Intelligence Surveillance Act of 1978

You wouldn't think that spies would have very many rights, particularly the foreign ones out to steal state secrets, but because the United States is a democracy built on the foundation of the Constitution, there are a number of little-known legal provisions for dealing with espionage and other nefarious acts committed by foreign powers.

In 1978, Congress passed the Foreign Intelligence Surveillance Act (Title 50 U.S.C., Sections 1801–1811), or FISA. The purpose of this act was to separate the rules of criminal surveillance, as specified in the Title III Wiretap Act, from how the government would handle surveillance related to domestic security, specifically in cases of espionage committed by foreign powers. FISA was originally designed to address issues relating to electronic eavesdropping, but was expanded in the

1990s to include covert physical entries during investigations and using pen registers and trap-and-trace devices.

FISA regulates the collection of "foreign intelligence," which is any information that relates to the United State's capability to protect itself against the following:

✓ Possible hostile acts of a foreign power or an agent of a foreign power

✓ Sabotage or terrorism by a foreign power or agent

✓ Clandestine intelligence activities by a foreign power or agent

Essentially if there's foreign involvement that relates to the national defense, national security, or the conduct of foreign affairs of the United States, FISA can be used.

Under the Fourth Amendment of the Constitution, for a search warrant to be granted it has to be based on probable cause that a crime has been or is being committed. Under FISA, however, surveillance activities can be authorized if there is probable cause that a person is a foreign power or an agent of a foreign power, even if a crime hasn't been committed or isn't being planned. FISA doesn't apply only to foreign nationals; a U.S. citizen can also be targeted under FISA as long as there is probable cause to believe that the individual is involved in espionage activities on the behalf of a foreign power.

Although the purpose of FISA surveillance is to gather foreign intelligence, FISA-obtained evidence can be used in criminal trials. However, there is a *minimization* requirement. Minimization means keeping foreign intelligence information separate from routine criminal investigations, and it is necessary because FISA grants broader surveillance powers. However, because there are times when there is an overlap between FISA and criminal investigations, there are "information-screening walls" in place, such as having an official not involved in a criminal investigation reviewing FISA information and then passing on only relevant data to the criminal investigators.

FISA established a special court, called the Foreign Intelligence Surveillance Court (FISC), which is composed of seven federal district court judges. FISC meets two days every month and reviews government requests for electronic surveillance in order to provide foreign intelligence information. (All requests for FISA warrants, no matter which agency is involved — including the CIA — are funneled through the Department of Justice for review. The Attorney General must personally approve each application to FISC.)

FISC is essentially a secret court because all records and files of the cases are sealed and usually aren't available even to individuals whose prosecutions were based on evidence gathered under FISA warrants. There is also a Foreign Intelligence Surveillance Court of Appeals, which secretly reviews and rules on any contentious issues that have come from the lower FISC. (The Foreign Intelligence Surveillance Court of Appeals met for the first time in the history of FISA in September 2002 to review the Department of Justice's request to change the minimization requirement.)

For the complete text of FISA, see www.law.cornell.edu/uscode/50/ch36.html.

Tactics: CALEA

CALEA stands for the Communications Assistance for Law Enforcement Act of 1994 (Public Law 103–414, 47 U.S.C, 1001–1010). Although this act isn't specifically computer related, it's worth mentioning because it involves electronic eavesdropping.

Title III, the Wiretap Act, required telecommunications carriers to provide "any assistance necessary to accomplish an electronic interception." However, the question of whether companies had an obligation to design their networks so they couldn't impede a lawful interception was never addressed.

CALEA changed this by amending the ECPA and requiring that telecommunications carriers ensure that their equipment complies with authorized electronic surveillance techniques. You've seen hardware that says "Microsoft Windows-compatible"; for the telephone companies, all their internal switching hardware has to say "wiretap-compatible."

A unit within the FBI's Laboratory Division called CIS (CALEA Implementation Section) currently drives CALEA implementation. Its mission is to "provide effective collection, surveillance, and tactical communications systems to support investigative and intelligence priorities." In addition to telephones, there are suggestions that the FBI is also talking to other standards organizations about including surveillance capabilities into DSL, Internet Protocol telephony, and wireless networking protocols.

CALEA isn't cheap. It's estimated that wireline telecommunication companies in the U.S. will spend somewhere between a half a billion dollars to $2.7 billion in CALEA operating expenses over a five-year period. It's no wonder that making a call on a payphone doesn't cost a quarter anymore.

The telecommunications industry obviously doesn't like CALEA, and has done everything in its power to avoid complying. Finally, in June 2002, the Federal Communications Commission ordered the telecoms to upgrade their systems to FBI specifications. The industry and privacy groups fought a similar order by the FCC three years prior and brought it to a standstill in the courts. This time, in a post-9/11 environment in which no one wants to be viewed as anti-government or unpatriotic, there were no organized challenges.

For more information on CALEA, see `www.askcalea.net`; to see the full act, go to `www.law.cornell.edu/uscode/18/2522.html`.

Electronic Communications Privacy Act of 1986

In 1986, a surprisingly forward-thinking Congress expanded the scope of the Title III wiretapping laws to incorporate electronic conversations including radio paging devices, electronic mail, cellular telephones, private communication carriers, and computer transmissions. The expanded act became known as the Electronic Communications Privacy Act of 1986, or ECPA (pronounced "ek-pah") for short.

Some of the key provisions in ECPA include the following:

✓ All individuals, not just the government and law enforcement, are prohibited from unauthorized eavesdropping of digital and analog communications.

✓ Privacy of all types of digital communication, including the transfer of text and images between individuals, is protected.

✓ Privacy of electronic communications doesn't just extend to intercepted messages, but also to the authorized access of messages stored on a computer.

ECPA states three exceptions to Title III that don't require court authorization to intercept electronic communications. They are as follows:

✓ An individual can monitor or authorize the government to monitor communications on his or her computer if it has been cracked and is being used for unauthorized purposes. For example, if a spy breaks into a server and creates an e-mail account to communicate with other spies, the owner of the server can give permission to a law enforcement agency to monitor the e-mail to gather evidence against the spy.

✓ If a banner (a text message that appears when accessing the system) is displayed that alerts all users of a computer system that it is private, and by entering, the user agrees to be monitored; implied consent is given to any monitoring activities.

✓ The final exception permits a private party to monitor system activities to prevent the misuse of the system through damage, fraud, or theft of services. For the exception to be valid, it must be done by the private party and not by the government. (In many cases as long as one or more of the communicating parties consents to the monitoring, it is viewed as legal.)

ECPA not only addresses the real-time interception of communications, but the Stored Communications Act (Title II of ECPA) also has privacy provisions for stored communications. The act prohibits a third party from obtaining stored wire or electronic communications, such as voice-mail or e-mail, without a court order (law enforcement agencies require a search warrant to access these types of data, which is considerably easier to get than a wiretap order). ECPA has both criminal and civil penalties, depending on the offense.

Just like with intercepted communications, there are some exceptions that allow stored communications to be accessed without court authorization. These exceptions include the following:

✓ **Implied consent.** If a service provider or employer publicizes a policy stating that stored communications may be monitored, users or employees give implied consent to monitoring.

✓ **Communication provider access.** The provider of the electronic communication service can legally view communications that have been stored on the service.

In terms of employee monitoring, some attorneys believe that the wording of the Stored Communications Act gives employers greater rights to access stored communications, such as saved e-mail, versus intercepting e-mail as they are sent.

Tactics: Wiretapping Statistics

If you watch TV or movies, you probably think that wiretaps are about as common as shared MP3 files. The reality is that they're not. In 2001, there were fewer than 1,500 criminal wiretaps authorized in the entire United States.

Part of Title III requires the Administrative Office of the United States Courts to prepare a yearly report on the number of state and federal wiretaps that were authorized. These reports come out each spring and have quite a bit of interesting information in them.

For example, here are the total numbers of wiretaps authorized over the past several years. Remember, a wiretap order can apply to a telephone, pager, fax, computer, or any communication device.

2001 — 1,491

2000 — 1,190

1999 — 1,350

1998 — 1,329

1997 — 1,186

Judges approved all the wiretaps requested in 2001 (it's rare for a judge to turn down a wiretap request). The largest number of wiretaps, a whopping 78 percent, was for drug-related investigations.

More than 23 million conversations were intercepted in 2001, which resulted in 3,683 arrests. Only one in five of those arrested were convicted, which many privacy groups point to as evidence that wiretapping isn't that effective as an investigation tool since in most cases the evidence it's providing isn't strong enough to contribute to an overall guilty verdict by a judge or jury.

Encryption was encountered in 16 of the wiretaps that were authorized in 2001, all from state or local jurisdictions (interestingly, the feds didn't report any cases). In none of these instances was encryption reported to have prevented law enforcement officials from obtaining the plain text of communications intercepted. Does that mean the cops can break PGP (Pretty Good Privacy, the free, de facto strong encryption utility)? It's pretty doubtful. It's more likely that the bad guys were using weak encryption, using poor passwords, or practicing bad security habits, such as writing down a password on a Post-it® and sticking it on a computer monitor.

The wiretap reports make for fascinating spy reading. They're available from www.uscourts.gov/wiretap.html.

Although ECPA was progressive back in 1986, despite all of the technological changes over the past 16 years, it was the last significant update to the privacy standards of the electronic surveillance laws.

For the ECPA wiretap provisions go to `www.law.cornell.edu/uscode/18/`
`pIch119.html`. For the Stored Communications Act, see `www.law.cornell.edu/`
`uscode/18/pIch121.html`.

Computer Fraud and Abuse Act of 1986

The Counterfeit Access Device and Computer Fraud and Abuse Act (18 U.S.C. 1030 or CFAA) was enacted in 1986 (it reinforced an earlier 1984 Fraud and Abuse Act). This was really the first major computer crime law targeted directly at crackers. It was designed to do the following:

- ✓ Criminalize unauthorized access of federal government computers

- ✓ Criminalize unauthorized access to computers owned by large financial institutions

- ✓ Give the Secret Service jurisdiction to investigate computer crime (the FBI now has this lead federal role)

The original act resulted in only a few prosecutions, most notably Robert Morris, the Cornell graduate student whose experimental worm got out of control and rapidly spread through the Internet. Under the CFAA, Morris was sentenced to three years of probation, 400 hours of community service, a fine of $10,050, and the costs of his supervision.

Since 1986, the act has been amended many times to include a number a different elements of computer crime. For example, the National Information Infrastructure Protection Act of 1996 significantly amended the CFAA. It expanded the definition of "protected computer" to cover any computer connected to the Internet.

The CFAA prohibits the following (any of these violations can take place during the course of computer espionage):

- ✓ Accessing a "protected computer" (a computer used for communication or in interstate or foreign commerce)

- ✓ Accessing a computer without authorization and subsequently transmitting classified government information

- ✓ Computer extortion

- ✓ Computer fraud

- ✓ Theft of financial information

- ✓ Trafficking in computer passwords for the purpose of affecting interstate commerce or a government computer

- ✓ Transmitting code that causes damage to a computer system

From a prosecution standpoint, this is one of the primary laws that an attorney general will go after crackers and computer spies with. At least $5,000 worth of damages (this can also include recovery costs) must be done to incur possible prosecution under CFAA. However, this amount is

Busted: Konop vs. Hawaiian Airlines, Inc.

Robert Konop was a pilot for Hawaiian Airlines. In 1995, the airline was negotiating contracts for their pilots with the Air Line Pilots Association. Konop felt that certain labor concessions in the bargaining were unfair, so he created a password-protected Web site that he gave only certain employees access to. When someone entered Konop's site, a list of terms and conditions was displayed that the user had to agree to before he was granted access. One of the terms was not revealing information on the site to Hawaiian Airlines management.

Hawaiian Airlines Vice President James Davis heard about the site and convinced a pilot who had access to the site to let him use his user name to log on. Davis logged onto the site 34 times, pretending he was the pilot, and agreed to the displayed terms.

Davis passed on information about Konop and what was on the site to the President of Hawaiian and the pilots' union. A union representative contacted Konop and expressed his displeasure with the Web site, without revealing his sources. Konop played detective and was able to use the system logs to track the access back to Davis.

Konop eventually sued Hawaiian on the grounds that unauthorized Hawaiian management staff entered his Web site and violated the Wiretap Act and other laws. The District Court dismissed these claims, but in January 2001, the Ninth Circuit Court of Appeals reinstated them, affirming that when the contents of a password-protected Web site are viewed without the permission of the owner, it is a violation of both the Wiretap and Stored Communications Acts.

However, in an unusual turn of events, the same court withdrew its opinion nine months later; in August 2002, it reversed the decision, stating that the Wiretap Act wasn't violated because it applied only to information that was intercepted while it was being transmitted, not stored. The court did hold that Hawaiian Airlines' actions still could have violated the Stored Communications Act.

For complete details of the case and the different rulings see `www.ca9.uscourts.gov/ca9/newopinions.nsf/DD51CB5C3834F00F88256C1E0002A94D/$file/9955106.pdf?openelement`.

waived if the incident harmed someone, impacted medical care, or posed a threat to national security. Convictions under the CFAA include a maximum sentence of 20 years in prison and a fine of up to $250,000.

For the complete CFAA text, see `www.law.cornell.edu/uscode/18/1030.html`.

Economic Espionage Act of 1996

Up until 1996, there were no federal laws that dealt specifically with the theft of trade secrets. Some states had laws, but the U.S. government didn't have anything on its books to prosecute economic spies. This changed with the enactment of the Economic Espionage Act (18 U.S.C., Sections 1831–1839) or EEA.

There are two key provisions of the act:

✓ It authorized the FBI to conduct investigations in which foreign governments are suspected of being involved in the theft of American business information. Although the FBI has always had the lead counterintelligence role when it comes to foreign espionage, up until 1996 it dealt only with national security issues, not those of an economic nature.

✓ It redefined the term "goods, wares, or merchandise" in federal laws relating to stolen property to include a company's "proprietary economic information." This opened the door for expanded federal investigation and prosecution.

Violations of the EEA have some serious penalties — with a maximum of 15 years in prison and up to $500,000 fines for individuals, and up to a $10 million fine for a business found guilty of supporting espionage activities. It's important to note that EEA doesn't just apply to foreign economic espionage, but also to spying performed by U.S. companies against each other.

The feds are serious about this law, unlike some other statutes; in 1997 for example, a Florida couple violated ECPA by eavesdropping on and taping then-Speaker of the House Newt Gingrich's cell-phone conversations and were each slapped on the hands with a $500 fine. Since the EEA came into being, there have been 35 cases involving violations of the act, many of these with significant fines and prison terms.

x-ref

Mark Halligan, a lawyer who specializes in trade secret work, tracks violations of the EEA and has the complete text of the act as well as a list of arrests and convictions at http://my.execpc.com/~mhallign/indict.html.

State Laws

Although federal laws are important, the majority of law enforcement takes place at the state and local levels. Most states have laws on their books that are very similar to the federal computer crime, wiretap, and privacy laws. (Some are even stricter, such as California's Privacy Act, which has provisions that exceed the protections of the federal Title III Wiretap Act.)

State laws are limited in scope, though, because they are set up to deal with criminal activities and civil complaints within the political boundaries of the state. When it comes to computer espionage that might be conducted remotely from out of the state, state governments aren't equipped to handle the extraterritoriality because their law enforcement agencies can't execute search warrants, subpoena witnesses, or make arrests beyond their own borders. This is where the federal agencies get involved.

If both state and federal laws are broken, state Attorneys General or local District Attorneys get together with their regional U.S. Attorney General counterparts and decide which entity is going to go after the guilty party.

The laws from state to state vary widely in structure and wording, but not in intent. Almost all of them criminalize the unauthorized access to or use of computers and databases, using a computer as an instrument of fraud, and known and foreseeable acts of computer sabotage. Do some research and take these laws into consideration (for example, in Virginia only a single party needs to consent to a monitored communication, while in Maryland both parties need to consent) if you plan on eavesdropping or happen to catch an eavesdropper.

It's beyond the scope of this book to cover all the state laws relating to computer eavesdropping. Every state has its own official Web site, and most have online, searchable versions of their state codes. Other sources of information on state law are the National Conference of State Legislatures (www.ncsl.org/programs/lis/CIP/surveillance.htm), which has a summary of state laws relating to surveillance, and the National Security Institute (http://nsi.org/Library/Compsec/computerlaw/statelaws.html), which has a site with links to state computer crime laws.

Implications of the USA Patriot Act of 2001

In response to the September 11, 2001 terrorist attacks on the United States, President Bush signed the USA Patriot Act (USAPA) into law on October 26, 2001. The law makes amendments to 15 statutes, including many of the federal laws discussed previously. (Spy trivia: USA PATRIOT is actually an acronym for "Uniting and Strengthening America by Providing Appropriate Tools Required to Intercept and Obstruct Terrorism.")

The USA Patriot Act has two implications for those involved with computer eavesdropping:

✓ It gives the government much broader powers to conduct surveillance and investigations, which has worried many privacy advocates.

✓ It provides harsher penalties for some activities that could be associated with computer spying.

Organizations such as the Center for Democracy and Technology, Electronic Frontier Foundation, American Civil Liberties Union, and the Electronic Privacy Information Center voiced concerns that politicians rushed the act through Congress without much oversight due to the emotions of the September 11 attacks. There is a sunset provision in USAPA that calls for many electronic surveillance amendments to expire on December 31, 2005. However, due to the fluid nature of the asymmetrical conflict, it's unlikely that the war against terrorism will be won within the next three years, so the amendments will be renewed.

A year after the bill was signed, the House Judiciary Committee released the Department of Justice's (DOJ) response for a request for information about how USAPA was being implemented (the letter is available at www.house.gov/judiciary/patriotresponses101702.pdf). DOJ classified a large amount of the information, and a number of organizations have filed Freedom of Information Act suits trying to disclose some of the implementation details. USAPA will always remain controversial, and there's a good chance that future terrorist attacks on the United States will bring even more changes to surveillance-related laws, causing even more contention.

This section discusses some of the key changes that USAPA has made to various laws that could apply to computer eavesdropping.

The USA Patriot Act is more than 300 pages long and contains many amendments. For a complete analysis of the act, refer to `www.cdt.org/security/010911response.shtml`.

Wiretap and Stored Communications Access Acts

With the advent of USAPA, the Title III Wiretap Act and the Stored Communications Access Act (discussed earlier in this chapter) were amended with some important computer-related changes, including the following:

- ✓ A cable company must comply with the laws governing interception and disclosure of communications by other telephone companies or ISPs when it provides telephone or Internet services. Previously cable companies that provided Internet services were covered by a different set of rules than phone companies.

- ✓ Voice-mail can now be obtained with a search warrant instead of a more stringent wiretap order (messages stored on answering-machine tapes still continue to have a higher level of protection, though).

- ✓ Terrorism and violation of the Computer Fraud and Abuse Act have been added as crimes that can be investigated with a wiretap.

- ✓ Pen register/trap-and-trace authority has been clarified to apply to Internet traffic.

- ✓ The government is now protected from liability for warrant-less interceptions of crackers and similar "trespassers" at the request of a service provider.

- ✓ The ECPA has been amended to allow a single court having jurisdiction over an offense to issue a search warrant for stored data such as e-mail that would be valid anywhere in the U.S. (previously, judges could issue warrants only within their own jurisdiction).

Foreign Intelligence Surveillance Act

Because the purpose of USAPA was to enhance law enforcement's capability to counter foreign terrorism, a number of changes were logically made to FISA, including the following:

- ✓ **Roving wiretaps.** Normally, when a wiretap order is granted, it specifies the communication means to be monitored, such as a phone line or Internet connection. Under USAPA, FISA was expanded to permit "roving wiretaps on intelligence targets." This means that a single court order can grant permission to eavesdrop on any communications method without specifying the type. It also means that in the course of the surveillance, other people who use the communication device may also be eavesdropped on, regardless of whether they are involved in espionage. For example, if a suspected terrorist is known to use a public library Internet connection, the FBI could monitor all of the Net activity at the library. Another provision in the amendment would prevent the library, or whichever third party was asked by the government to cooperate in the surveillance, from revealing that monitoring was taking place. (The American Library Association even offers advice to librarians about this at `www.ala.org/alaorg/oif/usapatriotact.html`.) Privacy advocates have raised serious Fourth Amendment issues about this provision.

✓ **Pen register/trap-and-trace devices.** Under FISA, the government had to provide enough evidence to convince the Foreign Intelligence Surveillance Court that a surveillance target was an agent of a foreign power before a pen register/trap-and-trace device could be used. USAPA eliminated that requirement, and now the government can use the surveillance devices "for any investigation to gather foreign intelligence information." There is a provision that prevents the use of these devices on U.S. citizens based only on "the basics of activities protected by the First Amendment." This means just because you were Muslim and there was no evidence you were involved in any espionage activities, a FISA request for a pen register/trap-and-trace would be rejected.

✓ **More FISC judges.** The act designates five more judges to sit on the Foreign Intelligence Surveillance Court to provide increased capacity and oversight for FISA surveillance requests.

✓ **Standards for surveillance.** Previously, FISA surveillance was granted when foreign intelligence gathering was the primary or only purpose of an investigation. USAPA changed the wording and lowered the standards by stating that when foreign intelligence gathering is "a significant" purpose of the investigation a request shall be approved. The word "significant" isn't defined, and the vagueness of the term leads to concerns.

Computer Fraud and Abuse Act

In addition to the clearly terrorist-related amendments, the USAPA also included modifications to the CFAA. Many electronic rights advocates questioned these changes, viewing them as a government attempt to add strengthened computer crime laws under the umbrella of terrorist legislation. Key new provisions that could relate to computer eavesdropping include the following:

✓ Classifying an "attempt to commit an offense" under the CFAA as having the same penalties as an offense.

✓ Applying the CFAA to computers outside the United States if damage is done that impacts U.S. Interstate commerce.

✓ Including state convictions under similar statutes as prior convictions for the purpose of giving increased penalties for more than one conviction.

✓ Increasing penalties for violations of the statute — maximum penalty of ten years for the first offense and 20 years for a second offense.

✓ Redefining "loss" to include time spent responding and assessing damage; restoring data, programs, systems, or information; any revenue lost; any cost incurred; or other consequential damages. (This makes it relatively easy to reach the $5,000 damage threshold for prosecution.)

✓ Classifying computer crime as a terrorist offense when it affects national security or causes damage that results in physical injury, causes disruption in medical care, and impacts public health or safety issues.

Earlier versions of the act would have classified low-level computer intrusions and Web site defacement as terrorist offenses, but these definitions were removed from the final version of the act.

Busted: FISA Abuses

The Department of Justice wants to be able to share more information between law enforcement and intelligence agencies, but this would go against the concept of *minimization*, discussed earlier in the chapter (minimization is the practice of keeping criminal investigation information separate from intelligence information). The reason why the DOJ wants to combine the information gathering of law enforcement and intelligence agencies is that it would then be easier for law enforcement to get authorization to conduct surveillance if they could say it's against a foreign power versus your garden-variety criminal. However, by combining the two investigative branches, it would be all too easy for law enforcement to abuse FISA to spy on someone who isn't engaged in suspected terrorist or foreign espionage activities.

The DOJ wanted to minimize minimization, but the Foreign Intelligence Surveillance Court (FISC) had second thoughts about that. In August 2002, a FISC decision previously made in May came into public view.

The presiding judge of the FISC, U.S. District Court Judge Royce Lamberth, stated that the FBI had made an "alarming number" of errors in seeking and using national security warrants in terrorism investigations since 2000. "In virtually every instance, the government's misstatements and omissions in FISA applications and violations of the court's orders involved information sharing and unauthorized dissemination to criminal investigators and prosecutors," the court ruling said. Those are some pretty strong words.

Attorney General John Ashcroft pressed forward with his bid for greater information sharing for national security reasons and took his case to the Foreign Intelligence Surveillance Court of Review in hopes of reversing FISC's decision. On November 18, 2002, the Court of Review issued its first-ever opinion granting the Justice Department new powers to use wiretaps in criminal cases. The Court of Review reversed an earlier decision by the Foreign Intelligence Surveillance Court, which had limited those powers out of concern for citizens' privacy.

Other Provisions

USAPA has a number of other provisions, many of which deal with terrorism and don't have much relevance to computer espionage. There are a few notable items to mention, though, that don't fit into the framework of federal surveillance-related laws. These items include the following:

- ✓ Information obtained from grand juries and wiretaps can be shared among a wider range of government offices and officials.

- ✓ The scope of subpoenas is expanded, and investigators can access Internet subscriber information, such as method of payment, session time and duration, and temporarily assigned network addresses.

- ✓ Service providers (including ISPs) can disclose the content of stored e-mail messages and other customer information whenever the provider "reasonably believes" that an emergency involving immediate danger of "death or serious physical injury to any person" requires such disclosure.

- ✓ Rules for law enforcement to conduct "secret searches" during the investigation of any federal offense are liberalized, including delaying notice of the warrant to the person it is served on. During most criminal investigations, a subject is served with a copy of the search warrant. With a "sneak and peek" warrant, the court allows notifying the suspect in a "reasonable time" if immediate notice could jeopardize an investigation.

State Laws

Although USAPA is a federal act, a number of states have followed suit and changed their own laws to mirror those of the U.S. government. State "homeland defense," "anti-terrorist," or "whatever name makes political hay" acts started popping up right after USAPA was signed into law. These laws generally follow the federal lead in expanded law enforcement surveillance activities and increasing penalties for various crimes. Be sure to consult your own state laws for more information.

For the complete text of the USA Patriot Act, see `http://thomas.loc.gov/cgi-bin/bdquery/z?d107:HR03162:%5D`.

The Realities of Enforcement

The effectiveness of a law correlates directly to how rigorously it is enforced. Although computer espionage activities are illegal under a variety of statutes, the reality is that there haven't been that many prosecutions, especially considering the amount of spying that's estimated to be going on.

Some of the reasons why enforcement hasn't been so strict include the following:

✓ An overburdened legal system

✓ Not enough law enforcement officers qualified to properly investigate computer espionage

✓ The difficulty of detecting eavesdropping activities

✓ Lack of adequate evidence

✓ Victims not wanting to report espionage because of negative public relations and diminished stockholder confidence

✓ More attention and resources being devoted to the "war on terrorism" versus other crimes, which might involve computer espionage

Don't think that spying is as safe as driving 60 mph in a 55 mph zone, however. There have been an increasing number of cases at the state and local levels that involve computer eavesdropping. Although these cases seem very minor when compared with high-profile government and business espionage episodes, they are setting legal precedents and getting prosecutors comfortable with

Countermeasures: Kinder, Gentler FBI

The FBI recognizes that cyber-crime, including computer espionage, is a growing problem. In an October 2002 speech to an industry trade group, FBI Director Robert Mueller told attendees that only an estimated one-third of computer intrusions were being reported to the agency. Recognizing that many corporations shun law enforcement because of possible negative publicity if an intrusion is revealed, Mueller went on to reassure industry, and said:

"Let me first tell you what will not happen if you report a cyber-crime or intrusion. We will not surround your building with agents clad in jackets emblazoned with the letters F.B.I. We understand the value of a low-key approach in these matters. We are coming to assist the victim company, not prosecute it. Our specialists will come in plainclothes, perhaps in the guise of contractors or consultants, if needed.

We will not hold a press conference or issue a press release. At no time do we hold press conferences on pending cases. As for leaks — they are forbidden. If one happens, whoever is responsible will answer to me personally.

We will not take over your system or attach foreign machines to your networks.

And we will not read your files to study your regulatory compliance plan. I assure you we are not interested in your files."

The FBI wants to encourage industry reporting incidents, and to do that, they have to gain industry's trust. Whether they will succeed remains to be seen.

handling such crimes. Increasingly, computer-savvy law enforcement and prosecutors coupled with "get tough on crime" political motivations are starting to turn up the heat on computer-related crime.

Also, if you're considering doing any type of eavesdropping, give some careful consideration to whether your actions might be viewed as associated with real or potential terrorism, even in the remotest circumstances. The scrutiny that everyday activities are currently coming under is getting fairly intense. For example, during the summer of 2002, federal investigators quietly requested the membership records from diving organizations and customer records from dive shops for anyone who had went through SCUBA training. The reason was a fear that minimally trained, recreational divers might try to blow up ships in U.S. ports; a theory dismissed by both many divers and security professionals.

Even though you might not be a card-carrying member of Al Qaeda, if you're doing something illegal with a computer, your activities could put you on state and federal law enforcement radar.

Civil versus Criminal Court

So far, most of the discussion in this chapter has focused on criminal law. However, when it comes to corporate espionage, in addition to criminal proceedings there's a good chance a blown spying operation could also wind up in civil court.

Civil proceedings take place when a person or legal entity (a company, organization, or government) accuses another person or legal entity of causing injury and then seeks compensation in court. Each party uses his own lawyers, and a judge or jury resolves the matter. For example, if a spy was working on behalf of a competitor and was caught, the victimized company could file suit against both the spy and the competitor in an attempt to recover lost revenue caused by the espionage activities.

There are two important distinctions between civil and criminal court:

- ✓ **Penalties.** In criminal court, jail time, monetary fines, or both can be levied against a guilty party. In civil court, penalties usually involve only monetary damages.

- ✓ **Required proof.** For criminal cases, prosecutors must establish "beyond a reasonable doubt" that a party is guilty. That means there has to be enough evidence for an average person to think, "Yes, there's no reasonable doubt in my mind that he's guilty." Civil cases have a lesser standard of proof required, called "preponderance of the evidence." This means that there needs to be just enough evidence to make guilt more likely than not. The classic nonespionage examples of required proof are the O.J. Simpson cases. Simpson was found not guilty by a jury in his 1995 criminal trial because the prosecution couldn't establish his guilt beyond a reasonable doubt. However, during his 1997 civil trial, a jury believed there was enough evidence to make Simpson liable for the deaths of Ronald Goldman and Nicole Brown Simpson, and they awarded $8.5 million to the deceased's families.

It's also worth noting that the court can issue seizure orders in civil cases. For example, if a judge believes that a defendant (the entity that compensation is being sought from) company has evidence of espionage on its corporate servers, he can issue an order to seize the servers, having

Busted: Raiders of the Lost Amazon

In November 1999, Internet bookseller Alibris settled federal charges that it eavesdropped on e-mail sent by Amazon.com and possessed unauthorized computer passwords. The company was faced with ten counts of violating the ECPA and one count of unauthorized possession of passwords with intent to defraud. Each of the charges had up to a $250,000 penalty, but Alibris was able to settle for a single $250,000 fine.

The company's corporate predecessor, a defunct business named Interloc, Inc., was a Massachusetts online bookseller that had a subsidiary Internet service provider business running under the name of Valinet. During 1998, Interloc intercepted and stored thousands of e-mails from Amazon to customers who were using the ISP's services, many of whom were booksellers. Although no financial or proprietary information was revealed, prosecutors alleged that the interceptions were designed, in part, to gain a competitive advantage for Alibris' online bookselling business. (Prosecutors also stated that Interloc kept unauthorized copies of confidential password files and customer lists of its competitor Internet service providers.)

Because Amazon wasn't significantly harmed, no additional criminal or civil charges were brought against Alibris. When asked about the federal charges at the time, Martin Manley, Alibris' president said, "We're a different company in a different business now, and it was just time to clean this stuff up." Alibris is still in business, and is one of the leaders in online sales of used and hard-to-find books.

the order executed by law enforcement officers and representatives of the plaintiff (the entity seeking compensation). The seizure can also involve information. For example, a corporation could file a "John Doe" suit against some unknown person and then compel an Internet service provider to turn over subscriber data that might be relevant to the suit.

Bosses and Employees — Legal Spying

Under ECPA, an employer can't monitor employee telephone calls or e-mail when employees have a reasonable expectation of privacy—an example of a reasonable expectation of privacy would be restrooms without surveillance cameras. However, ECPA does allow employer eavesdropping if employees are notified in advance or if the employer has reason to believe the company's interests are in jeopardy. These are pretty broad exemptions, so if you're an employee, it's best just to assume that anything you do on your computer may be monitored. There are a few exceptions though, including:

✓ **Public employees.** The First, Fourth, and Fourteenth Amendments of the Constitution give government employees rights and remedies that private sector employees don't have. For example, federal, state, and local employers typically must respect their employees' free speech rights and generally cannot conduct unreasonable employee searches and seizures.

✓ **Union employees.** The National Labor Relations Act (NLRA) applies in an organized or organizing workplace. Under the NRLA, a collective bargaining agreement could limit an employer's right to intercept employees' communications, even if Title III or state law allows the eavesdropping. The NLRA could also limit an employer's right to intercept employees' communications if that interception affects "the right to self-organization" or "concerted activities."

Although there are currently no federal workplace privacy statutes, be sure to check with an attorney to make sure you're within legal bounds if you plan on monitoring your employees. Some states have expanded privacy laws, such as California's Privacy Act, or are considering them. Because the public's demand for privacy appears to be growing, it's wise to keep up with current workplace legislation.

Although laws tend to be on the employer's side, a prudent business should consider taking additional steps to reduce any potential litigation under privacy laws. Three low-cost, simple techniques include the following:

✓ **Using implied consent.** Utilize a login banner, software "nag" screen (found on many keyloggers), or some other apparent method of informing employees that all e-mail, Internet use, and other computer communications may be monitored.

✓ **Using express consent.** Create and distribute employee agreements or other documents in which the employees expressly consent to monitoring.

✓ **Using e-mail signatures.** Attach a brief paragraph to the end of all outgoing e-mails that states all e-mail may be monitored. Although this practice may seem excessive, it does inform anyone that replies to an outgoing e-mail that any exchanged messages aren't private.

In addition to protecting yourself from lawsuits, a publicized monitoring policy may actually be a deterrent against employee misuse of resources. If an employee knows that computer monitoring is taking place, they may be less likely to try pilfering company data.

Legal Issues with Family Members

In 1976, the National Commission for the Review of Federal and State Laws Relating to Wiretapping and Electronic Surveillance reported that 68 percent of all reported wiretapping involved an attempt by a spouse to obtain evidence for use against the other spouse in a domestic matter. Another 11 percent were the result of other domestic surveillance, including "parental and courtship" eavesdropping. That means almost 80 percent of reported wiretapping was taking place in a family context. Although the report was issued in the pre-PC days and focused on telephone taps, there's no reason to think that the statistics have changed much over the years. Only now, in addition to a telephone, a suspicious spouse can use a keylogger or a sniffer for wiretap purposes.

There is a fair amount of case law that deals with interspousal wiretapping, and although most of it has to do with secretly recorded phone conversations, remember that Title III also applies to computer eavesdropping. Although there haven't yet been any widely publicized cases that involve the use of keyloggers and sniffers that set legal precedent, the results of the earlier telephone-oriented cases are viewed as relevant by attorneys and judges.

Generally, the courts have followed two paths regarding violations of Title III by a husband or wife:

- ✓ **"Marital Home" Exception.** In the 1974 Simpson vs. Simpson case (which didn't involve O.J. or Homer), in which a husband secretly recorded his wife's phone calls, a federal court established a "marital home" exception to Title III, believing the intent of the act wasn't to intervene in the home, even though there was no exception stated in the statute. Several other court decisions have been based on Simpson vs. Simpson.

- ✓ **No Exception.** In the 1976 United States vs. Jones case, a federal court of appeals reversed a district court decision that dismissed a Title III indictment of a husband who intercepted telephone conversations of his estranged wife. The court stated, "If Congress had intended to create another exception to Title III's blanket prohibition of unauthorized wiretaps, they would have included a specific exception for interspousal wiretaps in the statute." Although the federal courts haven't heard a large number of these trials, a majority of state and federal cases have gone with the Jones viewpoint.

So if you use a keylogger on your spouse and intercept his or her e-mail, although it's not a sure thing, you're definitely flirting with a Title III violation. The one certainty in this matter is that the courts have made it very clear that a third party who wiretaps a spouse in his or her home at the request of the other spouse definitely violates Title III. (If you don't have a recognized legal relationship with your significant other and you eavesdrop, you're definitely on thin ice if you get caught and your partner is of a litigious nature.)

How about eavesdropping on your children? There's case law here too, most of it based on divorce-related incidents in which a parent secretly tape-recorded a phone conversation between a child and the other parent. Many of the court cases have created a parent-child exception to Title III based on vicarious consent. Generally, the courts have stated that a custodial parent can monitor a minor child's communications as long as the parent has a good faith, objectively reasonable belief that the monitoring is done in the best interests of the child. Using the keylogger example again, although Title III doesn't have a parental exclusion, you certainly aren't at as much legal risk if you eavesdrop on your children's computer activities compared to snooping on your spouse's. However, once junior reaches the age of majority, all bets are off. (Note to spy kids: Your age is probably going to save you from jail time if you computer snoop on Mom and Dad and get caught. Just remember that sometimes parents aren't as lenient as the courts when it comes to punishing children.)

Summary

As you can see, there are a number of federal and state laws that relate to computer eavesdropping. You don't need to be a lawyer to have a general awareness of these laws, but you should leave it up to attorneys to deal with the details and nuances.

There are three important points to consider when it comes to computer-related legislation (espionage-related or not):

- ✓ **Law hasn't kept pace with technology.** Both the written laws and precedent-setting cases have lagged behind advances in networking, hardware, and software technology. There seems to be at least a several-year lag when it comes to legal matters and contemporary technology. Attorneys and the courts are starting to catch up, but the adoption of new technologies will also put the legal system behind the curve.

- ✓ **Laws may not be "pure."** The notion that laws are passed solely to benefit society is a bit naive (we know what's best for you, so trust us). The USA Patriot Act was rushed through Congress with minimal review due to patriotic emotion. The Homeland Security Act, passed in December 2002, contains even more surveillance-related provisions with no subpoenas or court oversight required. A draft proposal marked confidential of something the Justice Department calls the Domestic Security Enhancement Act, dubbed Patriot II, surfaced in February 2003 and gives the government even more spying powers. Technology users should expect laws that, to quote Spock, "seem highly illogical."

- ✓ **Laws change.** Change is inevitable, and this also applies to law. Although legal change isn't as blindingly fast as technology change, things might not be the same tomorrow as they were yesterday. New laws and legal opinions and precedent-setting cases regarding old laws keep lawyers on their toes. The same should apply to you or someone in your organization. What might be a current electronic surveillance law today could be something completely new next year.

Now, with this general introduction to legal matters out of the way, let's get into the more interesting parts (no offense to attorneys) of the book: how to spy and how to stop spies from eavesdropping on you.

Chapter 3

Black Bag Jobs

"I work at night."
  —Anonymous FBI agent assigned to a surreptitious entry team, when asked what he did
    for a living

A Look Inside the Black Bag

A "black bag job" is spook-speak for covertly breaking and entering into a building to gather information or evidence or to plant some type of surveillance device. The term came from the World War II era, when FBI agents used black leather doctor's bags to carry equipment in and out of a burgled home or office. The more politically correct law enforcement term for a black bag job (or its shortened form, "bag job") is "surreptitious entry," which just doesn't have that criminal ring to it.

Although breaking into places where you're not supposed to be and stealing other people's secrets has been going on for thousands of years, the first modern organized break-ins for intelligence purposes started in the 1920s when the U.S. Navy financed a series of black bag jobs against the Japanese government. In a joint effort between the Office of Naval Intelligence, FBI, and New York City police, agents broke into the Japanese Consulate in New York, cracked a safe, and photographed a Japanese Naval codebook. This gave the U.S. a significant advantage in the prewar years because it could read intercepted Japanese messages that were encoded. The black bag jobs against the Japanese continued up until 1939, with a series of successful burglaries carried out against other Japanese government offices in New York.

Since the early days of black bag jobs, advances in security technology have caused them to become more sophisticated. Throughout the world, there are government and private schools that teach specialized surreptitious entry skills to military, law enforcement, and intelligence community personnel. These skills often find their way to the private sector through former agents who have had practical field experience.

Black bag jobs can be legal, such as when a court grants a warrant to a law enforcement agency to carry out a covert entry to search for evidence or when a business conducts an investigation on its own premises that it doesn't want its employees to know about; or illegal, when a surreptitious entry takes place without authorization. (Remember that if you do this kind of thing illegally, you're now treading into criminal offenses such as breaking and entering and burglary, which the police and courts usually don't take too lightly.)

Black bag jobs are especially suited to computer espionage for a number of reasons:

✓ Because of the large amount of data that's stored on a hard drive and the relative ease and speed in which it can be covertly duplicated, surreptitious entries can provide a wealth of information in a short amount of time.

✓ From a technical standpoint, as strong encryption that's difficult, if not impossible, to crack becomes more widely used, black bag jobs such as the ones used to bug the keyboard of mobster Nicodermo Scarfo may be law enforcement's investigative tool of last resort. (The relaxing of the legal requirements for such "sneak-and-peek" operations under the provisions of the USA Patriot Act may also cause the number of bag jobs to increase in the coming years.)

See Chapter 8 for more on the Nicodermo Scarfo, Jr. case.

In this chapter, you learn about different types of bag jobs, how they're performed, and some general ways to defend yourself against them.

Physical and Network Black Bag Jobs

A black bag job can take place anywhere — in a target's house, office, car, or hotel room. For example, when the FBI was investigating whether CIA employee Harold Nicholson was spying for the Russians, they covertly searched his Chevrolet Lumina sports van and discovered a personally owned laptop computer. The agents imaged the hard drive and later found deleted classified CIA documents. A floppy disk was also found in the van that contained information about access agents, unpaid American citizens who frequently travel abroad and provide information to the CIA. The evidence played a key role in convicting Nicholson.

When it comes to computer espionage, there are two general types of black bag jobs:

✓ **Physical attacks.** This is a traditional break-in in which a spy enters someplace he's not supposed to be. Think lock picks, alarm systems, and Tom Cruise hanging upside down on a trapeze over a computer. There's more at stake and to risk during a physical black bag job because there's a greater chance of being discovered by people who are suspicious about your activities. In addition, law enforcement is very good at investigating and responding to burglaries because residential and business property crime break-ins are relatively common.

✓ **Network attacks.** Instead of targeting a physical location, a spy might break in through a network connection to collect information. If done correctly, network bag jobs have considerably less risk than a physical bag job because it's much easier to cover your tracks in the virtual world compared to the real world. Law enforcement typically doesn't have the training, experience, or personnel to deal as well with network break-ins as they do

Busted: Watergate "Plumbers"

Probably the most famous publicly known black bag job in history happened at the Democratic National Committee Headquarters in the Washington, D.C. Watergate apartment-office complex. The White House–sanctioned burglary took place on June 17, 1972. The White House was already sponsoring illegal break-ins with its Special Investigations Unit or "Plumbers," a group of former intelligence and law enforcement agents assigned to locate and plug sources of government leaks to the media.

The five men who performed the Watergate bag job carried sophisticated espionage gear used by the CIA, including cameras, lock picks, miniature tear-gas dispensers, bugging equipment, and radios. They had broken into the office complex during the previous Memorial Day weekend and installed bugs, but they returned when one of the listening devices didn't work. Although the "Plumbers" were all either former employees of the CIA and FBI or had CIA connections, sloppy tradecraft led to their downfall. One of them forgot to remove tape from a door latch holding it open, and a security guard discovered it and called the police. The rest, including the downfall of Richard Nixon, is history.

Eugenio R. Martinez, one of the burglars, wrote an excellent account of the break-in, with details of the tradecraft and operational bungling. It is available at `www.watergate.info/index.php?itemid=18`.

with physical break-ins. The downside to a network attack is that only information on the computer can be compromised, in comparison to a physical attack where all sorts of interesting nondigital information may be present.

Because this chapter focuses more on physical bag jobs, go to Chapter 10 for more information on the techniques a spy would use in a network bag job.

Planned and Opportunistic Black Bag Jobs

Black bag jobs also come in two different flavors: planned and opportunistic. One of the primary goals of a bag job is to perform it completely undetected; a target should never know that his or her security was compromised (until it's perhaps too late). There are two approaches to carrying out a bag job:

✓ **Planned.** The hallmark of a good black bag job is extensive planning. The entire operation is completely thought-out ahead of time. Planning is especially crucial if the operation is complex due to alarm systems, guards, dogs, or strong physical security measures. The more countermeasures and defenses a target has in place, the more planning and resources are required to carry out the bag job. (Of course, even with lots of planning and experienced operatives, a bag job can still fail; consider Watergate, for example.)

✓ **Opportunistic.** Opportunistic bag jobs are simply stealing information when an opportunity presents itself. Either the spy is directed to acquire specific types of information or he feels his employer or a potential employer might be interested in the information. There is little to no planning that takes place with these bag jobs. The chances of successful opportunistic attacks can be greatly reduced when security policies are put in place, enforced, and adopted as second nature by employees. There's more about this in the "Countermeasures" section later in this chapter.

Ultimately, whether a bag job is performed or not can come down to a matter of economics. The circumstances may make an operation too costly to perform, whether in terms of time, money, or risk.

Spy Tactics

In many of the following chapters of this book, there's a section like this one called "Spy Tactics" that describes how spies go about compromising sensitive information. Quite often, you are asked to step into the shoes of a spy to better understand how he or she operates. In some cases, you pretend you're a good guy; at other times you'll be up to no good. Thinking like a spy is a very important step in developing defenses to use against one.

Spy Games

For this first bit of role-playing, imagine that you're a consultant employed by a security company that specializes in penetration testing. Penetration testing, or "pentest" for short, is the evaluation of an organization's physical or computer security, or both. The military and government have been successfully using penetration testing for a number of years to assess the security of nuclear facilities, military installations, and classified networks. "Tiger teams" or "red teams" are assigned to stage attacks against secure facilities or computer networks to test detection and response reactions. Following the penetration testing, reports are written that outline the security strengths and weaknesses with the eventual goal of shoring up attack defenses and countermeasures. Computer network penetration testing in the private sector has become popular over the past several years as businesses and the government try to keep crackers out of their networks.

Your assigned target is the sales-training division of a large software company. It's housed in a six-story office building several miles away from the company's corporate campus headquarters. The vice president of sales has been worried that competitors have somehow gotten hold of internal sales-training material on new, yet-to-be-released products and are using the proprietary information to their advantage. He's hired your company to perform an internal audit. Although another team focuses on possible network vulnerabilities, your job is to probe and assess the physical security of the building and attempt a black bag job on the office.

Because you've been authorized and contracted to perform the spying, you've got a "get-out-of-jail-free" letter signed by a senior vice president as well as his personal cell phone and pager phone numbers. It's a reassuring safety blanket in case you get caught, but no one from your company has ever been caught doing an assessment, and you'd like to keep it that way.

Because you're a little new at all of this, before you start thinking about your upcoming assignment, it's worthwhile to take a quick look at how the pros work. Pay attention; you might get some ideas.

Inside a Government Black Bag Job

There's not a whole lot of information in the public domain about black bag jobs. That's because the people who do them most often (military, law enforcement, and intelligence agencies) like to protect their "sources and methods." The rationale is if bag job techniques are revealed, the bad guys will be able to come up with ways to effectively counter them. (There are definitely merits to maintaining operational security, OPSEC, but as with most forms of security through obscurity, it leaves law-abiding citizens and businesses that could be victims of illegal black bag jobs rather defenseless because they don't know what they are up against.)

Wes Swearingen, who worked as an FBI agent from 1951 to 1977 and wrote a tell-all book called *FBI Secrets: An Agent's Exposé*, participated in numerous black bag jobs for the Bureau. In his book and during various media interviews, he has provided details on the "logistics of a black bag job." Although the information is somewhat dated and oriented toward bag jobs of private citizens' homes, most of the tradecraft still applies today, and provides a general framework for how to perform surreptitious entries of offices, warehouses, and other facilities.

TEAMS

The FBI and other law enforcement and intelligence agencies have the luxury of using a number of people during a black bag job, each with different responsibilities. While it's possible for a lone agent to perform a bag job, it's much safer to use at least a handful of agents for the operation to perform different jobs. There can be up to five functional teams involved with a black bag job, including the following:

✓ **Surveillance.** The surveillance team covertly follows people (anyone who lives in or is visiting the residence) after they leave the premises. The surveillance team's responsibility is to keep other teams informed of the whereabouts of the people they are trailing, so they don't unexpectedly return to the residence and surprise agents.

✓ **Inside.** The inside team is responsible for entering the residence and installing surveillance devices or gathering evidence. Specialists in electronic surveillance, computers, photography, and other fields may be included on this team, depending on the needs.

✓ **Pickup.** The pickup team drops off and picks up the inside team at a location selected to draw the least amount of attention to the operation.

✓ **Observation.** The observation team watches the vicinity of the residence for any people or activities that might compromise the operation.

✓ **Command.** The command team directs and coordinates the black bag job from outside the residence. In some cases the command team can also perform observation duties.

The number of people assigned to each team depends on the target and the circumstances. For example, a single person might share command and observation duties on a simple operation, whereas a more sophisticated operation could involve multiple surveillance teams monitoring subjects while on foot, in vehicles, and in the air.

Tactics: FBI Surreptitious Entry Teams

In his 1996 book, *Above the Law*, author David Burnham briefly describes the FBI's Surreptitious Entry Program. This program involves highly trained agents whose job is to covertly break and enter into all sorts of places to collect evidence and plant surveillance devices. There are two acronyms associated with FBI surveillance: SOG stands for Special Operations Groups, which are responsible for physical and electronic surveillance; and TTAs refers to Technically Trained Agents, who have electronic surveillance or computer skills required to carry out these covert operations.

Although the FBI refuses to discuss the covert entry program, from various publicly released affidavits, we do know that it's been very effective. In high-profile espionage cases, such as those involving Aldrich Ames, Robert Hanssen, Ana Belen Montes, and Brian Regan — as well as in criminal cases, such as that of Nicodermo Scarfo — the FBI has performed bag jobs on homes, offices, and vehicles in order to gather evidence on suspects.

All of these FBI bag jobs, whether performed for the Bureau, DEA, or other federal agencies, are carried out under a court order. Generally, there are four steps involved:

✓ The FBI field office or other federal agency that wants electronic surveillance states its requests.

✓ Technical agents covertly inspect the target and gather architectural blueprints and drawings.

✓ The team assembles whatever tools they need for the job, including specially designed surveillance equipment.

✓ The team performs the entry.

The Surreptitious Entry Program will definitely see more action in the wake of the terrorist attacks of 9/11. In the FBI's proposed Fiscal Year 2003 budget, there is a request for $12,162,000 for something referred to as "Tactical Operations." This item is described as being designed, " . . . to enhance the FBI's ability to respond to increasing physical search requests and to address changes in technology through research, development, and engineering."

In addition, the FBI is interested in beefing up its TTA program, as quoted in the Fiscal Year 2003 budget request, "The widespread use of digital telecommunications technologies and the incorporation of privacy features/capabilities through the use of cryptography pose a serious technical challenge to the FBI. Terrorists are using this technology to shroud their operation in secrecy and to thwart the efforts of law enforcement. The FY 2003 request of $10,027,000 includes personnel funding for new TTAs to support the administration of all monitoring functions and to provide necessary equipment for existing TTAs as well as to support training initiatives to ensure TTAs have the technical skills to implement electronic surveillance and to respond quickly and effectively to emerging technologies."

With the passage of the USA Patriot Act, many civil liberties groups are concerned about the relaxed surveillance restrictions and possible abuses based on past history. From World War II until the mid-1970s, the FBI performed hundreds, probably thousands, of illegal black bag jobs on politicians, civil rights activists and organizations, and citizens. Only time will tell if history repeats itself.

RESEARCH AND PLANNING

After a decision has been made to perform a black bag job (and has been approved by a judge), agents just don't rush out and immediately start the operation. A considerable amount of research and planning can go into the bag job. There's a negative correlation between risk and planning; as the amount of planning increases, the risk decreases, and vice versa. Although you can never eliminate risk completely, research and planning mitigates it and increases your chances of success.

Some of the key information to be identified during the research and planning phase includes the following:

- ✓ **The target.** Who the operation is going to be carried out against. A profile of the subject is created from records and surveillance, including driving routes, regularly attended meetings and events, and habits and patterns that allow the target to be easily followed.

- ✓ **The target's type and place of work.** Residential black bag jobs frequently take place while the subject is at work. Knowing where and when he works as well as what he does is important.

- ✓ **People who live in the house with the target (or who are visiting).** Before a team stages a break-in, it needs to know if the residence is unoccupied. The number of people living with the subject should be known, with profiles available for each occupant.

- ✓ **The landlord of the property (if it's not privately owned).** Because of the mystique of the FBI, people tend to cooperate with agents, even when there's no warrant involved. A discreet, cooperative landlord may simply let agents inside a rented property.

- ✓ **Information about the residence.** This information includes photographs and written notes about doors, locks, lighting, architectural plans, pets, neighbors, and any other details that might be useful in planning the operation. This information should be covertly gathered so you don't tip a target off that he's under surveillance.

Based on this research, a plan is developed to accomplish a certain objective, such as planting a bug or recovering possible evidence from a computer. Contingency plans are produced in case the bag job doesn't go as planned, and specialized tools and equipment are identified that are needed for the operation. The number of agents required, including those with special skills, is determined, and agents selected for the team are fully briefed on the plan.

TRIAL RUN

Practice makes perfect, and the FBI wants a black bag job to go as smoothly as possible to avoid detection. Because of this, the next step often is to perform a trial run before the actual operation. The trial-run sequence of events generally goes like this:

✓ The surveillance team follows the target and any members of the residence as they leave the house. Depending on the circumstances, no fewer than two agents may be used to follow each person. This is to provide backup as well as to continue surveillance if one of the agents believes his cover has been blown in tailing the person.

✓ All members of the surveillance team stay in constant radio contact. If radio contact is broken, the bag job is aborted. (To avoid eavesdropping by people with scanners, all radio communications use predetermined codes whenever encrypted radios aren't available.)

✓ After the target and other occupants of the residence have been followed away from the house or accounted for elsewhere, the dry run is ready to go.

✓ Agents make false pretense phone calls to neighbors, who might be in a position to view the entry in order to distract them from the operation. The "outside man" (command), who is serving as a lookout and directing the operation, specifies the precise time when the phone calls are made.

✓ The "outside man" (part of the command team) directs the "inside team" into position and informs the surveillance teams that the job is about to start. On the trial run, a two-person team is used, one to pick the lock and bypass any security systems, the other to communicate with the "outside man" over a radio. (Technician specialists may also be included, depending on the circumstances.)

✓ The "pickup team," which may consist of only a single agent, drives the "inside team" to a predetermined location where they won't be observed getting out of the vehicle; the "pickup team" then immediately leaves the area.

✓ The "inside team" approaches the entrance and looks for obvious alarm systems. If no alarms are present, the team enters the residence. If alarms are discovered that can't be bypassed, information about them is noted for a future attempt. The radio person informs the "outside man" that the team is inside. (Swearingen uses baseball jargon as codes, such as "the players are on the field" to indicate that the "inside team" is in place. Codes will almost certainly vary, depending on the team.)

✓ The trial run starts with an immediate search of all rooms for anyone who may still be in the residence. The "inside team" describes events to the "outside man" as they are taking place. A photographer may be called in to take pictures of evidence or to document the interior for future black bag jobs (especially those involving placing surveillance devices; for example, a bug may need to be custom-designed and built to match a piece of furniture or some other item in the house). Depending on how much time the "inside team" needs, the surveillance team communicates whether their followed subjects are headed back to the residence or not.

✓ The "inside team" gives progress reports to the "outside man" every few minutes, and when they are finished, the team requests to be picked up.

✓ After the "inside team" is clear of the residence, the "outside man" contacts the agents performing surveillance and observation and has them break surveillance and return to the office.

THE JOB

After a trial run takes place, the teams are debriefed, any kinks are worked out of the plan, and the actual bag job is carried out. The operation follows the general format of the trial run, with the possible addition of more technical specialists to be on the "inside" team.

Successful, undetected black bag jobs require skill, experience, and a high level of organization. Not everyone has the resources and skills to pull off something like this; even the FBI has only a limited number of agents for this type of work. Because of the time commitment and relative expense of a bag job, these operations are used judiciously in cases in which other evidence-gathering techniques haven't worked or won't work.

Exploiting the Vulnerabilities

Now that you have a general idea of the way the professionals operate, let's go back to our penetration test scenario and step through how you might plan and execute a black bag job against your software company client. We won't get into the details, such as how to defeat alarm sensors or pick a high-security Medeco lock (though there are some references listed in this section that might tell you how), instead, we'll focus on exploiting general, commonly encountered vulnerabilities. Whenever you see text in *italics*, it is something that directly relates to the scenario.

In a way, black bag jobs are the same as breaching a computer security system: You find a vulnerability and figure out how to exploit it. However, bag jobs are more complicated because they involve many different security elements that can't easily be identified or exploited with software tools.

Researching and Planning the Operation

To quote the old saying, "Proper Prior Planning Prevents Poor Performance," and with the "6 Ps" there are also "6 Ts" when it comes to black bag job planning. They include the following:

✓ **Target.** The target is who or what the black bag job will be carried out against. You should always establish what the goals and objectives of the job are and gather as much information about the target as possible; this information can include personal habits, whether an alarm system is installed, the model of door locks, or the type of computer the target uses.

✓ **Time.** You'll only have a limited amount of time to carry out a black bag job, so it's important to understand how much time each part of the job will take. Although timing may not be everything, it certainly is very important.

✓ **Talk.** Talk refers to communications, both using radios in a secure fashion during the operation and ensuring that team members are briefed and have a clear understanding of their roles and responsibilities.

✓ **Tools.** Make sure that you have the right tools for the job. For computer espionage, these tools could include software utilities that breach operating system and application security, examine files, or copy hard drives (don't forget something to copy the data to). You might also include hardware or software for monitoring keystrokes or tapping into networks.

✓ **Tactics.** A thorough plan should always be developed with built-in contingencies in case of unexpected events.

✓ **Tale.** You should always have a cover story in place that's both plausible and well rehearsed in case you're compromised.

It's time to apply some of this knowledge and come up with a black bag job plan for the scenario. You have two other people assigned to you to assist with the penetration test. Here's the initial information you've gathered about your target:

✓ *The office building has two entrances: a main lobby on the first floor and a basement-parking-level entrance. Both have cardkey-type locks that require you to swipe an identification card through a reader to unlock the door. Cardkey readers secure elevators during nonbusiness hours and are coded to the card; for example, if you work on the fourth floor, the elevator will take you only to that floor. Stairwells have alarmed doors, which are always locked from the outside, except when a fire alarm is activated.*

✓ *During business hours, weekdays from 7:30 a.m. to 6:00 p.m., a receptionist staffs a desk in the main lobby. If you're not an employee, she'll either buzz you through a locked door (again controlled by a cardkey reader) or call someone who works in the office to come down and escort you to an appointment.*

✓ *During nonbusiness hours, a security guard staffs the lobby desk. There are three video monitors at the desk connected to two cameras showing the opposite sides of the parking garage and another showing the parking garage building entrance. There is only one guard, who is supposed to make rounds of the building every hour. When he's not making rounds, he sits at the desk reading, watching television, or playing computer games.*

✓ *Janitorial service takes place every weekday evening around 10:00 p.m. with a contracted maintenance crew.*

✓ *The sales-training division takes up the entire fourth floor. All the employees have offices with locking doors instead of cubicles. The employees of the division tend to be older, have families, and don't put in the long overtime hours like the rest of the company does.*

Start thinking about what other information you might need and about possible approaches to breaching the office building's physical security.

Gaining Entry

Obviously, you will need to have a computer in front of you before you can search it for information or evidence. This search can be trivial or extremely challenging because you may need to go through several different layers of physical security to finally get the data you want. For example, in an office building, this can mean getting through the lobby, up an elevator or set of stairs, in through a locked office suite door, and then into an individual office.

Generally, there are three approaches to covertly gaining physical access to a location. In order of least risky to most risky, they include using insiders, "elicitation" (social engineering), and breaking and entering.

USING INSIDERS

An insider is someone who already works, lives, or has a reason to be at the location you're trying to penetrate. When it comes to gaining access to sensitive information, insiders are always preferable because

✓ They already have access to a facility and information

✓ They're already known or familiar to others at the location

✓ There's considerably less risk compared to sending in an outsider

When government intelligence agencies try to recruit people to spy against their home countries, they look for MICE. This isn't the squeaky rodent or computer kind of mouse; in this context, MICE refers to four influencing factors — Money, Ideology, Compromise, and Ego — that can be played individually or collectively as powerful motivators in getting a person to spy. Types of insiders to target include the following:

✓ **Disgruntled employees.** Employees who have been overlooked for promotions, are undergoing disciplinary actions, or have had recent cuts in pay or benefits.

✓ **Vulnerable employees.** Employees who have overextended debt, drug or alcohol addictions, concealed extramarital affairs, mental health issues, or relationship problems.

✓ **Contractors.** Cleaning staff, security guards, consultants, or repair people who don't have the loyalty of full-time employees.

Although recruiting spies through the use of MICE has traditionally been a tactic of state-sponsored espionage, the reality is that it works equally well for corporate economic espionage.

 Treason 101 is an excellent Web resource hosted by the U.S. military's Defense Security Service. It provides an overview of why people spy, a discussion of contemporary espionage topics, examples of insider threats, information about how spies are caught, and demographic and statistical information about spies. Go to `www.dss.mil/training/csg/security/Treason/Intro.htm#Treason%20101`.

Busted: Mind of a Spy

Robert Hanssen was one of the most devastating spies in American history. Until he was caught in 2001, the high-level FBI agent sold the nation's secrets to Russia for 20 years, in return for more than $1.4 million in cash and diamonds.

Hanssen is also the first spy who's been publicly exposed who made extensive use of the Internet. A Linux user and technophile, he frequently posted queries to USENET newsgroups about hardware problems, GPS units, PDAs, and digital cameras (as well as some erotic stories about his wife). Hanssen was no dummy when it came to computer technology, and one has to wonder if at some point he was passing messages to the Russians over innocently appearing USENET messages, either under his own name or an alias.

Hanssen's USENET posts are still out there. For an interesting peek inside the mind of a spy, go to `http://groups.google.com`, and search for any of the e-mail addresses that Hanssen used, including: hanssen@orion.clark.net, hanssen@nova.org, hanssen@amelia.nas.nasa.gov, rphanssen@earthlink.net, or TBERRR1@aol.com.

"ELICITATION" — A.K.A. SOCIAL ENGINEERING

Commonly known as "social engineering" within the computer security and cracking communities, it's known as "elicitation" in the espionage trade, and it means to subtly extract information or get someone to do something for you during an apparently normal and innocent conversation.

As a spying technique, elicitation exploits several fundamental aspects of human nature:

✓ Most people want to be polite and helpful, so they answer questions; even from relative strangers.

✓ People often want to appear well-informed and important, and they sometimes say more than they should.

✓ People want to be appreciated and feel that they're doing something important and useful. As a result, they tend to open up in response to praise of their work.

✓ Because the American culture tends to be open and honest, people are often reluctant to withhold information, lie, or be suspicious of others' motives.

When conducted by a skillful practitioner, elicitation appears to be part of a normal social or professional conversation and can occur anywhere — in the workplace, at a social event, in a restaurant, at a conference, or during a visit to one's home. Certain types of elicitation may even be perfectly legal, with a spy piecing together bits of information from one or more people to use as a tool for compromising secure data.

Elicitation can be done over the phone (which is safer) or in person; for example, play-acting that you're a repairperson, delivery service worker, utility company representative, employee, or someone else who can get you close to your target (just be sure you have the right appearance and false credentials to get away with it). In-person and telephone elicitation are often used together as part of an overall plan to compromise information.

For an extensive discussion on social-engineering techniques, see *The Art of Deception: Controlling the Human Element of Security* by Kevin D. Mitnick and William L. Simon (Wiley, 2002).

BREAKING AND ENTERING

The last and most risky way of gaining entry to a location is by breaking and entering (B&E in cop jargon). This involves picking locks, stealing keys, bypassing security alarms, and using other burglary methods. The main difference between a typical criminal break-in and an espionage black bag job is that a burglar usually only cares about stealing something of value and doesn't care if he leaves evidence of his crime, whereas a spy doesn't want to leave any trace that might tip off his target that he's been a victim of a bag job. (In some cases, a bag job may be performed to look like a burglary to draw attention away from its actual purpose.)

Cardkey badges, push-button locks, tamper-proof alarm systems, guards, and biometric authentication systems that were once only found in high-security facilities are all becoming common. These security measures can pose a significant challenge to a spy. In fact, in several Congressional budget requests, the FBI has asked for additional research and development funding, stating that it is becoming increasingly difficult to perform surreptitious entries on residences and businesses due to advances in security technologies.

When it comes to B&E, windows and doors aren't the only entrance points to secure. During a sophisticated black bag job, especially launched against a hard target, a covert entry team may break through walls, ceilings, and up through floors to gain access. High-level teams may use restoration specialists to quickly repair a damaged entry point so it appears never to have been breached.

If you're interested in how locks work (and how they can be defeated), an excellent starting point is the USENET alt.locksmithing FAQ at www.indra.com/archives/alt-locksmithing/. The FAQ contains a number of resources, including links to the infamous *MIT Guide to Picking Locks*.

For more advanced information, check out the definitive *Locks, Safes, and Security* by Marc Tobias, which is available in both printed and CD-ROM formats. This 1,400-page, illustrated volume is the ultimate reference on locks and safes and how to bypass them. It's not cheap, but it's a must for the professional. For more information, including a searchable online version of the CD-ROM with limited content, go to www.security.org.

Getting back to our scenario, what method might you use to gain entry into the building? There are many different options, but one approach might consist of the following:

As part of the corporate benefits package, the employees of the target company are offered a membership in the company-owned health club. Through surveillance, you find out the sales-training manager works out at the club every day after work. (His name and his picture appeared in a magazine article you found on Google when you were researching the sales division, and he has a reserved parking spot with his name stenciled on it, so it was easy for one of your colleagues to follow him and see what his habits are.) You get a temporary membership to the club and strike up a conversation with the sales manager — of course, not revealing who you really are or what you're after. He plays racquetball, so on your next visit you bring your racquet and your goggles and end up playing a few matches with him. A three-day weekend is coming up, and he tells you about a ski trip to British Columbia he's planning.

What he doesn't know is that you plan to steal his cardkey from his club locker the day before his trip while he's in the shower. And because he's preoccupied with his ski trip, he either won't notice the card is missing, or if he does, he won't worry about it until he gets back to work on Tuesday.

You successfully steal his card, and on Saturday morning of the three-day weekend, you're dropped about a block away from the sales-training office and walk to the underground parking entrance. You have a female companion with you. In your pocket, you have the cardkey you stole and a replica of the card that has a photograph of you with the training manager's name under-neath it. It looks identical to the company ID card. You duck your head as you swipe the stolen cardkey through the reader to avoid being caught on the surveillance camera. The door unlocks, and you use the cardkey to access the elevator. Once inside, you put the stolen card in your pocket and clip the fake ID card on your front jacket pocket. You and your companion both have small radios with nearly undetectable earpieces. You're in contact with a colleague outside the building who's watching for anyone entering the building. He has a view of the front lobby and is watching the guard who sits behind the desk reading a newspaper.

Documenting the Scene

After you successfully gain entry to a location, it's important to document the scene. This simply means keeping a record of anything you encounter that's relevant during the black bag job (this obviously can be used as evidence against you if you're caught). There are two types of documentation:

- ✓ **Written.** Cops are taught to take extensive notes while working a case because if they testify in court, the adage is "If it's not in writing, it never happened." You should follow the same advice and take written notes on any information or evidence you find, whether for legal purposes or to refer back to later.

- ✓ **Photographic.** You should also photograph the scene, both for collecting information and ensuring the operation remains undetected. If anything is moved, it must be returned to the exact position it previously was in. Although most people aren't observant, there's always a chance a target could key in on something out of place. Although digital still and video cameras are excellent tools for documenting a room, Polaroid cameras offer the advantage of quickly being able to produce a hardcopy photograph that you can hold in your hand and use to compare how things looked before and after.

After you successfully gain entry to the building and the fourth floor, what will you do next? Here's one possibility.

The first thing you do is walk through the hallways, checking to see whether any of the offices are occupied. Your female companion sits on a couch in the reception area and pretends to read a magazine. She's young, attractive, wears a revealing outfit, and is an accomplished actress. If the guard shows up on his rounds, she'll say she's your wife and is waiting for you to pick up some papers to work on at home. She then will engage him in conversation. If someone who works in the office unexpectedly arrives, she'll say her husband works on the fifth floor, and she was bored waiting for him and started wandering around the building. In either case, her appearance and acting will buy you the time you need to finish whatever you are doing and come out to "find" her. She has a small voice activated microphone on the radio in her purse so you'll be able to hear her at all times. (If you're a female reader, substitute the actress with a boy-toy actor.)

You have your lock picks with you ready to open your target's office door, but you don't need them. Almost none of the office doors are locked. You make some brief notes about this and other security weaknesses you discovered. You pull a small digital video camera out of your pocket and begin recording, pointing the camera at a bookshelf you plan on searching.

GATHERING INFORMATION

The main purpose of a black bag job is to covertly gather information or evidence. The rest of this book discusses a number of ways to do this, especially if you have physical access to a computer. As part of your planning, you should have established exactly what the purpose of the bag job is, and whether you are looking for a specific type of information or are simply on a fishing expedition searching for anything that may be useful.

Because bytes are so easy to copy, you should have different types of storage media with you to duplicate anything of interest. These media can range from an entire hard drive to mirror the target's hard drive to floppy disks or CD-RWs to copy individual files.

Even though you're computer spying, never just focus on the computer as your only potential source of information. Take time to physically examine the area around the desk looking for slips of paper with passwords or any other sensitive information. Anything you find should be documented. Some other places to look for relevant information include the following:

- ✓ Trash containers (both in the office and outside in dumpsters)
- ✓ Desk drawers
- ✓ File cabinets
- ✓ Whiteboards
- ✓ Corkboards
- ✓ Rolodexes
- ✓ Wall calendars
- ✓ Appointment planners

Your target's computer is running, and a screen saver is dancing on the monitor. You jiggle the mouse and a Windows ME desktop appears. A file is open that describes a reseller-training program for a product that's due to ship six months from now. Stuck to the side of the monitor is a Post-it® with a password. You pull a floppy disk out of your briefcase and begin copying some interesting-looking files as you search through an unlocked desk drawer. You take notes on everything you've found and what you've done.

CLEANING UP AND GETTING AWAY

After you've gotten the information you came for, it's time to clean up. That means wherever you've been should be left exactly as you found it when you got there. This is where photographic documentation becomes essential because human memory is fallible, especially under stressful circumstances.

Everything you brought with you should be accounted for. If you used utility software on a floppy disk or CD-ROM to examine or duplicate the target's computer, be sure you remove it from the drive. Some spies use a written checklist of everything they carry just to ensure that something isn't left behind that could raise suspicions.

The last stage of a black bag job is successfully getting away. Leaving the scene of a bag job is just as risky as getting inside, and it's important to keep a high level of awareness throughout the entire operation.

You've gathered enough information to easily prove that the office's physical security measures are lacking. If someone working for a competitor could somehow gain access to the office, a considerable amount of proprietary information would be compromised. You watch the video you shot of the office on the camera's LCD screen and make sure everything is in place. You double-check your list and see that your notebook, pen, video camera, five floppy disks, and two CD-RWs are all in your briefcase. You let your partner know you're finished and are coming to pick her up.

You gave yourself a maximum of a half an hour in the office, and you're done in 20 minutes. Using a code word, you radio your outside colleague that you and your companion are heading for the elevator and the basement. He picks you up a block away from the target building, and the three of you return to your office, where you debrief. Later, you drop by the health club and turn in the sales manager's cardkey to lost-and-found, saying you found it in a locker.

You start working on a report that presents all the security weaknesses you discovered, including passwords stuck to monitors, computers left running with open sensitive documents, and unlocked office doors and file cabinets. You attach printed copies of the training files you copied as further evidence. Your boss will be very pleased.

Countermeasures

How do you go about countering black bag jobs? This section takes a look at the general countermeasures you can employ. (Other chapters in the book get rather detailed about countermeasures, but because physical security is such a broad topic, this section is more conceptual in nature. A number of online references are provided that give you more depth and breadth, though.)

One of the biggest security mistakes a system administrator can make is shoring up his or her network defenses while neglecting defenses that could prevent a physical attack. In your risk assessment, if you believe there's a viable threat of a black bag job that could compromise sensitive data, it's imperative that you take actions to "harden" the physical security of your location. Even if you don't think you may be the target of a bag job, it's still a worthwhile exercise to run penetration tests against your physical security measures to see if any holes exist.

Physical Security

Physical security is anything that protects a space containing a computer, storage media, or networking equipment (cables, routers, and switches) from natural disasters, environmental conditions (fires, floods, and hurricanes), accidents, sabotage, and espionage. When it relates to espionage, physical security measures serve one or more of the following purposes:

- ✓ **Deterrence.** Any measure that prevents an intrusion by its presence, such as a guard, a video surveillance camera, lighting, or a sign that says a building is protected by an alarm. How effective the measure is depends on how determined the spy is.

- ✓ **Detection.** Any measure that detects an unauthorized intrusion, such as a sensor with an alarm, a monitored video surveillance camera, or a guard checking IDs at an entrance.

- ✓ **Defense.** Any measure that prevents or slows down an intruder from gaining entry, such as locks, reinforced doors, or an audible alarm. When it comes to countermeasures, time is on your side, and the longer you can delay an attack from being successful, the greater the chances are that your opponent will be caught or give up.

Based on the three "Ds," physical security measures fall into several different categories:

- ✓ **Access control.** Access control is a security measure that limits access to a facility or locations within the facility to authorized people. ID cards or badges, biometric devices such as fingerprint scanners, and proximity card readers (entrances that unlock with a "card key" that emits a radio frequency when close by) all can be components of an access control system.

- ✓ **Architectural design.** Elements of a building's design can increase security (for example, reinforced doors, walls that extend over dropped ceilings, air ducts that are too small to be crawled through, and routing of communications cables so they can't easily be tapped).

- ✓ **Electronic security systems.** These systems provide an early warning that an intrusion has taken place. These security systems are made up of sensors (such as motion detectors, magnetic switches, or pressure mats) that interface with alarms. Alarms can be audible sirens or bells, or they can be inaudible and silently alert a police department or private security company. Closed Circuit Television (CCTV) systems can also be used to monitor important locations within a building.

- ✓ **Guards.** Guards are uniformed personnel who staff primary entrances, monitor security systems, and make rounds through a building.

- ✓ **Lighting.** Lighting includes exterior lighting that illuminates a building's entry points, making it difficult for an intruder to gain access at night.

- ✓ **Lock and key systems.** These systems include the installation and maintenance of secure locking devices on building and room entrances, as well as containers (file cabinets, desk drawers, and safes).

- ✓ **Protective barriers.** These barriers are security measures, such as fences or gates that form the outer perimeter security zone of a building.

These physical security measures are usually used in different combinations to form an integrated security system. Physical security can be expensive, and it's important to perform a risk assessment and understand the cost/benefit ratio that goes with a particular type of security measure before you implement it.

It's worthwhile to spend some time determining whether your current physical security systems are adequate; this not only applies to defenses against espionage, but also to other measures such as disaster-recovery plans, backup plans, and offsite storage. (If you're using an offsite storage service, make sure that it has good security because it could be an easier target for a black bag job than your main facility.)

If you don't have much experience with physical security, some good online resources include the following:

- ✓ **American Society for Industrial Security (ASIS).** ASIS is the primary trade association for professionals involved with corporate security. For more information on ASIS, as well as a number of excellent papers on different security issues, go to `www.asisonline.org`.

- ✓ **Security Industry Buyers Guide.** This guide is a comprehensive manufacturer directory published by ASIS that contains listings for just about any physical security product or service that you can think of. Both print and free online versions are available at `www.sibgonline.com`.

- ✓ **FM 3-19.30 Physical Security.** This is the Army's recently revised physical security field manual. Although targeted toward the military, if you can wade through some of the acronyms, many basic concepts and techniques are applicable to the civilian world. It's available at `www.adtdl.army.mil/cgi-bin/atdl.dll/fm/3-19.30/toc.htm`. (Note that because the military and government have been removing various Web sites that are deemed to be national security risks, you may need to refer to a Google cache if a Web site is no longer available.)

- ✓ **Department of Defense Lock Program.** This program provides military and government specifications and other information on locks and physical security components. Go to `http://locks.nfesc.navy.mil`.

- ✓ **Physical Security Requirements for NSA/CSS Sensitive Compartmented Information Facilities.** This is a 1979 unclassified NSA document on physical security that was leaked over the Internet. It's a bit dated, but there is some good information on extreme physical security. The document is available at `cryptome.org/nsa-scif.htm`.

Security Policies

If you could pick one countermeasure to help you defeat black bag jobs or just about any type of espionage threat, what would it be? Armed guards, strong encryption, biometric authentication, or maybe laser alarm systems? No, probably the most effective — yet boring — countermeasure is a written security policy.

A policy is a clear, comprehensive, and well-defined set of plans, rules, and practices — in this case, those that relate to information security. Although bad policies are often the hallmark of ineffective, rule-bound bureaucracies, well-implemented policies that are understood and adhered to by employees are an effective organizational firewall against information theft.

Risk: Travel Abroad

Although large corporations usually have security policies in place, one area in which some fall down on is travel outside the United States. Be aware that a number of foreign governments sponsor economic espionage operations against business travelers. These spying attempts may be fairly crude — for example, hotel rooms that have clearly been searched and unattended computers that have been examined. The government's National Counterintelligence Executive (www.ncix.org) offers the following information-protection tips for business travelers heading abroad:

- ✓ Keep all sensitive documents in your personal possession and physical control at all times.

- ✓ Hotel rooms and restaurants are rarely suitable places for sensitive discussions. If possible, conduct sensitive discussions outdoors in a spot where you are not vulnerable to bugging and conversations cannot be overheard.

- ✓ Recognize that your laptop computer is a major target for theft. If you must take it, always keep it as carry-on baggage; never check it with other luggage. Leaving it in your hotel room or a hotel safe also presents a significant risk. If you must leave your computer in your room, lock it in your suitcase so it is out of sight while you are out or asleep at night. If possible, copy sensitive material to a floppy disk, CD-RW, or external hard drive and delete it from the main hard drive prior to travel. Carry the storage media on your person, and not with the computer.

- ✓ If secure communications equipment is accessible, use it for any discussion of sensitive matters. Don't use computer or FAX facilities at foreign hotels or businesses for sensitive matters.

- ✓ Use encryption to protect sensitive files and directories.

- ✓ Use a file "wiping" utility to securely delete files. In case the laptop is stolen, sensitive deleted data won't be able to be restored.

- ✓ Protect unwanted sensitive material until it can be disposed of securely by burning or crosscut shredding. Cut floppy disks into small pieces.

For example, a security policy might clearly state that whiteboards need to be erased after meetings, sensitive documents shouldn't be left unattended on desks, confidential papers should be shredded, file cabinets and desks should be locked, strong encryption should be used, and secure screen savers should be used on computers left running and unattended.

The two places where policies typically fail are employee buy-in and enforcement. Make sure employees understand why measures described in security policies are important; their jobs could theoretically be on the line if an unethical competitor resorted to economic espionage and hurt the company's bottom line. Also remember that if you don't enforce a policy, its effectiveness is diluted, and you probably ended up wasting your time developing it. And if you've never enforced a policy and eventually fire someone for a security breach that the policy could have prevented, it's very likely the termination could be challenged.

Policy writing is both an art and a science, and you should turn to experienced staff to help you develop policies. A few useful resources that should give you some general ideas on framing a security policy include the following:

✓ **Safeguard Your Technology, Practical Guidelines for Electronic Education Security.** This clearly written primer on security targeted toward education administrators and managers is produced by the National Center for Education Statistics (use this guide as a resource for your nontechnical colleagues). An online version is available at `http://nces.ed.gov/pubs98/safetech/`.

✓ **National Industrial Security Program Operating Manual (NISPOM).** NISPOM contains all the requirements, restrictions, classifications, and guidelines to prevent classified information from being disclosed by unauthorized sources. Although targeted toward government agencies and contractors, this manual is a must-read for anyone interested in securing a facility from espionage activities. NISPOM can be downloaded from `www.dss.mil/isec/nispom.htm`.

✓ **National Security Agency Security Manual.** This NSA employee manual was supposedly retyped from a photocopied hard copy and then leaked on the Internet. It appears to be real, but it is a good model for how to disseminate a security policy in any case. It's available at `www.cl.cam.ac.uk/ftp/users/rja14/nsaman.pdf`.

✓ **Site Security Handbook (RFC2196), IETF Site Security Task Force.** This is an Internet Engineering Task Force guide for developing computer security policies and procedures for sites that have systems connected to the Internet. Download it from `ftp://ftp.isi.edu/in-notes/rfc2196.txt`.

Summary

Many people focus on network security and completely forget that a spy who bypasses physical security can just as easily compromise sensitive information. In fact, an eavesdropper who has physical access to a computer is probably more dangerous than a spy who breaks in through an unsecured network because he can look at information stored on a computer as well as papers, documents, photos, and other nondigital forms of information.

Sophisticated black bag jobs are usually carried out by law enforcement agencies, government intelligence agencies, the military, or individuals engaged in high-level economic espionage. Even if you don't think you're the potential target of one of these groups, you still should pay attention to your physical security. The same methods used to keep you safe from spies also work against more common criminals who aren't so much interested in your data, but in selling your hardware for a quick buck.

Chapter 4

Breaching the System

"When the walls came tumbling down . . ."
— Def Leppard, "When the Walls Came Tumbling Down," *All*

JUST BECAUSE YOU BREACHED THE PHYSICAL SECURITY that protects a computer, it doesn't necessarily mean you can unlock its secrets. System-level authentication methods, such as a computer's startup BIOS passwords and the Windows logon process, are stumbling blocks to a spy interested in compromising data.

Despite the best intentions of hardware and software vendors, there are a number of ways a computer system can be breached, and that's what this chapter is about. You'll learn about system-level vulnerabilities and the tools and techniques for exploiting them (some have the finesse of using a lock pick, whereas others are more like kicking in a door). You are also provided with some basic countermeasures you can use to "harden" your computer against eavesdroppers who are interested in what's on your hard drive.

Spy Tactics

In this chapter, your role-playing assignment is to take the guise of a KGB agent who's fallen on hard times. (Technically, the KGB was dissolved with the rest of the Soviet Union in 1991, and the old KGB First Chief Directorate, which was responsible for foreign espionage, was renamed the SVR for Sluzhba Vneshney Razvedki, or the Foreign Intelligence Service.) Morale and pay in Russian public service have hit rock bottom over the years, and colleagues have told you about lucrative business opportunities in private industry. You specialized in economic espionage for the KGB/SVR in the Directorate T (responsible for acquiring Western strategic, military, and industrial technology) and were trained to perform black bag jobs and penetrate computer systems. When a friend tells you about a large European corporation that's recruiting people with "security skills," you make some guarded inquiries and are immediately offered a position on retainer to teach tradecraft to shadowy third-party contractors the company occasionally uses. The pay certainly beats a government salary; as a colonel, you were making the equivalent of a few hundred dollars (U.S.) a month, plus whatever you could take in on the side. You turn in your formal resignation, and several weeks later find yourself in a conference room in the La Defense district of Paris, lecturing a dozen students.

You hold up a matryoshka (a traditional Russian nesting doll, in which smaller and smaller wooden dolls are found nested inside a larger doll) and explain that computer security is like a matryoshka. To get to the innermost layer where the secrets are, you have to peel open the outer layers one at a time; sometimes during the course of this process, you find that the larger dolls on the outside are painted identically to the smaller ones inside (which is an inscrutable Russian way of saying that the passwords used for system-level authentication are sometimes used to secure other types of information). Setting the doll down, you explain that today's lesson focuses on the outer two layers of a computer's security system, the BIOS password and the operating system's authentication process.

Exploiting the Vulnerabilities

Before you can exploit vulnerabilities in the outer layers of security, you need to know what you're dealing with, including the following:

- ✓ **Identifying the BIOS.** You need to know the BIOS type and version because some tools and techniques are dependent on them. When the computer powers on, the BIOS manufacturer and version usually display on the screen, along with the processor type and the memory. If they do not, you may need to go into the BIOS setup (if it's not password-protected) to view the information. Holding down a key, such as Del, or a combination of keys allows you to enter the setup mode when the computer is powered-on. This startup key(s) varies by manufacturer. In addition to the BIOS, be sure to note the manufacturer and the model of the computer you're attacking.

- ✓ **Identifying the operating system.** As with the BIOS, different versions of Windows have different vulnerabilities, and which release of Windows the target computer is running should also be noted. You can tell which version of Windows is being used by paying attention to the startup screen as the operating system loads or the desktop appearance while Windows is running.

With this information in hand, consider that when you attack a computer, it can be in one of two states, either running or powered-off. Depending on the computer's state, you'll use different tools and methods to breach it.

BIOS PASSWORDS

The BIOS (Basic Input/Output System) is low-level code on a chip of the motherboard that controls the keyboard, display, disk drives, serial communications, and a number of other functions. BIOS parameters such as the date, time, and system setup information, are stored in CMOS (Complementary Metal Oxide Semiconductor) memory, usually in the computer's Real Time Clock (RTC) chip.

Wim Bervoets has an excellent reference site for those interested in more-detailed BIOS information. Go to www.wimsbios.com.

Tactics: Das Boot

It's useful to understand what happens during a computer's boot sequence. The steps include the following:

1. The CPU reads code in the BIOS chip, which runs a series of tests (called POST, for Power On Self Test) that ensures system devices are working correctly. During POST, the BIOS does the following:

   - Initializes system hardware and chipset registers

   - Initializes power management

   - Tests Random Access Memory (RAM)

   - Enables the keyboard

   - Tests the serial and parallel ports

   - Initializes the floppy disk drives and hard disk drive controllers

   - Displays system information

2. The BIOS compares system configuration data during the self-test with information stored in CMOS. (CMOS is updated whenever new system components are added.)

3. After POST, the BIOS searches for a boot program that loads the operating system. The BIOS usually looks on the A: floppy drive followed by the C: hard drive (although this setting can be changed).

4. At this point, the boot sequence shifts responsibilities from BIOS to Windows, which loads Windows system configuration information and device drivers (including the logon authentication code in Windows NT/2000/XP).

If the boot sequence is successful, any startup programs are loaded and run.

There are at least two authentication security options found in the BIOS, which can be enabled in the BIOS setup when the computer starts up. They include the following:

✓ **Boot password.** A password is required when the computer is powered-on before the boot sequence can continue. This password is also known as a user password.

✓ **BIOS setup password.** A password is required to access the BIOS setup to change settings such as power management, hard drive support, and time and date. This password is also known as a supervisor password.

The passwords are stored in CMOS, along with the rest of the BIOS parameters.

Although BIOS passwords seem like a good security measure, they really aren't that effective against a dedicated eavesdropper. BIOS passwords may keep the average snoop out of your computer, but they are only a minor inconvenience to someone with the right tools and knowledge.

You ask your students for ways they might breach a system protected with a BIOS password. You get a few responses and start to elaborate on the various attack methods you've used in the past.

caution

Some of the methods for defeating BIOS passwords involve hardware-related attacks. If you don't have experience with opening up a computer and swapping internal components, think about sticking with software attacks instead. Static electricity and unbridled enthusiasm can easily damage electronic components. Even modifying the BIOS with software utilities can cause unforeseen consequences if you're not careful.

RESEARCH   You begin by telling your students that with a black bag job or any type of espionage activity, one of the first things you should do as a spy is research your target. For attacks on computers that have BIOS passwords, this research should include the following steps:

✓ Visit the manufacturer Web site of the computer you have targeted to see if there is any information on disabling or resetting a BIOS password.

✓ Directly contact the manufacturer's technical support and try to get information on how to bypass the password. Most manufacturers ask you for information in an attempt to identify you as the legitimate owner, so you may need to resort to some social engineering skills.

✓ Perform a Google search on the computer you're planning to attack, such as "dell latitude BIOS password." These searches can locate utilities or data you might be able to use when breaching a specific type of computer.

Information gathered during the research phase can save you a considerable amount of time and effort in attacking a BIOS-protected system.

BACKDOOR PASSWORDS   Backdoor BIOS passwords aren't a secret conspiracy. People are forgetful, and it's bad business to have a customer locked out of his computer because he forgot the password. For this reason, most BIOS manufacturers put backdoor passwords in their products that let you sneak into a protected system that you don't have the password for. Computer vendors also often implement their own backdoor BIOS passwords. (BIOS manufacturers provide computer makers with utilities so they can modify certain settings to customize their own systems.) If a default password works, you can later change the user password in the BIOS setup, or use a software tool to reveal the password after Windows is running.

Tables 4-1, 4-2, 4-3, and 4-4 show common backdoor passwords, listed by manufacturer, which have been successfully used to bypass BIOS startup passwords.

TABLE 4-1 AMI (American Megatrends, Inc.) BIOS Passwords

A.M.I	AAAMMMIII	Aammii	AM
AMI	AMI!SW	AMI.KEY	AMI.KEZ
AMI?SW	AMI_SW	AMI~	AMIAMI
AMIDECOD	Amipswd	AMIPSWD	AMISETUP
BIOS	BIOSPASS	CONDO	HEWITT RAND
LKWPETER	PASSWORD		

TABLE 4-2 Award BIOS Passwords

?award	_award	01322222	01322222
256256	589589	589721	595595
598598	admin	Alfarome	ALFAROME
Ally	aLLY	ALLy	ALLY
APAf	award	Award	AWARD PW
AWARD SW	AWARD?SW	AWARD_SW	Awkward
AWKWARD	BIOS	Biosstar	Biostar
BIOSTAR	CONCAT	Condo	Condo
CONDO	d8on	Djonet	g6PJ
h6BB	HELGA-S	HEWITT RAND	HLT
j09F	j256	j262	j322
j332	J64	KDD	Lkw peter
Lkwpeter	Lkwpeter	LKWPETER	PASSWORD
Pint	PINT	SER	Setup
SKY_FOX	SWITCHES_SW	Sxyz	Syxz
SYXZ	SZYX	t0ch20x	t0ch88
TTPTHA	TzqF	Wodj	ZAAADA
Zbaaaca	ZBAAACA	ZJAAADC	

TABLE 4-3 Phoenix Technologies Passwords

Phoenix	PHOENIX	CMOS	BIOS

TABLE 4-4 Other Passwords by Manufacturer

Manufacturer	Password
Biostar	Biostar
Compaq	Compaq
Dell	Dell
Enox	xo11nE
Epox	Central
Freetech	Posterie
IBM and VOBIS	Merlin
IBM (Aptiva)	(Press both mouse buttons on boot up.)
Iwill	Iwill
Jetway	Spooml
Packard Bell	bell9
QDI	QDI
Siemens	SKY_FOX
TMC	BIGO
Toshiba	Toshiba

Trying a series of backdoor passwords can be very time-consuming, and there's no guarantee that these backdoors will work on a specific computer (the backdoor passwords are all for desktop systems; at the present time, there aren't any widely distributed lists of backdoor passwords for laptops). Also keep in mind that some systems may have additional security features. For example, some Dell products power down after three unsuccessful password attempts, which makes password-guessing a very slow and tedious process.

GUESSING THE PASSWORD   If a backdoor password attack doesn't work, another related approach is to simply guess the password. Refer to Chapter 6 for more information on password guessing and clues that can help you attack a BIOS or any other type of password.

RECOVERING THE PASSWORD   BIOS passwords don't tend to be protected with strong encryption and can be revealed quite easily with specialized tools. Several utilities, which are listed in the "System Breaching Tools" section of this chapter, can recover a BIOS password if the system has already been booted and is running.

PULLING THE HARD DRIVE   One of the easiest techniques for defeating a BIOS password that your students can employ is to simply remove the hard drive from a protected computer and install it in another computer. Because the BIOS is part of the motherboard, the password protection applies only to that particular computer and has nothing to do with its hard drive or any other storage media. (There are some BIOS products, particularly associated with newer laptops, that "lock" a hard drive. If this type of security is in place, you won't be able to view data on the drive by moving it to another computer.)

Another BIOS security feature to be aware of, particularly with computers configured as servers, is a "chassis intrusion detection" option. If this setting is enabled, a message is displayed during the boot sequence if the computer case has been opened. In the future, expect computers in enterprise environments to start incorporating Alert Standard Format (ASF) technology, which involves a networked computer sending messages to a central control console about its status. For example, if you opened up a computer to pull its hard drive in the middle of the night, you might be greeted by security guards who were dispatched to the office when they got a chassis intrusion message from the BIOS. (Removing the network cable or powering down the computer can defeat ASF, but both these acts can theoretically trigger other alerts.)

ZAPPING THE CMOS   Another hardware-related attack is to wipe out the settings stored in the CMOS. If BIOS information is missing or corrupted, the default settings, which include disabled password protection, will be applied. You can literally short-circuit password security with a couple of techniques (refer to Figure 4-1 to see what the various BIOS components look like):

✓ **Batteries.** Data stored in the CMOS chip requires power, which is provided by a small battery. Disconnect the computer's main power source; then locate and remove the CMOS battery (it looks like a flat, round watch battery). Some manufacturers solder in the battery, which can make things a bit challenging if you don't know how to desolder. After the power is removed, all the data in memory will eventually go away. Discharging the CMOS may take a few minutes or up to several days due to capacitance in the circuit (one way to quickly and safely discharge the CMOS is to touch a 10k-ohm resistor to the battery connectors). When the computer is booted, the BIOS checks the CMOS for system settings, doesn't find any, and then uses the default settings, writing them to the CMOS. Shorting out certain pins on the CMOS chip can also zap the settings. Typically the documentation for the motherboard tells you how to do this.

✓ **Jumpers.** Another way to reset the CMOS is with a jumper (a pair of prongs that are electrical contact points on the motherboard used to change hardware settings) called a "password bypass control jumper." When this jumper is moved to the closed position, the BIOS password is reset the next time the computer is powered-on. The jumper is usually labeled Clear RTC, Clear CMOS, or PWRD. The jumper configuration varies from computer to computer; this is where your research about the target computer comes in handy.

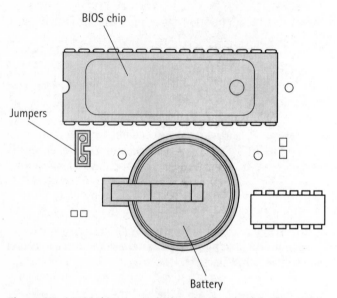

Figure 4-1: A BIOS chip on a motherboard at the top of the figure with the battery that provides power for stored CMOS settings and jumpers for resetting the CMOS.

These hardware attacks work against a computer that isn't powered-on. If the computer has already booted and is running, you can clear the stored CMOS settings with one of two different types of software attacks:

✓ **Use a CMOS zapping tool.** Utilities such as Cmospwd, which is described in the "System Breaching Tools" section of this chapter, can recover BIOS passwords as well as clear CMOS data.

✓ **Flash the BIOS.** Most modern BIOSes are upgradeable by flashing the memory with a factory utility. A flash upgrade clears the CMOS settings as well as upgrades the BIOS. Use caution with this method, since a failure could possibly damage the motherboard.

The main disadvantage of zapping CMOS settings is that a user may become suspicious if the BIOS passwords no longer are present. You should clear CMOS only as a last resort if other techniques don't work.

Mucking about with BIOS and CMOS settings is not for the faint-of-heart or nontechnical spy because you might accidentally change a setting that could render the system unusable (usually just temporarily). If possible, always back up the contents of the CMOS before trying to modify it. There are a number of utility programs that will save and restore CMOS settings, which can come in handy if you unintentionally mess something up.

LAPTOP BIOS ISSUES   Laptops deserve special mention in your lecture when it comes to BIOS security. Compromising a laptop BIOS password is more difficult than attacking its desktop cousin. There are a number of issues that complicate an attack on a laptop's BIOS, including the following:

- ✓ **Chassis design.** Even if setting a jumper or removing a battery clears a BIOS password, laptops are more difficult to open up and access the hardware components for the average spy.

- ✓ **EEPROMs.** Instead of CMOS, most laptops store BIOS settings, including the password, in an Electrically Erasable Programmable Read-Only Memory (EEPROM). To access the BIOS parameters, the EEPROM must first be desoldered from the motherboard and then read with a PROM reader. This type of attack requires special skills and tools.

- ✓ **Batteries.** Removing a battery inside the case can reset the password on some laptops. Just remember that there may be two batteries: one for the CMOS (if present) and another that acts as a power buffer during battery swaps.

- ✓ **Hard drive passwords.** Some manufacturers include a hard drive password that prevents the hard drive from being swapped into another laptop.

If you're dealing with laptop BIOS security, you should spend time researching approaches to breaching the system. Enhanced laptop security is not insurmountable, however. Depending on the manufacturer, there are different approaches to bypassing BIOS passwords. Some examples include the following:

- ✓ **Hardware devices.** Laptop vendors sometimes use different types of hardware devices to reset BIOS passwords. For example, the passwords on some models of Toshiba and Compaq laptops can be reset with a "loop-back" device, which is simply a DB-25 connecter that connects to the computer's parallel port. On some Toshibas, if the following pins are jumpered — 1-5-10, 2-11, 3-17, 4-12, 6-16, 7-13, 8-14, 9-15, 18-25 — and the BIOS detects this pattern during startup, it clears the password.

- ✓ **Keyboard combinations.** Some manufacturers use secret keyboard combinations to skip security settings. For example, various Toshiba laptops bypass the password security if the left Shift key is held down during the boot process.

Countermeasures: Laptops

Laptop theft is the second most common type of corporate security breach by outsiders. The money a laptop can bring on the street motivates most thefts, but a more serious motivation is when the hard drive data is the primary target. Stealing laptops is often a quick and easy path to government, military, or business secrets.

✓ According to the Computer Security Institute and the FBI, there were 591,000 laptops stolen in the U.S.A. during 2001, and usually 97 percent of these laptops are never recovered.

✓ In a recent report, the Inspector General of the Department of Justice stated, "Five agencies, including the FBI and DEA, have lost track of 400 laptop computers, more than half of which may have contained sensitive national security data."

✓ Six hundred laptops have gone missing from the U.K.'s Ministry of Defense since 1997, some with sensitive government and military information.

There are several steps you can take to keep your laptop's data out of a spy's hands:

✓ Don't let your laptop leave your sight or person (handcuffed to your wrist is optional).

✓ Lock your laptop in a secure place when you're not using it.

✓ Use strong encryption to protect sensitive data as discussed in the "Countermeasures" section of Chapter 5.

✓ Use as many BIOS security options as possible; although doing so may not provide absolute security against a dedicated opponent, it is an important first line of defense. (Just keep the passwords in some secure location. Internet forums are filled with tales of woe about forgotten laptop passwords.)

✓ **Key disks.** Some older Toshiba models used a "key disk" to reset the BIOS password. Factory service centers were provided with a special floppy disk that was inserted in the laptop drive. The technician would then boot the computer, press Enter when prompted for a password, and then press Y and Enter when asked to set the password. The BIOS setup screen would appear next, in which a new password could be entered. The magic password recovery disk turned out to be a formatted floppy disk with the first five bytes of sector 2 set to: 4B 45 59 00 00. You can use a hex editor to manually make your own disk or search for a utility called KeyDisk that automatically creates a disk for you.

✓ **Commercial recovery services.** Many laptop manufacturers and a few legitimate businesses offer services to owners of laptops who for whatever reason are locked out of their systems. Password Crackers, Inc. (www.pwcrack.com) sells "security chips" that replace those found in a number of popular laptops, thus resetting the security. You pull out the EEPROM, and they send you back one with the default BIOS settings for your computer. You can also send them the chip, and they'll recover the password from it. Nortek Computers, Ltd. (www.nortek.on.ca) specializes in the removal of ThinkPad power-on passwords and hard disk passwords, including full data recovery on protected hard drives. The Canadian company is extremely scrupulous and requires proof of ownership before recovering a locked laptop.

WINDOWS 3.X/9X/ME

If BIOS security is the outer doll of a matryoshka, once you get it open, it reveals the next doll: the operating system. Although Windows XP was released in the fall of 2001, by the end of 2002, Windows 98 still held a commanding lead as being the most-used operating system. This is good news for computer spies because the Windows 3.x/9x/ME operating system family doesn't have much in the way of authentication security.

Relying on the logon dialog box of older versions of Windows for security is about as smart as drinking samogon (moonshine vodka) purchased from a Moscow street vendor. Though economical, both can hurt you over the long term.

If you're confronted with a Windows 3.x/9x/ME logon dialog box, just dismiss it with the Cancel button. The Windows desktop appears, and you have full access to the system and the files on it. All the logon dialog box does is restore the desktop appearance and connect to any networked resources based on the user account and an associated password. These settings are stored in a profile (.PWL file).

See Chapter 6 for more information about profiles and how to retrieve passwords stored in them.

The only real system-level security measure that older versions of Windows provide (that don't involve networking) are password-protected screensavers. A user can specify that a password needs to be entered when a screensaver is running to return to the desktop. If a wrong password is used, the screensaver continues to run. Although a seemingly good privacy measure, protected screensavers provide users with a false sense of security because there are several ways to bypass a screensaver that's running. These types of attacks apply only to Windows 3.x/9x/ME because the Windows NT/2000/XP screensavers use the considerably more-secure operating-system authentication routines. Additionally, some third-party screensavers offer higher levels of security than the default versions that ship with Windows 3.x/9x/ME. Types of screensaver attacks include the following:

✓ **Reboot.** The simplest technique is to press the computer's reset switch or power it down and then turn it on. After the system reboots, you'll have full access to files and applications once Windows is running again. When you're done, just activate the screensaver again. The downside to this type of attack is that an observant user may wonder why applications and files that were previously on-screen aren't there any more when she enters a password to return to the desktop. A clever user may place a command to run the screensaver in the Startup folder. This automatically loads and executes the screensaver when Windows first starts. If this happens, hold down the left Shift key while Windows is loading. This prevents any programs in the Startup folder from being run.

✓ **Autorun.inf.** A more sneaky way to bypass a running screensaver is to take advantage of Windows' auto-run CD feature. When a CD-ROM is inserted in the drive, Windows checks to see whether a file named Autorun.inf is in the root directory of the CD-ROM. This file lists an application that is automatically run when the CD-ROM is inserted, even when the screensaver is active. Just create a text file named Autorun.inf with a single line containing the application you want to run and then burn the file to a CD-ROM. For example, if Explorer.exe was on the first line of the Autorun.inf file, the Windows Explorer file manager would automatically run and appear over the screensaver.

✓ **Password cracking.** Older versions of Windows used very weak encryption to store the contents of screensaver passwords. A variety of tools can extract and crack the password (several are mentioned in the "System Breaching Tools" section of this chapter). These utilities can be used in conjunction with Autorun.inf, so you can insert a CD-ROM and have it provide you with the password of the screensaver that's running.

WINDOWS NT/2000/XP

If the security in Windows 3.x/9x/ME is weak, the security measures in Windows NT/2000/XP are a bit more like Lubyanka, the notorious yellow-brick former Moscow headquarters of the KGB and prison. Although daunting on the outside with what appears to be impenetrable security, it's still vulnerable from the inside. (In a covert operation code-named CK-TAW during the early 1980s, the CIA intercepted phone, fax, and telex messages in a tunnel that connected Lubyanka, a secret communications center in Troitsk, and KGB First Chief Directorate headquarters at Yasenevo. The operation provided a wealth of information until CIA turncoats Edward Howard Lee and Aldrich Ames compromised it. Former KGB Major General Oleg Kalugin called it, "The CIA's greatest coup. They heard every conversation. Everything.")

As you end your history lesson you tell your students it's imperative to learn about some of the vulnerabilities in the Windows NT/2000/XP authentication process during an "interactive logon" (Microsoft's term for a non-networked, direct-from-computer logon), so they can stage their own Operation TAW against the system.

MANUALLY GUESSING PASSWORDS   The simplest attack to use on a computer running Windows NT/2000/XP is to manually guess the logon password (although you may get lucky and encounter a system where the user has Automatic Logon turned on, which automatically enters a valid user account and password when Windows starts up). Window's default configuration is to display the user account name of the last person who logged on to the system, so all you need is a password to go with it.

Windows XP systems can be even easier to launch guessing attacks against. In an effort to make the system more user-friendly, Microsoft included a password-hint feature during the logon process. Users not well-versed in proper security procedures might have a hint that can readily be guessed.

Windows has two default accounts: Administrator and Guest, described as follows:

✓ The Administrator account, or another account with a different name that has administrative privileges, should be one of your primary targets (this account is equivalent to "root" in Unix-style operating systems). As Administrator, you have access to all the files on the computer, with a few exceptions if the Encrypting File System (EFS) is in use. Administrator privileges are also important because they are required to extract accounts and passwords in Windows NT/2000/XP systems.

✓ The Guest account is used to allow people to have restricted access to the computer if they don't have an account. By default, the Guest account is disabled.

You should attempt a manual guessing attack on both of these accounts. Some common passwords to try include: Administrator, Guest, or leaving the password field blank.

See Chapter 6 for more detailed information about manual password-guessing.

ALTERNATE OPERATING SYSTEM BOOTING   One of the easiest and most effective attacks is to completely bypass Windows and boot the computer with a different operating system. This gives you complete access to files stored on the hard drive through the other operating system.

If the targeted drive is formatted as FAT or FAT32, you can use a DOS boot disk to start the computer and then access files on the C: drive. More than likely, however, the drive will be formatted as NTFS, which DOS doesn't recognize (NTFS provides enhanced file security by establishing file ownership permissions). In this case, you'll need to use a tool such as NTFSDOS, which allows DOS to access the drive or use a version of Linux that supports NTFS.

Several utilities that support this type of an attack are listed in the "System Breaching Tools" section later in this chapter.

SYSTEM PASSWORD-RESET DISKS   Windows XP has an option for creating a password-reset disk. Because users often forget their passwords, Microsoft has a Forgotten Password Wizard that writes data to a floppy disk. If a user can't remember his password during the logon sequence, he just inserts the disk, which allows him to reset the existing password with a new one.

Although there's no guarantee your target has created a password-reset disk, you should still take the time to search his office for a disk. If you find a disk labeled Password, Windows Password, or Windows XP Password, you're probably in luck.

Tactics: Intelligence Sources

A good spy understands the strengths and weaknesses of his opponent (or at least relies on someone in his organization to do so). Your opponent is the Windows operating system, particularly the security features that keep you out of the system. New vulnerabilities are discovered on a weekly (sometimes daily) basis, and you need to be aware of new holes so you can exploit them (or plug them if you're on the counterintelligence side of the house).

Why do software vendors release buggy code with so many vulnerabilities? Briefly consider the Windows operating system.

It's estimated that Windows NT had 20 million lines of source code, Windows 2000 had 35 million lines, and Windows XP has 40 million lines. This book has about 40 lines of text per page, so the source code for XP would roughly be equivalent to a single one-million-page book or 2,500 books of a similar size to this one. How would you like to be the proofreader for that collection of works?

According to the Software Engineering Institute, there will be 5 to 15 bugs for every 1,000 lines of code. If you apply that number to Windows XP, there's the potential for 200,000 to 600,000 bugs to be present. (Economics are definitely at play here because it's cheaper to write post-release patches than to spend months poring over every line of code.) Although all the bugs won't have an impact on security, a fair number will. This is why security flaws are so common in large, complex applications and operating systems.

Some of the best resources to stay up-to-speed on new vulnerabilities that can be exploited for espionage purposes include the following:

- ✓ **BugTraq.** This is the definitive, full-disclosure security e-mail list. New vulnerabilities and exploits for a variety of operating systems show up here. The list is often criticized (mostly by manufacturers whose bugs are identified) for providing too much information. For details, go to www.securityfocus.com/popups/forums/bugtraq/intro.shtml.

- ✓ **NTBugTraq.** This list is devoted solely to Windows NT/2000/XP security issues. To subscribe and access the archives, go to www.ntbugtraq.com.

- ✓ **Microsoft.** For a complete list of Microsoft's security bulletins (as well as information on how to subscribe), go to www.microsoft.com/technet/security/current.asp.

- ✓ **CERT.** Carnegie Mellon University's quasi-federal Computer Emergency Response Team's (CERT) list of advisories and vulnerabilities was one of the first vulnerability lists, but now it's typically surpassed in detail and timeliness by information that appears in BugTraq. Go to www.cert.org.

- ✓ **NIPC.** The U.S. government's National Infrastructure Protection Center (NIPC) collects and disseminates information on new vulnerabilities. The information is boiled down and lacks detail, but it is useful as a starting point for identifying topics to Google search for more comprehensive information. Go to www.nipc.gov.

ATTACKING THE SECURITY ACCOUNTS MANAGER   The Security Accounts Manager (SAM) file is one of the prime targets for breaching Windows security. Before discussing how to attack the SAM, it's useful to understand how the Windows logon authentication process works. After the computer starts and goes through the BIOS boot sequence, the following steps take place:

1. Winlogon.exe runs as the last step of the boot process.

2. Winlogon.exe makes a call to the Msgina.dll to display the logon Welcome screen in Windows XP or the logon dialog box in Windows NT/2000.

3. Winlogon.exe passes the user account and password to the Local Security Authority (LSA) subsystem, which checks the SAM file to see if the account and password are valid.

4. If the account and password are valid, the SAM returns the user's Security Identifier (SID) and the SIDs of any groups the user belongs to.

5. The LSA creates an access token based on this information. The access token grants access to protected resources based on the user's privileges and permissions.

6. Winlogon.exe loads the Windows shell along with the user's token.

The SAM file is one of the crown jewels of Windows security because it contains all the user account names and passwords. The file is kept scrambled by using a one-way hash function so password information can't readily be revealed. The SAM is located at winnt\system32\config\sam for Windows NT and 2000 and windows\system32\config\sam for Windows XP systems. (On Windows 2000 servers set up as domain controllers, the account and password information is stored in the Active Directory and not in the SAM file.)

If the SAM file can be compromised, various utilities can give a spy complete access to the system. Some techniques for attacking the SAM include:

✓ **Deleting or renaming the SAM file.** If the computer is booted with another operating system and you have read-write access to the hard drive, you can delete or rename the SAM file. Because there are now no accounts after you reboot, you can log on as Administrator when Windows starts up again and leave the password field blank. (Anytime you physically alter the SAM file, whether deleting it or modifying it, make a backup copy of it first.)

✓ **Cracking the SAM file in real time.** If the target computer is already running, you can install and run a SAM-cracking utility (you'll need Administrator privileges) in an attempt to compromise accounts on the machine.

✓ **Cracking the SAM file offline.** For this attack, you get the SAM information from the target computer and then run a cracking utility on it offsite. With older versions of NT, you could boot with another operating system and then copy the SAM file to disk. With Windows 2000 or XP, which has better password hash security, you need to have Administrator privileges and run a utility that extracts the SAM hashes from the target computer and then saves them to disk.

✓ **Modifying the SAM file.** There are several utilities that can readily change account passwords in the SAM. Just boot from a utility disk, select the account you want to compromise (for example, Administrator), and assign a new password.

From a vulnerability standpoint, the one-way hashing in Windows NT was weak and proved susceptible to cracking attacks that compared the hashed account passwords against those of guessed passwords. Microsoft responded to this weakness by implementing something called Syskey in Service Pack 3 for NT 4.0 and subsequent versions of Windows 2000 and XP.

Syskey, which stands for System Key, adds another layer of protection to the SAM file by encrypting it with a 128-bit key. This makes Syskey-encrypted SAM files nearly impossible to crack. Syskey had to be manually enabled in NT 4.0, but it is turned on by default in Windows 2000 and XP. (Up until recently, cracking utilities didn't recognize the difference between a SAM file that had Syskey applied and one without it, and they would happily churn through CPU cycles for days and weeks on end, attempting to find passwords that were impossible to discover because of the extra layer of encryption.)

Although Syskey protects against someone directly compromising the SAM file, it doesn't provide protection against extracting the password hashes from memory (if you have Administrator privileges) or from networking authentication traffic. In networks that have a mixture of Windows 9x/ME and Windows NT/2000/XP computers, the older, less secure LAN Manager (LM) password hashes are used for authentication. Hashes stored in memory or sniffed from a network can easily be saved and then fed to a password-cracking utility.

> **caution**
>
> If the Encrypting File System (EFS) is running under Windows XP Professional and you attempt to defeat the SAM by deleting it or modifying the password of an account protected by EFS, you risk losing access to any encrypted data. This isn't true with EFS-protected files and folders in Windows 2000, in which someone with Administrator privileges can access the encrypted files simply by changing the associated account's password. Windows XP Home doesn't support EFS.

ESCALATING PRIVILEGES Let's say you can log on to a computer with an unsecured Guest account. There's really not much you can do because the NTFS file permissions keep you out of other people's files, and you need administrative privileges to use any of the SAM password utilities.

However, if you have your foot in the door with some type of a nonprivileged user account, you may be able to perform a privilege escalation attack. This attack involves taking advantage of some known system flaw that lets you perform an action the operating system believes you're privileged to but actually aren't. With privilege escalation, you can add, delete, or modify data on the system; create or delete user accounts; or add accounts to the administrators group.

For example, a popular exploit under Windows 2000 involved the NetDDE service. It was discovered that when the service was running, you could run commands with SYSTEM privileges. (These are privileges granted to processes that run at the operating-system level; think of them as super Administrator privileges.) For example, by entering the following at the command line, any user that was interactively logged onto the system, no matter what his or her privileges, could run cmd.exe and have access to all of the files on the hard drive:

```
C:\>netddemsg -s Chat$ cmd.exe
```

As new privilege escalation attacks are publicized, Microsoft makes security patches available to address the problem. (The response time can vary from quick to glacial; for example, an escalation attack that involved the WM_TIMER event that was widely publicized in August 2002 and allowed any logged-on user to potentially take control of the system was finally acknowledged and patched by Microsoft in December 2002.) Consider that users often aren't aware of patches or even if they are, they don't install them. Obviously, this can work in your favor.

System-Breaching Tools

You tell your students there's no sense trying to open up a matryoshka by hand when there are many free and commercial tools that make the job quicker and easier. You pass out a list of some of the more popular utilities for breaching system security and briefly discuss each of them.

TOOLS FOR ATTACKING BIOS PASSWORDS

There are a number of utilities available for compromising BIOS passwords. Remember, these tools work only if the computer has successfully booted and is running. If you're faced with a BIOS password during the boot process, you'll have to rely on another method of accessing the hard drive, as described in the "Exploiting the Vulnerabilities" section earlier in this chapter.

CMOSPWD   One of the best-known and most-used BIOS utilities is a command-line tool called Cmospwd, written by Christophe Grenier. Cmospwd can retrieve passwords from the following BIOS versions:

Acer/IBM	IBM Thinkpad boot password
AMI BIOS	Packard Bell Supervisor/User
AMI WinBIOS (12/15/93)	Phoenix 1.00.09.AC0 (1994)
AMI WinBIOS 2.5	Phoenix 1.04
Award 4.5x	Phoenix 1.10 A03/Dell GXi
Award Medallion 6	Phoenix 4 release 6 (User)
Compaq	Phoenix 4.05 rev 1.02.943
Compaq (1992)	Phoenix 4.06 rev 1.13.1107
Gateway Solo — Phoenix 4.0 r6	Phoenix A08, 1993
IBM (PS/2, Activa)	Toshiba
IBM 300 GL	Zenith AMI

If the utility can't compromise a password, it has a "kill" option that deletes the password. Cmospwd is easy to use, effective, and well-documented; the Readme file has a wealth of information relating to BIOS attacks. To download the tool, go to `www.cgsecurity.org/index. html?cmospwd.html`.

OTHER TOOLS   There are a number of other utilities available that work on specific BIOS versions, and it's worthwhile to have a collection of such tools because one utility may perform better than another. A good starting place for building your system-breaching toolbox is with the BIOS password crackers listed at `www.packetstormsecurity.org/Crackers/bios/`.

TOOLS FOR ATTACKING WINDOWS 3.X/9X/ME
Because there's no logon authentication security in the Windows 3.x/9x/ME operating system family, the only real non-network system-level attacks occur when a screensaver is running. (Other attack tools that can compromise application encryption and network security in all versions of Windows are discussed in Chapters 6 and 10.) Screensaver attack tools include the following:

- ✓ **Ratware Win9x Screen Saver Buster.** When this free tool is burned to a CD-ROM and used in conjunction with Autorun.inf, it automatically turns off a running screensaver. The tool can be downloaded from `http://packetstormsecurity.org/Win/ RWSaverBust.zip`.

- ✓ **Scrsavpw.** This free screensaver password cracker, written by Matthias Bockelkamp, is available at `www.geocities.com/mbockelkamp/`.

TOOLS FOR ATTACKING WINDOWS NT/2000/XP
With the popularity of Windows in corporate environments and the need for administrators to perform security audits and recover data from locked systems, a number of commercial and free tools are available that can be used for less-than-savory espionage purposes. Some Windows NT/2000/XP tools that are popular with both spies and system administrators are discussed as follows.

LC (L0PHTCRACK)   L0phtCrack (named after the L0pht Heavy Industries hacking group before they became part of the corporate security consultancy @Stake) is the most popular Windows NT/2000/XP password-cracking utility. The latest 4.0 version of the tool is named a more politically correct LC4 in an effort to distance itself from its freewheeling hacker origins.

LC, which was originally written by Peiter Zatko (alias Mudge), started out in 1997 as a simple brute-force password-cracking utility. Since then it has evolved into a sophisticated tool with an easy-to-use interface (see Figure 4-2), the ability to distribute a brute-force attack across multiple computers, and a number of ways to acquire password hashes, including the following:

- ✓ **Import from the local machine.** LC can retrieve all accounts and password hashes from the local computer; administrative privileges are required.

✓ **Import from remote registry.** If a computer has remote registry access enabled, you can import the hashes from systems in which Syskey is not being used.

✓ **SAM files.** LC directly reads hashes from SAM files copied from systems that don't have Syskey enabled.

✓ **Sniffing.** LC can capture password hashes from the challenge/response sequence when one computer authenticates to another over an Ethernet network.

✓ **Pwdump.** LC can import the output of the password hash gathering tool Pwdump; see a description of this utility following.

✓ **Import files from previous versions of LC.** The current version of LC supports older versions, which used a different file format for storing account and password information.

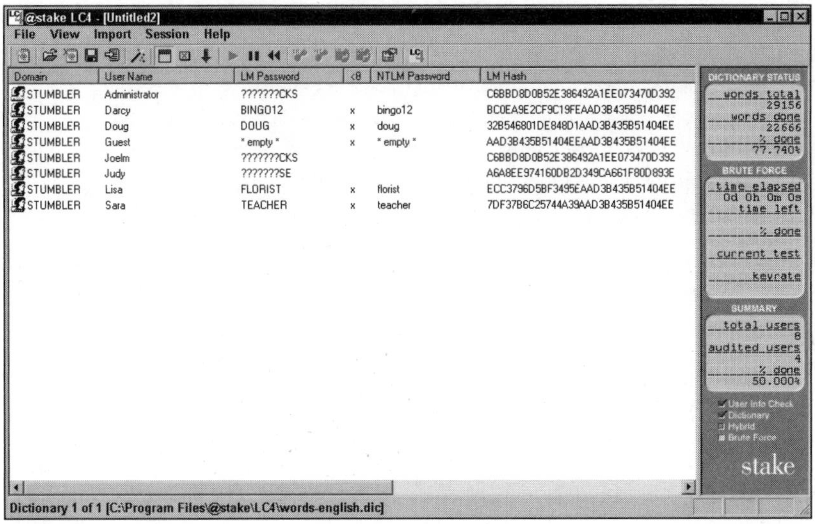

Figure 4-2: LC4 (L0phtCrack) password cracker in action against a collection of password hashes. Some accounts have been compromised by a dictionary attack, whereas others are undergoing a brute-force attack.

After the password hashes are loaded into LC, the utility can launch a dictionary attack, a hybrid dictionary attack that appends, prepends, or replaces commonly used letters in words; or a brute-force attack (a brute-force attack averaged around 2.8 million passwords per second on a 1000-MHz, mobile Pentium III).

LC isn't cheap at $350, but it's one of the premier tools for breaching system security (or legitimately auditing passwords). For more information, as well as a downloadable evaluation copy of LC, go to www.atstake.com.

Tactics: I Dream of GINA

GINA is the Graphical Identification and Authorization mechanism for Windows NT/ 2000/XP. GINA sits between the user and the operating system's Winlogon authentication service and displays the logon dialog box.

One way of attacking an operating system is with a fake logon application. An unsuspecting user would think he was logging on to a system just as he did every day, but in reality a Trojan horse application (set up by an attacker) would be recording the account and password before actually logging the user onto the system. Microsoft believed that if a Ctrl+Alt+Del key combination was built into the logon process, this would defeat Trojan logon applications because this is the key sequence for a hardware soft reboot.

However, Microsoft didn't account for clever programmers such as Arne Vidstrom, who wrote something called FakeGINA. FakeGINA intercepts communications between Winlogon and the normal GINA; captures the domain, username, and password from any successful logons; and writes the information to a text file. Unfortunately, this was exactly what Microsoft was trying to avoid in the first place. FakeGINA works by copying a small .DLL to the \system32 directory and modifying the Registry so the GinaDLL key points to the fakegina.dll. When a user logs on to Windows NT 4.0 or Windows 2000, the account name and password are captured and saved to a file called passlist.txt. FakeGINA is available at www.ntsecurity.nu/toolbox/fakegina/.

ADVANCED NT SECURITY EXPLORER   Advanced NT Security Explorer is a commercial password-cracker that can perform dictionary attacks, masked-character attacks (if certain characters in a password are known, they can be entered, and only the unknown characters are guessed), and brute-force attacks. Password hashes can be extracted from memory, the Registry, or be imported from password-extraction tools such as Pwdump. Performance-wise, a brute-force attack averaged around two million passwords per second on a 1,000-MHz, mobile Pentium III. Advanced NT Security Explorer is priced at $49 for a single user license, and a trial version is available from www.elcomsoft.com/antexp.html.

PWDUMP   Pwdump is a command-line tool for dumping Windows NT/2000/XP password hashes. The utility, which was originally written by Jeremy Allison, is designed to extract account and password information from the SAM using a technique known as DLL injection. Without getting into the technical details, Pwdump forces the Local Security Authority service process to load a DLL and execute code in the process's address space in order to access the password hashes. When Microsoft introduced Syskey as a way to further secure the SAM, it defeated Pwdump attacks. In response to this, Todd Sabin developed Pwdump2, which extracts the password hashes even if Syskey is enabled. There's also a Pwdump3, written by Phil Staubs and Erik Hjelmstad that is based on Pwdump2, which can extract password hashes from remote computers over the network. After Pwdump extracts the hashes, they can be fed into a password-cracking tool such as LC or Advanced NT Security Explorer. You do need Administrator privileges to use any version of Pwdump to successfully extract the password hashes.

All of the versions of Pwdump are free and can be downloaded from

- ✓ Pwdump2 (`http://razor.bindview.com/tools/index.shtml`)
- ✓ Pwdump3 (`www.polivec.com/pwdump3.html`)

ERD COMMANDER   ERD Commander is a multipurpose Windows NT/2000/XP tool that ships as a bootable CD-ROM. The product is designed to aid system administrators in repairing and diagnosing damaged systems, but it has a number of features that can benefit a spy, including the capability to reset passwords; edit the Registry; copy, move, and delete files; and execute system commands. ERD Commander is especially suited to less-technical users because it has a very easy-to-use interface that makes it appear as if you're using the Windows desktop. The current version, ERD Commander 2002, is priced at $399, and you can get more information about it from `www.winternals.com`.

CIA COMMANDER   CIA Commander is a German utility developed by Datapol that lives up to its spy name. The utility overwrites account passwords in the SAM, saves passwords to be replaced so they can later be restored, can modify the GINA to bypass alternate authentication systems such as smart card readers, and incorporates a tree-type file manager to easily copy and delete files on the target hard drive. CIA Commander is small enough to fit on a floppy disk and has an easy-to-use interface. It's priced at $249 with a trial version available from `www.ciacommander.com`.

Tactics: *The Wall Street Journal* vs. Al Qaeda

In January 2002, *The Wall Street Journal* announced that it had cracked files on Windows 2000 computers looted from Al Qaeda headquarters in Kabul. The computers were using Encrypting File System (EFS), but they were older exported versions of Windows with a relatively weak 40-bit key, versus the much stronger 128-bit encryption found in United States' versions of the operating system. According to press reports, the passwords were cracked in five days using a "cluster" of computers.

Under Windows 2000, EFS has some serious weaknesses. By default, the Administrator account has access to all encrypted files and folders, no matter who created them. If a spy successfully compromises the Administrator password, he wins. Additionally, if the user password associated with the encrypted files is changed with a utility such as Chntpw, the files are also accessible.

It's curious that *The Wall Street Journal* didn't use such attacks, but because the exact details weren't revealed, we'll give it the benefit of the doubt. One possibility is that it was just as interested in figuring out what the password was as much as gaining access to the files protected by EFS.

LOG "CLEANERS"   Windows NT/2000/XP all include the capability to log events (although security event logging is not enabled, by default). Offline attacks, where you use another operating system to boot the system and then manipulate files on the target hard drive, won't leave any traces in logs. However, attacks that are launched while Windows is running may leave clues to your activities. If you're careful, you'll want to remove any evidence of your actions.

Arne Vidstrom is a Swedish security expert and prolific developer of free Windows security tools. His Web site, www.ntsecurity.nu, has a number of tools useful for spying (or legitimate system administration). Vidstrom offers two log-cleaning tools:

- ✓ **ClearLogs.** ClearLogs is a command-line tool that clears the Security, System, or Application event logs.

- ✓ **WinZapper.** This tool lets you selectively erase events in the Security log on systems running Windows NT 4.0 and 2000.

Remember that an empty log might raise the suspicions of a system administrator or user who is security conscious. Another approach is to purposely corrupt the log file in an effort to lead the user to believe he has file system problems such as corrupt media. However, if you can, it's always better to selectively delete individual log entries to cover your tracks.

ALTERNATE OPERATING SYSTEM TOOLS   Other operating systems, such as DOS or Linux, can be used to boot a Windows NT/2000/XP system. You create a boot disk with the appropriate drivers or utilities for NTFS support and then attack the system, either by viewing, modifying, or copying files on the hard drive. (Windows NT/2000/XP hard drives and partitions can be formatted as FAT, FAT32, or NTFS. If the target hard drive is formatted as FAT or FAT32, it can be accessed with a DOS boot disk.)

Newer computers that have Windows 2000/XP preinstalled will likely be formatted as NTFS and can't be accessed with a DOS disk without a special utility called NTFSDOS. After NTFSDOS runs, you can mount NTFS volumes from DOS. There are two versions of NTFSDOS: a free release that provides read-only access and a commercial version that provides read-write capabilities. The read-only version is useful for snooping through a hard drive and viewing and copying files. (If files or folders have been protected with EFS, you can't read them with either version.)

- ✓ The free version of NTFSDOS is available from www.sysinternals.com.

- ✓ The commercial version, NTFSDOS Professional, is priced at $299 and is available from www.winternals.com.

There are also two Linux utilities you can use in attacks against Windows NT/2000/XP systems:

- ✓ **Chntpw (Change NT password).** This is a Linux command-line utility, written by Petter Nordahl-Hagen, which allows you to change the password of a user account in the SAM. Hagen has made it easy for non-Linux users by including a Linux boot disk image with NTFS support that can easily be written to the floppy disk or burned to a CD-ROM. Just boot the target machine with the provided disk image and run the utility. Chntpw is free and available from http://home.eunet.no/~pnordahl/ntpasswd/.

Tactics: Screensaver or Sorrier?

If you have read-write access to the target hard drive, another way to attack the system is to take advantage of Logon.scr. When the Windows NT/2000/XP logon dialog box is displayed and if there's no mouse or keyboard activity after awhile, the Logon.scr file is executed, displaying a default screensaver.

Boot the target computer with another operating system and rename the Logon.scr file in the \winnt\system32 (Windows NT/2000) or \windows\system32 (Windows XP) folder. Now make a copy of Cmd.exe, and rename it Logon.scr.

Restart the computer again, but this time let Windows boot. When the logon dialog box appears, don't enter any text or move the mouse. After up to 15 minutes of inactivity, the Logon.scr will launch. But now instead of the screensaver appearing, the Cmd.exe shell appears, running as a System process. At this point, you can do just about anything with the system at the command line, including creating a new account for yourself with Administrator privileges.

✓ **John the Ripper.** This is a popular UNIX password-cracking utility that runs under a number of different operating systems and has a rich set of features. The Linux source code is provided, and you can compile a third-party patch that will crack SAM passwords. John is available at `www.openwall.com/john/`.

Countermeasures

There are a number of countermeasures you can employ to keep wily ex-KGB agents and other spies from breaching your system security. Probably the most basic countermeasure is to ensure that your physical security is hardened, as discussed in Chapter 3. Keeping the bad guys from having physical access to your computer is a major part of the battle. And if you can't keep them away, there are still some techniques you can apply to make it extremely difficult for them to compromise your data.

Security Settings

There are a number of BIOS and operating system security settings you can use to reduce the chances of someone getting sensitive data from your computer. But before you change any of your settings, no matter what version of Windows you're running, always make sure that you have the latest service pack and security-related hot fixes installed. A good computer spy will be keeping track of any and all vulnerabilities he can exploit to take down your system. Having the latest patches installed reduces the chances of both local and remote attacks being successful.

Microsoft offers a variety of free tools and information sources for keeping its products protected from known vulnerabilities. They include the following:

✓ **Microsoft Security Bulletins.** Microsoft releases security bulletins as vulnerabilities are discovered and fixes are released. Security bulletins and other resources are available at www.microsoft.com/technet/security. You can stay even more current by sending a blank e-mail to securbas@microsoft.com, which subscribes you to Microsoft's Security Notification Service.

✓ **Windows Automatic Updates.** Windows XP and 2000 have an option that automatically downloads and updates any released security patch. When you turn this option on, your computer periodically connects to Microsoft over the Internet, checks for any new fixes, and downloads and installs them. (In the past, there have been delays of days or weeks between the time a security bulletin is published and when it appears on Windows Update. If you're concerned about security, don't rely solely on Windows Update to keep you current.)

✓ **Microsoft Network Security Hotfix Checker (Hfnetchk.exe).** This is a command-line utility that checks for the absence of security patches (in December 2002, the command-line functionality of the utility was integrated into Microsoft's Baseline Security Advisor tool). You can download the utility and get more information on how to use it from http://support.microsoft.com/default.aspx?scid=KB;en-us;q303215.

After you've ensured that your operating system and any potentially vulnerable applications are up-to-date, consider using the following security settings.

BIOS

Even though there are a number of different ways to compromise BIOS security, you still should use BIOS passwords if you're concerned about espionage. A BIOS password will keep casual snoopers or inexperienced eavesdroppers out of your computer and will at least delay a professional for a while. You should set passwords both for booting as well as changing any BIOS settings.

The other BIOS security measure to use is to prevent the computer from booting from the A: drive. This will stop a spy from booting with an alternate operating system and then accessing the hard drive. Remember that modern BIOSes may have a number of different boot sequence options that allow booting from CD-ROMs and USB devices. Be sure to disable any of these devices from booting. In the event your hard drive becomes corrupted and you need to use a rescue disk, you'll need to go into the BIOS setup first and change the boot sequence so the floppy disk is recognized.

WINDOWS 3.X/9X/ME

If you're using Windows 3.x/9x/ME, there's really not much you can do in the way of enhanced security settings. (You can at least prevent a CD from bypassing your screensaver, as previously discussed, by displaying the properties for My Computer and then disabling the Auto Insert Notification setting for the CD-ROM in the Device Manager tab.)

If a spy has physical access to a computer running an older version of Windows, there's no real system security measure to keep him from snooping through your files. The best you can do is use the countermeasures discussed throughout this book that don't depend on the operating system. If you're serious about security, consider upgrading to Windows 2000/XP or giving Linux a try.

WINDOWS NT/2000/XP

Unlike the older, consumer-oriented versions of Windows, the Windows NT/2000/XP operating system family offers considerably more security. However, many of the security settings required to really harden the system from attack aren't turned on, by default. You should spend some time fine-tuning the security of your system to ensure that it has a better chance of keeping the bad guys out.

The Microsoft Baseline Security Advisor is a free tool that examines configurations on Windows 2000/XP systems and offers suggestions on how to make them more secure. The utility is available from `www.microsoft.com/technet/security/tools/Tools/MBSA home.asp`.

Some security measures you should consider to reduce the chances of someone breaching your system include the following (many of these options are turned on and off through Local Security Settings, which you can access by typing **secpol.msc** in the Run dialog box):

✓ **Use NTFS formatting.** FAT and FAT32 file systems offer no file- or folder-level security and are easily accessed with a DOS boot disk.

✓ **Disable the Guest account.** Don't give a spy a foothold into the system where he can try to escalate his privileges.

✓ **Rename the Administrator account.** A good spy knows the name of the default Administrator account and likely will direct his efforts there. Use a different account name for Administrator (something that doesn't sound like an administrative account); then consider having a bogus account named Administrator with no privileges and a strong password. This bit of misdirection may focus a spy on the wrong account to attack.

✓ **Prevent the last logged-in user name from being displayed.** In the Security Options section of Local Policies, there's a setting that prevents the account name of the user who last successfully logged on to the computer from being displayed in the logon dialog box. This makes it more difficult for a spy trying to manually log on because he needs to determine both an account name and password to access the computer.

✓ **Use strong password policies.** There is a Password Policy section in Local Security Settings in which you can specify minimum password length, password complexity, and when passwords should be changed. Passwords should be a minimum of eight characters; have a mix of characters, numbers, and symbols; and be changed at least every 90 days.

✓ **Enable account lockout.** There is an Account Lockout Policy section in the Local Security Settings that prevents further logon attempts to an account after a specified number of failed logons (you can't lockout the built-in Administrator account though).

The Account Lockout Duration setting defines how long logons will no longer be permitted. For example, if the Threshold was set to 3 and the Duration was set to 15 minutes, a spy who was unsuccessful on the fourth password guess couldn't try any other guesses until after 15 minutes had passed.

✓ **Enable event logging.** By default, a number of security-related events aren't logged. You should enable events and periodically check the logs to see if there have been any intrusion attempts. Events and their statuses that you should audit include the following:

- Account logon events (success, failure)

- Account management (success, failure)

- Logon events (success, failure)

- Object access (success)

- Policy change (success, failure)

- Privilege use (success, failure)

- System events (success, failure)

✓ **Consider using additional Syskey security measures.** Although the extra encryption provided by Syskey improves the security of password hashes, you can increase the security even further by requiring a password or floppy disk startup key. Normally, the Syskey startup key is stored on the hard drive, but you can configure the system to require a password or disk key to unlock the passwords before the logon process starts. Exercise caution with this feature because if you lose the disk you won't be able to boot into Windows and will be forced to completely rebuild the system.

✓ **Be careful using logon password hints in Windows XP.** An easy-to-guess password hint coupled with a known user account name is an invitation to having your system compromised.

✓ **Password-protect the screensaver.** You should always enable password protection for your screensaver to prevent someone from easily accessing your computer while it's unattended.

Additional details on how to implement these as well as other security settings can be found in the security section of `http://labmice.net`; an excellent Web resource for Windows NT/ 2000/XP administrators and users.

In addition to spying, the National Security Agency (NSA) is also responsible for helping to keep the government's computer system secure. The NSA publishes a series of Security Recommendation Guides for Windows NT, 2000, and XP, which include .inf files that apply suggested security policy settings. The guides and files are available from `www.nsa.gov/snac/index.html`.

Countermeasures: More Is Better

Although you should always use a password that is at least eight characters long, consider using a password at least 15 characters in length for Windows 2000 and XP logon purposes. Longer passwords are always harder to attack, but they also add an extra layer of protection in this case.

In a mixed network with Windows 3.x/9x/ME computers, the operating system uses LAN Manager (LM) hashes for all computers. LM password hashes are considerably easier to crack than the more secure NTLM or Kerberos authentication methods, and even a password that's eight characters or more can be compromised because of the weak LM hashing scheme.

However, there's a flaw in the Windows 2000 and XP authentication process: If you use a password with 15 or more characters, the LM hash is set to a fixed value, no matter what the password is. This makes it considerably more difficult for a utility such as LC to be successful (in LC4, the LM hash of a 15+-character password is displayed as "empty"). This likely has something to do with the fact that the maximum length of a password under Windows NT was 14 characters (under 2000 and XP, it's 127).

Effective Passwords

When it comes to authentication (or any form of security), never use weak passwords! Your computer is extremely vulnerable if you use an easy-to-guess or short password, and you are essentially doomed if someone wants to compromise your system. See the "Countermeasures" section in Chapter 6 for more information on the risks of weak passwords and how to select strong passwords.

Encryption

Any sensitive data on your hard drive should be encrypted. In case the BIOS and operating system authentication security measures are defeated, critical information can still be protected if you use strong encryption. Microsoft's Encrypting File System (EFS) provides a reasonable amount of security as implemented in Windows XP Professional—although EFS under Windows 2000 is vulnerable to several different types of attacks. See the "Countermeasures" section of Chapter 6 for more information about strong encryption and some suggestions on which encryption utilities to use.

Summary

The BIOS and operating system are your first two lines of defense against a spy that gains physical access to your computer. Although it's possible to counter system security measures with a number of different techniques and tools, you should always ensure that your BIOS and Windows security settings are configured as strongly as possible. This prevents a casual snoop from compromising your data, and may prove to be enough of a deterrent to a more determined spy to prompt him to seek a softer target elsewhere. Don't become so focused on network attacks that you neglect physical and local computer security defenses.

Chapter 5

Searching for Evidence

"Just like watching the detectives. Don't get cute!"
— Elvis Costello, "Watching the Detectives," *My Aim Is True*

Legal Spying

Some people get paid to legally spy on other people's computers. Computer cops and forensic examiners sift through bits and bytes stored on hard drives and other storage media, looking for information and evidence that may either help convict or exonerate a suspect.

Computer cops work for law enforcement agencies. They may be sworn police officers or civilian technicians. Their private sector counterparts are computer forensic examiners, who perform the same type of work, but for corporations and attorneys. Forensic examiners don't get to carry a badge and a gun, but they do get paid quite a bit more than most computer cops.

Forget any James Bond danger, intrigue, and romance with this type of spying. Computer forensics is a tedious, painstakingly detail-oriented job. It can involve viewing screen after screen of hexadecimal output from hard drive sectors, looking for evidence that may or may not be there. For computer cops it can also mean journeying to some of the darkest sides of human nature, especially during child pornography investigations.

This chapter discusses how computer cops and forensic examiners operate and what applications and techniques they use to discover information and evidence. After presenting some of their tricks and tools of the trade, countermeasures that are used to thwart evidence-gathering attempts are listed.

How Computer Cops Work

Computer cops and private forensics examiners both have the same job: to determine if evidence exists on a computer relating to some suspected activity or to find some relevant bits of information that could eventually turn into evidence. For a cop, it might mean looking for gambling records on a bookie's seized computer; for a private forensics examiner, it could mean recovering deleted files associated with a corrupt accounting firm scandal.

Both types of investigators follow the same general processes and procedures. The biggest difference is that cops have a stricter set of rules of engagement when it comes to accessing computers that may hold evidence. For example, although a cop would need a court-issued search warrant to enter an office to look for evidence on a computer, a forensic examiner working for a corporation simply would need a company official's permission to search a computer in an employee's cubicle.

Busted: Regional Computer Forensics Laboratories

In November 2000, the FBI opened its first Regional Computer Forensics Laboratory (RCFL) in San Diego, California. The San Diego RCFL was set up to be a multi-agency, multijurisdictional entity with 18 computer cops from different agencies available to investigate computer-related crime in the San Diego area. In its first year, the lab handled nearly 400 cases and has served as a model for other RCFLs opening around the country.

Some of the cases the San Diego RCFL has helped gather evidence for include the following:

✓ Michael Craig Dickman, the "Gap-Toothed Bandit" who was sentenced to nine years in prison for robbing 12 area banks. Computer-forensics investigators found copies of the former bio-tech executive's holdup notes he gave to tellers in deleted print spool files on a laptop he had asked his sister to remove from his apartment.

✓ Arthur Gerardo and Valerie Beidler, who were convicted for the torture and murder of a roommate who helped them forge checks and make fake identification cards. A seized computer contained pictures of checks and driver's licenses that had been digitally scanned and then altered.

✓ Charles "Andy" Williams, a teenager who was convicted on charges of killing two classmates and wounding 13 others at Santana High School in March 2001. Williams' computer was seized as part of the investigation.

✓ David Westerfield, convicted in August 2002 of kidnapping and murdering his seven-year-old neighbor, Danielle van Dam. Westerfield's computers contained about 64,000 photo files and 2,200 video clips (85 images were recovered of naked girls and young teens being raped).

This section focuses primarily on the computer cop. However, keep in mind that because there's an overlap between the skills and techniques used by both computer cops and computer forensic examiners, much of the information described also applies to forensic examiners.

To start out with, a computer cop's skill level and technical depth can vary tremendously. A few computer cops may be capable of reverse-engineering an encryption utility, whereas others rely solely on turnkey Windows forensic examination software tools to do their work. At this point in time, most computer cops were cops first and didn't enter law enforcement with a technology background. (However, law enforcement agencies do hire technicians who aren't sworn officers who may have technology-related degrees and industry experience, and private forensic examiners generally have more of a technology background than their computer cop counterparts. Also because of the backlog of cases, some government agencies are turning to private consulting firms to process computer evidence.)

In July 2001, the Department of Justice published an excellent reference called *Electronic Crime Scene Investigation: A Guide for First Responders*. The easy-to-read, short manual is targeted toward nontechnical law enforcement officers, but it does contain worthwhile information for more technically adept readers. The guide is available at `www.ncjrs.org/pdffiles1/nij/187736.pdf`.

Because most computer cops don't start out with a strong technical background, there are a number of private and government sources that offer computer forensics training and certification programs. Certification is important for establishing credibility on the witness stand because cops frequently testify in court.

Computer cops tend to work out of offices and labs that have specialized hardware and software to process evidence. In the recent past, only federal and large municipal agencies staffed and equipped computer investigation teams and facilities, but now with PCs as an everyday part of life, even smaller departments are budgeting for full- or part-time computer cops and equipment.

Unlike other spies, in most cases police officers aren't worried about being stealthy unless they're involved with a black bag job (a court-sanctioned covert entry of a premise to gather evidence). They already have access to a suspected criminal's hardware and software and are primarily interested in discovering whether any evidence exists to connect the suspect with a crime.

Countermeasures: Getting Certified

Some of the more recognized providers of computer investigation training and certifications include the following:

✓ **International Association of Computer Investigative Specialists (IACIS).** IACIS is a nonprofit organization for law enforcement computer investigators. Its training and certification programs are widely recognized. For more information on IACIS, see `www.cops.org`.

✓ **High Technology Crime Investigative Association (HTCIA).** HTCIA is a trade organization composed of both law enforcement and civilian investigators. The association has regional chapters and puts on conferences and training events. To learn more about HTCIA, go to `www.htcia.org`.

✓ **National White Collar Crime Center (NWCC).** NWCC provides free computer forensics training to law enforcement personnel. The Center offers a variety of courses taught throughout the United States. See `www.cybercrime.org`.

✓ **New Technologies Inc.** NTI is a commercial forensics software manufacturer in Oregon that also offers forensics training to both law enforcement and civilians. For more information, go to `www.forensics-intl.com`.

There is a big demand for the services of computer cops (and forensics examiners, too), and it's doubtful that the supply will catch up with the demand in the coming years. Even though law enforcement agencies are recognizing the importance of trained cops who can take a "byte" out of crime, they face a number of challenges going into the future, which will put them even further behind the curve. Some of these challenges include the following:

- ✓ **Larger hard drives.** Bigger hard drives mean more bytes to process and search. With hard drives in the 100- to 200-gigabyte range becoming common and affordable, duplicating a suspect's hard drive takes longer, searching for evidence takes longer, and more storage media are required to back up evidence. All these extras increase departmental budgets.

- ✓ **Increased caseloads.** Computers are increasingly used in all manners of crimes. Ten years ago, computer cops just had to worry about white-collar criminals and crackers. Today, these same cops have to process evidence found on computers for drug cases, homicides, suicides, fraud, and just about any other crime in which a computer is present.

- ✓ **Techno-savvy criminals.** It's a statistical given that a certain percentage of the population will become involved with crime, and as a new generation grows up more computer-literate than the last, those who choose a criminal path will be familiar with a number of technologies that can impede or challenge law enforcement investigations.

Although the job of a computer cop has many elements, it can be broken down into three general components: seizure, forensic duplication, and examination. Let's examine each of these elements.

Seizure

Before you can search for evidence of a crime on a computer, you obviously need access to the computer first, which generally means seizing the computer and any other electronic or nonelectronic items that may be relevant to the case. (Forensic examiners may in rare cases be involved in computer seizures.)

The Constitution prevents law enforcement from kicking in doors and seizing computers whenever they think a crime has been committed. Before a seizure can take place, a judge must approve a search warrant. In cases dealing with computers, the computer cop either writes the search warrant or helps with the wording. Search warrants must be precisely written to stand up in court during the prosecution of a suspect, so the computer cop has to specifically state what computers and related equipment will be searched, with probable cause for why they need to be examined.

After a search warrant has been granted, it is executed. Depending on the crime and the suspect, this may be a simple knock on the door or a knock accompanied by battering rams and drawn guns in the early morning hours.

Because examination of evidence rarely takes place in the field, there are a series of steps that cops go through when it comes to seizing computers and electronic evidence. The steps and some guidelines that go with them include the following:

- ✓ **Secure the scene.** Remove all persons from the immediate area where the evidence will be collected. If the computer is powered on, leave it on. If it's turned off, don't turn it on. (If the computer is powered-on, the contents of the screen are recorded, and the power cord is typically pulled at the computer, not at the wall socket.)

✓ **Protect perishable data.** Any device that stores data in battery-powered memory (pagers, cell phones, PDAs, and so on) should be secured and documented.

✓ **Identify telephone lines and network cables attached to the computer.** Document, disconnect at the wall, and label all cables.

✓ **Conduct preliminary interviews.** After separating and identifying all persons at the scene (witnesses, suspects, or others), ask questions and document information about computer ownership, passwords, and any security devices; you should also find out whether data is being stored offsite. (It's amazing how much information people will volunteer.)

✓ **Document the scene.** Before examining or moving anything, photograph or videotape the entire scene, including close-ups of the computer, monitor, and any peripherals. Take notes in addition to the photographs.

✓ **Collect evidence.** Evidence comes in electronic and nonelectronic forms. Any paper notes, passwords, manuals, or documents relating to the crime should be collected. Remove the power cord from the computer, and in the case of a laptop, remove the battery (to prevent any software booby traps that might erase data during a normal shutdown procedure). Place pieces of tape over all drive slots and the power outlet. Record the make, model, and serial number of the computer.

✓ **Package and transport the evidence.** All collected evidence should be labeled and inventoried. Cables should be labeled to match which jacks they plug into on the computer (for example, place a label with an "M" on the PC's mouse port and another label with an "M" on the mouse cable). If there are multiple computers, ensure that peripherals and cables are labeled so they match the computer they were attached to. Any magnetic media should be placed in paper or anti-static plastic bags. During transportation of the evidence, protect equipment from shock and excessive vibration. Also avoid exposure to magnetic fields (radios, speaker magnets, or heated seats) and excessive heat, cold, or humidity.

✓ **Store the evidence.** Departmental policy dictates how evidence is stored, but it's important that computers and peripherals be protected from heat, humidity, moisture, dust, and magnetic sources. In a high-profile child pornography case, evidence was stored in a Post Office basement. After several floods, the computers had rusted, and floppy disks were covered with mildew.

After the evidence has been seized, transported, and stored, the next thing a computer cop does is duplicate all of the storage media associated with the case.

The Department of Justice's "Searching and Seizing Computers and Obtaining Electronic Evidence in Criminal Investigations" is available at www.cybercrime.gov/s&smanual2002.htm.

Tactics: Chain of Possession

Chain of possession (also called *chain of custody*) is a critical concept in criminal and civil investigations. It simply means that there is an unbroken chain that documents everyone who had possession of a piece of evidence from the time it was gathered to when it was placed in storage. The purpose of a chain of possession is to ensure accountability among those who have access to the evidence and to reduce the potential of evidence tampering. This is especially crucial when dealing with computer cases in which bits and bytes are easy to change and someone could potentially alter evidence.

Chain of possession is typically documented by using logs that track who had access to evidence, labels that clearly identify a piece of evidence, and secure storage locations for collected evidence.

Forensic Duplication

Before a computer cop examines a computer, he makes a forensic duplicate of the hard drive and any other storage media that have been seized as evidence. The cardinal rule of computer forensics is to never conduct an examination of the original media, but to always use a bit-for-bit mirror copy of the original. There are two reasons for this:

- ✓ When searching through a hard drive while running Windows, opening files may unintentionally modify evidence. Even booting Windows results in a number of files being altered.

- ✓ Because digital data can be so easily changed, a judge or defense attorney may raise the question of possible tampering if the original media are directly examined and serve as the only evidence.

Duplication can be performed at the site where the evidence was seized or at the agency office or lab. Most cops opt for back at the office, where they have access to all of their tools and equipment. Under certain circumstances, however, such as a black bag job, on-scene duplication may be required.

To ensure that evidence will be valid and will hold up in court, the following procedures are performed:

1. Boot the evidence computer with another operating system, such as DOS or Linux; then use a checksum or secure hash (for example, SHA-1 or MD5) application to create file and directory signatures. (Using an alternate operating system prevents Windows from making file changes when it starts up.)

2. Use a DOS or Linux application to make an identical copy of the hard drive (several are listed in the "Evidence-Gathering Tools" section later in this chapter). The copy should be made on sterile media (either a new hard drive or tape) or media that has been "wiped" to ensure that there are no residual data left.

3. After the copying is complete, use the checksum or hash utility to verify that the copy is identical to the original.

4. Be sure that the entire process is documented and then store the original hard drive in a secure location.

The next step is to start the search for evidence on the duplicated hard drive. If there is suspected evidence on other storage media, such as floppy disks, CD-Rs, or tapes, a similar set of procedures is used to duplicate the original media before an examination is performed.

There are several companies that manufacture workstations specifically designed for hard drive duplication and computer forensics evidence analysis and processing. These workstations contain features such as multiple hard drive bays, different storage media hardware, and bundled forensics software. Some of the key manufacturers include Digital Intelligence (www.digitalintel.com), DIBS USA (www.dibsusa.com), and Forensics Computers (www.forensic-computers.com).

Examination

After the media is duplicated, the computer cop starts his examination, which usually involves attaching the duplicated hard drive to a forensic workstation. (The seized computer is booted with a floppy disk to get CMOS information, which is important for establishing file creation or modification dates and times, but other than that, is never allowed to boot from the hard drive since evidence may be altered.) The forensic workstation contains analysis software and is ideally used only for dealing with suspected evidence — no playing Doom or instant messaging.

The main tasks to be completed in a forensic examination, regardless of the storage media, include the following:

✓ **The system is examined.** The boot record and system configuration files (such as Config.sys, Autoexec.bat, or Registry values) are examined.

✓ **Deleted files are recovered.** All deleted files are recovered. (The first character of the file name of any restored files should be changed from a hex E5 to another unique character to ensure consistency; this is discussed in more detail a little later in the chapter.)

✓ **Files are listed.** A list of all files on the media, whether they contain evidence or not, is recorded.

✓ **Unallocated space is examined.** A search of the unallocated space for any relevant evidence is made.

✓ **Slack space is examined.** A search of the file slack space (the unused space on a storage medium) is made for any relevant evidence.

✓ **Files are examined.** Document files are opened and viewed.

✓ **Files are decrypted.** An attempt is made to decrypt any protected documents. If successful, the contents are viewed.

✓ **Everything is documented.** A hardcopy printout is made of any evidence. The entire examination process is scrupulously documented.

There are two approaches to this process. The cop can manually perform all of these tasks using various software utilities or he can use automated evidence-gathering and analysis software, which is considerably faster and easier to use. A number of applications used for computer forensics are discussed in the "Evidence-Gathering Tools" section later in this chapter. In any case, the same exact process is used for each examination, which assures consistency during investigations.

An important point to make about the examination phase is that the cop will search for specific evidence associated with a specific crime. He may stumble on additional evidence that links a suspect to other criminal activities, but his main focus will be searching for evidence that ties a suspect with whatever crime he has been charged with.

After the examination is complete, the cop writes a report with his findings. How long the examination takes depends on the severity and the importance of the crime and the backlog of electronic evidence that must be processed from other cases. It's not unusual for state crime labs to take many months to turn around evidence due to backlogs because smaller police agencies don't have the resources to perform their own processing.

If the case goes to trial, it's likely that the computer cop will testify as a witness for the prosecution. A cop's ability to explain complex technical terms to a jury in an easy-to-understand manner is often just as critical to his job as discovering evidence on a hard drive. It's also during trials that the computer cop may meet up with his counterpart, the private forensic examiner, who may be working for the defense, trying to cast doubt on the cop's credibility when it comes to the way evidence was processed and examined.

Spy Tactics

It's time to play spy again, only this time you'll be wearing a white hat. Put yourself in the shoes of a police detective who's working a case related to a serious crime. Perhaps it's a child abduction, or maybe it's a homicide. A computer has been seized from a suspect, and it's your job to see if there's any evidence on it to help solve the case. (For now, mostly concentrate on the contents of the computer itself, and don't worry about performing any network-related forensics. Some of this is covered in Chapter 10.)

We'll assume that you've already made a forensic backup of the hard drive and are working on the duplicated copy. You'll be manually checking some common places on the hard drive where evidence might reside.

Remember: Even if you've got your white hat on and are one of the good guys, these tactics don't apply only to computer cops and forensic examiners; they also work for anyone interested in teasing out information from a hard drive or other storage media.

Exploiting the Vulnerabilities

A computer is like a leaky sieve when it comes to storing information and evidence (electronic data qualifies as "writings" or "recording" under Federal Rule of Evidence 1001, which includes data stored in magnetic impulse or by mechanical or electronic recording). There are a large number of places to look for data that could be evidence and be relevant to your case. Ideally, you should take the computer back to your office or lab, where you can duplicate the hard drive and then start searching for evidence. Here are some of the places you should look and what you should be looking for.

FILES

You don't need a degree in computer science to know you're going to want to examine the contents of certain documents. For example, files named 2002drugdeals.doc, nudekids.jpg, or secretevilplans.xls hopefully will catch your attention, depending on what you're looking for, and you'll open them up.

But when it comes to evidence, there's much more to files than simply examining the content of documents. Some other file-related evidence that can equally be as valuable includes the following:

MAC TIMES   Windows records the time a file was Modified, last Accessed, and Created; these are known as MAC times and can be shown in Windows Explorer by selecting a file and then displaying its properties. File MAC times are valuable when collecting evidence because they give a snapshot history of the file. For example, if a suspected corporate spy said she accidentally downloaded a budget forecast spreadsheet at a certain date and time but never looked at it, the MAC times could hint at whether she was lying or telling the truth.

SHORTCUTS   Shortcuts are references to applications, files, or devices (printers, external storage devices, and network nodes). Shortcuts have a .LNK file extension, but Windows hides this from the user so only the name of the shortcut appears on the desktop or within Windows Explorer. Shortcuts are designed to be timesavers. For example, a sales rep could create a shortcut that points to a customer list that she frequently uses. She saves time by double-clicking the shortcut icon on the desktop instead of navigating through numerous folders to get to the file.

In addition to user-created shortcuts, Windows also saves its own shortcuts in a number of places, specifically in the Desktop, Recent, Start Menu, and SendTo folders.

- ✓ **Desktop.** This folder stores all of the shortcuts that appear on the Windows desktop.

- ✓ **Recent.** The Recent folder contains shortcuts to recently opened files that appear in the Documents menu item when a user presses the Start button.

- ✓ **Start Menu.** This folder contains shortcuts to applications that appear in the Programs menu item when a user presses the Start button.

- ✓ **SendTo.** The SendTo folder contains shortcuts to applications and devices a user can send data to, such as a floppy drive or an e-mail application.

In Windows 9x/ME, these folders are located in the Windows folder; in Windows NT/2000/XP, these folders are located in the user Documents and Settings folders.

Shortcuts can be very important for evidence gathering for the following reasons:

- ✓ A shortcut that points to an external storage device or network node may indicate there is additional evidence than what is present on the hard drive.

- ✓ Shortcuts in the Start Menu can provide evidence that a particular application has been installed on the computer at some time.

- ✓ Shortcuts in the Recent folder can display information about recently accessed documents, even though they may have been deleted.

- ✓ Shortcuts contain the MAC times of the files they reference in the data portion of the .LNK file, specifically at byte offsets 28, 36, and 44.

HIDDEN FILES AND FOLDERS   Some computer users who think they are clever will try to conceal evidence by setting a file or folder attribute to make it hidden. The original purpose of hidden or invisible files and folders was to hide system files from users who don't need to access them, but anyone can make any file or folder invisible.

In Windows Explorer, right-click on a file or folder, and select Properties from the pop-up menu to display the attributes. If the Hidden box is checked, the file or folder won't be shown in Windows Explorer or when a File Open dialog box is displayed.

Inexperienced computer users without a full understanding of how a file system works often assume that they can take advantage of this feature, to keep other people from snooping in their documents. Unfortunately, they never made it to evil criminal mastermind school. Hidden files and folders can be displayed a number of different ways:

✓ **Windows Explorer.** The default setting in Windows Explorer is not to show hidden files and folders, but this can easily be changed in Folder Options to show all files.

✓ **Command line.** The DOS `dir` command in command-line sessions does not show hidden files; `dir /a` does show them, however.

✓ **Applications.** Hidden files and folders are easily discovered using computer forensics applications or other programs written specifically to list every file and folder, regardless of its attributes.

Using hidden file and folder attributes might keep out a casual spy who is just poking around in folders, but it won't stop anyone who is serious about hunting for evidence.

TEMPORARY FILES   Windows and most applications make extensive use of temporary files, which are files that are created and deleted by the application without the user knowing about it. Temporary files usually are created as part of the save process and can contain all sorts of interesting information that could be useful as evidence. For example, temporary files created by Microsoft Word are named ~WRLxxxxxx.tmp and can be renamed with a .DOC extension so they can be opened directly from Word.

Temporary files are typically located in

✓ The Temp folder of the Windows folder

✓ Any folder that contains an application or a document created by an application

Many applications don't do a very good job of cleaning up temporary files and deleting them, and the files are clearly shown in Windows Explorer, often with a .TMP file extension. Even if a temporary file has been deleted, it still may be resurrected with a file recovery utility.

If you do a search for .TMP files and don't find any, there's a good chance that the user is running evidence-eliminating software (this kind of software is covered in more detail later in this chapter). Another possibility is if the Windows temporary environmental variables TMP and TEMP have been set to point to a RAM disk (a volume that exists in memory that's contents disappear when the computer is turned off) or to an encrypted folder. If this is the case, temporary files would disappear when the computer is shut down or be stored in a password-protected volume that would need to be mounted to access the files.

CHANGED FILE EXTENSIONS   File extensions (the three letters after the dot in a filename) show what type of document a file is. For example, .DOC is a Microsoft Word file, .XLS is a Microsoft Excel spreadsheet, and .BMP is a bitmap graphics file.

People sometimes try to conceal evidence with the mistaken belief that simply by changing the file extension they can hide what information a file actually contains; this is a common tactic used by collectors of child pornography in an attempt to conceal .JPG or .GIF files.

To demonstrate that this doesn't work, use Paintbrush to create a graphics file and save it as SPY.BMP. Now use Windows Explorer and rename the file to SPY.INI. Based on the name and icon, no one would ever guess that the document is really a graphics file. Or would they?

Now use Paintbrush to open SPY.INI. Just because it appears to be an .INI file, Paint doesn't immediately dismiss it. Instead, Paint checks whether the document contains information that identifies it as a graphics file and if it does, successfully opens the file.

With the exception of simple text files, all documents have a unique file format. The format contains header information that allows an application to recognize a particular file format so it can either process the document or display an error message, saying that it can't read it. It's relatively easy to write a program that traverses hard drive directories, listing files that have a particular header regardless of what the file extension says. This feature is found in several commercial computer forensics applications.

Checking for files that may have had their extensions changed should be done anytime you think a suspect may have above-average computer knowledge.

To learn more about the exact file formats of different types of files, see www.wotsit.org. To find out what application is associated with a file extension, see http://filext.com.

DELETED FILES   On the surface, deleting files is a two-step process in Windows. First, you put the file in the Recycle Bin and then you empty it. Before you empty the Recycle Bin, you can always restore a file to its original location by selecting the file in the Recycle Bin and using the Restore command. But what happens to the file after the Recycle Bin is emptied?

If you've worked with computers for awhile, you probably already know that when a file is deleted, it really doesn't vanish off the face of the hard drive. Windows replaces the first character of a deleted file's directory entry with a sigma character (hexadecimal E5), indicating that the file shouldn't be displayed in any directory listings. In addition, the File Allocation Table entries are changed, setting the deleted file's entries to zero. This tells the file system that the space the file occupies is now available for use. A new file, a copied file, or a file that grows all could overwrite the location where the data from the deleted file was located.

Using a hex editor (a utility that can view the hexadecimal data that makes up a file), it's possible to examine the sectors of a hard drive and manually reconstruct a deleted file based on the sector information. This can be a tedious task because files typically don't occupy contiguous space and may be scattered all over a hard drive. It's much simpler to use an automated file recovery utility to restore deleted files.

There's a greater chance of being able to recover a more recently deleted file than a file that was deleted six months ago. This is because over time it's likely that the space has been overwritten with the data from other files.

Obviously, deleted files are an excellent source of evidence, and you should always do the following:

✓ Check the Recycle Bin to see if there's anything in it.

✓ Use a file recovery utility, such as those discussed in the "Evidence-Gathering Tools" section later in this chapter to see if you can restore any deleted files. Even if you can't recover the entire file, you may still be able to salvage pieces of the file that have relevant evidence.

PRINT SPOOLER FILES   Windows uses print spooling when a document is printed, which means that the document prints in the background and the user can continue working with the document while it prints.

Print spooling works by relying on temporary files that contain the data to be printed as well as information required to complete the print job. There are two print spooling types: EMF and RAW.

✓ **EMF.** EMF, or enhanced metafile, is the default Windows print-spool data type. A document is changed into a metafile format before it is printed.

✓ **RAW.** RAW is the spool data type used by non-Windows applications. It indicates that the data is ready to print as-is and won't be converted into a metafile.

In both EMF and RAW formats, files with .SPL and .SHD extensions are created for each print job. .SHD ("shadow") files contain information about the print job. .SPL files contain either the data to be printed or the names of data files to be printed. Usually, these files are named with the print-spool data type and a .TMP extension; for example, ~EMFxxxxxx.TMP. All of the .SHD, .SPL, and .TMP files are deleted after the print job is completed.

Deleted print-spool files can be important evidence. For example, a user might claim he never printed a document that was found on his hard drive, but a recovered metafile would prove otherwise. Or perhaps an original document was wiped before it was deleted, but the metafile from when it was printed could still be on the hard drive.

You can learn more about print spooling by searching for EMF and RAW at Microsoft's TechNet site: www.microsoft.com/technet/.

SCAN DISK TEMPORARY FILES   Whenever a Windows session ends improperly, such as in the case of a system crash or turning the computer's power off instead of shutting down first, the Scan Disk utility runs at startup to ensure that the file system hasn't been damaged. As it runs, the utility may create temporary files with a .CHK extension in the root directory. Scan Disk doesn't do a good job of cleaning up after itself and often leaves these temporary files in place. Any .CHK file should be examined because it may contain fragments of evidence that have come from other files.

Alternate Data Streams   With the Windows NT/2000/XP NTFS file system, you can bind additional data to a file or folder; this is known as an Alternate Data Stream (ADS). An ADS can hide text or even an executable file without being detected by Windows Explorer or the DOS dir command. The hidden data in the ADS can't be removed unless the parent file or directory is deleted.

Tactics: Recycling Pays

Having an understanding of how the Recycle Bin works can pay off for an investigator more than returning cans for deposit money.

The Recycle Bin is actually a hidden system folder named Recycled in Windows 9x/ME and Recycler in Windows NT/2000/XP. When a user places a file in the Recycle Bin, Windows deletes the file's entry from the folder it came from, creates a new file entry in the Recycled folder, and adds information about the file to a hidden file named INFO or INFO2. For Windows NT/2000/XP, a subfolder is also created in the Recycled folder with the security identifier (SID) of the account that's currently logged in.

Information stored in the INFO file includes the following:

- ✓ The name of the file to be deleted
- ✓ The date and time the file was placed in the Recycled folder
- ✓ The location of where the file was previously located

This can be powerful data when it comes to evidence-gathering because it can prove whether a user knowingly deleted files (the operating system and applications don't use the Recycle Bin for deleting files), when files were deleted, and where they were previously located.

The INFO file is deleted each time the Recycle Bin is emptied, but as with any file, this may be restored with a file recovery utility.

For more information on Windows recycling, see Microsoft Knowledgebase Article 136517 at `http://support.microsoft.com/default.aspx?scid=kb;` `EN-US;136517.`

Most users and computer cops don't know about ADSs, and this feature provides a stealthy way to conceal information. To see for yourself, follow these steps:

1. Use Notepad to create a file named test.txt in the root directory, enter some text, and save the file.

2. In Windows Explorer, check the size of the file.

3. Now at the Run command dialog box, type the following: **notepad test.txt:alternate.txt.** Notepad asks you if you want to create the file; answer yes. Enter some text and then save it.

4. Now look for alternate.txt. The file doesn't appear in any directory listing, a search for the file based on the text you typed won't find a match, opening up test.txt with a hex editor shows only whatever you typed in that file, and even the size of test.txt remains the same even though new data has been bound to it. Pretty sneaky stuff.

5. To confirm that the alternate.txt file still exists, enter **notepad test.txt:alternate.txt** at the Run command. You can now access the ADS.

If your suspect is a sophisticated computer user and is using a Windows 2000/XP NTFS file system, you should check for any ADSs. Crucial Security, which has a free utility called Crucial ADS that detects alternate data streams, is available at www.crucialsecurity.com.

SLACK SPACE

The Windows operating system operates on fixed-sized chunks of data called clusters. Clusters are the smallest-sized units that Windows can store data to; a file is made up of a series of clusters. If a file or part of a file that occupies a cluster is smaller than the cluster size, the entire cluster is still reserved for the file. The unused space between where the file data ends and the end of the cluster it occupies is known as "slack space." As an example, DOS and older versions of Windows used a 16-bit File Allocation Table (FAT) that had very large cluster sizes. With a 2GB hard drive, each cluster was 32K. If a text file took up only 10K of space, the entire 32K would still be allocated to the file, meaning there would be 22K of slack space associated with the file. Current versions of Windows are much more efficient and have considerably smaller cluster sizes.

Slack space can be valuable to the investigator because it might contain pieces of long-deleted files whose clusters were reallocated and then partially written to by a newer file (some computer-forensics professionals state that 25 percent of hard drive space is slack). There are tools that collect all of the slack space data on a hard drive and create a single large file that can be viewed and searched.

UNALLOCATED SPACE

Unallocated space on a hard drive or other storage media are clusters that currently aren't being used by a file. This space has either never had data written to it or is occupied by files or pieces of files that have been deleted. As with slack space, unallocated space can provide valuable evidence for an investigator. There are forensic utilities that collect any ASCII data found in the unallocated space and write the potential evidence to a single file that can be examined.

WINDOWS SWAP FILE

All versions of Windows make use of a swap file (also called a page file). The swap file resides on the hard drive and is part of the operating system's memory management system. Data is "swapped" to and from Random Access Memory (RAM) to the swap file as needed.

Let's say you use Outlook to access your e-mail but are also surfing the Web and using a word processor to write up a business proposal. There's a pretty good chance that some data from your e-mail, the Web sites you're visiting, and the business proposal could all wind up in the swap file. This means that all sorts of evidence, including passwords, credit card numbers and other personal data can reside in a swap file.

Depending on what version of Windows you're using, the swap file is named

- ✓ Win386.swp for Windows 9x/ME systems

- ✓ Pagefile.sys for Windows NT/2000/XP systems

Swap files, which range in size from tens to hundreds of megabytes, are always in use by the operating system. If you want to open the swap file and see what's inside, you need to boot the computer with a non-Windows operating system (DOS or Linux) and then use a utility to view the data.

Most computer cops use some type of string search utility on a swap file, looking for evidence that they believe is related to a case; for example, known names of graphics files commonly associated with child pornography or a list of drug-related terms. In some instances, though, it may be necessary to manually page through the entire swap file, tediously looking for some obscure piece of evidence that could mean breaking a case.

Keep in mind that with affordable memory prices, a user could install a large amount of memory in his computer and turn swapping off without affecting system performance. Additionally, a savvy user could delete the swap file before using Windows again (the swap file can't be deleted while Windows is running).

WINDOWS REGISTRY

The Registry can be a gold mine for someone searching for evidence on a Windows computer. The Registry can contain passwords, lists of recently used files, evidence of previously installed applications, and all sorts of potentially valuable information. Most users have no idea what the Registry is or what's contained within it. Before discussing how the Registry can be exploited, its important to have a general understanding of what the Registry is and how it works.

For more detailed information about the Windows Registry, go to www.regedit.com.

Starting with Windows 95, Microsoft started using database files collectively known as the Registry to store operating system and application data. Prior to that time, application and system settings were stored in text .INI files. This simple storage technique lacked in both efficiency and performance, which the Registry improved on:

✓ In Windows 9x/ME, the Registry is contained in two hidden files in the Windows directory, called USER.DAT and SYSTEM.DAT.

✓ In Windows NT/2000/XP, the Registry is stored in several files (including NTUSER.DAT and USRCLASS.DAT) located in the \windows\system32\config and \Documents and Settings\{username} folders.

The Registry has a hierarchal structure, with each branch called a "key." Each key can have other keys as well as "values." A value contains the actual data stored in the Registry. Values can be String, Binary, or DWORD data types.

There are five main branches in the Registry (six in Windows 9x/ME), and each of the branches contains a certain type of information. The branches include the following:

✓ **HKEY_CLASSES_ROOT.** File types and OLE information for OLE-aware applications.

✓ **HKEY_CURRENT_USER.** Points to the part of HKEY_USERS associated with the current user.

✓ **HKEY_LOCAL_MACHINE.** Information about all of the hardware and software on the computer. The current hardware configuration is specified in HKEY_CURRENT_CONFIG.

✓ **HKEY_USERS.** Preferences for each of the users of the computer. In Windows 9x/ME, the default branch contains the currently logged user. In Windows NT/2000/XP, the default branch contains a template for newly added users.

✓ **HKEY_CURRENT_CONFIG.** Points to the part of HKEY_LOCAL_MACHINE associated with the current hardware configuration.

✓ **HKEY_DYN_DATA (Windows 9x/ME only).** Points to Windows Plug and Play information in HKEY_LOCAL_MACHINE.

Windows and applications are constantly accessing the Registry with API calls, reading data, and writing new data to branches and keys. You can view and edit the contents of the Registry with the RegEdit utility. RegEdit has a tree structure similar to Windows Explorer, as illustrated in Figure 5-1; you can click through the branches and keys to view information.

Changing key values in the Registry without knowing what you're doing can corrupt both Windows and installed applications.

When Registry keys and values are deleted, they still can exist in the actual Registry files, although they don't appear when viewed with RegEdit. Searching these files with a hex editor may reveal unexpected evidence. The only way a user can be assured that keys and values are removed when they are deleted with RegEdit or other utilities is to rebuild and compress the Registry.

Instead of using RegEdit to individually examine Registry entries, get a copy of SomarSoft's free DumpReg utility to dump the entire Registry out as an easily-read text file. Download the tool from www.systemtools.com/somarsoft/.

MOST RECENTLY USED FILE LISTS

Many applications have a Most Recently Used (MRU) file list. This is a list that typically appears at the bottom of the File menu that contains the names and paths of files that have been most recently opened with the application. This information can be valuable in seeing what documents a user has been working on. MRU information is often stored as values in the Registry.

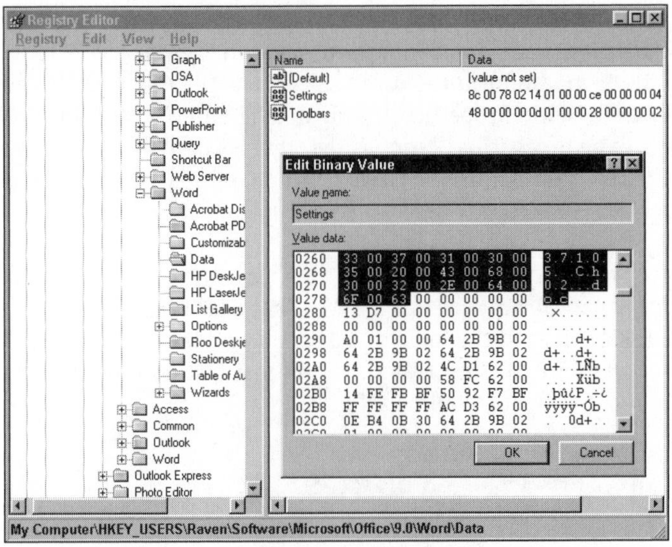

Figure 5-1: The Windows Registry opened with RegEdit, displaying the name of a recently opened Word document in the Settings key.

CLIPBOARD

If a computer is still powered on when you examine it, check the clipboard for any information that may have been recently copied or cut. Keep in mind that the contents of the clipboard aren't persistent, and when Windows is shut down, clipboard data isn't kept for the next time the computer is powered-up. Windows comes with a clipboard viewer that displays text and bitmap images currently in the clipboard. Search for the hard drive for Clipbrd.exe and run the viewer.

BROWSER ARTIFACTS

Web browsers leave a number of breadcrumb trails you can use to learn about someone's Net-surfing habits. Browsers retain a remarkable amount of information and should be one of the first places you look when you're seeking evidence.

CACHE   Caching means instead of having to download frequently viewed Web pages and graphics, the browser keeps a local copy of the content on the hard drive. Users are happy because of faster load times. You're happy because a copy of all of the Web content a suspect has viewed is now easily accessible.

Browser caches work on a first-in, first-out basis. New content is constantly being added to the cache until it reaches a certain threshold; then the oldest data is deleted to make room for the newer cached content. Most default browser caches are set at a ridiculously high size and store a long back-history of files.

With Internet Explorer, cached files are stored in a folder named \Temporary Internet Files. The files aren't compressed and can be opened with any Web browser.

FAVORITES   The Web sites that a suspect commonly visits can provide clues and evidence for the crime you're investigating. In Internet Explorer, click the Favorites icon in the upper toolbar. A window is displayed that contains all of the Uniform Resource Locators (URLs) that have been marked as favorites. Right-click a URL and select Properties. Information about when the link was entered as a favorite as well as how many times it has been visited (this bit of information isn't always present) is displayed. Web site favorites can also be viewed outside of Internet Explorer by looking inside of the Favorites folder.

HISTORY   All browsers have a history feature that lists Web sites that have been visited over the past several days or weeks. History automatically catalogs all the Web sites a user has visited. With Internet Explorer, click the sundial History icon in the toolbar to display a window that contains a list of all visited URLs, as shown in Figure 5-2. It goes without saying that history can provide a tremendous amount of information about someone's online activities.

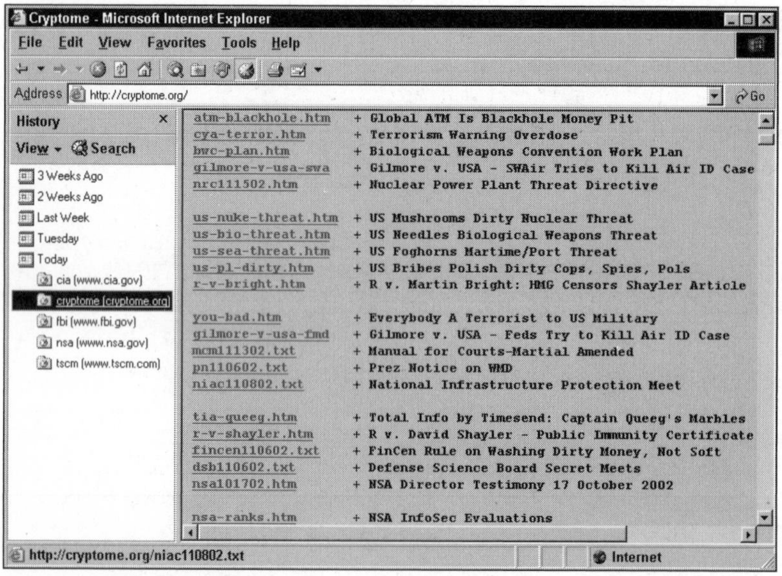

Figure 5-2: Internet Explorer History can provide valuable information about the Web-surfing habits of a suspect.

AUTOCOMPLETE INFORMATION   By default, Internet Explorer saves everything a user types into a form on a Web page. This information can include accounts, passwords, addresses, and all sorts of other personal information. When the user visits the Web site a second time, all of the information on the form is filled in. This is convenient for the user and also convenient for an investigator looking for evidence. AutoComplete data can be retrieved by visiting Web sites that are listed in History or by examining keys and values associated with Internet Explorer in the Registry. (Check the HKEY_CURRENT_USER or HKEY_LOCAL_MACHINE\Software\Microsoft\Windows\CurrentVersion and look for keys named "Explorer" and "Internet Settings" or look in subkeys of the HKEY_CURRENT_USER or HKEY_LOCAL_MACHINE\Software\Microsoft\Internet Explorer keys.)

COOKIES   Without getting into the details, cookies are small amounts of data that a Web server stores on a local computer. When the Internet started to become popular in the 1990s, there was a heated debate about cookies and how companies could track individual Web usage using them. Although this is true to an extent, the controversy died down considerably when people realized that cookies didn't pose a great privacy threat (or if they did, only a few people seemed to care). Although cookies are meant for use with Web servers, you can also use them to track a suspect's Web-surfing habits because cookies have a reference to the Web site visited, as well as when the cookie was last modified and accessed.

The default setting of most Web browsers is to accept cookies. With Internet Explorer, cookies can be found in a folder named \Cookies, and they can individually be opened with Notepad or any word processor.

E-MAIL CLIENTS

E-mail client applications can be another valuable source of evidence. E-mail is ubiquitous, with an estimated 31 billion e-mail messages sent daily throughout the world. Many people don't think twice about the contents of e-mail they send and receive, even though it can provide an investigator with direct and indirect information regarding their activities.

Tactics: .DATs All Folks

Internet Explorer creates a hidden file named Index.dat in the cache, cookies, and history folders. This file contains Internet Explorer indexing information. It also contains a detailed history of a user's Net activity. Index.dat is written to three folders:

- ✓ **Cache folder.** Index.dat in the \Temporary Internet Files folder contains URL names, date- and time-stamps, and pointers to cache that are spread among several randomly named cache subfolders.

- ✓ **Cookie folder.** Index.dat in the \Cookies folder contains URL names, date- and time-stamps, and pointers to Cookie files that are stored in the Cookie folder.

- ✓ **History folder.** Index.dat in the History folder stores visited URLs, as well as date- and time-stamps. Internet Explorer uses this data for AutoComplete and identifying whether links in the currently displayed Web page have been visited.

The location of these folders depends on what version of Windows you're running:

- ✓ Windows 9x/ME systems: \WINDOWS

- ✓ Windows 9x/ME systems with profiles: \WINDOWS\PROFILES\user_name

- ✓ Windows NT/2000/XP systems: DOCUMENTS AND SETTINGS\user_name\LOCAL SETTINGS

Although the Index.dat files aren't text files, they can be opened in WordPad or another word processor to view some of the data. There are also tools such as Index.dat Viewer (www.exits.ro/index-dat-viewer.html) that display the contents of the file.

The first step in using e-mail as evidence is to become familiar with a suspect's e-mail client application. You should know how the application works, what features there are, and commonly used commands. Be sure you have a basic understanding of the e-mail client before you attempt to use it to discover evidence. The good news is that although there are many e-mail clients available, only about a half a dozen are widely used. They include Microsoft Outlook and Outlook Express, AOL Mail, Eudora, Pegasus, and Netscape Communicator e-mail clients.

Regardless of the software you're investigating, one of the primary vulnerabilities of most e-mail applications is that password protection typically applies only to logging in to the e-mail account. If you have physical access to the computer, most e-mail applications lack security features that prevent someone from viewing e-mail that's already been downloaded, temporarily deleted, or sent (if saved copies are being kept).

An additional vulnerability is that most e-mail applications have an option to store a commonly entered account name and password so it isn't entered each time. Although this option is convenient, it also presents a significant security risk because anyone who has access to the computer can run the e-mail application and both send and receive messages.

In looking for e-mail-related evidence, there are five places you should consider:

- ✓ **Inbox.** The Inbox is the first place you should look in an e-mail application for evidence because it contains all the e-mail the suspect has received. Be sure to view the full headers of messages because information relating to the origin of the message might be discovered.

- ✓ **Sent messages.** Many e-mail applications have an option to keep a copy of sent messages. This can be an evidence gold mine if the option is enabled because you can view all your target's sent e-mail.

- ✓ **Saved attachments.** Whenever a user sends an attachment, the e-mail application converts a copy of the attached file into a format that can be sent over the Internet; typically Multipurpose Internet Mail Extensions (MIME). The converted MIME files are automatically deleted after the e-mail is successfully sent. If these deleted files are recovered, they can be converted back to their original format from MIME using the Munpack.exe utility (enter **munpack** in a search engine to find download locations). It's also worth looking in temporary folders for e-mail attachments.

- ✓ **Pending and draft messages folders.** Another place to look for evidence is in the pending or draft message folder, which contains messages that haven't been sent yet.

- ✓ **Deleted messages.** Most e-mail applications use a Trash or Recycle Bin approach to deleting messages. A message that's deleted is kept in a separate folder or storage location until the user "empties the trash" or purges the deleted e-mail. Until that time, the messages can be viewed.

INSTANT MESSAGING

The popularity of instant messaging (IM), whether Internet Relay Chat (IRC) or the proprietary America Online, Yahoo, and Microsoft versions, has increased dramatically over the past several years. If an IM application is installed on a hard drive, there can be valuable information associated

Busted: Cops vs. Kopp

James Kopp, an anti-abortion activist who was indicted for the October 23, 1998 murder of Dr. Barnett A. Slepian, was arrested in France in April 2001. Kopp allegedly shot and killed Slepian in his home with a Russian-made carbine.

The FBI wanted Kopp caught badly, and in June 1999, they added him to its "10 Most Wanted List;" interestingly enough, Osama bin Laden was added at the same time.

Kopp managed to leave the United States and led law enforcement on a chase throughout Europe before being caught. Following Kopp's arrest, the FBI arrested two alleged accomplices, Loretta Marra and Dennis Malvasi of Brooklyn, New York. The two were indicted after the FBI tapped their phone, bugged their apartment, and monitored their e-mail.

Apparently, Kopp and Marra were using a Web-based e-mail system to communicate. Instead of sending e-mail to each other, they used the same account, leaving messages for each other in the draft message folder. They obviously had enough operational security sense to realize that e-mail sent over the Internet could be intercepted and thought they could avoid this threat by never sending messages. What they didn't realize was that the IP addresses of the computers they used to access the Web e-mail are routinely logged and that Web-hosted mail providers routinely cooperate with law enforcement. The FBI stated that it used a pen register/trap-and-trace order on an e-mail account in conjunction with the investigation. It probably was for the e-mail Web site, and the logs likely pointed directly back to a French cyber-cafe. From there, conventional physical surveillance took place until Kopp was spotted and arrested.

Kopp was found guilty of intentional murder in March 2003 and prosecutors announced they would be seeking a maximum prison term of 25 years to life when he is sentenced.

with it. "Buddy" lists, account names of people who have recently sent instant messages, and saved message logs all can provide evidence.

If you can find out the password of an IM account, which is fairly easy if you use some of the tools listed in Chapter 7, you may be able to gather evidence by masquerading as the suspect and having conversations with other people shown in the Buddy list.

HARD DRIVES

Sometimes you might encounter a hard drive that you can't access during the course of an investigation. It might have crashed, been damaged by fire or water, or been reformatted in an attempt to destroy possible evidence. Even under such extreme circumstances, it still may be possible to retrieve evidence from the hard drive.

There are two restoration methods for recovering data from a hard drive: recovery software and commercial recovery services.

✓ **Recovery software.** If the hard drive hasn't been physically damaged, a data recovery application may do the trick in resurrecting it. These utilities can recover deleted partitions, restore deleted logical drives, and locate and recover deleted files and folders. See the "Evidence-Gathering Tools" section later in this chapter for examples of several recovery applications.

✓ **Commercial recovery services.** The other option is to send the hard drive to a company that specializes in data recovery. Instead of just using commercial recovery software, these companies employ technicians that take apart a hard drive in clean rooms and extract data with specialized equipment and software. Even if the hard drive platter is physically damaged, there's still a chance some of the data can be recovered. The companies extract the original data and place the recovered files on DVD-R, CD-ROM, or tape. Using a data recovery company isn't cheap, and you can expect to pay somewhere from $500 to $1,500 for a typical successful hard drive failure recovery (unsuccessful attempts are considerably cheaper).

x-ref

A fairly comprehensive list of United States and European data recovery businesses can be viewed at: www.datarecoverylinks.com. Two of the largest and most well-known companies that get a lot of business from both corporations and law enforcement are Ontrack Data International (one of the leaders in data recovery, acquired by security conglomerate Kroll, Inc. in June of 2002 — see www.ontrack.com for more information) and DriveSavers Data Recovery (founded in 1985, DriveSavers can turn around recovered data in 24 to 48 hours — for company details go to www.drivesavers.com).

FLOPPY DISKS

With their limited storage capacity, floppy disks are pretty passé as storage media. However, the ubiquitous floppy lives on and likely will be encountered during most computer-related investigations. File recovery software that's used for resurrecting files on hard drives can also be used on floppies, as can the services of professional data recovery companies.

There are two points worth mentioning regarding floppy disks and investigations:

✓ If a suspect uses file wiping (overwriting files with data to ensure that their contents can't be recovered after deleting), he may not be as successful at erasing files on floppy disks versus a hard drive. Floppy disk data tracks are so wide and the drive mechanisms so forgiving when it comes to head alignment that some software utilities can recover data on either side of the location overwritten.

✓ The Department of Defense Computer Forensics Laboratory (DCFL) in Maryland has developed disk-splicing techniques for reconstructing 3.5-inch and 5.25-inch floppy disks that have been cut, segmented, bent, torn, melted, or removed from the disk hub. After the disks are put back together, data can be recovered from them. DCFL offers a "law-enforcement-only" paper that describes the process. The DCFL Web site is at www.dcfl.gov.

MEMORY

If the computer is still powered-on, you may want to view the contents of Random Access Memory (RAM) or perform a complete system memory dump to disk for later examination. Passwords, documents, and other pieces of evidence may be residing in memory and not be present on the hard drive. (Remember that saving memory to the hard drive isn't a preferred forensic practice because you're altering the original storage media.)

Evidence-Gathering Tools

There are a number of tools available to help you gather and analyze digital evidence. Many of these tools are general-purpose in nature and were originally designed for system administration use. There are a handful of utilities that have been exclusively built for computer forensics work. Although some of the simple command-line forensics tools are free, other commercial software designed expressly for investigative use comes at an expensive price. At this point in time, computer forensics is a niche market, but as the need for forensics tools expands over the coming years and as competition increases (especially from free utilities produced by the open-source community), expect more and cheaper tools to become available.

Dan Mares has been in the computer forensics business for a long time and produces some widely used software tools. He also maintains a list of forensic hardware and software at www.maresware.com/maresware/linksto_forensic_tools.htm.

FORENSIC DUPLICATION TOOLS

Forensic duplication tools are designed to make a mirror image of a hard drive. Instead of just copying files, an exact bit-for-bit copy of the drive is made. Generally, the suspect's hard drive and a "sterile" hard drive (one that has had all of the data wiped from it) are connected to a computer. The computer is booted with a non-Windows operating system, and the duplication software is run. Several popular copying tools used in computer forensics are discussed in the following sections.

SAFEBACK   SafeBack is a DOS-based duplication tool that has been around since 1990. It can directly access IDE hard drives without checking BIOS drive geometry settings; duplicate a hard drive to another hard drive, tape, or removable storage media; and add checksum information to the drive image files that ensures data integrity. SafeBack is widely used by law enforcement, the military, and intelligence agencies; it even has a GSA product number for ease of government ordering. At $595, it's not cheap, but it is effective. For more information about SafeBack, go to www.forensics-intl.com/safeback.html.

NORTON GHOST   Norton Ghost was originally designed for system administrators to make backups of hard drives. Because of its ease of use, low cost, and versatility, the application has become popular with computer cops and forensics examiners. Ghost costs $69.95. For more information, see www.symantec.com.

LINUX DD   For someone familiar with Linux or for an investigator on a tight budget, the dd (data dumper) utility is an evidence-copying alternative. Although traditionally used for transferring data between files, dd also works well for duplicating hard drives. The biggest drawback to dd is it doesn't have a very friendly user interface, and its commands will be extremely cryptic to a computer cop who only has Windows experience. For example, to duplicate a hard drive to a tape backup system with dd, you'd type **dd if=/dev/had of=/dev/rst0** at the command line.

The Department of Justice released a special report in August 2002 on using dd for forensic duplication. See `www.ncjrs.org/pdffiles1/nij/196352.pdf`.

AUTOMATED EVIDENCE-GATHERING TOOLS

Gathering and analyzing evidence from a hard drive or any storage media can be a time-consuming and tedious process. Traditionally, investigators relied on a series of command-line tools to extract and examine computer evidence. It's only been within the past five or so years that stand-alone, easy-to-use Windows-based evidence-gathering and processing tools have started to appear. These applications considerably shorten the length of time it takes to gather and analyze evidence and decrease the number of technical skills an examiner needs to be able to perform effective computer investigations. Currently, there are three forensics tools that combine a number of features into a single package.

ENCASE   EnCase is the most popular and widely used stand-alone computer forensics tools on the market today (currently, more than 2,000 law enforcement agencies throughout the world use the product). Because EnCase is one of the de facto forensics analysis tools, let's give it a detailed look.

From a hardware perspective, EnCase runs on most modern PCs with Windows 98/ME or NT/2000/XP. For its copy protection scheme, EnCase requires that a dongle be attached to a USB or parallel port (a dongle is a small hardware device used as part of a software copy protection scheme). The application can acquire data without the dongle but won't analyze it.

EnCase creates a DOS boot disk, which is used on the computer to be examined. A parallel port, null modem cable, or crossover network cable connects the suspect's computer with the computer running EnCase. With the suspect computer booted with the DOS disk and EnCase running on the other computer, an investigator can use the preview feature to view the contents of the suspect computer without altering any evidence. Preview can be used for establishing probable cause or just performing a cursory examination of a system.

EnCase also has an acquire feature for saving evidence. Instead of performing a forensic duplication of the suspect's storage media, EnCase creates an evidence file, which is a read-only, tamper-proof file that contains an accurate representation of data that exist on the storage media (the courts widely recognize these files as acceptable evidence). Acquiring evidence files can be done by directly connecting the suspect's computer to another computer, physically removing the suspect's hard drive and chaining it to a forensic workstation's hard drive, or transferring the data over a network.

EnCase has a number of features to analyze evidence, including advanced string searches, searching and displaying graphics files (as shown in Figure 5-3), examining files to determine whether a file extension has been changed to conceal evidence, viewing deleted files, and showing timelines with MAC file information. Because an investigator examines files and unallocated and slack space, he can make notes about evidence he discovers. EnCase also has a feature for creating case reports based on the evidence that has been found.

EnCase isn't cheap, priced at $2,495 ($1,995 for government agencies), but if you perform a lot of investigations, the cost is easily offset by the overall time saved. For more information about EnCase, go to www.encase.com.

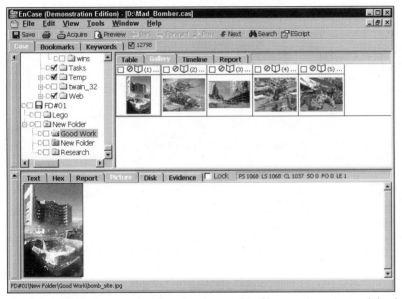

Figure 5-3: The EnCase user interface, showing graphics files stored on a suspect's hard drive.

FORENSIC TOOLKIT   AccessData, one of the leaders in password-recovery tools, recently entered the evidence analysis market with its Forensic Toolkit (FTK). FTK can perform advanced searches, display more than 270 different file types, undelete files and partitions, and analyze compressed and e-mail files. Forensic Toolkit is priced at $595, and a trial version is available for download at www.accessdata.com.

ILOOK   If you're a computer cop on a budget, you may want to check out ILook. Developed by Elliot Spencer for the Criminal Investigation Division of the Internal Revenue Service, U. S. Treasury Department, ILook is a free "law-enforcement-only" tool that contains a number of search and analysis features found in commercial products. For more information about ILook, go to www.ilook-forensics.org.

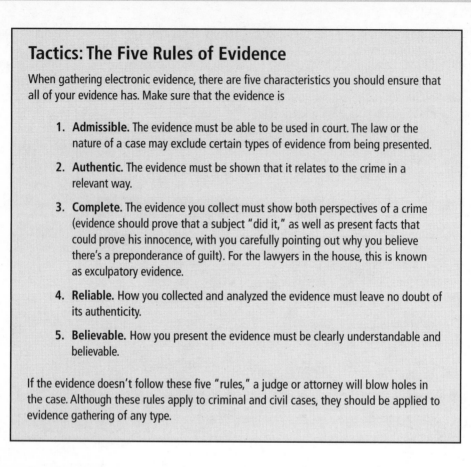

Tactics: The Five Rules of Evidence

When gathering electronic evidence, there are five characteristics you should ensure that all of your evidence has. Make sure that the evidence is

1. **Admissible.** The evidence must be able to be used in court. The law or the nature of a case may exclude certain types of evidence from being presented.

2. **Authentic.** The evidence must be shown that it relates to the crime in a relevant way.

3. **Complete.** The evidence you collect must show both perspectives of a crime (evidence should prove that a subject "did it," as well as present facts that could prove his innocence, with you carefully pointing out why you believe there's a preponderance of guilt). For the lawyers in the house, this is known as exculpatory evidence.

4. **Reliable.** How you collected and analyzed the evidence must leave no doubt of its authenticity.

5. **Believable.** How you present the evidence must be clearly understandable and believable.

If the evidence doesn't follow these five "rules," a judge or attorney will blow holes in the case. Although these rules apply to criminal and civil cases, they should be applied to evidence gathering of any type.

EXAMINATION TOOLS

Even if you have automated evidence-gathering software, it's important to also have a few general-purpose tools to assist you in investigations. Two important types of examination tools to have on hand include the following:

✓ **Disk editor.** Also known as a hex editor, this tool allows you to search for text on hard drives and other storage media as well as to open and view files in hexadecimal and ASCII formats.

✓ **File viewer.** This tool allows you to view many different file formats without requiring the application that created the file.

Two versions of these tools that are very popular with computer cops and forensics examiners include the following:

WINHEX   WinHex started out as a disk editor, but has gained a number of powerful features over the years. WinHex can view and read memory, recover deleted files, clone drives, collect slack and unused space, and perform text searches (as shown in Figure 5-4). The utility is small enough to fit on a single floppy disk. The specialist version of WinHex, which contains forensics features, is priced around $100. Evaluation copies are available from www.winhex.com.

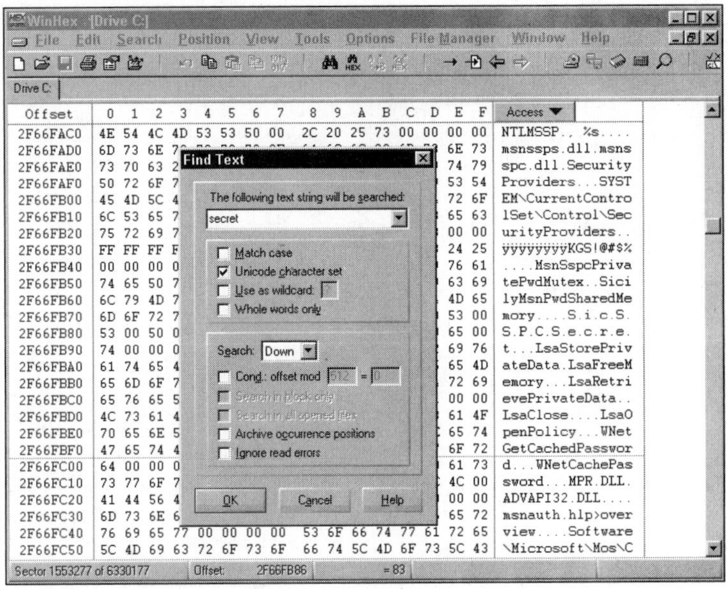

Figure 5-4: The WinHex disk editor performing a string search on a hard drive. The window in the back shows both the hexadecimal and ASCII representations of data on a hard drive sector.

QUICK VIEW PLUS   Jasc's Quick View Plus is a popular forensics tool for quickly viewing and printing more than 200 different file formats (graphics, word-processing documents, spreadsheets, databases, presentations, and compressed files). Quick View Plus is $35, with an evaluation version available from www.jasc.com.

RECOVERY TOOLS

There are a number of recovery tools on the market that can resurrect deleted files, fix problems with inaccessible storage media, and extract data from damaged media. Every investigator should have one or two data recovery utilities in their toolbox. Two popular applications include:

NORTON UTILITIES   Symantec's Norton Utilities has been around for years, and many computer cops use this Swiss Army knife set of integrated tools for file and data recovery. Norton Utilities is priced at $49.95, with a trial version available at www.symantec.com.

EASYRECOVERY PROFESSIONAL EDITION   OnTrack's EasyRecovery Professional is a dedicated, advanced data recovery utility. In addition to recovering data from deleted files and damaged drives, it can also fix corrupted Microsoft Office documents and restore deleted e-mails from Microsoft Outlook .PST and .OST files (the file types used to store Outlook data). EasyRecovery is priced at $499. A free trial version that lists what data can be recovered (without resurrecting it) can be downloaded at www.ontrack.com.

Countermeasures

This section isn't meant to be a how-to for circumventing justice by outsmarting computer cops. The reality is that most technically savvy bad guys already know all about encryption, file wipers, and other related evidence-busters. If you're a computer cop or forensic examiner, you need to be aware of some of these countermeasures in case you encounter them. In instances where these countermeasures are employed correctly, you may need to focus on other parts of the investigation that don't rely on the computer as an evidence source. (The good news is that virtually all these countermeasures take a measure of discipline to use all the time, and a majority of criminals tend to be lazy and not too bright. Look at the number of crimes that are solved by fingerprints. If bad guys can't use a simple countermeasure such as wearing gloves, it's pretty unlikely they'll all suddenly start using technical countermeasures to defeat computer cops.)

Even if you're not a cop (or a criminal who's trying not to get caught), it's important to understand that a spy engaged in illegal eavesdropping is going to use some of the same techniques a computer cop uses in trying to extract information and evidence out of your computer. You may be engaged in perfectly legal and legitimate activities and want to employ countermeasures to protect yourself from unauthorized snooping.

Encryption

Unless you've been living in a cave for the past eight years, you've probably heard about encryption. Quite simply, encryption is using a mathematical algorithm to turn information that's normally understandable into data that can't be understood without using the correct key (which can be a password, a smart card, or some other token). While we're defining terms, *cryptography* is the science of making codes and ciphers, *cryptanalysis* is the science of breaking them, and *crypto* is slang that refers to anything related to either of the two previous terms.

This section does not discuss the basics of how cryptosystems work, the nuances of s-boxes, the implications of quantum cryptography, or any of the many technical issues related to encryption (which tend to take up entire books or simply serve as filler material). Instead, it provides a quick history of modern cryptography, some guidelines for using encryption applications, and a list of recommended encryption products.

x-ref

To learn more about cryptography, check out these Web resources: Cryptography (http://world.std.com/~franl/crypto.html) has general information links; Crypto-Gram (www.counterpane.com/crypto-gram.html) offers an excellent monthly newsletter on security and cryptography; and the Center for Democracy and Technology, Encryption Issues (www.cdt.org/crypto/) presents cryptography from a legislative standpoint.

A VERY BRIEF MODERN HISTORY

Up until the 1990s, governments had a monopoly on cryptography. They made the codes and they broke the codes. The banking industry had the Data Encryption Standard (DES), but the National Security Agency (NSA) and other members of the United States intelligence community generally had a lock on all things crypto.

In the mid-1990s, the crypto genie was let out of the bottle. Thanks to PGP (Pretty Good Privacy, a strong encryption utility)—and cryptographers such as Phil Zimmermann, Bruce

Schneier, Whitfield Diffie, and Ron Rivest, to mention a few — suddenly the public had access to military-grade encryption that the government couldn't even crack. In fact, cryptographic technology was classified in the same category as missiles and other weapons, and was under heavy export restrictions.

The fact that people could electronically communicate with each other in complete privacy upset a fair number of people in government, especially the FBI, who spent most of the late 1990s trying to get legislation in place that called for "key escrow." This meant that any commercial encryption products would either need to have a backdoor so the government could have access to the encrypted data, or else a copy of the key used to decrypt data would be held by the government or some trusted third party and be made available to law enforcement in case of a criminal investigation. Key escrow withered on the vine, the export restrictions on crypto were relaxed, and encryption is freely and readily available to anyone who wants to protect data or communications, even in the current post-9/11 environment.

Where this brief bit of history ends up is that if you're a computer cop or some other type of spy, people will have access to encryption products that you — the FBI, the NSA, or (insert your favorite alphabet soup agency) — will not be able to break. That's pretty much the way it goes, and you will need to be creative when it comes to compromising evidence that may be protected (this book should give you all sorts of ideas).

GENERAL GUIDELINES

Although encryption is bad news for the snoop, it's good news for anyone interested in protecting the privacy of his or her personal or business activities. Strong encryption used with other security measures can effectively thwart spies in their efforts to gather information or evidence.

If you use encryption or plan on using it, you should follow these simple guidelines:

- ✓ Applications with published and peer-reviewed encryption algorithms (AES, 3DES, Blowfish, IDEA, and so on) should be used. Don't trust products with proprietary, secret algorithms; these are usually snake-oil and should be avoided.

- ✓ Open-source applications are preferred. Open-source code promotes peer review for discovering potential security flaws and gives individuals concerned about programs with backdoors that provide secret access a chance to examine and compile the code on their own.

- ✓ 128-bit keys for symmetric encryption and 1,024-bit keys for asymmetric encryption (this second type of encryption is also known as public-key cryptography) are good for the present. Use a larger key size if you're concerned about the future.

- ✓ Use strong passwords and good password policies!

- ✓ Depending on your circumstances, you may want to keep your encryption software on a floppy disk or CD-ROM. If an encryption application is discovered on your hard drive, this may raise someone's suspicions or cause him to try to compromise the application.

- ✓ Encryption isn't the silver bullet to all security issues. Bruce Schneier, noted cryptographer and security guru, has been saying this for years, and he's right. Encryption should be part of a multilayered series of countermeasures.

Encryption software can be divided into three broad categories: e-mail encryption applications, file encryption applications, and on-the-fly encryption applications.

E-MAIL ENCRYPTION SOFTWARE

Although any encryption application can be used to send secure messages back and forth between two people, the gold standard is Pretty Good Privacy (PGP). There are other secure e-mail protocols out there, but because of its international acceptance and wide use, PGP has turned into the de facto standard for secure e-mail communication.

PGP   Developed by Phil Zimmermann in the 1990s, this free open-source encryption application gained notoriety and widespread use because it couldn't be readily cracked, even by government intelligence agencies (see Zimmermann's Web page at `www.philzimmermann.com` for more background information about PGP). Although originally developed in the United States and at the time subject to cryptographic export laws, PGP slipped outside the U.S. and soon spread all over the world through the Internet.

PGP uses something known as public-key encryption (also known as asymmetric encryption). Public-key encryption is based on your having two keys: a public key that can be given out to anyone who wants to securely communicate with you and a private key that you use to decrypt messages that are sent to you. (You can't decrypt a message with someone's public key.) This contrasts with symmetric encryption applications, which use a single key to encrypt and decrypt data.

You generate both a public and private key the first time you use PGP (it's easy to generate the keys which are stored in files). For example, if you want to securely communicate with Alice, who also uses PGP, you first exchange public keys (PGP makes it easy to exchange public keys through e-mail). Then to send Alice an encrypted e-mail, you compose the message and then encrypt it with PGP using her public key. When Alice receives your e-mail, she decrypts it with her private key by entering the password associated with the private key. (If you start reading about cryptography you'll no doubt encounter Alice, Bob, Carol, and perhaps Eve. These characters have no relation to the 1969 movie *Bob & Carol & Ted & Alice,* but are simply a more friendly way of describing communications between multiple parties instead of using A, B, C, D, and so on.)

PGP is available for just about any computer operating system you can think of — which is another reason for its popularity. In its early days, PGP was DOS-based and a pain for most people to use. Since then, very friendly, easy-to-use Windows versions have evolved. There is even a number of plug-ins available for popular e-mail applications so PGP can integrate directly into your e-mail client.

Commercial versions of PGP were formerly available from Network Associates; in 2002, however, the company decided to no longer offer the product. A new independent company, PGP Corporation, was formed, which acquired the PGP assets from Network Associates in July 2002. PGP Corp. plans to release a new commercial version of the product that's fully compatible with Windows XP by the end of 2002. For more information about PGP Corp., go to `www.pgp.com`.

Free, open-source versions of PGP, which lack some of the features found in the commercial versions, can be downloaded from `www.pgpi.org`.

GNUPG   GNU stands for "GNU's Not Unix. The GNU project was started in 1984 to provide a Unix-like operating system composed of free software (for more information on GNU see `www.gnu.org`). In the spirit of GNU and free open-source software (abiding by the Free Software Foundation's General Public License), GnuPG (Gnu Privacy Guard) was born.

One of the issues with the original PGP was that it used algorithms licensed from RSA (the security company that holds a number of cryptography patents) and from the patented IDEA (International Data Encryption Algorithm) encryption algorithm. A design goal of GnuPG was to eliminate reliance on code that had restrictions, while having general compatibility with PGP. GnuPG is currently a command-line program, although there are Windows front ends and plugins available. To get more information on GnuPG and to download it, go to www.gnupg.org.

FILE ENCRYPTION SOFTWARE

Unlike e-mail encryption, in which the goal is to protect the secrecy of messages that may be intercepted, with file encryption software, you're protecting data that resides on a hard drive, CD-R, or some other form of storage media.

This type of software uses symmetric encryption, in which a single key encrypts and decrypts data. With file encryption software, you use the application to encrypt a file and then decrypt it when you want to access it. For example, let's say you had a spreadsheet file that contained sensitive financial information. After you were done working on the file, you'd save it and then encrypt it. When you wanted to work on the file again, you'd decrypt the file so the spreadsheet application could open the document. If some unauthorized person accessed your hard drive, she wouldn't be able to open the encrypted document and snoop through your financial information unless she had the password.

PGP also offers symmetric encryption for files, but it lacks a number of advanced features that make regular file encrypting and decrypting easy. Two other alternatives to consider are described in the following sections.

BLOWFISH ADVANCED CS   Blowfish Advanced CS is a free open-source file encryption utility written by Markus Hahn. It can encrypt files and folders with 11 different modern encryption algorithms (obviously including the popular Blowfish), as shown in Figure 5-5. The application also has file wiping and a number of other file-handling features. The utility and all its required files are small enough to fit on a single floppy disk, which makes it very portable. Blowfish Advanced CS can be downloaded from http://members.tripod.com/markus_hahn/software.html.

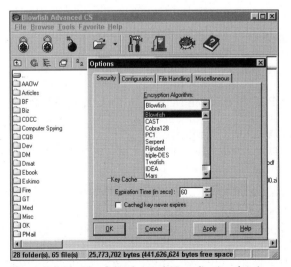

Figure 5-5: The Blowfish Advanced CS application showing user-selectable encryption algorithms.

ABI-CODER   Abi-Coder is a popular file encryption application that uses Blowfish, 3DES, and AES. The utility can encrypt multiple files and folders and has a feature to create secure, self-decrypting files. A full version of Abi-Coder can be downloaded from www.abisoft.net/bd.html. If you like the application, the developer requests a $12.99 licensing fee.

To find other free and shareware encryption and security applications, check out the Security/Privacy sections at www.webattack.com.

ON-THE-FLY ENCRYPTION SOFTWARE

A major drawback to file encryption applications is you have to manually select which files or folders you want to encrypt, you have to encrypt them, and then you have to decrypt them when you're ready to use the files again. On-the-fly (OTF) encryption solves this problem by creating a secure, encrypted volume on your hard drive or some other storage media. Using the software, you create a fixed-size volume, which is then encrypted and can only be mounted by running the OTF application and providing the correct password. After a volume has been successfully mounted, existing files can be moved to the volume or new files saved to it, with all of the encryption and decryption transparently performed. Most OTF software has features that automatically unmount a volume by pressing a hotkey or after a set amount of time has passed.

OTF encryption packages save you quite a bit of time and effort because you don't have to manually encrypt and decrypt files and folders all of the time. The software also tends to be easy to use: After it's installed, it's just like having another hard drive or floppy disk mounted by the system when it comes to file management.

STEGANOS SECURITY SUITE   Steganos Security Suite is a popular European application that includes an OTF encryption utility, a file wiper, an evidence eliminator, and a number of other security tools. The application employs the strong AES and Blowfish encryption algorithms and is very easy to use. Steganos Security Suite is priced at $29.95, with a trial version available from www.steganos.com.

BESTCRYPT   BestCrypt is one of the oldest OTF encryption utilities on the market, providing transparent encryption with AES, GOST (the Russian encryption standard), Blowfish, and Twofish. Jetico, the manufacturer, sells Windows and Linux versions of BestCrypt, so encrypted container files are compatible between operating systems. BestCrypt costs $89.95, with an evaluation version available from www.jetico.com.

DRIVECRYPT   DriveCrypt is a commercial disk encryption utility that evolved from the free, open-source Scramdisk and E4M applications. Scramdisk (which works with Windows 9x/ME) and E4M (Encryption for the Masses, which runs under Windows 9x/ME/NT/2000) are both available from www.samsimpson.com/scramdisk.php. In addition to the basic product, there is also a version that uses a USB token as a key and another that encrypts an entire Windows NT/2000/XP hard drive. DriveCrypt is priced starting at $49.95; a trial version and more information can be downloaded from www.drivecrypt.com.

Countermeasures: EFS

Windows 2000/XP Professional has a feature called EFS (Encrypted File System). This is Microsoft's version of on-the-fly encryption, and it allows you to transparently encrypt files and folders, with documents available only to someone who successfully logs in under your account. There are two significant weaknesses of EFS under Windows 2000:

✓ The original version of Windows 2000 shipped with 56-bit encryption to meet export requirements, which is very weak from a security standpoint. If you have an old version of 2000, you should upgrade to at least the Service Pack 2 and install the 128-bit High Encryption Pack, which can be downloaded from `www.microsoft.com/windows2000/downloads/recommended/encryption/`.

✓ With all versions of Windows 2000, anyone who has Administrator privileges can access EFS-protected files and directories without a password. This was changed under Windows XP Professional, so now only the user who enters the correct password can access protected data.

Although EFS looks good on paper and there have been no significant holes discovered, you may want to consider a third-party, stand-alone application to protect your files instead because of Microsoft's less-than-stellar reputation when it comes to security and the fact that the encryption system is integrated tightly with the operating system (in which known or unknown bugs could compromise integrity).

Sarah Dean has compiled a comprehensive (although a bit dated) listing of on-the-fly encryption software at `www.fortunecity.com/skyscraper/true/882/Comparison_OTFCrypto.htm`.

Steganography

Steganography is the art and science of hiding secret messages within some other form that is usually visible or out in the open for anyone to see. As a concept, steganography, abbreviated "stego" by some security practitioners, isn't all that new.

✓ Twenty-five thousand years ago, the Greeks removed the wax from writing tablets and scratched messages into the underlying wood. A fresh layer of wax was applied over the wood to conceal the message. They also tattooed messages on a slave's shaved head and let his hair grow back before sending him out as a secret messenger.

✓ During World War I, both sides used stego for passing spy messages. For example, a German agent sent the following message, "Apparently neutral's protest is thoroughly discounted and ignored. Isman hard hit. Blockade issue affects pretext for embargo on byproducts, ejecting suets and vegetable oils." Perhaps a bit cryptic, but if you take the second letter in each word, it reveals, "Pershing sails from NY June 1."

✓ During World War II, the Germans developed the microdot, a technology that could shrink down a message to the size of a typewriter period. A microdot would be affixed to a period at the end of a sentence, and only the receiver would know it was there.

Modern implementations of steganography rely on digital media to hide information. For example, you could take a digital photo .JPG image file and embed an encrypted text message in it with special software. The photo would appear normal when opened with a graphics application. Only if someone knew the message was there and had the right software to extract the text would the message be discovered. Graphics and sound files work especially well for steganography because their file formats support low-order bits that can be used to hide the message content with only slight (usually unnoticeable) distortion in the original file. Some of the "carrier" file types that different steganography applications use to conceal data include the following:

✓ .AU

✓ .BMP

✓ .GIF

✓ .HTML

✓ .JPG

✓ .MP3

✓ .PCX

✓ .PDF

✓ .PNG

✓ .WAV

As with the World War I German spy's message, information can also be hidden in text files. An example of this is the SpamMimic Web site. You can enter a short message, and the Web site will conceal the information in what appears to be an e-mail spam message. Simply copy and paste the spam into your e-mail application (or preferably a hard-to-trace Web e-mail account) and mail it to whomever you want to secretly communicate with. When she receives it, she can visit the SpamMimic site to decode the message. You can check out SpamMimic at www.spammimic.com.

Steganography can be used as a countermeasure against evidence gathering by hiding key pieces of information within other documents. This can be critical in countries that have outlawed encryption software or in situations in which the presence of encrypted files might raise suspicions and cause further scrutiny.

Tactics: Osama bit Mappen?

In February 2001, steganography emerged from the shadowy world of spooks and geeks and made headline news. *USA Today* reported that Osama bin Laden was using steganography to communicate with his operatives over the Internet. With more than two billion Web sites and an estimated 28 billion images spread over the Internet, Al Qaeda was using stego-ed images to pass communications on, literally hiding them in plain sight.

Following the September 11 terrorist attacks, the rumors heated up again. There were reports that Bin Laden's followers were sending hundreds of encrypted e-mail messages hidden in digital photographs on eBay; the Islamic Web site Azzam.com had stego-ed images; Al-Qaeda was concealing messages in pornographic images on adult Web sites; and there was an alleged link between suspected stego-ed images and Internet traffic from Pakistani cyber-cafes and public libraries throughout the world.

However, no government officials have ever come forward and officially stated that Al Qaeda or any other terrorist group is using steganography. (They probably are to a limited extent, but nowhere near the large-scale proportions alluded to by the media.)

University of Michigan computer researcher Niels Provos led a November 2001 study that attempted to find stego-ed images in USENET newsgroups. Distributing hidden messages through USENET would be a more secure communication method because it would be considerably more difficult to detect both the person who sent and the person who potentially received a secret message. Provos' team scanned more than two million images and found no evidence of hidden messages in any of the files.

Provos' research paper can be viewed at `www.citi.umich.edu/u/provos/stego/usenet.php`.

If you use steganography, here are some things to keep in mind:

✓ Don't leave evidence that you've used a steganographic utility. If an investigator finds a copy of S-Tools (a utility that's described later in this section) on your hard drive, he's likely going to suspect that there may be stego-ed files present.

✓ Always encrypt any messages or information you conceal.

✓ Make sure that the carrier file isn't going to draw suspicion. Using a message hidden in an MP3 file and making it available over a P2P (Peer to Peer) file sharing network such as Kazaa is much stealthier than exchanging e-mail with someone with stego-ed text in attached images of Jupiter (unless you're both astronomers, of course).

✓ Don't use carrier files that are commonly available elsewhere. You don't want to provide your opponent with a way to easily detect differences by comparing the carrier file with the original source. For example, a photograph that's been widely distributed over the Internet would probably not be the best carrier file.

✓ Don't put all your eggs in the stego basket if you're up against a government intelligence agency. In 1999, Andreas Westfeld and Andreas Pfitzmann (`http://os.inf.tu-dresden.de/~westfeld/publikationen/ihw99.pdf`) described how images could be attacked both visually and statistically to reveal whether embedded messages were present. At the University of Michigan, Niels Provos has developed a utility called Stegdetect that detects the presence of messages hidden by a number of popular steganography tools (the utility can be downloaded from `www.outguess.org`). It's not a very large leap to assume that government intelligence agencies have some sophisticated capabilities in detecting the use of different types of digital steganography.

There are a number of steganographic utilities available, but with the following two popular and easy-to-use applications, you can experiment with steganography and get a better understanding of how it works.

S-TOOLS

S-Tools, written by Andrew Brown, was one of the first steganography tools written for Windows. Although it hasn't been updated in a number of years, it's still quite powerful and easy to use. S-Tools can hide files in .BMP, .GIF, and .WAV carrier files, either in plaintext or encrypted format. S-Tools is free and can be downloaded from `ftp.uni-stuttgart.de/pub/rus/security/win95/s-tools4.zip`.

WBSTEGO

wbStego4, developed by Werner Bailer, hides data inside bitmap images, ASCII and ANSI text files, .HTML files, and Adobe Acrobat (.PDF) files. The utility has a friendly user interface and supports encryption. wbStego is $20, and an evaluation copy is available at `http://wbstego.wbailer.com/`.

For a comprehensive listing of steganographic software, go to `http://stegoarchive.com`.

File Wipers

Obviously, you can't rely on Windows to effectively delete files so they can't be recovered. If you want to securely remove files, you need to use a file-wiping utility. These applications work by overwriting the file with data before deleting the file. If the deleted file is recovered, it won't contain any of its original data because it has been overwritten with new data.

There are four general approaches to permanently erasing files on hard drives: DoD NISPOM, DoD 5200.28 STD, Gutmann, and overwriting with pseudo-random data.

✓ The Department of Defense (DoD) National Industrial Security Program Operating Manual (NISPOM) gives guidelines on how to sanitize different storage media (an online version of the manual is available at `www.dss.mil/isec/chapter8.htm`). To sanitize hard drives, you can degauss with a Type I or II degausser, overwrite data on the drive with a character, its complement, then a random character, and then verify. If there's "Top Secret" information the drive should be disintegrated, incinerated, pulverized, shredded, or melted. Many file wipers use the DoD standard for permanently deleting data (just note that the government clearly states that the standard isn't good enough for erasing "top secret" information).

✓ The 1985 standard DoD Trusted Computer System Evaluation Criteria — 5200.28 STD comes from the Orange book of the government's "rainbow" series of computer security standards. It involves writing multiple passes of data to the file before it is deleted. (An excellent resource with detailed information on securely sanitizing all types of media is the U.S. Navy's 1993 Remanence Security Guidebook, available from `www.fas.org/irp/doddir/navy/5239_26.htm`.)

✓ In 1996, Peter Gutmann released a paper called "Secure Deletion of Data from Magnetic and Solid-State Memory" (the paper is available at `www.cs.auckland.ac.nz/~pgut001/pubs/secure_del.html`). Gutmann postulated that considering how hard drives were encoded, it was possible to recover data that had previously been overwritten by using electron microscopy. He suggested that by overwriting data upward of 30 times, this would defeat an attack by a well-funded opponent with an electron microscope. As with the DoD's method, Gutmann's approach is used by many file wipers.

✓ Another method found in file wipers is simply to write pseudo-random data to the media. Most wipers support this along with specifying how many overwriting passes to make.

Which file-wiping method should you use? Consider who may be interested in your data and what type of resources they have. Unless you're going up against a government-class spying operation, a single-pass wiping is probably adequate. (Also remember that the more wipe passes the utility makes, the longer the process takes.)

One of the tools that a well-funded opponent could use for recovery is an electron microscope. In Gutmann's paper, he describes that even after data is overwritten, there still may be some remaining magnetic remanence (traces of magnetic data) that could be recovered under lab conditions with an electron microscope. Although electron microscopy was definitely a threat when the paper was released in 1996, hard drive encoding has evolved since then, with most manufacturers now using the Extended PRML (a hard disk coding and decoding method) and newer design technologies. This makes it considerably more difficult to recover data from a new hard drive versus a drive manufactured five years ago.

Busted: Ana Belen Montes

Ana Belen Montes was a senior intelligence analyst with the Defense Intelligence Agency (DIA) in Washington, D.C. She started working for the DIA in 1985, and beginning in 1992 specialized in matters relating to Cuba. Because of her job responsibilities, Montes had access to a variety of classified information that made her a good candidate to be a spy for the Cuban Intelligence Service (CuIS).

Cuban intelligence tradecraft involves the use of what are called "numbers stations." As the name suggests, numbers stations broadcast a series of numbers over shortwave radio frequencies from undisclosed locations. An anonymous voice, often female, slowly reads a series of numbers over the air. Numbers stations exist all over the world, with the numbers read in different languages. The numbers are a way to secretly communicate with spies. Although anyone with a shortwave radio receiver can listen in, only the spy knows how to decode the numbers to reveal a message. (Go to www.spynumbers.com for more on numbers stations and actual recordings of broadcasts.)

Montes was receiving instructions from the Cubans by listening to a numbers station on a portable Sony shortwave radio receiver. As she listened, she keyed in the numbers on her Toshiba laptop and decrypted the messages.

The FBI suspected her of spying, and in May 2001 they performed a court-sanctioned black bag job on her residence, which included making a forensic duplicate of her hard drive. Technicians recovered deleted files on the hard drive that helped convict Montes of espionage. One of the files included the following Spanish text:

"You should go to the WIPE program and destroy that file according to the steps which we discussed during the contact. This is a basic step to take every time you receive a radio message or some disk."

Montes obviously didn't follow her control agent's instructions, and is now serving a 25-year term in a federal prison.

Floppy disks are another matter entirely. Because of the way they're encoded, it's possible to recover original data that has been overwritten. Don't bother wiping floppies; follow the NISPOM guidelines and destroy them completely.

There are many file wipers available, most of them free. One of the best is Eraser, a popular, free open-source file wiper, originally written by Sami Tolvanen. In addition to securely deleting individual files, Eraser can also erase unused space on a hard drive, and it can be downloaded at www.heidi.ie/eraser/.

For a comprehensive listing and review of file wipers, go to www.fortunecity.com/skyscraper/true/882/Comparison_Shredders.htm.

Evidence-Eliminating Software

Although you can take a do-it-yourself approach and manually remove evidence such as browser artifacts, temporary files, and Registry entries with a file wiper, RegEdit, and a set of batch files, there are a number of commercial utilities that automatically delete evidence found on your hard drive. Most of these applications have the same set of features, such as removing browser artifacts, deleting most recently used file lists, wiping temporary files, and eliminating other forms of common electronic evidence. Any of these utilities can save you a considerable amount of time and effort when it comes to purging your system of potential evidence.

One word of caution about using these types of utilities (and any application that states it can get rid of digital evidence): Be careful of marketing hype. Evidence-eliminating software is growing in popularity, and software claiming to erase all of your tracks is prominently advertised on many Web sites, some of it using rather questionable advertising techniques. Although the manufacturer likely has good intentions, there's no guarantee that a product can keep someone from discovering evidence after the utility has been run. Because there's no *Consumer Reports* for these types of tools, if you have sensitive information on your hard drive that you think someone may try to recover, it's worthwhile using an evidence-eliminating application and then seeing if you can recover any data. This chapter provides you with enough information, resources, and tools that you should be able to put yourself in the shoes of an opponent and spy on yourself to test your own countermeasures. (Just remember "probable" opponent versus "possible" opponent. That means most people won't need to run out and buy a $50,000 electron microscope to see if they can recover wiped data from a hard drive.)

A few popular evidence-eliminating applications include the following:

WINDOW WASHER

Window Washer was one of the first utilities to remove browser artifacts, and now it has evolved to incorporate features such as slack space deleting; the capability to clean user-specified files, folders, and Registry keys; and scheduled automatic evidence cleaning. Window Washer has more than 150 free plug-ins that work with different applications to remove any evidence that is left on your hard drive. Window Washer is $29.95 with a trial version available from www.webroot.com/washer.htm.

SURFSECRET PRIVACY PROTECTOR

SurfSecret Privacy Protector offers advanced features such as scheduled interval cleaning and stealth mode. It's priced at $39.95, with a trial version available from www.surfsecret.com.

CYBERSCRUB

CyberScrub is another cleaning application that removes browser information and other electronic evidence. The professional version of Cyberscrub is $49.95, and a trial version can be downloaded from www.cyberscrub.com.

Summary

As you can see, there is a tremendous amount of evidence that can be extracted from a computer. Computer cops and forensic examiners are pros when it comes to getting at this data, and the same techniques and tools can be used by anyone interested in spying on you.

There are three general countermeasures that can protect you from someone gathering evidence from your hard drive or other storage media. They include the following:

✓ Encrypting sensitive e-mail messages

✓ Encrypting sensitive documents

✓ Ensuring that any operating system and application artifacts are erased

It's important that you just don't blissfully rely on technology to address your security needs. In addition to the tools, you also need to put security policies in place — such as those involving passwords, encryption use, and evidence removal. These policies need to be enforced and adhered to, whether on a personal or organizational basis (remember a policy is simply a set of guiding principles; you don't need to be a large corporation to come up with your own security policies). Consider that in most cases, it's often human failure versus technology failure that causes data to be compromised.

Chapter 6

Unprotecting Data

"What's the frequency, Kenneth?"
— R.E.M., "What's the Frequency, Kenneth?" *Monster*

JUST BECAUSE YOU BREACH A COMPUTER SYSTEM, doesn't necessarily mean you will have immediate access to all the information or evidence that's on the hard drive. Savvy, cautious, or paranoid users concerned about their privacy will often encrypt their data, possibly with some of the tools discussed in Chapter 5 or more commonly with password-protection features found in most business and productivity software packages.

The two factors that trip users up most often when it comes to protecting data are weak encryption that's easy to crack and poorly selected passwords that are easy to guess. These two factors directly impact each other: Easily cracked encryption totally negates hard-to-guess passwords, and weak passwords completely void the effectiveness of strong encryption. All a spy needs is for one of these conditions to exist, and your data is at risk.

This chapter discusses how data can be unprotected by taking advantage of both human and technical vulnerabilities and the steps you can take to ensure that your sensitive information remains safe from prying eyes.

Spy Tactics

Just because a file has been encrypted doesn't mean the protected information can't be compromised. An experienced computer spy is comfortable in the knowledge that there are a number of espionage tools and techniques for dealing with protected data. Let's give you a chance to get some experience.

Put on your dark sunglasses and a suitable disguise, and imagine you're an undercover agent for an unnamed government intelligence agency who is tasked with penetrating an international terrorist organization in a third-world country (sounds rather timely, doesn't it?). You have a lead on a suspect who may be supplying weapons and support to a known terrorist group, and with the help of the local authorities, you break into the suspect's apartment for a little sneak-and-peek while he's out shopping for groceries. Using the skills on black bag jobs you learned in Chapter 3, you enter the apartment. On a desk sits an older Compaq laptop computer running Windows 95 (it's not a sophisticated terrorist organization). The suspect is only going to be out for 15 minutes at the most. You don't have time to duplicate the entire hard drive so you quickly copy the contents of several interestingly named folders onto a few floppies. You take pictures of the room and plan to come back later when you have more time to duplicate the hard drive for a complete analysis.

You make sure you haven't left any evidence of your break-in, and take a circuitous route back to the safe house. After removing your disguise, you put one of the floppies in your PC and double-click on one of the Excel spreadsheet documents you copied. It loads, but you're greeted with a dialog box that asks you to enter a password. You curse under your breath. You didn't find any passwords written down near the desk when you were in the suspect's apartment, and you have no clue what the password might be, so you click on the Cancel button and exit the spreadsheet application. You decide to examine the file with a hex editor to see if any usable information might be present, but the file appears to be hopelessly scrambled. All the other word-processing and spreadsheet documents also seem to be encrypted. Time is running out because intelligence sources have been picking up an increased number of coded conversations in online chat rooms thought to be frequented by terrorists that suggest a possible upcoming terrorist attack. The documents you copied may contain information that's related. Technical analysis staff isn't available in-country, the encrypted link back to Langley is down, and there have been delays getting things back to the U.S. through the diplomatic pouch. What are you going to do to try to unprotect the files?

Exploiting Vulnerabilities

You actually have several options in trying to solve your problem. When it comes to protected data, both technical and human vulnerabilities can be exploited to compromise information. You need to have a general understanding of how applications protect data as well as how human nature can diminish the effectiveness of a protection method.

WEAK ENCRYPTION

At the top of the technical exploitation list is weak encryption. This is where information is seemingly protected by cryptographic software, but in reality it can still be compromised, which can be due to several factors:

✓ **Insecure encryption algorithms.** The programmer (or his employer) just didn't cut it when it came to implementing security. He either didn't know much about cryptography or never really intended to make the product secure. If customers weren't demanding high security, why should the company have bothered? For example, most business software produced in the early and mid-1990s used a simple XOR scheme (an exclusive or logical operation performed on the text to be encrypted) to protect documents that could be cracked in a matter of seconds. Eric Thompson, the founder of AccessData, a pioneer in the password-recovery business, was quoted as saying he put delay loops in his early password-cracking programs so customers would think compromising the weak encryption was more difficult and time-consuming than it really was.

✓ **Flaws or weaknesses in the encryption algorithm.** This is different from the insecure algorithm mentioned previously, in that the software developers thought they were creating a secure algorithm but missed something either subtle or obvious. An example is the Content Scrambling System (CSS), the data-encryption method used to protect DVDs from piracy and to enforce region-based viewing restrictions. The proprietary algorithm turned out to be extremely weak, when in 1999 a 15-year-old Norwegian student reverse-engineered the algorithm and developed a decryption utility called DeCSS that cracked an encrypted DVD file and saved it unencrypted to a hard drive.

✓ **A "trapdoor" version of a cryptographic application.** The last way to compromise protected data is to modify the source code of a strong cryptographic application so that it weakly encrypts data (making it easy for an adversary to crack) or perhaps saves the password to disk. For example, a copy of PGP (Pretty Good Privacy) could be modified so that it uses only the first 40-bits of a 1,024-bit key, producing messages that could easily be cracked. A spy would then replace the original version of the cryptographic application on his target's computer, with the watered-down version, allowing him to compromise any data that's subsequently encrypted.

The widespread and rapid dissemination of new information over the Internet, particularly related to security issues, makes it easy for a spy to keep up on new vulnerabilities and tools for compromising weakly encrypted data. In the case of CSS, although in 2001 a federal judge ruled that *2600* magazine couldn't distribute DeCSS through its Web site, the utility, source code, and detailed analysis of CSS had already widely spread over the Internet, making it impossible to put the genie back in the bottle.

When it comes to cryptography, every spy should read two nontechnical papers, written by Bruce Schneier, which discuss the strengths, weaknesses, and pitfalls of cryptography. The papers are "Why Cryptography Is Harder Than It Looks" (www.counterpane.com/whycrypto.html) and "Security Pitfalls in Cryptography" (www.counterpane.com/pitfalls.html).

WEAK PASSWORDS

On the human side of exploitation are passwords, which serve as a means to authenticate a user. If you know the right one, you must be the right person to have access to the data. Because most applications rely on passwords to protect information through encryption and decryption, passwords are a logical place for a spy to attack. (The same holds true for trying to breach security at the operating system level, as discussed in Chapter 4.)

Passwords are binary in nature; they're either right or wrong. This same modality also applies to whether a password is weak or strong. A weak password could be your wife's first name, your iguana's birthday, any word that's found in a dictionary, your last name with a 1 added to the end of it, or any combination of letters and numbers that's fewer than seven or eight characters long. Weak passwords can be revealed without too much difficulty, either by manually guessing or by using an automated attack tool. Strong passwords, on the other hand, don't fall victim to such attacks.

If weak passwords are such a security risk, why do people continue to use them? To answer that question, we need to delve a little into the psychology of password selection. With no offense to the Jedis, "The Force can have a strong influence over a weak password."

Here's some more required spy reading. Although these papers might seem like they're ancient history and discuss UNIX login passwords, they provide the basis for a contemporary understanding of the problems with passwords. The papers include Thompson, Ken and Morris, Robert, "Password Security: A Case History," 1979 (`http://lambda.cs.yale.edu/cs422/doc/unix-sec.pdf`); Feldmeier, David C., Karn, Philip R. "UNIX Password Security Ten Years Later," 1990 (`http://dsns.csie.nctu.edu.tw/research/crypto/HTML/PDF/C89/44.PDF`); and Klein, Daniel V., "Foiling the Cracker: A Survey of, and Improvements to, Password Security," 1991 (`http://geodsoft.com/howto/password/klein.pdf`).

HOW PEOPLE SELECT PASSWORDS   Understanding the way people select passwords is important if you want to compromise their protected data. Considering that a typical spell checker can have upwards of 100,000 words in it, what motivates some to select one of those words or some combination thereof? Let's start with some relevant general observations before we get too deep into the psyche of the average computer user.

- ✓ **Security is an imposition.** The majority of computer users find security measures such as passwords a complete pain and will do anything to avoid them or decrease the amount of time and effort it takes to deal with them. This attitude produces short, easy-to-remember passwords such as common terms or easily typed keyboard patterns (such as Qwerty or 12345).

- ✓ **People have limited memories.** Although the human brain is one powerful supercomputer, it comes up a little short in the RAM department; remembering passwords is just one of those things we're not very good at. And again, this promotes the use of short and easy-to-remember passwords.

- ✓ **Security awareness isn't a priority.** Let's face it, if you're reading this book, you're not the average computer user who doesn't use a firewall on his cable modem, is running an antivirus program that hasn't been updated in a year, and likely is responsible for accidentally infecting half of the East Coast with the Klez virus. The majority of computer users either don't understand how vulnerable they are to certain security vulnerabilities or just don't care. This again means weak passwords.

Now let's get into the Jedi mind tricks. Up until a few years ago, there wasn't much research done regarding the psychological aspects of the password-selection process. However, some work is starting to appear in this arena and offers some unique insights to a spy interested in compromising a password to unprotect data. Let's focus on one recent study, in which British psychologists polled more than 1,200 office workers about their passwords and found some interesting results.

- ✓ Thirty percent of the users were classified as "fans," and passwords could often be predicted by personality type based on what appeared on a desk. Let's say that in snooping through our terrorist suspect's apartment at the beginning of the chapter, you see an autographed Seattle Mariner's baseball, an Ichiro Suzuki poster, and a bat signed by Lou Pinella. Ah ha. The British research found that "fans" used a variation of the name of a sports team or an athlete or a real or fictional entertainment figure as their password.

Considering this and the baseball memorabilia you saw scattered around the apartment, a good place to start guessing might be baseball-related passwords.

✓ Fifty percent of the passwords were based on the name of a family member, partner, or a pet. That information is pretty easy to come by if you know where to look. Google searches and online credit reporting companies can provide a wealth of information about family members. The research found that these folks tended not to be very computer-literate. Keep this in mind when you're spying on an AOL user versus someone running multiple Linux boxes sharing a single DSL connection.

✓ Eleven percent of the users were classified as "self-obsessed," using passwords such as "sexy," "stud," or "goddess." Oh, the egos that some people have. Just remember the old saying that "pride goes before a fall"; in this case, the password falls in a dictionary attack because it's so common (more about this in the next section).

✓ The remaining nine percent were considered "cryptics." These users didn't use common terms as passwords, instead opting for hard-to-guess sequences of letters, numbers, and symbols. "Cryptic" is probably more of a polite term for "geek" because this category tended to be experienced computer users who were much more dialed-in to basic computer security procedures. This will likely be the type of password you'll face when dealing with the user mentioned previously who set up a Linux network on his own.

Obviously, there are exceptions to the preceding groups, so don't assume that everyone with an AOL account will be using their significant other's name as a password. Even with the different user classifications, one common theme emerged from the study: 90 percent of the survey respondents had passwords that could relatively be easily guessed. That number is considerably higher than some of the other earlier studies relating to UNIX passwords and could be attributed to a larger population of users who are both less technically proficient and less concerned with security. Bad news for system administrators; good news for spies. (For more details on the study, go to www.centralnic.com/page.php?cid=77.)

THE PASSWORD HOUSE OF CARDS   Although probably a bit dated and mundane of a pastime for 20- and 30-somethings, in the old days when a kid got tired of playing Solitaire with real cards, he might start stacking the cards precariously on top of each other, starting with a shed and trying to make it a high-rise. It took lots of patience and precise skills to balance the cards while building walls, floors, and roofs. And all it took was one little mistake, and the carefully built house of cards came tumbling down.

The same holds true for passwords. Security experts, bosses, magazine articles, and books all urge users to use strong passwords that are hard to guess and resistant to manual or automated guessing attacks, but there's one dirty little secret they often neglect to mention: the ultimate level of security depends on where the strong password is used.

Let's say our hypothetical terrorist suspect is using PGP to encrypt and decrypt his e-mail, and is smart enough to use a strong password. You desperately want to find out what his messages say. You snagged a copy of his private key during one of your black bag jobs, but you're out of luck without the password. So, you start eavesdropping on his Internet connection and find out he used the password "D2fitHPoR<" to log on to an online chat forum. Those encrypted Microsoft Word and Excel documents you copied earlier in this chapter, were protected using a pretty lousy

Busted: FBI vs. Russian Crackers, Part II

In the first chapter of this book, there's an account of a sting operation the FBI mounted against two Russian crackers (see the sidebar called "Busted: Good Cop, Bad Cop?" in Chapter 1). The Russians were lured to the United States with job offers from a bogus computer security company and then they were busted when the FBI used a keylogger that revealed accounts and passwords of computers in Russia (which were then logged into by the G-men in order to gather evidence).

One of the suspects, Alexy Ivanov, had his personal Toshiba laptop with him. After the FBI announced he was under arrest, Ivanov gave permission to one of the agents to search the computer. However, Ivanov had protected the system with a BIOS password. The agent asked Ivanov for his password, which he gave him. (You'd be surprised how often people comply with a request for information like this during an investigation.)

The password was "FynjyKj[," which by anyone's standards was a strong password because it was eight characters long and contained a seemingly random mix of characters. The FBI knew Ivanov had the nickname of "subbsta," and they knew the address of one of the remote computers he had accessed in Russia. But they didn't have an account/password pair for the remote computer.

One of the lead agents used Telnet to connect to the Russian computer and entered "subbsta" as the account name and "FynjyKj[" as the password. It worked, and the agent was logged in on the Russian computer. This is a classic example of a collapsing house of cards based on the compromise of a single strong password.

encryption scheme that with readily available utilities you can crack the password in less than a second (and that password also happens to be "D2fitHPoR<"). "D2fitHPoR<" is a pretty good hard-to-guess password, but what if our suspect is also using it with PGP? Bingo! When you use that password on his intercepted messages, you now easily decrypt them. For your efforts, you're awarded the Intelligence Commendation Medal.

Using the same password in applications that offer strong and weak levels of protection is potentially asking for trouble. Frequently using the same password again and again is one of those human nature traits that you can exploit. Rachna Dhamija, a researcher at the University of California at Berkeley, found that a typical user might have to enter a password for 10 to 100 different things, but would only use between one and seven passwords over and over again. And once one password is revealed, parts of or perhaps the entire house of cards comes tumbling down.

ATTACKS ON PROTECTED DATA

The easiest way to attack protected data is to find a password that's been written down and taped to a computer monitor or tucked inside a desk drawer. Game over; your job is done. However, because our terrorist suspect didn't make things easy for you and now seems to have changed all his passwords and upgraded his version of Microsoft Word, you need to figure out some other ways to reveal his password. Some possibilities include the following (in no particular order):

✓ Court orders (at least in the United States)

✓ Blackmail

✓ Bribery

✓ Sex

✓ Drugs

✓ Technical surveillance (bugging)

✓ Social engineering

✓ Torture (rubber-hose cryptanalysis)

But your operational budget and resources are stretched a bit thin (plus, this is a book about computer espionage), so you're left with four classic ways of attacking the protected data: manual-guessing attacks, dictionary attacks, brute-force attacks, and cryptanalysis.

MANUAL-GUESSING ATTACKS   The very first password attack most people think of is simple guessing; manually trying what seem like good password possibilities. When an application asks you for a password, you enter one that seems logical. Logical guessing attacks should be based on a user's predicted behavior patterns, including the following:

✓ **General behavior.** Most computer users are fairly predictable when it comes to pass-words: They use their account names, the word "password," no password at all, default passwords, or the same password over and over again. (Because you're a government agent, you'll likely have access to behavioral characteristics of non-Western, non-English-speaking computer users.)

✓ **Specific behavior.** If you've gathered information about your target and profiled him or her, you can try passwords such as a spouse's or child's name, social security number, anniversary or birthday dates, or other significant bits of information the target is going to frequently be able to remember. (The classic fictional example of this is the early 1980s movie *War Games*, in which Matthew Broderick breaks into a NORAD computer using the name of a scientist's deceased son, Joshua.)

Guessing attacks can be surprisingly successful, but they can also be slow and tedious as you manually enter each possible password in an application dialog box. There's also the possibility that the application can lock you out after a certain number of unsuccessful guesses. If you don't initially succeed after a few tries or minutes, you're better off launching a dictionary attack with specialized software, as described in the following section. If you've gathered profile information on your target, you can easily add it to a word list to automate guessing during a dictionary attack.

Paul Bobby wrote an excellent paper on creating focused dictionaries to help determine a user's password. This involves gathering information about the targeted user and then hybridizing possible passwords based on different rule sets. The paper is available at rr.sans.org/authentic/cracking.php.

Tactics: Saddam, You've Got Mail!

In October 2002, freelance reporter/security researcher Brian McWilliams visited the official Iraqi government Web site at www.uruklink.net/iraq. He noticed that there was a link where you could send an e-mail message to Iraqi President Saddam Hussein. The e-mail account associated with the link was press@uruklink.net. (It's unknown whether "press" literally meant press or was an abbreviation for President Saddam.)

McWilliams also saw there was a way users who had accounts on the site could check their e-mail while online. Relying on a classic manual-guessing attack, he entered "press" as the account name and "press" as the password. Just when he was about ready to give up, thinking his attempt had failed, he was rewarded when the inbox of Saddam Hussein appeared, chock-full of e-mail messages.

The e-mails in there were from June to August 2002. No messages had been read or replied to, and the mailbox appeared to have reached its maximum capacity and wasn't accepting new mail. McWilliams downloaded over 1,000 messages addressed to Hussein. In addition to spam, threats, and messages from fans requesting autographs and photos, McWilliams reported several American companies had made business overtures to Hussein in an attempt to sell their products or services, a no-no when it came to U.S. trade policies.

Despite the fact that the incident was widely publicized on various Internet news sources, McWilliams reported that government authorities hadn't contacted him about the messages he downloaded. Considering the lack of federal interest, it's likely that one American intelligence agency or another had already cracked Hussein's e-mail account and was actively monitoring it.

McWilliams changed the password before he publicized his findings, and then someone at uruklink.net changed the password again. The swift fall of Hussein's regime in April 2003 didn't leave much time for volunteer civilian crackers to break in to other Iraqi Web sites on their own during the war. Remember that while cracking Axis of Evil servers may seem patriotic, it's still illegal.

DICTIONARY ATTACKS   A more effective means of compromising a password is with a dictionary attack, in which a list of words is checked to see if one of the words matches the password. This type of attack is especially quick to reveal weak passwords that are composed of common terms. Most password-cracking utilities give you the option of specifying one or more word list files, either a pre-made list or one you create yourself. The utility reads a word from the list and then checks it against the encrypted documents to see whether it matches the password required to decrypt the document. If a match is found, the attack ends, and the password is displayed.

There are hundreds of word lists available on the Internet that contain words; common names; science fiction characters; religious terms; and references to popular entertainers, movies, and TV shows. There are even Japanese, Russian, Croatian, French, German, and a host of other language word lists to deal with someone who speaks another language. If you've done a good deal of research on your target, you should have a pretty good idea about which word lists might be appropriate to use for a dictionary attack.

Many cracking programs offer advanced features, such as taking each word from a selected list and capitalizing the first letter, replacing an "o" with a zero, or adding a symbol or punctuation mark to the end of the word (all relatively common techniques that an above-average computer user might use in an attempt to make a difficult-to-guess password).

Dictionary attacks provide the highest return rate when it comes to compromising passwords — as various studies have shown, anywhere between 50 percent to 90 percent of computer users rely on common words to secure their data or protect their access.

You should use a dictionary attack early on in your attempts to unprotect data. Before you ever launch an attack, spend some time gathering as many word lists as you can find and either burn them to a CD-R or copy them to a hard drive partition (this makes attacks slightly quicker due to the faster read access times of hard drives).

Word lists are cheap and abundant on the Internet. A few sources that offer free downloadable collections of English and foreign language word lists that are perfect for dictionary attacks include **AccessData** (`www.accessdata.com/dictionaries.htm`), **ElcomSoft** (`www.elcomsoft.com/prs.html`), and **University of Oxford** (`ftp.ox.ac.uk/pub/wordlists/`).

BRUTE-FORCE ATTACKS   If your target is smart about his passwords and a dictionary attack fails, the next approach to try is a brute-force attack. This is where every possible combination of letters, numbers, punctuation marks, and symbols (or some subset) are tried in an effort to reveal a password. It works just like a dictionary attack, except that combinations of characters are compared against the password until a match is found instead of checking words in a word list.

The success of a brute-force attack entirely depends on the size of the password. The longer the password, the less realistic it is that the attack will succeed. In fact, after passwords reach a certain length, the time requirements of an exhaustive search prevent such attacks from ever being successful.

Let's do a quick math review. There are 95 possible characters that can compose a password (128 ASCII characters minus the 33 unprintable ones, such as the ASCII 7 control character which rings a bell). There are an additional 128 extended ASCII characters (characters other than standard letters, numbers, and symbols; for example an ASCII 142 would produce an Ä character), but the vast majority of English-speaking users never even consider using these in their passwords (which can be a countermeasure in itself). It's also possible that the extended characters might not be supported by an application.

Let's say that our hypothetical terrorist suspect decided to use an eight-character password with a strong encryption application to encrypt and decrypt his data. If he selected only from the printable ASCII characters, there would be 6.6×10^{15} unique combinations to choose from. If you attempt a brute-force attack on his password, assuming a million guesses per second, you will need to rely on several future generations of your relatives to help you with the attack: It will take more than 200 years to exhaust all the possible combinations. (Of course, this isn't factoring in Moore's Law, which states that the number of transistors per square inch on integrated circuits doubles every year thus increasing computing power, or possible breakthroughs in cryptanalysis.)

But now, suppose that our terrorist hasn't followed security procedures and uses only a five-character password out of 95 possible characters. That shrinks down the number of password

Tactics: More Is Better

Obviously, there are limitations to carrying out a brute-force password attack with a single computer. However, what happens if you enlist other computers in your quest to compromise data? This is called a distributed-attack approach, in which you have many computers, each working on small portions of the total number of possible passwords or keys.

Up until the late 1990s, the Data Encryption Standard (DES) was the gold standard for encrypting data, but although the algorithm was strong, there were increasing suspicions that because of increases in computer horsepower, DES could be vulnerable to a brute-force attack. (It had long been rumored that the NSA already had computers capable of cracking DES.)

In January 1997, RSA, Inc. issued a series of public challenges to crack DES, with varying cash prizes for different key lengths. The $1,000 prize for cracking the paltry 40-bit exportable version of DES was promptly handed out to a University of California at Berkeley researcher who used 250 campus workstations to crack the key in 3.5 hours. The next challenge would be significantly more difficult, consisting of a 56-bit key with a prize of $10,000 for whomever could crack it first. (A general rule of thumb is that the number of possible keys doubles for each additional bit.)

Rocke Verser, Matt Curtin, and Justin Dolske started a project called DESCHALL that relied on computers connected to the Internet to perform the brute-force attack. There were 2^{56} (more than 72 quadrillion) keys that would need to be checked, and software was written for a variety of operating systems and hardware platforms that would connect to a central server, download a portion of the key space to be searched, check for the key, and then report the results back to the server.

Other groups started similar projects, but DESCHALL had the most participants. During the effort, more than 78,000 IP addresses were registered that assisted with the challenge. In one peak 24-hour period, more than 14,000 hosts were working on the attack at once. Finally, on June 17, 1997, with 24.6 percent of the key space searched (18 quadrillion keys) the key was discovered in 96 days. (A detailed paper on the project is available at www.interhack.net/pubs/des-key-crack/.)

Since DESCHALL, other distributed cracking projects have been run, attacking progressively larger and larger key sizes. The main purpose of these events has been to demonstrate the strengths and weaknesses of different encryption algorithms to brute-force attacks (there are also other noncryptographic distributed computing projects such as SETI@home, which is looking for extraterrestrial life, and Folding@home, which studies protein folding and related diseases).

If you have some spare computer cycles and want to be involved in one of the cracking projects, visit Distributed.net, which is currently sponsoring a 72-bit RC5 challenge. Barring an initial lucky key find, this one will probably take awhile.

possibilities to 7.7×10^9, which at one million attempts per second will take a little over two hours to exhaust all the possible password combinations.

With any brute-force attack, there's a point of diminishing returns based on the computing resources you have available to carry out the attack. This rule applies to everyone, regardless whether you have access to a NSA supercomputer or a single PC. At a certain size, the password or key will make an attack impractical because of the amount of time it will take. You may not know the actual password length, but it's important to establish a maximum threshold to limit your search based on your computing resources and how much time you're willing to devote to trying to discover the password.

It's also important to determine how valuable the data is that you're trying to unprotect. Is it critical enough to spend months trying to compromise? Will the information still have value when or if it's finally compromised? For example, suppose you're a computer cop who intercepted an encrypted message from a suspected drug supplier to his dealer, and it takes you six months to crack the message that talks about the details of a shipment that took place a week after the message was originally sent. Does eventually learning the contents justify the time and effort spent to compromise the message? (We'll assume that the criminal is smart and changes his password regularly, so if a single message is compromised, it probably won't impact past or future messages.)

CRYPTANALYSIS Cryptanalysis is the study of encryption algorithms, cryptosystems (a system for encrypting and decrypting data), and encrypted text with the goal of being able to retrieve plaintext (unencrypted) information from the encrypted data. Cryptanalysis is both an art and science, whose practitioners blend mathematics, inquisitiveness, intuition, persistence, and luck to solve cryptographic problems.

There are generally two types of people who break codes and ciphers:

✓ **Government.** The National Security Agency (NSA) employs more mathematicians and cryptographers than any other private corporation or government agency (it's also the largest purchaser of computer equipment in the world). There are also cryptanalysts employed by the military and a smattering of other government intelligence and law enforcement agencies. Virtually all the cryptographic work and research the government does (with the exception of the National Institute of Standards and Technology) is classified and never sees the light of day.

✓ **Academic or corporate.** Up until recently, the government has had a monopoly on cryptographers and has generally controlled their work. However, government influence has decreased considerably due to a growing interest in cryptography by mathematicians (who stay in academia) and expanded private-industry need for cryptographers, especially in the financial, communications, and computer security sectors. These cryptographers are much more open with their work, giving presentations and publishing papers on encryption algorithm weaknesses. Sometimes when a weakness is publicized, other programmers who may not be cryptographers write tools that exploit a newly discovered vulnerability. A classic example is the 802.11b Wired Equivalent Privacy security protocol. Shortly following the release of an academic paper that described its weaknesses, several tools appeared on the Internet that could compromise WEP keys. Although many programmers may lack the skills or experience to identify technical flaws in an encryption algorithm, they often have the skills to transform a theoretical concept to a real-world utility.

It's really beyond the scope of this book to delve into the details of cryptanalysis and how crypt-analysts attack encrypted data. There are a few important points to consider, though:

- ✓ Cryptanalysis takes a considerable amount of skill and knowledge (particularly in mathematics) that tends to go way beyond what an average spy or cracker possesses.

- ✓ There are skilled professionals who either are being paid to find weaknesses in cryptosystems or are doing so out of academic curiosity. Their work can potentially compromise what was commonly thought to be a secure cryptosystem.

- ✓ Although there are more talented cryptographers now (not employed by the government) who can make logical guesses about the capabilities of the NSA and other agencies that break codes, never underestimate government-class opposition. Governments have a tremendous amount of resources at their disposal and are probably at least several years ahead of academia and the private sector when it comes to cryptography.

- ✓ New research and faster processors can turn strong cryptosystems into weak ones, and it's important to stay current in these areas by paying attention to print and online security-related news sources. Just don't panic when you see a headline about someone discovering a vulnerability in an encryption algorithm. From an academic standpoint it may exist, but in the real world it still may be secure because an effective exploit just isn't practical to take advantage of the weakness.

There are a number of Internet sources that explore cryptanalysis in more detail. A few good places to start include RSA Laboratories' Frequently Asked Questions About Today's Cryptography (www.rsasecurity.com/rsalabs/faq/), Basic Cryptanalysis (Army Field Manual 34-40-2) (www.fas.org/irp/doddir/army/fm34-40-2/), and A Self-Study Course in Block-Cipher Cryptanalysis (www.counterpane.com/cryptanalysis.pdf).

Cracking Tools

So you're sitting on all these protected documents you managed to acquire from your terrorist suspect, and now you know that there are tools out there to help you crack them. Your grandmother was a code clerk during World War II and told you stories about mathematicians and other codebreakers using pencils, paper, and primitive computers to crack encrypted messages, but today you know you don't need to be a cryptanalyst to compromise common forms of protected data. Let's examine some of the commercial and free, easy-to-use automated utilities that can easily circumvent the security of encrypted files.

APPLICATION PASSWORD CRACKING

Password cracking is a relatively specialized niche market, and there are a handful of companies that make software designed to reveal the passwords. They do this by first reverse-engineering the applications that create protected documents to understand what type of encryption algorithm is used. Based on this information, a programmer writes a utility that either directly exploits the weak encryption and reveals the password or performs a dictionary or brute-force attack on a protected file.

Just about every popular software application that uses a password to protect data has a corresponding third-party tool that can unprotect the data. Depending on the encryption method, a password can be immediately revealed or take several weeks to compromise. To give you an idea of how easy it is to crack protected documents, here is a list of file types and products that ElcomSoft, one of the leaders in the password-recovery business, offers password crackers for the following:

- ✓ Adobe Acrobat: PDF files

- ✓ Archiving software: Zip, RAR, ACE, and ARJ files

- ✓ Corel products: WordPerfect, QuattroPro, and Paradox

- ✓ E-mail clients: Microsoft Internet Mail and News, Eudora, TheBat!, Netscape Navigator/ Communicator Mail, Pegasus, Calypso, FoxMail, Phoenix Mail, IncrediMail, @nyMail, and QuickMail Pro

- ✓ Instant Messengers: ICQ, Yahoo, AOL AIM, MSN Messenger, Excite Messenger, Odigo, Trillian, AT&T IM Anywhere, T-Online Messenger, Match Messenger, Praize IM, ScreenFIRE, ACD Express Communicator, Imici Messenger, Prodigy IM, PowWow Messenger, Jabber IM, Kellster IM, PalTalk, Indiatimes Messenger, Miranda, and Tiscali

- ✓ Intuit products: Quicken, Quicken Lawyer, and QuickBooks

- ✓ Lotus products: SmartSuite, Organizer, WordPro, 1-2-3, and Approach

- ✓ Microsoft products: Office, Access, Excel, Outlook, Word, Excel, Outlook Express, Internet Explorer, Project, Money, Backup, and Visual Basic for Applications

- ✓ Symantec ACT!

Those of you who aren't spies might be feeling a little morally outraged right now at how companies can produce and sell espionage software such as these. Take a deep breath and remember that like any technology, password crackers can be used both legitimately and illegitimately. On the positive side, for example, they can recover protected documents when a password has been forgotten, misplaced, or lost. They are also helpful for discovering evidence during criminal investigations (law enforcement agencies are a big customer of these companies).

The general rule of thumb with application-cracking software is the faster the CPU, the quicker a dictionary or brute-force attack can be performed. The megahertz speed directly relates to the number of passwords the program tries per second. The more megahertz, the more attempts per second.

All the password-cracking applications run in the background while you're working on other things; however, the more processes you have running and the more the CPU is taxed by other applications, the slower the cracking tool will be. With some cracking applications, you can set the process priority to ensure that the utility gets the maximum number of possible CPU cycles, but overall you're probably better off dedicating one or more computers to the cracking effort.

Password-cracking companies frequently update their products, increasing the utilities' speed and effectiveness and addressing new protection and encryption methods used by application manufacturers. In addition to the password-recovery software companies, there are also some service companies that will unprotect documents you send them. Most of the commercial recovery software isn't that expensive, though, and would be a worthwhile investment to have at your disposal.

Some of the key players in the commercial password-cracking business are discussed in the following sections.

Tools of the Trade: Cracking Hardware

Another brute-force option available to governments and well-funded spying operations is dedicated hardware that's specifically designed to crack encrypted data.

Although specialized cracking hardware sounds pretty exotic and something only the NSA might have, in 1998 the Electronic Frontier Foundation (EFF) built a computer designed exclusively for cracking DES-encrypted data. The machine consisted of 1,500 chips, each with 24 identical search engines capable of trying 2.5 million keys per second. The DES cracker could test an astounding 90 billion keys per second, and would only take about nine days to perform an exhaustive search of all possible combinations (often referred to as the key space).

On its official debut, the machine was able to crack a message encrypted with a 56-bit key in less than 56 hours (at the time, the previous record using a distributed attack was 39 days). This record was eventually beat by using the DES-cracking hardware in conjunction with a distributed cracking effort. Testing more than 245 billion keys a second, the correct key was discovered in a little over 22 hours. (For more on the EFF DES cracker, including photos, go to www.cryptography.com/resources/whitepapers/DES.html.)

Consider that if a nonprofit advocacy group could build a fairly low-tech yet effective cracking device for less than $250,000, it stands to reason that government intelligence and law enforcement agencies also have such hardware at their disposal.

Could specialized hardware be developed to accomplish the same with stronger cryptosystems, such as the Advanced Encryption Standard (AES) that uses a 128-bit key? Let's say you could harness enough computing power to build a machine that could recover a 56-bit DES key in a second. Even with that horsepower, it would take about 149 trillion years for the machine to exhaustively search through all of the possible 128-bit AES keys. That's a long time, especially because most scientists believe the universe is less than 20 billion years old.

ACCESSDATA   AccessData, founded in 1987, is one of the pioneer password-recovery firms. The company has provided consulting services and software to the U.S. government, federal and local law enforcement agencies, and corporate America; as a result, AccessData has a trusted reputation among its customers. Password-cracking modules for a number of popular applications are priced from $35 to $99, with all of the modules sold together for $495 as the Password Recovery Toolkit.

AccessData also has a product called Distributed Network Attack (DNA) for attacks on protected Microsoft Office 97/2000 documents and .PDF files. DNA has a central server and multiple network clients so each of the clients can check an assigned set of possible passwords, thus decreasing the total amount of time to perform an exhaustive search. A ten-client version is available for $249, with a 100-client version priced at $995.

For more information and to download a demo version of the Password Recovery Toolkit, go to www.accessdata.com.

ELCOMSOFT   ElcomSoft, Ltd. is a controversial Russian software company that specializes in password-recovery software. The company released its first password-cracking utility for protected ZIP files in 1997 and since then has developed a number of password crackers for many popular applications. The individual utilities range in price from $30 to $79 for personal licenses.

ElcomSoft became widely known in digital rights and computer security circles during the summer of 2001, when employee Dmitry Sklyarov was arrested at a Las Vegas hacker convention after giving a presentation on how the encryption Adobe used for protecting e-books was fundamentally weak. Sklyarov developed a product for ElcomSoft that decrypted Adobe formatted e-books, and Adobe pressed the government to arrest Sklyarov on charges of violating the Digital Millennium Copyright Act (DMCA).

Sklyarov spent several weeks in jail before being freed on $50,000 bail and was eventually allowed to return to Russia. (Alexander Katalov, president of ElcomSoft who used to work for the KGB, later stated it was ironic that the FBI had arrested Sklyarov, considering that the federal law enforcement agency was one of his customers.) Although the charges against Sklyarov were dropped, the government still decided to go after ElcomSoft on the same grounds, but a jury cleared the company of charges in December 2002. (Adobe, which was originally vocal in its support of the prosecution, quietly stepped out of the picture, coincidentally after several activist groups threatened to organize a boycott of the company's products.)

Serving as a test case for international enforcement of the DMCA hasn't stopped ElcomSoft from producing a number of innovative password-recovery utilities. Evaluation software and more information can be downloaded from www.elcomsoft.com.

PASSWARE   Passware is another newer European company that's quickly risen as one of the top password-cracking tool vendors. Founded in Estonia in 1998 (the former Soviet Union has produced some excellent programmers with a penchant for computer security), the company offers cracking utilities for a number of popular applications, available individually and priced from $45 to $195 or all bundled together as the Passware Kit for $395. One of the password-cracking utilities is shown in Figure 6-1. For demo software and more details, go to www.lost-password.com.

OTHER CRACKING UTILITIES   In addition to utilities produced by these three companies, there are also a number of other commercial and free utilities that can compromise password-protected documents. Some of the free tools work just as well as their commercial cousins in recovering passwords. Some resources to check include the following:

✓ One of the best, most comprehensive sources for password-cracking utilities is Pavel Semjanov's "Russian Password Crackers" Web site. Semjanov has an extensive listing of free and commercial password utilities, with brief descriptions and comments on how effective the application is. Go to www.password-crackers.com.

✓ Another excellent source of information on password crackers, weak encryption, and general security-related topics is Joe Peschel's "D.O.E. SysWorks" Web site at http://members.aol.com/jpeschel/.

✓ Finally, a number of password crackers for many different operating systems and applications can be downloaded from the venerable Packetstorm security Web site at www.packetstormsecurity.org/assess.html.

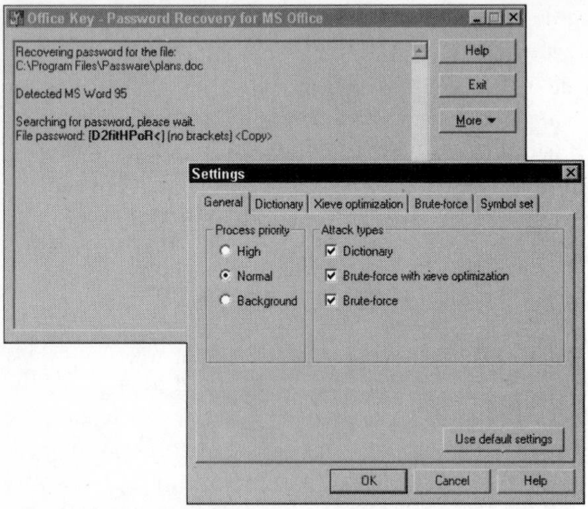

Figure 6-1: Passware utility that cracked a password-protected document created by an old version of Microsoft Word 95 (from our suspected terrorist scenario at the beginning of the chapter) in less than a second. The password was D2fitHPoR<. Documents created and protected with newer versions of Word take longer to crack but are still vulnerable. Go to `http://support.microsoft.com/default.aspx?scid=KB;en-us;q290112` for complete information on the encryption algorithms Microsoft uses.

WINDOWS 3.X, 9X, ME .PWL PROFILE CRACKING

As discussed in Chapter 4, the Microsoft Windows 3.x, 9x, and ME family really doesn't offer much in the way of operating system security. The Windows login dialog box doesn't restrict access to the computer because you can press the Cancel button and Windows still happily loads and displays the desktop, giving you full access to all of the files on the hard drive.

All the login sequence does is change the appearance settings based on the user name and restores access to shared directories, printer queues, and network shares. To make it easy, instead of entering a password each time to access these resources, an encrypted list of passwords is kept in a .PWL file and then decrypted with the login password.

The main purpose of attacking a profile is to reveal any passwords that might be stored in the file, just in case these passwords might be used to protect data elsewhere. Knowing this, it would have been worthwhile copying any .PWL files that were on our suspected terrorist's laptop and then attacking the files once you got back to the safe house.

It's worthwhile knowing a little bit about the history of the encryption schemes Microsoft used because they vary depending on the operating system.

✓ Windows for Workgroups (3.11) and Windows 95 had a very weak implementation of the RC4 encryption algorithm, and free utilities such as Glide made it easy to quickly reveal any stored passwords.

✓ Microsoft addressed this security flaw in the OSR2 release of Windows 95 and carried the fix over to Windows 98 and ME. Glide and first-generation PWL utilities won't expose passwords in these later operating systems; however, there are still two avenues for attack. All the passwords stored in the .PWL file are cached as plaintext in memory. If an unattended computer is already running, you can run a tool such as PWLView to view all the passwords. If the computer isn't running, simply boot it and copy all the files with a .PWL extension to a floppy disk. Then use a utility such as PWLHack or PWLTool to launch a brute-force or dictionary attack against the PWL file.

PWL cracking tools are available from a number of security and cracker sites. You can download some of the more popular and effective tools from the following:

✓ **Glide:** free, download at `http://members.aol.com/jpeschel/Glidepwl.zip`

✓ **PWLView:** free, available from `http://lastbit.com/vitas/pwlview.asp`

✓ **PWLTool:** $40, available from `http://lastbit.com/vitas/pwltool.asp` (trial version available)

✓ **PWLHack:** free, available from `www.pilabs.org.ua/wisdom/download/pwlhack/pwl_h410.rar`

PASSWORD DIALOG BOX CRACKING

Another way to possibly compromise passwords that are being used for multiple purposes is to use the software version of x-ray vision on certain dialog boxes. Windows has a dialog box security feature that replaces any password text that's entered with asterisks (*). This prevents someone nearby from watching you enter your password on the screen (commonly known as "shoulder surfing").

In applications with this feature, the programmer simply sets an edit control style to ES_PASSWORD, and whenever a user types text into the edit control, the text appears as asterisks. However, because the "real" text is still present in memory, it's possible to retrieve the text by accessing the control's handle (a memory reference).

Many applications that use passwords employ this security feature. For example, the popular WS_FTP utility lets users save passwords associated with FTP accounts to avoid entering the data each time they log in; a dialog box shows the host computer, the account name, and the password (which is displayed with asterisks).

Just like Superman with his x-ray vision, free tools such as Revelation and Snitch access the hidden password text and quickly show you what's under the asterisks. You just run the tool and move the cursor over the asterisks, and presto, the password is displayed.

With Windows 2000 and XP, Microsoft changed the way the password edit control works, and a number of utilities that worked with earlier versions of Windows no longer reveal passwords. Two tools that work on all versions of Windows are the commercial iOpus Password Recovery XP and the free open-source PasswordSpy, shown in Figure 6-2.

Password dialog box cracking doesn't work with all applications (some application developers are aware of this and wrote code to prevent the vulnerability from being exploited), but this is a quick and easy way to reveal passwords that may be used elsewhere to secure data for an application that it does work with.

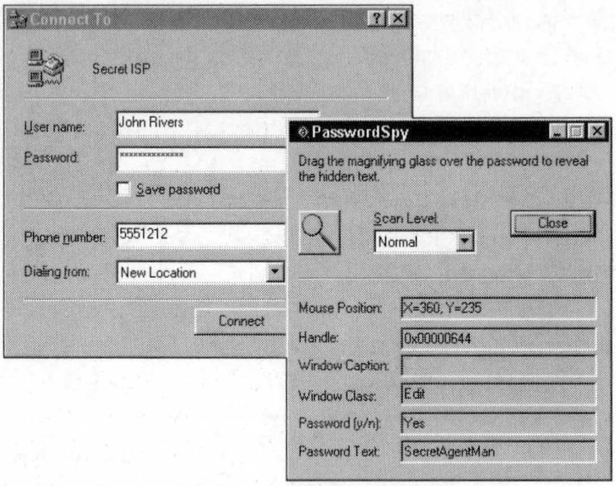

Figure 6-2: PasswordSpy reveals a protected password in a Windows 98 Dial-Up Networking dialog box.

Here are some popular password dialog-cracking tools and where you can download them:

✓ **Revelation:** free, available from `www.snadboy.com`

✓ **Snitch:** free, available from `http://ntsecurity.nu/toolbox/snitch/`

✓ **iOpus Password Recovery XP:** $29.95, from `www.iopus.com/password_recovery.htm` (trial version available)

✓ **PasswordSpy:** free, available from `www.csc.calpoly.edu/~bfriesen/software/ pwdspy.shtml` (with source code)

DIAL-UP NETWORKING CRACKING

One other place to look for compromising weak passwords is Windows Dial-Up Networking (DUN). This service lets modem users easily set up accounts for Internet service providers and other online services. One of DUN's convenient features is a Save password option that remembers your password each time you connect to an account so you don't have to enter it. DUN is especially insecure under Windows 9x/ME, and there are several command-line tools available that can crack the weakly encrypted account and password information, including the following:

✓ **Dialpwd:** free, available from `www.password-crackers.com/DOWNLOAD/dialpwd.zip`

✓ **PhoneBook Viewer v1.01c:** free, available from `www.password-crackers.com/ DOWNLOAD/phbv101c.zip`

CRYPTOSYSTEM CRACKING

Cracking protected application documents is pretty much a snap, but what if your target is using strong cryptographic software? Unless you get lucky, you will probably have great difficulties trying to compromise his or her protected data. Modern cryptosystems such as PGP and Blowfish Advanced CS (and others described in the "Countermeasures" section of Chapter 5) are highly resistant to attacks that succeed against applications using weak encryption.

Although it's currently impossible to perform a fully exhaustive brute-force attack on data protected by a strong encryption algorithm and an adequately sized key, it's very possible to perform a limited brute-force or dictionary attack on the data in hope that the target has used a weak password. There are brute-force or dictionary attack tools that work against common encryption algorithms, but they tend not to be as readily available as application password-cracking utilities. If you're technically inclined, you'll probably end up writing your own tool to attack whatever encryption algorithm was used to protect the data. (Or in our hypothetical government spy example, you can just hand the data off to a technical analysis group for them to attempt to crack.)

One of the complications in cracking strongly encrypted data is you may not know which type of encryption algorithm was used to protect the data. Although some applications, such as PGP, place a header in an encrypted message, which readily identifies which application was used to protect the information, other cryptosystems leave no clues whatsoever. Not knowing whether the data was protected with IDEA, 3DES, Blowfish, or any number of other encryption algorithms severely hampers any dictionary or brute-force attacks. You should always look on the hard drive or other storage media to see if there are any encryption tools present. With this information and a search engine, you may be able to find published weaknesses associated with the tool or even utilities to help you compromise data protected by it.

The good news is that targets that use strong crypto are few and far between. And if you do encounter protected data that's difficult to compromise with a cracking utility, stay flexible and consider your other options. It may be much easier and less time-consuming to use a keylogger, surveillance camera, or Trojan horse application to get at the data you want.

Countermeasures

So you decided to ditch the shades and the disguise because corporate work pays a whole lot better than public service spying does (and is a heck of a lot less risky), and now you're gainfully employed doing computer security work for a Fortune 500 company. One of your responsibilities is to protect sensitive company data from the likes of your former self; specifically when it comes to economic espionage.

Let's review several simple, low-cost countermeasures that rely on strong encryption and good passwords that you'll employ as part of your plan to prevent spies from accessing critical corporate data.

Strong Encryption

This is pretty much a no-brainer. If you have data you want to protect, don't rely on "password-protection" features found in many commercial software packages. Use strong file and "on-the-fly" encryption applications, such as those discussed in Chapter 5. However, don't let the strength of an encryption algorithm provide you with a false sense of security. As you've seen from examples throughout this book, there are many ways to encrypt information.

Password Policies

You'd think that computer espionage should be about sexy, risky, interesting topics — not boring bureaucratic policies. However, good security policies are a primary countermeasure against spying, and a password policy is extremely important because passwords are such a weak link that can easily be exploited by a spy.

You don't need to be a large corporation to establish your own security policies. You don't even need to write the policy down (although it's a good idea so you can remember it or easily share it with others if you work for an organization). This section should give you some ideas for creating your own password policy.

Just remember that the key to a successful policy is compliance. If you or others don't follow the policy religiously, you're leaving yourself open for attacks that could compromise your data.

"STRONG" PASSWORDS

You should have a pretty good idea of what a strong password is by now. Not to belabor the point, it's not your wife's name, your birthday, a word that appears in the dictionary, your user account name, or other clearly weak passwords that can readily be attacked. Characteristics of a strong password are as follows:

- ✓ It's at least eight characters in length (the more the better, especially if you're going up against an opponent with considerable resources).

- ✓ It isn't a word (in any language).

- ✓ It isn't based on personal information.

- ✓ It contains both upper- and lowercase characters (for example, a–z and A–Z).

- ✓ It contains digits and punctuation characters as well as letters (for example, 0–9 and any of the following: !@#$%^&*()_+|~-=\{}[]:";'<>?,./).

- ✓ It's easy to remember (you don't need to write it down).

- ✓ It's never written down or saved in electronic format unless it's encrypted.

One of the best methods of selecting a strong password is to use something called a *passphrase*. This is a series of words and/or characters that form a memorable phrase — for example, Mycat$Is1Fatty or Iht1tAM* (I hate traffic in the AM). Because of the potential length and mix of characters, passphrases are extremely resistant to brute-force attacks.

However, always remember that a strong password is only as good as the encryption algorithm it's used with. Our hypothetical terrorist could have used one of the strong passwords mentioned previously and would have instantly been compromised if he used it to protect a document using an older version of Microsoft Word, which had very weak encryption.

RANDOMLY GENERATED PASSWORDS

Some security experts advise clients to use randomly generated passwords; a semi-random (remember, true randomness is usually difficult to achieve) selected sequence of letters, numbers, and symbols. The rationale is that this prevents users from choosing weak passwords, which they're often prone to do. You can use your favorite Web search engine to find a number of free utilities that create random passwords.

Although this approach seems reasonable, studies have shown that the tactic may be a bit flawed. Users have more difficulty remembering randomly generated passwords, and the passwords seem just as strong as those created by a user based on a mnemonic phrase in various tests. If you're using randomly generated passwords, the costs associated with generating them and remembering them likely exceed the perceived security benefits.

Jianxin Yan, Alan Blackwell, Ross Anderson, and Alasdair Grant wrote an excellent paper called "The Memorability and Security of Passwords — Some Empirical Results," which debunks the notion that random passwords are superior and provides other interesting information about password use. Download it from www.cl.cam.ac.uk/ftp/users/rja14/tr500.pdf.

PASSWORD USE

Always remember the password house of cards (or dominoes, chain reaction, ripple effect, or whatever metaphor makes the most sense for you). If you're using the same strong password for everything and it somehow becomes revealed, you can probably kiss all of your protected data good-bye.

One approach to minimizing the total number of remembered passwords is to take a cue from government intelligence agencies and use compartmentalized passwords. With compartmentalized passwords, you use several different passwords for different information and activities. For example, sending encrypted messages to your lawyer is a high-security activity, and logging on to various fly-fishing Web site forums is a low-security activity. If the password for the low-security activity gets compromised, it won't impact any of your higher-security activities.

SOCIAL-ENGINEERING PROTECTION

As mentioned earlier, a good spy tries to exploit both technical and human weaknesses in order to attack a security system. In many cases, passwords can be more effectively and efficiently compromised using social engineering attacks that prey on human nature and behavior. Your password policy should incorporate the following protections against social engineering:

- ✓ Don't reveal your password over the phone to anyone.

- ✓ Don't reveal your password in an e-mail message.

- ✓ Don't reveal your password to your coworkers or manager.

- ✓ Don't mention your password in front of other people.

- ✓ Don't mention the subject of your password, such as "my wife's name."

- ✓ Don't reveal your password on questionnaires or security forms.

- ✓ Don't share a password with family members.

- ✓ Don't use easily guessed password "hints" in applications or Web sites that grant you access in case you forget your password. Simple hints are clues that can narrow the number of possibilities for a spy trying to compromise a Web account.

- ✓ Don't use the same password to secure sensitive information that you would to enter a Web site.

CHANGING PASSWORDS ON A REGULAR BASIS

The longer you use a password, the greater the chances that it might be deliberately or accidentally compromised. You should change your password on a regular basis, at least every three to six months. (One old saying is you should change your password as often as you change your toothbrush; which should be every three to four months as recommended by nine out of ten dentists.)

When you change your password, try to be creative and use a password you've never used before. Many people fall into the trap of recycling their passwords and using the same two or three passwords over and over again when it comes time to change them. This is obviously a big security risk.

Password Lists

Modern life is tough. You have to remember login passwords, e-mail passwords, Web site passwords, bank ATM Personal Identification Numbers, as well as birthdays and anniversaries (which may be the most critical pieces of data). It's no wonder people resort to a series of commonly used, easy-to-remember (and compromise) passwords.

The simplest solution to this problem is to keep an encrypted list of all your passwords. This can be a text file with all of the passwords you use and what they're for, secured with a strong encryption algorithm such as AES, BlowFish, or IDEA. If you forget a password, simply decrypt the list and look it up. When you change a password, decrypt the file, make the edit, and re-encrypt. You can handily store the file on a floppy disk, a PDA, or your hard drive. If you're paranoid, real or imagined, you could even hide the password list in another file with one of the steganography utilities discussed in the "Countermeasures" section of Chapter 5.

Just remember what your grandmother told you about putting all of your eggs in one basket. You obviously don't want a spy getting a hold of this information, so you should do the following:

✓ Ensure that the encryption application you're using is trustworthy and secure.

✓ Use a strong password.

✓ Ensure that there's no possible way the application or operating system is leaking plain-text data from the encrypted file.

One way to check for leakage is to use a hex editor, after encrypting the document, to search the entire hard drive for a unique string that you know exists only in the protected document, such as one of your passwords. If you find the string, either the application is "leaking" information by writing data to a temporary file you don't know about or the operating system is "leaking" data by saving information to the swap file. If this is the case, consider creating a DOS boot disk that contains a simple text editor and a command-line version of an encryption utility. Boot your computer with this disk and maintain the encrypted list of passwords on it.

Another alternative is to use a commercial or free password manager application. These programs store an encrypted database of your passwords and other sensitive information. (Free Windows password managers can be found at `www.webattack.com/Freeware/security/fwpass.shtml`.) Although password managers are convenient and easy to use, you have to put your trust in an unknown programmer and his or her skills in developing a secure product.

Password Alternatives

A password is simply an authentication method, a way to distinguish one computer user from another. Because weak, text-based passwords are easy to attack and it's difficult to convince people to use strong passwords, other authentication methods hold the promise of better security. Let's briefly cover several different types of authentication devices you may be using now or in the near future.

BIOMETRICS

Many alternative authentication devices are based on biometrics. Instead of a typical password system that relies on what you know (the password), biometric devices are based on some unique physical characteristic you have, essentially what you are.

Currently, there's quite a bit of media and marketing hype about biometrics, mostly as a security mechanism for identifying known or suspected terrorists. When it comes to widespread use, biometric systems are still in their infancy, however, and there are a number of kinks to be worked out before systems can widely be deployed. There are two terms you should be familiar with when it comes to the accuracy of biometric systems:

✓ False Rejection Rate (FRR) is when a device doesn't correctly authenticate an authorized user.

✓ False Acceptance Rate (FAR) is when a device erroneously authenticates an unauthorized user.

Both FRR and FAR values are important to know, particularly if the numbers have come from lab tests or more complex and rigorous real-world use. You should also understand some potential system vulnerabilities if you're considering a biometric system, including the following:

✓ **Replay attacks.** The hardware component of the biometric system must pass data to the software component of the system to authenticate a user. If this verified data is captured, it can potentially be played back to the software component of the system to gain access. For example, with a fingerprint scanner that attaches to a USB port, it's possible for a successful authentication sequence to be captured and then replayed through the port at some later point in time.

✓ **Spoofing.** Because biometric authentication devices work by identifying some physical characteristic of a person, it's possible to spoof the device by using a facsimile of that characteristic. For example, a voice recognition system can be spoofed by using a bug and a digital tape recorder to copy a user's spoken words.

✓ **Database manipulation.** Biometric signatures need to be stored in a database for comparison during the authentication process. It's possible a spy could manipulate the database and covertly add an entry to give an unauthorized person permission to access a system.

✓ **Reverse-engineering.** All biometric authentication devices consist of hardware and some type of software that communicates with the operating system or an application. It's possible to reverse-engineer the software and patch it so the recognition algorithm would always authenticate the identity of a user, even if she didn't appear in the system's database. For years, software copy-protection schemes have been circumvented by crackers who simply change the hex value of an assembly language conditional branch statement or replace a piece of code with a null operation (NOP) instruction. If a teenage cracker can reverse-engineer and defeat a complicated software-protection scheme, it goes without saying that an authentication system program can also be short-circuited.

Consider that as biometric devices become popular and more widely used, new weaknesses and exploits will be discovered and publicized. Just like any other technology, biometrics shouldn't be relied on for exclusively protecting sensitive data. Instead, they should be part of an integrated, layered security system.

 The German computer magazine *c't* featured an article in its November 2002 issue in which a group of testers tried to outwit 11 biometric devices. They ended up successfully defeating the devices with a series of simple attacks. An English translation of the article is available at `http://heise.de/ct/english/02/11/114/`.

FINGERPRINT SCANNERS   Fingerprint scanners are currently the most widely used biometric authentication devices. Consumer-grade models, which retail from $100 to $150, work by recognizing patterns in the finger ridges using external hardware scanners with some types built into keyboards and mice, as shown in Figure 6-3. An authorized fingerprint is first scanned and stored in a database (a digital image of the fingerprint, like the police would take, isn't stored; instead, the fingerprint is registered as a series of points and stored as a 256-byte "minutia file"). The authentication system scans subsequent fingerprints and checks for a match. If your fingerprint is in the database, you can access the computer or the data. If it's not, you're out of luck.

Fingerprint-recognition systems aren't perfect and can be affected by normal wear on the finger ridges, scarring, sweat, and dirt. In addition, if an opponent has access to your finger (either attached or severed) or a close replica of it, there's a good chance your security may be compromised.

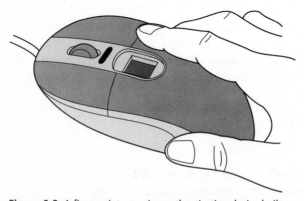

Figure 6-3: A fingerprint-scanning authentication device built into a mouse.

Tactics: Gumming Up the Works

In May 2002, researcher Tsutomu Matsumoto from the Yokohama National University gave a presentation (and subsequently released a paper) on fingerprint scanner vulnerabilities. With under $10 of commonly available household supplies, he created a fake finger made of gelatin that fooled a number of commercially available fingerprint scanners.

Matsumoto made plastic molds of volunteers' fingers and then filled the molds with gelatin (the same ingredients Gummi Bears are made of). The prints lifted from the mold were good enough that the "Gummi Fingers" fooled fingerprint readers up to 80 percent of the time. Matsumoto also tried capturing latent fingerprints left on a glass and was equally successful at creating fake fingers based on the prints that could fool the authentication scanners.

Fingerprint scanner manufacturers were quick to dismiss Matsumoto's work, saying that it was performed under lab conditions. Most security experts shook their heads, though, and considered the researcher's discovery an excellent reason not to rely on fingerprint biometrics as a sole method of securing sensitive data.

Matsumoto's PowerPoint presentation, including color photos and instructions for making your own artificial and "Gummi" fingers, can be viewed at `www.itu.int/itudoc/itu-t/workshop/security/present/s5p4.pdf`.

EYE SCANNERS   Long a favorite of spy movies and TV shows, eye-scanning authentication devices come in two different types. Retina scanners, priced from $400 to $500, work by directing a low-intensity infrared light through the pupil to the blood vessel patterns on the back of the eye. These devices, which are extremely accurate, are often found in high-security installations. Iris scanners, such as the one shown in Figure 6-4, rely on proprietary technology and cost from $200 to $300. They are less intrusive than retina scanners because they passively record the pattern of flecks and other features that appear on an eye's iris. Unlike retina scanners, which have proven to be secure, iris scanners have been defeated by using detailed photographs of the human eye.

VOICE SCANNERS   Voice-scanning devices capture characteristics of a person's voice, such as the pitch, tone, and frequency. Because most computers have sound cards with microphone jacks, this technology can be cheaply and easily deployed. Noisy environments, poor-quality microphones, and illnesses that affect the voice, such as a cold, all can affect the accuracy of biometric voice devices. Voice scanners are currently priced from $150 to $200.

For more information on biometric authentication systems, go to Biometric Consortium (`www.biometrics.org`) or Michigan State University Biometrics Research (`http://biometrics.cse.msu.edu`).

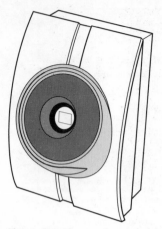

Figure 6-4: Iris-scanning authentication hardware records iris patterns and features when you look into the lens. Unlike retina scanners, iris scanners don't project a light beam into the eye.

SMART CARDS

A smart card is a credit-card-size plastic card with a microprocessor embedded in it. The cards are called "smart" because they have their own CPU, memory, and operating system. For security purposes, the cards work on two authentication principles: something you have and something you know. When a card is inserted into an external reader (a number of smart cards now plug directly into ubiquitous USB ports, eliminating the need for a reader), the card identifies itself to software as part of the authentication process; then the user must enter a correct personal identification number (PIN) to access a computer or network.

Although smart cards are generally a secure approach to authentication, there are attacks that a technically skilled opponent can carry out against them. Bo Lavare maintains a comprehensive site devoted to smart card security at www.geocities.com/ResearchTriangle/Lab/1578/smart.htm.

SYMBOL RECOGNITION

A final nonbiometric authentication method is based on symbol, image, or pattern recognition. Instead of typing in a text password, a series of images randomly appears in a window. The user selects the correct images or sequence of images by using a mouse and the cursor to be authenticated. Studies have shown that symbols are easier to remember than text-based passwords and are obviously less susceptible to dictionary attacks (although not enough research has been done to determine whether some images are generally aesthetically pleasing to most people and could therefore be considered weak). Rachna Dhamija and Adrian Perrig developed an experimental system called Déjà Vu, shown in Figure 6-5, which illustrates this authentication concept. For more information, go to www.sims.berkeley.edu/~rachna/dejavu/.

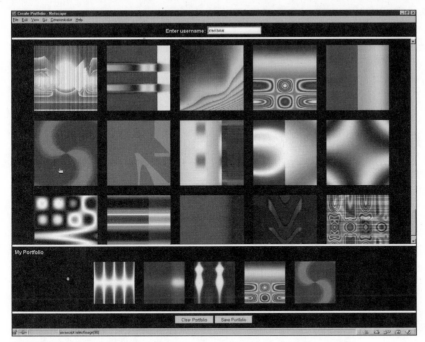

Figure 6-5: The Déjà Vu recognition system, showing user-selectable graphics.

Summary

Information and evidence that you've seemingly protected may not be as secure as you thought. Weak encryption and poor passwords make it a snap for a spy to compromise protected data using a variety of widely available, easy-to-use tools.

If you have sensitive documents on your computer, don't rely on the protection schemes found in business and productivity software to safeguard your data. Instead, use strong encryption applications. You should also fully understand the risks associated with passwords and adopt a password policy that reduces the risk of attacks that rely on poorly chosen and weak passwords.

Chapter 7

Copying Data

" . . . Write it down in your notebook, my wannabe, Harriet the spy."
— Indigo Girls, "Caramia," *Shaming of the Sun*

ONCE A SPY HAS PHYSICAL ACCESS TO A COMPUTER, he or she is probably going to want to copy key information from it. You're probably thinking this seems rather straightforward and shouldn't warrant an entire chapter of discussion, but the reality is that there are a number of considerations and options when it comes to copying data and computer spying.

Storage media such as floppy disks, CD-Rs, and ZIP disks all have their own strengths and weaknesses when it comes to espionage. In addition, you should be familiar with a number of external hardware devices that connect to a target computer that are specifically designed for duplicating data. Many of these products are cheap, unobtrusive, and would fit right into a James Bond movie.

Unlike most of the chapters in this book that have a "Countermeasures" section following the "Spy Tactics," this one doesn't. This is because if you do a good job of applying the defenses presented in other chapters, such as physical security, encryption, and strong passwords, you'll prevent a spy from either gaining access to a target computer or viewing the data stored on it.

With that said, let's move on and look at duplicating data from a spy's perspective.

Spy Tactics

Before we discuss storage media and high-tech gadgets, there are four data-copying guidelines you should always keep in mind before you even step foot in front of a target computer:

✓ **Use available resources.** Take advantage of storage devices that are already present to copy data.

✓ **Use compression tools.** Be sure to have compression utilities with you in case data doesn't fit on storage media.

✓ **Consider other data.** Don't just focus on the hard drive as the only source of data.

✓ **Understand what's involved in copying data.** Practice copying data ahead of time.

Use Available Resources

The Chinese strategist Sun Tzu advocated always using your enemy's resources to your own advantage, and when it comes to copying data, you should think along these same lines. At the very minimum, your target computer will have a floppy disk drive. If you're lucky, it will have a CD burner or a ZIP drive. There might even be backup software installed on the computer.

Unless you need a forensic image of the hard drive, use these resources to your advantage in copying files. You should always bring a collection of blank floppy disks, CD-Rs, CD-RWs, and perhaps a ZIP and Jaz disk with you so you can duplicate the data in case there are no devices around to "borrow."

Use Compression Tools

In addition to bringing blank storage media with you, your handy-dandy spy utility disk or CD-ROM should include some type of a compression tool (such as Gzip, WinZip, or WinRAR), in case the data on the target hard drive is too big to fit on your storage media. Just remember that compressing data adds time to the copying process, and sometimes every second may count.

All compression tools aren't created equal when it comes to speed and shrinking efficiency. See Martin Tsachev's comparison of archiving tools at martin.f2o.org/windows/archivers.

Consider Other Data

Remember that the hard drive isn't the only place where data resides. Floppy disks, CDs, or backup tapes lying on a desk, stashed in a drawer, or archived in a file cabinet all could hold useful information, and should either be copied on-site or pilfered if you don't think they will be missed. If based on the labels, you believe that storage media contain the backed-up contents of a hard drive, examine the target computer to see what type of archival software is being used, so you know what type of application to use to restore the data after you leave the scene.

Understand What's Involved in Copying Data

The longer it takes you to copy data on-site, the greater your chances are of being discovered. Just because a spy on TV can copy a couple hundred gigabytes of data onto a floppy disk in a few seconds doesn't mean you (or any other nonfictional character) can. You need to have a good understanding of the capabilities and limitations of different copying techniques and storage media.

When it comes to copying data, it's important to consider the *transfer rate*. This is the theoretical maximum amount of data that can be transferred to a device in one second; MBps is megabytes-per-second, Mbps is megabits-per-second, and Kbps is kilobytes-per-second (these three abbreviations are used throughout the rest of the chapter as different storage media are described). You may only have a limited amount of time in front of a computer, and the storage device you're using dictates how long copying a certain amount of data will take. (There are also other things

Risk: Low-Tech, High Stakes

On Saturday, December 14, 2002, someone broke into the offices of TriWest Healthcare Alliance Corp. in Phoenix, Arizona. It wasn't a typical smash-and-grab burglary. The thief first gained access to a property manager's office, stole a master card key, and then entered the TriWest facilities. There were no surveillance cameras to record the break-in, but the electronic door logs showed that the thief or thieves made two trips in and out of the TriWest office located in a Northwest Phoenix industrial park.

Whoever performed the break-in seemed to know what they were doing. They stole hard drives out of servers used to store insurance enrollment and claims information. The records contained personal data on more than 550,000 beneficiaries of the U.S. military's TRICARE managed care network, across a 16-state region. (No one is commenting on whether the stolen data was encrypted or not.)

The FBI and Defense Criminal Investigative Service are investigating the theft, TriWest ponied up a $100,000 reward for information leading to arrests and sent out mail to the affected beneficiaries warning about possible identity theft, and the Department of Defense is reviewing its data storage security procedures for civilian contractors. At this point, there are no suspects, the motive is unknown, and everyone is being tight-lipped about the investigation (the criminal and national security implications are both considerable).

Even if the theft doesn't prove to be espionage-related, it does demonstrate how vulnerable sensitive high-tech data can be to old-fashioned, low-tech physical attacks. A stealthier attack could have involved replacing the stolen hard disks with damaged or unformatted drives of the same type. The system administrator could have written the disks off to an unusual power-surge that caused multiple head crashes and simply replaced the damaged drives and restored data from backups. If done correctly, the company likely would never have suspected that its data had been compromised.

that impact the amount of time it takes to duplicate data such as hardware bus speed and the type of media the target data resides on, but you don't have much control over these factors.)

You should practice copying data ahead of time with different copying utilities and storage devices to give yourself a better understanding of the amount of time and effort it takes to duplicate data.

Storage Media to Target

Keeping the preceding guidelines in mind, now let's examine some of the commonly used and portable storage media that you can copy data with (the large, high-end, and exotic storage media are beyond the scope of this book).

Floppy Disks

Spies take for granted that they can easily slip a small 3.5-inch floppy disk filled with secrets into a shirt pocket and casually stroll out of a building undetected. This hasn't always been the case.

In 1971, IBM introduced the "memory disk;" the first floppy disk (named because it was flexible instead of rigid) was eight inches, was read-only, and could store a paltry 100K of data. The product was revolutionary because it was small and portable; you didn't need to lug card decks or magnetic tapes around to transfer data between computers. A few years later, IBM released a read/write version of the disk, which held 250K. The basic technology in these early disk drives is still present in contemporary floppy drives.

From that point, floppy disks got both smaller and bigger. The 5.25-inch disk debuted in 1976, and could store only about 100K. However, researchers soon discovered how to write to both sides of the disk and increase the density, and storage capacities jumped to 1.2MB.

In 1981, Sony introduced the 3.5-inch floppy disk and drive, which eventually replaced the 5.25-inch drive as an industry standard. The small, hard-cased, double-sided, double-density disks store 1.44MB of data, have a transfer rate of 500 Kbps, and are priced at under 20 cents each.

Most people think that floppies have gone the way of the dinosaur because of their limited storage capacity. This is true when it comes to copying large amounts of data or big files, but the floppy is still very useful for duplicating smaller amounts of data and for use in other espionage activities. Convicted spies Robert Hanssen, Aldrich Ames, and Ana Belen Montes all used floppy disks in their spying against the United States to receive instructions from their handlers and to pass stolen information on in "dead drops" (a predetermined location where information or equipment is secretly left for the spy by his handler, or by the handler for the spy, without either having physical contact with each other).

CD-R/CD-RWs

For many computer users, the CD (compact disc) has replaced the ubiquitous floppy disk as the storage medium of choice. Rewriteable CD drives (commonly known as *burners*) have rapidly become a standard feature in new computers, fueled by the popularity of downloading music from P2P (peer-to-peer) networks. Some characteristics of this storage media include the following:

- ✓ A single, standard-sized CD can store between 650MB and 870MB of data. CD-R discs can have data written to them only once, whereas CD-RWs can have data written and erased multiple times.

- ✓ CD-Rs and CD-RWs are cheap, and depending on quantity can respectively cost less than 50 cents to a dollar each.

- ✓ Transfer rates, which depend on the CD burner, are typically expressed in write speed. The bigger the number, the faster the writes (writing data to CD-R discs is quicker than writing to CD-RWs). For example, an ancient burner with a write speed of 8x (about a 1,200 Kbps transfer rate) would take about 10 minutes to duplicate a CD, whereas a common 24x (about 3,600 Kbps) write drive could do the same in a little over four minutes. 52x drives started to appear in late 2002, and are likely getting close to the top of the write speed ceiling.

Busted: Devious Disks

FBI documents state that convicted spy Robert Hanssen frequently used floppy disks to pass information back and forth to his Russian handlers. In his arrest warrant, there's an interesting and curious reference to floppy disks:

"On April 4, 1988, the KGB received an envelope from 'B' at an accommodation address in the Eastern District of Virginia. The envelope bore a return address of 'Jim Baker' in 'Alexandria' and was postmarked in Northern Virginia, on March 31, 1988. The envelope contained a note from 'B' reading: 'use 40 TRACK MODE. this letter is not a signal.'

The term 'use 40-track mode' refers to a technical process for re-formatting a computer diskette in order to conceal data by putting the data onto specific tracks on the diskette. Unless a person uses the correct codes to decrypt such a diskette, the diskette would appear to be blank."

The description the affidavit provides about "use 40-track mode" is pretty vague and probably misleading using the word "decrypt." Many of the exact details of Hanssen's spying activities have not been made public, but there are several things the 40-track reference could possibly point to showing what Hanssen was up to.

✓ By default, 5.25-inch, single-sided 320K floppy disks were formatted with 40 tracks. It's possible to format 5.25-inch, double-sided 760K and 1.2K disks that normally have 80 tracks to only have 40 tracks. Doing so could conceal data on the second side of the disk.

✓ A boot sector virus named Joshi created a 41st track, which would have been track 40, on a 5.25-inch, 320K disk to hide its code in. Hanssen could have been hiding data in an extra track. (Joshi was first discovered in 1990, though, two years after Hanssen's cryptic message.)

✓ The old Tandy TRS-80 used 35 track floppies, but hobbyists found they could also format them to a nonstandard 40 tracks. The TRS would have been old technology by 1988, but sometimes that can be advantageous in espionage if your opposition assumes that you're using some current communications method.

Until more definitive public information is released about Hanssen's computer-related tradecraft, all we can do is speculate exactly what the 40-track reference meant.

Most CD burners come with software that treats the CD-R the same as a floppy disk so you can copy or write files directly to it (for example, Roxio's popular DirectCD). If you're using a burner to copy data to a CD-R on a target machine, make sure that you specify that the CD is readable by other computers when you're done. The direct write software doesn't allow a CD that's being treated as a floppy to be accessed on another computer as a read-only CD could be. If you're using direct write software, before you remove the CD from the drive, you need to specify that the CD be written so other computers can read it (in ISSO 9660 format).

Tools of the Trade: USB and IEEE 1394

USB (Universal Serial Bus) and IEEE 1394 devices are a spy's dreams come true. When used with a modern Plug and Play operating system, all you need to do is plug a portable storage device such as a hard drive or CD burner into a computer and start copying files. Before you go out and buy one of these nifty peripherals, here's some background intelligence.

USB first appeared in 1997 as a new way to connect peripherals, but it didn't really take off until the introduction of Microsoft Windows 98 in June 1998. The original USB 1.0/1.1 standard supports only a relatively slow 12 Mbps (megabits-per-second, not to be confused with MBps, which is megabytes-per-second) transfer rate. Computers with the new USB 2.0 chipset started to be released in the summer of 2002, and all new computers will support USB 2.0 over the next several years. This version of USB is considerably faster and can transfer data at speeds of up to 480 Mbps. Speedier storage devices are appearing on the market that take advantage of USB 2.0 and are backward-compatible with 1.1, but for now most of the computers you'll encounter will support only USB 1.1 speeds.

USB's competitor is IEEE 1394 (commonly called FireWire, which is Apple's retail name for the standard, or i.Link, Sony's trademarked name). IEEE 1394 has been around since 1986, and was adopted by the IEEE (Institute of Electrical and Electronics Engineers) as a standard in 1995. Apple popularized the standard as a high-speed way to move digital video and audio data between Macintoshes and other devices. 1394 devices cruise along at up to 400 Mbps. The 1394b standard, whose products are starting to appear in the beginning of 2003, ups the ante against USB 2.0, with speeds of up to 800 Mbps.

Although Microsoft has provided IEEE 1394 support in Windows, you're far more likely to encounter USB ports on most computers you may be spying on. A good source of information about USB devices, including hard drives and CD burners, is EverythingUSB at www.everythingusb.com.

DVDs

DVDs (digital video discs or digital versatile discs) are the next generation of optical storage media. Think of a DVD as a faster CD that can hold 4.7GB of data. As prices go down (drives are falling under the $300 price point) and standards are adopted, DVDs will replace CDs as the computer storage medium of choice.

✓ At present, two groups are battling over whether DVD-R/DVD-RW or DVD+R/DVD+RW will become the predominant standard. Some manufacturers such as Sony are taking the middle ground and ensuring that their rewriteable DVD drives support both sets of standards.

✓ Data written to a DVD at 1x speed is equivalent to around 11 Mbps, which is about nine times the transfer rate of CD-ROM's 1x speed. Current drives can write up to 4x for DVD-Rs and 2x for DVD-RWs. (DVD burners can also write data to CD-Rs and CD-RWs.)

✓ Depending on the quantity, DVD-R prices range from $1.50 to $3.50 apiece, whereas DVD-RW discs are priced at $2.50 to $4.50. These prices will decrease as the media becomes widely adopted.

Currently, you're much more likely to encounter a computer with a CD burner versus a DVD burner, but you still should carry some blank DVD discs with you, just in case.

ZIP Disks

Before CD burners became inexpensive and popular, Iomega's ZIP drives (www.iomega.com) were poised to replace the floppy as the industry's next removable storage medium standard. The first ZIP drives introduced in 1994 offered 100MB of removable storage, in what looked like a fat, over-sized floppy disk. Later ZIP drive models offered up to 750MB of storage, with the Jaz drives holding up to 2GB of data.

The parallel port external versions of the ZIP drives were incredibly slow with 300- to 800-Kbps transfer rates while the internal IDE versions had quicker 1.4- to 2.4-MBps sustained rates. Although the Jaz drives and subsequent ZIP models had faster transfer rates, the expense of the media ($7 to over $10 per disk) and the advent of cheap CD burners and discs diminished the popularity of the devices. You still may encounter ZIP drives connected to older computers or in specialty business settings (the drives were very popular with graphic artists and creative departments).

Memory Storage Devices

If you don't have a lot of data to copy, your best bet might be some type of flash memory storage device. This storage medium is extremely stealthy due to its thin matchbook or even smaller size and the fact that an external power source isn't required because flash memory is nonvolatile.

Just plug a flash memory card with an adaptor into a laptop's PC Card slot (some laptops even have slots that directly accommodate certain types of memory cards) or plug the memory device into a card reader connected to a desktop PC and start copying files.

The digital camera, handheld computer, and audio player industries haven't standardized on a single type of flash memory so there are a number to choose from, including the following:

✓ **CompactFlash (CF).** The first flash memory device, introduced by SanDisk in 1994 (and still the most popular).

✓ **MemoryStick.** Sony's proprietary memory device, introduced in 1998.

✓ **Multimedia Memory Card (MMC).** A small memory card, about the size of a postage stamp.

✓ **Secure Digital.** A memory card with a write-protection tab to prevent you from accidentally erasing the contents.

✓ **SmartMedia.** Memory devices that are smaller and lighter than CF units.

CompactFlash memory cards are well-suited for spying because they can store considerably more data (in March 2003, SanDisk announced a 4GB CF card that starts shipping in the summer of 2003 with a $999 retail price) than the other devices and are very durable. SanDisk's new high-speed Ultra CF cards support up to a 2.8-MBps transfer rate, about twice as fast as a standard CF card. Current prices for 128K of memory are in the $50 to $60 price range (and falling).

In case you discover a flash memory card during a black bag job and want to copy the contents onto a hard drive, consider Imation's (www.imation.com) FlashGo! Card reader and writer. The portable USB device supports CompactFlash (Type I and II), SmartMedia, Multimedia Card, Secure Digital, and Memory Stick formats, and is priced around $55. First, plug the memory card into the small, handheld card reader; then plug the card reader into a USB port and start copying files.

Another new flash memory-based storage product that looks like it came out of a James Bond movie is the USB Flash Drive (see Figure 7-1). This is a small memory device, a bit bigger than the size of your thumb, which plugs into a USB port. With Windows ME, 2000, and XP, just connect it and start duplicating files (be sure to have your driver disk for older versions of Windows).

Flash drives come in bright colors with some models that look like a marking pen and others designed to function as a key chain. Due to their unobtrusive appearance and the fact they are fairly new on the market, the devices might pass unnoticed if you're caught spying. (If you're creative and good with small tools, you can take the flash drive out of the housing and put it into an even less-conspicuous object such as a large felt tip marker to really be sneaky.)

Storage size currently ranges from 8MB to 512MB, with prices depending on the capacity (between $40 and $260). Transfer rate is around 1 MBps, with some of the newer USB 2.0 models achieving 4.5-MBps write speeds.

For a list of different types of flash memory drives, see www.everythingusb.com/hardware/Storage/USB_Flash_Drives.htm.

Figure 7-1: Lexar's JumpDrive 2.0 Pro (www.lexarmedia.com),
256MB of sneaky storage with a transfer rate of 4.8 MBps.
Just plug it into a USB port and start copying files.

Tools of the Trade: Invasion of the iPod People

In February of 2002, *Wired News* had an article about an incident at a Dallas, Texas CompUSA. A teenager who was listening to an Apple iPod (for older generations, picture a shrunk-down Sony Walkman that plays MP3 music files "ripped" from a CD or downloaded from the Internet) hooked up the device to one of the store's Macs. A customer watched the kid as he copied Microsoft's new Office for OS X onto the iPod (www.apple.com/ipod/). With the FireWire connection, he was able to copy the 200MB product to his iPod in less than a minute.

Although this was clearly a blatant case of software piracy combined with shoplifting, it does point out the iPod (which comes in 5GB, 10GB, and 20GB versions and is advertised as being able to download an entire CD in 15 seconds) can also be used for performing black bag jobs on Macs or PCs with FireWire cards.

Similar products are available that work with PCs, such as Creative Labs Nomad Jukebox Zen (www.nomadworld.com/products/Jukebox_Zen/). These new Windows-compatible MP3 players that plug into a USB port hold considerable espionage promise; the Zen even has a microphone option for digitally recording audio eavesdropping.

MP3 players that plug into USB ports and support copying files to the player may be the perfect plausible deniability tool for a spy. "Who me? I was just cleaning up the office while listening to my tunes."

Hard Drives

The first hard drive was introduced in 1957 as part of an IBM mainframe (RAMAC 350). It had 50 24-inch disks that could store a whopping 5MB of data. It cost $35,000 a year to lease. Now fast-forward to 2003, when hard drives over 100GB are common and prices have dropped below the dollar-per-gigabyte threshold.

Hard drive duplication is extremely common in computer forensic work and at times is useful for on-site spying. Open up the computer case and chain a slave hard drive to the main internal drive. Then boot the computer with a duplication software disk and copy the entire contents of the main drive to the slave drive; you don't even need to worry about bypassing the Windows logon. After you're done, put everything back together and take the slave disk to a safe location for analysis.

Forensic hard drive duplication software is discussed in Chapter 5.

Tools of the Trade: Hardware Disk Duplicators

One of the FBI's (and other government law enforcement and intelligence agencies') favorite hard drive duplication tools is Logicube's SF-5000 (see Figure 7-2). Just connect the source hard drive and a blank destination drive to the unit, and it will faithfully image the contents of the source drive to the destination drive. The FBI has used these devices hundreds of times during the past several years and likes them because of their speed, portability, and ease of use. (Although the units work great for IDE drives, they slow down considerably when dealing with SCSI drives.) The base price of the handheld duplicator is $1,199 (the complete kit is $2,249), and you can get more information from www.logicube.com.

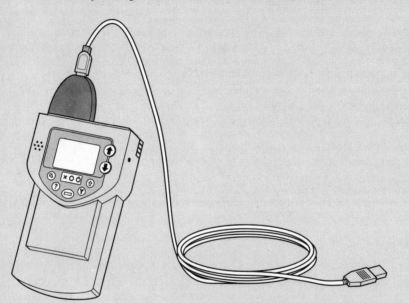

Figure 7-2: Logicube SF-5000 handheld hard drive duplicator with USB attachment; a favorite of the FBI and other government agencies.

Other hardware disk duplicators that are popular with law enforcement (and can certainly work for less-legal activities) include the following:

✓ **Corporate Systems Portable Pro Drive.** Although the Logicube is faster at duplicating IDE drives, the Corporate Systems unit supports copying IDE, SCSI, SCA, and 2.5" laptop drives. Not a small handheld duplicator, it comes in an oversized briefcase, but is regarded by many in the computer forensics business as an outstanding value at $995. For more information, see www.corpsys.com.

> ✓ **Intelligent Computer Solutions Image Masster Solo-2.** The Image Masster
> Solo-2 is another handheld duplicator that's very similar to the Logicube unit.
> Field reports suggest that Solo-2 does well in handling bad sectors, an issue
> that can create problems for some duplicators. The base price of the unit is
> $1,495. To learn more about it, go to www.ics-iq.com.
>
> Although these devices are well-suited for field duplication, you can also use a laptop and
> software such as the Linux dd command or Norton Ghost to achieve the same results.

The transfer rate of a conventional internal hard drive, especially the faster 7,200-RPM models with data caching, can reach speeds of up to 100 MBps. However, you also need to factor in the time opening up the target computer's case, installing the hard drive, performing the actual copy, removing the hard drive, and cleaning up. If you're pressed for time during a quick black bag job, using an internal drive for copying might not be an option. For covertly copying data, portable external drives such as USB hard drives and Microdrives are likely a better alternative.

USB HARD DRIVES

Plug-and-play USB (and IEEE 1394) hard drives are an excellent tool for copying data. Instead of taking a target computer apart and temporarily installing an internal drive to copy data, just plug the external hard drive into the USB port and start duplicating files (transfer rates are slower than an internal drive because the device is constrained to the maximum USB throughput speed). There are two types of drives available:

  ✓ **Standard.** Although these drives are portable enough to be used for spying, they definitely won't fit in your pocket (especially with an AC adapter and power cord). The hard
  drives store from 20GB to 200GB of data and are priced between $100 and $250.

  ✓ **Compact.** These small drives easily fit into a shirt pocket and can store between 5GB and
  60GB of data (see Figure 7-3). Priced between $175 and $400, they draw their power
  from the USB port, so you don't need an external power source.

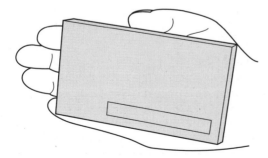

Figure 7-3: The Pockey DataStor (www.pocketec.net) fits in your pocket and
only weighs 5.5 ounces; the perfect covert tool for copying large amounts of data.

MICRODRIVES

If your target is a laptop or a desktop computer with a PC Card reader, consider using a Microdrive. The Microdrive is a PC Card with a built-in one-inch hard drive that can store 340MB, 500MB, 1GB, or 4GB of data (depending on the model). The drive works in any CompactFlash CF+ Type II- or PC Card-compliant slot and has a transfer rate of approximately 40 to 60 Mbps. A 1GB drive is priced at $350. Hitachi bought IBM's hard drive business at the end of 2002 and now manufacturers and markets the Microdrives. For more information, go to `www.hgst.com/products/microdrive/index.html`.

Tape Backup Systems

Tape systems are popular in corporate settings for backing up data, and although there are portable models available, they're not very well-suited for spying purposes (other than for backing up evidence in a forensics lab). Lower-end tape systems are slow when compared to other storage devices and require frequent tape changes. If you encounter a tape backup system on a target computer, use some other storage media to copy files. If you find backup tapes and decide to take them, be sure to note what types of backup hardware and software are being used so you can attempt to restore the data at some other location.

Alternate Methods of Copying Data

Don't get locked in to thinking that using floppies, CDs, hard drives, and memory devices are the only ways to copy data. A good spy always has the right tool for the job, and there are several alternative methods of copying data that a spy may consider using.

Transferring Data Over a Network

If the target computer is connected to a network (such as the Internet), you can send the data to another computer connected to the network instead of transferring data to a local storage device. Just remember the following:

- ✓ The data transfer rate completely depends on the speed of the network connection. A slower connection can leave you exposed as you wait for the data to upload.

- ✓ Network connections are likely to be logged (and may be monitored), and you'll possibly leave evidence of the intrusion. At the very least, be sure that the destination you're sending the data to isn't an IP address that can be tracked back to you.

If the circumstances are right for copying data over a network, there are three options:

- ✓ **FTP, Telnet, and SSH.** If you have access to an account that supports FTP, Telnet, or SSH, you can always connect to the account and then copy the local files to the remote machine. (You should have appropriate client applications with you on your spy utility disk.)

- ✓ **E-mail.** If you have access to the e-mail client on the target computer, you can simply send attachments to a disposable e-mail account you set up. This works with smaller amounts of data but may exceed mailbox size limits if you try to send large attachments.

✓ **NetCat.** NetCat is a Swiss Army knife, command-line tool that every spy should have. Developed by Hobbit and first released back in 1995, you can port scan, copy files, remotely execute commands, and perform all sorts of other useful networking activities. To copy files to another computer, make sure that Netcat is running on the destination, run Netcat on the source computer, specify the IP address and port number of the destination, and you're ready to start copying files. Versions of the free popular utility are available for Unix and Windows at `www.atstake.com/research/tools/network_util-ities/`. (Cryptcat, which is a modified version of Netcat that encrypts the data with the Twofish algorithm, is available from `www.farm9.org/Cryptcat/GetCryptcat.php`.)

Digital Cameras

Every computer spy should have a camera in his or her black bag of tools. Cameras are essential for snapping photographs of sensitive information that doesn't happen to be in a digital format that can be easily copied. They're also indispensable during black bag jobs to document a room, so you can make sure everything is put back the way you found it.

The quintessential spy camera is the Minox subminiature (for more information, go to `www.minox-web.de`). The tiny, 56-gram camera that shoots proprietary 8×11mm film has been around since the 1930s and still is popular with many intelligence agencies all over the world.

Although the Minox is a classic, digital cameras are considerably more versatile and in many cases better suited for spying these days. Although you can use a conventional, full-sized model, there are an increasing number of cameras that trade off image quality and features for size. Cameras such as the SiPix StyleCam Snap (`www.sipixdigital.com`; see Figure 7-4) and the Creative Labs Cardcam (`www.americas.creative.com`) can fit in the palm of your hand, are remarkably concealable, and are cheap (around $40 and $80, respectively). Although they don't have LCD display screens, flashes, zoom, or take resolution photos you'd expect in a more expensive camera, they do work well for many spying applications.

Figure 7-4: The SiPix StyleCam Snap, an inexpensive, ultra-concealable digital camera that weighs less than two ounces.

Summary

There are many options for copying data from target computers, and some are faster and stealthier than others. When duplicating data, your first consideration is how much time you'll have to copy whatever information you're interested in. This timeframe dictates what type of storage media you'll be able to use and how much data you'll be able to effectively copy. Before you duplicate any data, whether it's imaging a hard drive in a forensics lab or covertly copying a competitor's strategic business plan, be sure to practice with the storage device and media you plan to use. Practice sessions will make the process familiar (and identify any potential hitches) and give you an idea about how long copying the data will take.

On the other hand, physical security is the key to defending against illicit data copying. Obviously, the more difficult you can make it for the spy to gain access to a computer, the better your chances are for protecting sensitive information. As a countermeasure, time is on your side. Time directly correlates to the amount of data that can be copied, so if you can limit the amount of time a spy spends at a computer, you reduce the amount of data he can potentially copy. Alarm systems, monitored video surveillance cameras, and guards who regularly patrol a building are some of the defenses that can restrict a spy's activities. Treating time as a countermeasure works well when there's a large amount of data to copy, but often one or a few sensitive documents can be copied in a matter of seconds. This is where encryption plays a critical role in your layer of defenses. Even if a spy manages to copy data, if strong encryption was used to protect it (and you've followed a good password policy), there's a good chance that the spy won't be able to compromise your critical information.

Chapter 8

Snooping with Keyloggers

"I'm never to write on typewriter, my friend."
— The Posies, "Farewell Typewriter," *Success*

An Introduction to Keyloggers

A keylogger is software or hardware that records the keys you press on a computer keyboard. The collection of key-presses could reveal a password, evidence of an illicit affair, or other secret information you'd rather keep from other people. Spying on keys certainly isn't new. Monitoring keyboards in one form or another has probably been going on because E. Remington & Sons sold the first typewriter back in 1874. Some examples of keyboard espionage include the following:

✓ Because typewriters use ribbons, whatever letters are typed appear on the ribbon. Early–20th century law enforcement and intelligence agencies commonly fished discarded ribbons out of the trash. Even in the 1990s, the FBI used ribbons as key pieces of evidence to convict Russian double-agent Aldrich Ames.

✓ The cover of former CIA agent Phillip Agee's book, *Inside the Company: CIA Diary*, has a photo of a bugged portable Royal typewriter. During the 1970s, a supposed friend who was affiliated with the agency loaned Agee the typewriter so the CIA could monitor Agee while he was writing his tell-all book.

✓ The popularity of electric typewriters gave spies a built-in power source to connect monitoring devices. Even though electric typewriters had been around since 1902 with the Blickensderfer, they didn't reach commercial popularity until the 1920s. The modern IBM Selectric, which debuted in 1960, was a popular eavesdropping target because it was so common. A spy could easily swap a normal model for a bugged model, and a secretary wouldn't know the difference. (Typewriters can be eavesdropped on with a microphone to monitor the acoustics of key strikes or with electronics that record which key is pressed. A small transmitter sends the information to a nearby radio receiver, where the key-presses are recorded and then played back later for analysis.)

✓ In 1984, U.S. security officials discovered 13 bugged IBM typewriters in Russia. The typewriters were being used in secure areas of the United States embassy in Moscow as well as the Leningrad consulate. The surveillance devices had been transmitting information to the Russians for years. (Typewriters can be eavesdropped on with a microphone to monitor the acoustics of key strikes or with electronics that record which key is pressed. A small transmitter sends the information to a nearby radio receiver, where the key-presses are recorded and then played back later for analysis.)

Now let's fast-forward to the present. Although some of the same techniques used for bugging typewriters can be used with computer keyboards, it's considerably easier to use specialized software and hardware. In fact, over the past few years, there has been a literal explosion of both free and commercial keyloggers available on the Internet. (Many commercial keylogger vendors have affiliate programs with a number of unique Web sites marketing their products.)

Bosses are using keyloggers to spy on employees, significant others are using them to eavesdrop on their partners, parents are using them to monitor their children's activities, and even the FBI is using them to go after mobsters. If a spy has physical access to a computer, keyloggers are often a favorite tool of choice.

Spy Tactics

Are you ready to pretend you're a spy again? Good; keyloggers can be one of the most effective tools in your bag of tricks.

There are two ways to deploy a keylogger:

- ✓ **Locally.** You have access to the target computer so you install the monitoring software or hardware. You'll need to make sure that you have enough time alone with the computer. A software keylogger takes up to five minutes to install, whereas a hardware keylogger takes up to a minute.

- ✓ **Remotely.** If you don't have physical access to the computer, you send the target an e-mail with a Trojan horse attachment that contains a keylogger. There are a number of Trojan horse applications that contain keyloggers, as well as some dedicated keyloggers designed specifically for this type of an attack.

For more on Trojans and other remote control applications, turn to Chapter 9.

Once you have the keylogger in place, it monitors the target computer and records data. Depending on which keylogger you use, you either need to physically access the target computer to retrieve the collected data, or if you're using a sophisticated keylogger, you can have it e-mail the surveillance data to you. There are also certain keyloggers that open up a port on a target computer, so you can access the machine directly if you know its IP address. If you use a keylogger with an Internet-enabled way of getting the collected keystrokes, be sure to cover your tracks. It's not smart to have a key-press log file sent to your personal e-mail account or have your IP address revealed when you remotely access the target computer to retrieve the collected keystrokes.

Exploiting the Vulnerabilities

Any computer that uses a keyboard as an input device is vulnerable to a keylogger attack. Software keyloggers have been developed for just about any operating system you can think of. As long as people use keyboards to type text, you can use a keylogger to spy on them. (And before you ask about voice-recognition software, just use a conventional audio bug to record the spoken information. Audio eavesdropping devices are briefly discussed in Chapter 12.)

Let's examine how software and hardware keyloggers work and discuss some of their general features.

HOW SOFTWARE KEYLOGGERS WORK

Software keyloggers are fairly simple in nature—a programmer writes code to intercept each key as it's pressed and then writes the value of the key to a log file. There are three approaches to creating a software keylogger:

✓ **Low-level keyloggers.** These keyloggers are written in assembly language. They work by using a hook (an interface that allows a programmer to insert custom code) to the keyboard device interrupt (hardware signal that conveys key status) and redirecting the output to some custom code. Each key is logged and then the code calls the original handler to process the key as normal.

✓ **Operating system API keyloggers.** The advent of Windows made developing keyloggers much easier. Instead of requiring an in-depth knowledge of assembly programming and system internals, a spy can write a keylogger in just about any high-level programming language. (There is a large amount of Visual Basic keylogger source code available on the Internet; in fact, one popular commercial keylogger is written in VB.) A program that runs in the background can frequently check the key states for whether keys have been pressed by using the GetAsyncKeyState and GetKeyState Windows API calls. Once a key is pressed, the returned value is logged. A keylogger can also use the SetWindowsHookEx Windows API to trap system messages and process keyboard events with special handlers.

✓ **Device driver keyloggers.** These keyloggers are the mostly stealthy because they operate at the lowest level of the Windows operating system. For computers running Windows 9x/ME, these keyloggers are written as virtual device drivers (.vxds). For Windows 2000/XP computers, the keyloggers are written as kernel-mode Windows Driver Model (WDM) drivers. There aren't as many device driver keyloggers around due to the relative complexities of writing a device driver compared to hooking an API call.

Most spies don't want their target knowing that they're being eavesdropped on with a keylogger, and all keyloggers aren't created equal when it comes to being stealthy. A good keylogger employs a number of different techniques to prevent a user from discovering it. Some common crafty ways of avoiding detection include:

✓ **Hiding from the Task Manager.** In Windows 9x and ME, there's a kernel32.dll function called RegisterServiceProcess. As the name suggests, this function registers a process as a service, which makes the process exempt from automatic shutdown at logoff and doesn't display the process in the Task Manager. This tactic is commonly used by stealthy keyloggers and works against Windows 9x/ME (because of different architecture, these hidden processes show up under Windows NT/2000/XP). However, keyloggers that are installed as device drivers avoid detection by the Task Manager and other process viewers.

✓ **Using a deceptive process name.** Obviously having the name EvilKeylogger show up as a process kind of gives things away. Stealthy keyloggers have an inconspicuous filename and process name to avoid suspicion.

✓ **Using obscure file and Registry names.** Files that are part of the keylogger installation often have obscure filenames and Registry names designed to lull an unsuspecting user to think the files are part of the operating system. Some keyloggers even rename files after they have run to further avoid detection.

✓ **Concealing log files.** Keystroke log files are often encrypted to prevent a user from discovering the contents. In addition to encrypting the log, deceptive file extensions may be used, such as disguising a text log file with an .ocx extension, which would lead a casual observer to think it was an OLE custom control. Some keyloggers also change the log file dates to prevent users from searching for newly created or modified files.

How stealthy a keylogger should be depends on your target. With a sophisticated, suspicious user, you select as covert a keylogger as possible. For a semi-computer-literate family member, a very simple keylogger may be all that you need. Generally, commercial keyloggers tend to be sneakier than the many free versions available on the Internet.

THE AVAILABILITY OF KEYLOGGERS

Although keyloggers are designed to run covertly on a computer, their availability certainly isn't a secret. These eavesdropping tools have received extensive coverage in both the popular and computer media, and the commercial versions are heavily marketed. Keyloggers are just a click and a download away. A Google search for "keylogger" returned over 210,000 pages, including four sponsored links to commercial products. At the end of 2002, some spy Web sites listed more than 250 commercial and freeware keyloggers. Advertising for SpyCop, a commercial keylogger-detector, claims that the product can detect more than 300 different keyloggers. Just as with viruses, newer and more keyloggers appear on a regular basis, mostly because of the public availability of source code and the discovery of new stealth techniques to better hide the eavesdropping tools from their victims.

BEYOND JUST KEYS — ADVANCED LOGGERS

Early keyloggers did exactly what their name implied: they logged keystrokes. However, current keyloggers, especially the commercial varieties, have gotten much more sophisticated and now perform a number of other surveillance functions in addition to simply logging keystrokes.

Tactics: Thinking Beyond Passwords

When you use a keylogger, don't focus entirely on passwords, trade secrets, or evidence of some immoral activity. Information gleaned from keyloggers can also be put to work in conjunction with social-engineering attacks to expose even more information. Let's say you intercept the contents of an e-mail message from Vice President Frank Jordan to engineer Carla Knight. It discusses a new possible feature for the soon-to-be released XP-9000 vacuum cleaner. Wow, what's that? You've got the engineer's name and enough product details to call her up, say that you're working with Frank Jordan, and you've got some questions on the XP-9000.

Some of these features include the following:

- ✓ **Capturing screen contents.** Some programs use security techniques, such as virtual, on-screen keyboards that are designed to defeat keyloggers (an image of a keyboard appears on the screen and you click the keys with a mouse to enter text avoiding using the physical keyboard). These countermeasures can be thwarted by a keylogger that takes periodic screenshots during certain program activity.

- ✓ **Saving clipboard contents.** Any time text is put into the clipboard, it is recorded. Opening a text file with accounts and passwords, copying the text, and then pasting it into the entry field can defeat a simple keylogger because no keys are ever pressed. However, if the clipboard is being monitored, the information is logged.

- ✓ **Logging window text contents.** You may want to eavesdrop on more than just what someone is typing; an example would be the other side of a conversation during an instant messaging session. This feature captures all the text as it appears in a window.

- ✓ **Displaying Web cam output.** If a computer has a Web cam attached to, all video that is received from the Web cam is intercepted and saved. Someone a thousand miles away can be watching you or whatever your Web cam is pointed at without you even knowing it.

- ✓ **Logging file activity.** Any time a file is moved, renamed, copied, or deleted, the keylogger lists the activity. This feature is useful for gathering evidence.

- ✓ **Listing Web sites visited.** Instead of examining thousands of collected keystrokes, some products provide you with a convenient list of all the Web sites that a user has visited.

- ✓ **Generating reports.** Many commercial keyloggers save all collected evidence into an easy-to-read format that can be imported into a spreadsheet or database.

- ✓ **Accessing information remotely.** Some keyloggers can e-mail collected information to a spy-specified e-mail address, whereas others can even access a bugged computer over a LAN or the Internet.

Busted: Nicodermo Scarfo, Jr.

In January 1999, FBI agents secretly broke into the New Jersey business office of Nicodermo Scarfo, Jr., son of jailed Philadelphia mobster "Little Nicky" Scarfo. Armed with a search warrant to copy the contents of a computer, the feds were stymied when they later learned one of the files, named Factors, was protected with the popular encryption utility PGP (Pretty Good Privacy).

A U.S. magistrate then granted a second warrant for the FBI to covertly install a keylogger on the computer to snag the password Scarfo was using to encrypt what was suspected to be a file containing bookmaking and loan sharking information. FBI agents broke into Scarfo's business again in May 1999 and installed some type of a keylogger on his computer. The keylogger was in place for 14 days and successfully recorded a PGP passphrase. The problem was that the passphrase didn't decrypt the original file, but agents found a newer version of the file encrypted with the snagged passphrase and got the evidence they were looking for. Scarfo, Jr. was prosecuted, but the story doesn't stop there.

Scarfo's defense attorneys wanted details about the keylogger. The FBI didn't want to reveal any information about it, saying it was a matter of national security. Suddenly the case received national attention regarding the issue of personal computer privacy rights versus law enforcement's right to use secret computer spying technology. The judge in the case agreed with the government that the technology was too sensitive to be publicly disclosed, and Scarfo pleaded guilty to the charges in the spring of 2002.

The FBI did release some limited information about the keylogger in an affidavit, referring to it as KLS, or Key Logger System.

- ✓ KLS was devised and owned by the FBI and consisted of multiple components (which could be software, hardware, firmware, or a combination of all three).

- ✓ KLS didn't record keystrokes when the modem was being used (Scarfo had an America Online account). If the modem was being used and he was online, it would have classified the computer as an electronic communication device, which would have required an additional wiretap court order.

- ✓ The FBI appears to have gotten around this by examining the windows of running processes and logging keystrokes in programs that didn't interact with the modem. It seems likely that software running in the background looked for the presence of a PGP window and then started recording keystrokes.

- ✓ KLS required physical access to the computer to recover the keystrokes, and the FBI made five surreptitious entries to Scarfo's business. Four out of the five times, the computer was described as "inoperative or not present." (This is a curious statement that leads one to wonder whether the FBI was bugging a laptop. Scarfo had a laptop with him on Halloween night in 1989 when he survived an assassination attempt in a restaurant. However, in recorded FBI phone conversations at the start of the investigation, Scarfo bragged to an associate, "I got a monster. I got a f***ing DVD in there . . . 128 megs of ram, a Pentium III, 450 . . . a 19-inch monitor and Digital Surround Sound. The whole f***ing nine yards.")

There's been lots of speculation as to what KLS was, but no substantive information has leaked out to the public at this time.

In case it ever comes up in the spy version of Trivial Pursuit, Scarfo's PGP password was "nds09813-050," his father's Federal prison identification number.

When it comes to selecting an advanced keylogger, first determine which activities you want to monitor. Don't be tempted by marketing hype if all you need is a keylogger that just captures keystrokes. In many cases, you don't need all of the features a logger may offer, and it's better to use a tool that isn't bloated with unneeded add-ons.

HARDWARE KEYLOGGERS AND HOW THEY WORK

In addition to keyloggers that run in software, there are also hardware keyloggers. These devices consist of electronic circuitry that records keystrokes as they are sent from the keyboard to the computer's keyboard controller (two such keyloggers are shown in Figure 8-1). Just plug the device in and walk away. All of the capturing is done with the hardware, and no software is required (this usually will give a keylogger away because you can actually see the keylogger plugged into the keyboard port of your computer).

There are two types of commercial hardware keyloggers:

✓ **Inline.** Inline keyloggers plug into a computer's keyboard port. The keyboard cable then plugs into the keylogger. The keylogger looks like a connector plug or a cable with what appears to a balun type electronics filter (see Figure 8-1 for an example).

✓ **Keyboard.** Keyboard keyloggers have the keylogging circuitry built inside the keyboard. Unless you open up the keyboard (and know what you're looking for), these keyloggers are very difficult to detect.

Hardware keyloggers have built-in memory and they store keystrokes as they are entered. As the memory fills up, the oldest data is overwritten with the most recent keystrokes.

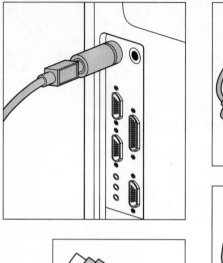
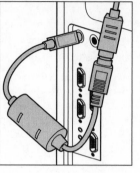
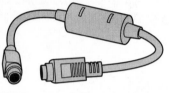
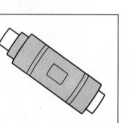

Figure 8-1: KeyKatcher and KeyGhost hardware keyloggers. If you see devices like these connected to the keyboard port of your computer, you're being spied on.

To manage the keylogger, because the circuitry is constantly monitoring keystrokes, whenever a user-defined password is entered in the text entry window of a word processor, the logger sends output back to the word processor that displays a text-based menu. By selecting menu options, you can view the recorded keys, change the password, and perform other administrative functions (see Figure 8-2).

You don't need to physically have access to the computer on which the keylogger was installed to view the captured keystrokes. Simply unplug the device from the target computer and attach it to another computer at your safe, secret spy lair to examine the collected keystrokes.

THE PROS AND CONS OF HARDWARE KEYLOGGERS

There are advantages and disadvantages of using hardware and software keyloggers. You should be aware of some of the general strengths and weaknesses of each before you decide which to use.

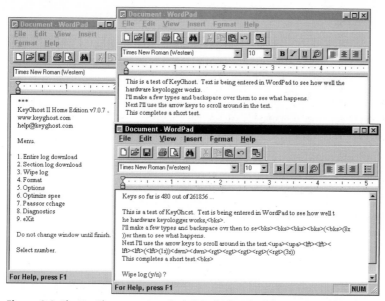

Figure 8-2: The KeyGhost menu on the left is displayed when you type the keylogger's password in a text editor. The window at the top shows text entered in WordPad. The window at the bottom shows what KeyGhost recorded, including backspaces and arrow key movements.

HARDWARE KEYLOGGER ADVANTAGES   Hardware keylogging devices have a number of advantages over their software cousins, including:

✓ These devices aren't detectable by software. Standard techniques and tools for discovering software keyloggers don't work because there are no files to install, no processes being run at the operating-system level, or any telltale signs of log files.

✓ Hardware loggers are extremely quick and easy to install. Just plug the keylogger into the computer keyboard port; then plug the keyboard cable into the keylogger, and the logger is ready to run. The computer doesn't even need to be powered-on to install the keylogger, which is very convenient if a smart user has protected the PC with a hard-to-guess BIOS or login password.

✓ Hardware keyloggers are operating-system-independent when running on Intel platform computers. This independence means that a device will work with DOS, Windows 95, Linux, Windows XP, or any other operating system that runs on a PC. These devices even log keys that are entered during the BIOS startup.

✓ Hardware loggers don't require separate power because the current coming from the keyboard port powers them.

HARDWARE KEYLOGGER DISADVANTAGES   Although hardware keyloggers seem like the perfect keyboard eavesdropping device, they do have some limitations.

✓ You need to have physical access to the computer. With some software keyloggers, remote attacks that offer less risk of detection are possible.

✓ Hardware keyloggers cost two to six times more than comparable software keyloggers. The devices are still relatively inexpensive though, with the most costly commercial devices priced under $300.

✓ The devices capture only keystrokes, unlike some sophisticated software keyloggers that capture screen displays as well as mouse movement, clicks, and other information.

✓ Unless they're installed in a keyboard, hardware keyloggers often aren't as stealthy as their software cousins. A savvy computer user may wonder what the extra connector is that's hanging off the keyboard port. Although the keyloggers are designed to look like a common connector or balun-type inline filter, they will instantly raise suspicions if a user knows what he is looking for.

✓ The devices don't have a way to automatically send the collected keystrokes to another computer over a network. To do this, you need to write a custom program to interact with the keylogger to covertly download the information and then send it elsewhere.

✓ Off-the-shelf commercial hardware keyloggers typically won't work with laptops. This is a big limitation if you're spying on traveling business executives.

✓ Currently none of the hardware keylogging products work with USB keyboards. The devices work only with PS/2 and older style AT keyboards. It's likely that the government and well-funded spies have access to custom USB keyloggers, but they're not available to the general public. Over the next few years, however, expect commercial USB versions of hardware keyloggers to reach the marketplace.

Keylogger Tools

Now that you have a basic understanding of keyloggers, let's review some examples of the software and hardware products you can use to spy on people. Keyloggers are inexpensive and a cheap investment for anyone interested in computer spying. You'll likely want to acquire several different types that will meet specific needs.

There's a lengthy list of more commercial and freeware/shareware keyloggers at this book's Web site: www.wiley.com/compbooks/mcnamara.

SOFTWARE KEYLOGGERS

There are so many keylogging programs floating around the Internet that it would take an entire book just to describe all of them (and that would be a pretty boring book for all but the most dedicated spies). This section discusses some of the more popular and well-known software keyloggers. The larger keylogger vendors typically offer a variety of eavesdropping products, ranging from those with limited features suitable for home use, to professional versions with advanced features such as remote data sending. Most of the commercial keyloggers have trial versions of their products so you can download and evaluate them to see whether they meet your needs (including applying some of the countermeasures mentioned later in the chapter to see how difficult it is for your target to detect your spying attempts).

Spector Professional Edition   Spector Professional Edition is SpectorSoft's top-of-the-line keylogger (interestingly, some of the code used in the company's keyloggers is based on the Netbus Trojan horse). It logs keys as well as e-mail, chat sessions, instant messages, and screens. SpectorSoft also makes a product called eBlaster that in addition to logging keystrokes, also covertly sends e-mail reports on what your target is doing as frequently as every 30 minutes. Some users have reported that encrypted data is sent back to SpectorSoft when their keyloggers are in use. SpectorSoft says this is for their e-mail alert system, but a paranoid spy might have some concerns with any data being sent to a third party. Both Spector Professional Edition and eBlaster are priced at $99 and are available from www.spectorsoft.com.

Invisible KeyLogger Stealth   As its name suggests, Invisible KeyLogger Stealth (IKS) is one of the more stealthy commercial keyloggers. IKS is a device driver keylogger, with different versions available for Windows 9x/ME, NT, and 2000/XP. Unlike some of the other commercial keyloggers that incorporate a "kitchen-sink" approach to including monitoring features, IKS just collects keystrokes. Separate utilities are available for viewing the log file and covertly sending the recorded data via e-mail. IKS is one of the few keyloggers that can capture keystrokes in the Windows 2000/XP Ctrl+Alt+Del login dialog box. The manufacturer even makes a "custom compile" version of the software available designed to fool keylogger detectors that perform a search for a specific file size or binary string to identify IKS. The Windows 2000/XP version of IKS is priced at $99 and can be ordered from www.amecisco.com.

Here are some sources for independent, in-depth reviews of keyloggers:

✓ In July 2001, the National Consortium for Justice Information and Statistics (www.search.org) published a review of commercial keyloggers designed to help probation officers select software to monitor the computer activity of those under their supervision for violations of their probation. The PDF version of this document used to be located on the organization's Web site, but doesn't seem to be available any more (fill in your own conspiracy theory). You can get a cached HTML version, though, by doing a Google search for: "Desktop Monitoring and Surveillance Software."

✓ *PC Magazine* did a review on commercial keyloggers in July 2002, and the results can be found online at www.pcmag.com/article2/0,4149,272723,00.asp.

WINWHATWHERE INVESTIGATOR   Investigator, which started out as a product called Win WhatWhere way back in 1993, was designed more as a project management tool for tracking time and software use. By 1998, the product was repositioned to take advantage of the growing interest in computer monitoring. Investigator, which is a full-featured monitor, can log keystrokes, screens, Web cams, and running applications. One particularly handy feature is that the program can automatically remove itself from the target computer after a set period of time. The main downside to Investigator is that it is quite large (written in Visual Basic), and unless you can convince a user to open a 3MB e-mail attachment, it really isn't suitable for remote deployment. Investigator is available from www.winwhatwhere.com and costs $100.

HARDWARE KEYLOGGERS

Unlike the hundreds of software keyloggers that are available through the Internet, there are only a few companies making commercial hardware keyloggers. Hardware products include the following:

Busted: From Russia with Love

During the FBI Invita sting operation (discussed in Chapter 1), which ended in the arrest of two Russian crackers, the government used the commercial keylogger WinWhatWhere Investigator to gather evidence. Although the affidavit filed by Special Agent Michael Schuler was originally requested to remain sealed, its contents eventually appeared on the Internet. It gives an interesting glimpse into the operation.

The FBI installed WinWhatWhere on two computers. Gorshkov, one of the suspects, used a bugged computer (an IBM Thinkpad) to telnet to the freebsd.tech.net.ru machine. He didn't know that his account ("kvakin") and password ("cfvlevfq") were recorded by the keylogger. After Gorshkov was arrested, Schuler unsuccessfully tried several times to telnet to the freebsd machine (it seems he was using the name instead of the IP address). He then went to the www.samspade.org site and used whois to determine that the freebsd machine was part of a network connected to tech.net.ru. Using telnet, Schuler successfully logged on to the tech.net.ru computer. He then used CuteFTP in an attempt to download the contents of the computer.

Schuler brought in a non–law enforcement security expert to assist with downloading the files. (From the affidavit, it sounds as if Schuler was over his head in dealing with Unix machines.) The security expert checked the amount of disk space used on each of the machines and then compressed the contents using tar and FTP-ed the archives back to the Seattle FBI office.

Note to prospective spies: Never trust someone else's computer or network before you demonstrate your skills for hire or you might just get duped like the Russians did thinking they were interviewing for high paying security jobs.

KEYGHOST   Interface Security, a New Zealand company, is one of the pioneers and innovators in the hardware keylogger business. Their KeyGhost product looks like a cable with an inline balun filter. The keyboard cable plugs into one end of the logger cable, and the other end plugs into the PC's keyboard port. Once you plug KeyGhost in, it starts capturing keystrokes. Typing in a user-specified password in a word processor configures the hardware. Because KeyGhost is monitoring all the keystrokes pressed, when it encounters the correct password, it sends a series of keystrokes back to the word processor that displays the command menu. Menu options include download and delete the current log, change the password, and other configuration actions.

A PC's keyboard interface isn't meant for high-speed communication, and downloading the contents of a hardware keylogger can be a slow process (at around 150 characters per second). If the logger has been collecting data for awhile, half a megabyte of keystrokes will take around an hour to download. The manufacturer addresses slow downloads with a separate product called the Turbo Download Adaptor, with which you plug one end into the keylogger and the other into a PC's serial port. With special software, the adaptor supports considerably faster 56-Kbps downloads of the keylogger data.

KeyGhost products are priced from $89 for a home edition that stores 128K of data to a Professional model for $199 that stores 2MB of data and encrypts the information it stores. Interface Security also offers keyboards with built-in hidden keyloggers. The products are available from www.keyghost.com.

KEYKATCHER   The developer of KeyKatcher likes to call his product a "tape recorder for your keyboard." This hardware keylogger is different in appearance from KeyGhost and KeyLogger. Instead of using a cable configuration, KeyKatcher has its circuitry built into a small connector that plugs into the computer's keyboard port. The keyboard cable plugs into the connector. KeyKatcher comes with a piece of heat shrink tubing that you can optionally attach to the keyboard cable and connector. This makes the product a bit stealthier than the inline cable-type products.

KeyKatcher operates just like the other hardware keyloggers when using a word processor and a password to access the command menu. KeyKatcher is somewhat underpowered in the memory department when compared to the other hardware keyloggers because it can store only up to 64K of data (less memory does mean a smaller size though). This product is appropriate for short-term monitoring or in situations in which the target is known to not input very much data. KeyKatcher is unique in that each unit has a serial number, recorded by the manufacturer, which can be useful in tracking down who originally purchased one of the devices that's been covertly installed.

The base model KeyKatcher with 8K of memory is $45; 32K and 64K versions are available for $59 and $79 from www.keykatcher.com.

HARDWARE KEYLOGGER   In addition to its IKS software product, Amecisco also makes hardware keylogging products. As with the KeyGhost product, the Hardware KeyLogger is a cable that attaches between the keyboard and the computer to record keystrokes. The keystrokes are stored in nonvolatile memory, between 512K to 2MB, depending on the model. A command menu is displayed in a word processor when a password is entered.

A much more intriguing product is Amecisco's Keyboard Edition of its Hardware KeyLogger. The vendor buys keyboards directly from manufacturers and installs its logging chip inside the keyboard. You can order a bugged version of many popular types of keyboards. Swapping entire keyboards works well for newer computers, but it gets complicated when replacing an older keyboard that may have an accumulation of grime and food stains. Amecisco offers slightly used keyboards on request that are harder to detect than brand new ones.

KeyLogger products are priced from $99 for a version that stores 512K of data to $199 for a version that stores 2MB of data. The Keyboard Edition models are priced between $129 and $299. Complete product information is available at www.amecisco.com.

CUSTOM HARDWARE   Commercial keyloggers work great, especially the stealthy keyboard versions, but there may be times when you have a hard target and need a keylogger that will really defy detection. If you have government or corporate resources at your disposal, custom-designed

Tools of the Trade: FBI's Magic Lantern

In 2001, information started to surface about an FBI project called Magic Lantern, which was described as a law enforcement keylogger that could be remotely installed on a computer if a user opened a Trojan horse e-mail attachment. Unfortunately, the media got some of the facts wrong and called the software a virus; then things started to get out of hand. Network Associates supposedly contacted the FBI and let it know that they would ensure that their McAfee virus-protection software wouldn't detect Magic Lantern so as not to compromise investigations. (Antivirus vendors Symantec and Sophos were quick to claim they wouldn't give preferential treatment to Magic Lantern and detect and delete it like any malicious program.) This caused an outrage with electronic privacy-rights advocates, and Network Associates denied any involvement with Magic Lantern in a statement. Some security analysts viewed the press release as very narrowly worded, leaving the door open for Network Associates to be involved with similar government projects, not specifically called Magic Lantern. Conspiracy theorists soon jumped on the bandwagon, speculating that Network Associates, which at the time sold the commercial line of PGP encryption products, was also putting backdoors in PGP at the government's request.

The flack over Magic Lantern did have its moments of humor. In one online discussion, a participant cynically joked about the surveillance program saying, "This only works if: a) The FBI kicks in your door and installs Outlook; b) You always open e-mail with the subject 'Snow White and the 7 FBI Agents'; c) You run the attachment called FBILOVESYOU.VBS."

Although lots of rumors made the rounds about Magic Lantern, no real details have emerged about it. The FBI did admit that Magic Lantern was a "workbench project," part of a collection of investigative software tools dubbed "Cyber Knight."

hardware may be appropriate to use against a technically savvy target. A custom keylogger can be designed to fit inside a keyboard, PC case, or laptop and be small enough and unobtrusive-looking to avoid detection. It's conceivable that a hardware keylogger could be used in tandem with specially designed networking hardware that could pass collected information through a network connection. Such a sophisticated eavesdropping device obviously wouldn't be cheap, but would be extremely effective in a high-stakes espionage operation.

Countermeasures

The best countermeasure against a spy using a keylogger is physical security. Adequately securing the computer against physical access reduces the chances of a keylogger being covertly installed on your computer. (There's still a risk of a keylogger being remotely installed, but if you use common sense when dealing with e-mail attachments and practice general network security, this risk is mitigated significantly.)

 For more on physical security, see Chapter 3.

For all of the sneakiness associated with keyloggers, they typically leave some telltale sign of their presence, and there are a number of countermeasures you can apply to discover and defeat the many different types of keyloggers.

Viewing Installed Programs

In the Windows Control Panel, run the Add/Remove Programs utility to list the programs that have been installed on your computer with an installer. Look for any programs mentioned that you didn't install or don't know the purpose of. Surprisingly enough, this simple countermeasure will catch some commercial keyloggers.

Examining Startup Programs

Obviously, for a software keylogger to operate, it needs to be run first. Keylogger installation programs typically put instructions for the logger to run in one of several places:

- ✓ Autoexec.bat
- ✓ Startup folder
- ✓ Registry

Countermeasures: Disinformation

So what should you do if you find a keylogger installed on your computer? Although you can immediately try to disable and uninstall it, you might consider using it as part of a disinformation campaign against the spy who installed it. Going back to fundamental questions discussed in Chapter 1, who do you think the spy is, and what do you think he or she is after? You should do some research and try to find out what type of keylogger is running. If you can locate the log file, check the creation date to see how long the key-logger has been gathering data on you (keep in mind, though, that the date can be spoofed). After you estimate how long the keylogger has been in place, try to assess how much damage might have been done while it's been running. What have you been working on? With whom have you been communicating? How often have you visited a Web site or used software that required a password?

If you will try to pass disinformation to the spy, you'll need to use another computer that you know is secure for your day-to-day work, and only use the compromised computer as part of your deception strategy. Alternatively, you can use the compromised machine, but be very careful not to reveal any sensitive information.

What type of information should go into a disinformation campaign? Documents and communications that mask your real activities, information that disputes what may have already been compromised by the keylogger, or mention of names of people you think may be affiliated with the spying activity — the classic false mole hunt, in which you make the adversary believe that trusted people in his organization are actually working for you. For example, if you suspect that information about an upcoming merger was compromised, you can easily create a series of false documents and e-mails that say the merger had broken down, and that your company was now pursuing the acquisition of some other competitor.

If you're dealing with a sophisticated adversary, disinformation may be suspected, so you'll need to carefully craft your plan. How long you run the disinformation depends on your goals and the amount of effort you want to put into the operation.

If you suspect someone had physical access to your computer, you may want to set up surveillance to see who planted the keylogger. This can be done with anything ranging from an expensive video camera setup to a cheap Web cam and motion detection software.

The Registry is often used to hide keylogger run instructions and information because most users never look inside the Registry. To check for startup programs in the Registry, use the RegEdit tool and look for suspicious entries in the following keys:

```
HKEY_LOCAL_MACHINE\SOFTWARE\Microsoft\Windows\CurrentVersion\Run
HKEY_LOCAL_MACHINE\SOFTWARE\Microsoft\Windows\CurrentVersion\RunOnce
HKEY_LOCAL_MACHINE\SOFTWARE\Microsoft\Windows\CurrentVersion\RunOnceEx
```

```
HKEY_LOCAL_MACHINE\SOFTWARE\Microsoft\Windows\CurrentVersion\RunServices
HKEY_LOCAL_MACHINE\SOFTWARE\Microsoft\Windows\CurrentVersion\RunServicesOnce
HKEY_LOCAL_MACHINE\SYSTEM\CurrentControlSet\Services
HKEY_CURRENT_USER\Software\Microsoft\Windows\CurrentVersion\Run
HKEY_CURRENT_USER\Software\Microsoft\Windows\CurrentVersion\RunOnce
```

Consider booting in Safe Mode before examining the Registry values. Some keyloggers alter the values of the Run keys after they're loaded, to prevent discovery with RegEdit. In Safe Mode, the keylogger won't load, and the Registry values that specify the keylogger file path will be shown.

Windows 9x and ME have a System Configuration Utility called MSCONFIG.EXE. The program lets you examine the contents of AUTOEXEC.BAT, Win.ini, and Startup programs. This tool is useful for discovering keyloggers that have been set to automatically run when Windows starts up.

Examining Running Processes

After seeing whether there are any unusual or unknown files running when Windows starts up, the next step is to determine whether any keyloggers are currently running as a process.

TASK MANAGER

The Task Manager utility is a quick way to see which processes are currently running in Windows. You can run it by doing the following:

✓ For Windows 3.x, 9x, and ME, press Ctrl+Alt+Del.

✓ For Windows NT, 2000, and XP, right-click on an empty spot on the Task Bar and select Task Manager (you can also press Ctrl+Alt+Del and select the Task Manager button in the dialog box).

The Task Manager supplies a limited amount of information under Windows 9x/ME. Also remember that in older versions of Windows, a stealthy keylogger won't show up in the Task Manager. This isn't the case with Windows NT, 2000, and XP, unless the keylogger has been installed as a driver.

PROCESS EXPLORER

A superior alternative to Task Manager is Sysinternals's free utility: Process Explorer. Process Explorer, which provides considerably more information than Task Manager, runs on all versions of Windows later than Windows 95. Process Explorer is a valuable detective tool for discovering software keyloggers because it can display what file a process was run from. Process Explorer can be downloaded from www.sysinternals.com.

As you examine processes, you'll no doubt encounter process names that you aren't familiar with. Don't immediately think that an unknown process is a keylogger. In all likelihood, it's probably a normal program or service, but you should spend some time doing some detective work to know for sure.

There are two approaches to correctly identifying malevolent processes:

✓ Simply enter the process or associated filename in Google, searching Web sites and USENET newsgroups, to see if there are any matches. The search engine usually returns information about the process.

✓ Consult a process reference Web site, such as `www.answersthatwork.com/Tasklist_pages/tasklist.htm`. These Web sites contain updated lists of processes, both Windows and third-party, which often appear in task lists.

MSINFO32

Another system utility that's useful for discovering keyloggers and other hidden programs is MSinfo32. This program provides a variety of system hardware and software information, including which drivers have been loaded, which tasks are running, and which startup programs have been run (see Figure 8-3). This is a very powerful yet underutilized discovery tool. To use the utility, follow these steps:

1. In the Start menu, select Run.

2. Enter msinfo32.

3. Select OK.

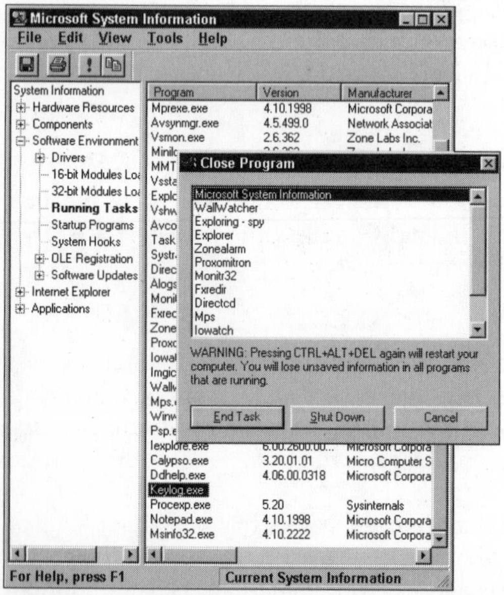

Figure 8-3: The Keylog.exe program doesn't appear in the Windows 98 Task Manager in the top window, but it does appear as a Running Task with the MSinfo32 utility.

You can find information that might point to an installed keylogger in the Software Environment folder.

Monitoring File Writes

Virtually all keyloggers store the collection of keystrokes in a file. This can be an important clue to help discover whether a keylogger has been installed on a computer. By monitoring which files are being written to, you can discover whether a keylogger is active.

File Monitor, commonly called Filemon, provides real-time system monitoring of file events. Any time a file is accessed, opened, or closed; has its attributes retrieved; or is read or written to, Filemon displays the time and date, the process that made the file call, what type of file request was made, and the path of the file. This is an extremely powerful tool for locating keyloggers, in that you can view the process that was responsible for writing the data to a file as well as the name of the file that holds all of the keystrokes (see Figure 8-4).

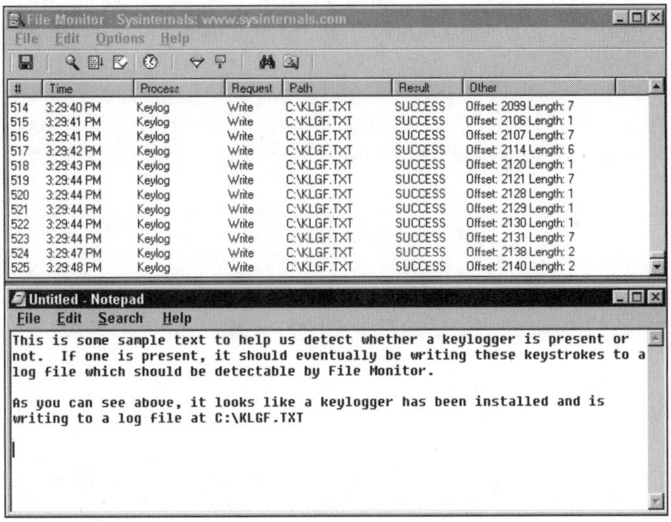

Figure 8-4: Filemon detecting writes to a keylogger key file while text is being input with Notepad.

To use the free utility, download FileMon from the www.sysinternals.com site and follow the installation instructions. (If you are running Windows NT, 2000, or XP, you need to be logged-in as Administrator for the tool to work correctly.) Follow these steps:

1. Close all running programs.

2. Run Filemon.

3. Select the Filter icon in the toolbar (or press Ctrl+L).

4. Select the Log Writes checkbox. This limits data displayed to only file writes.

5. Click the Apply button.

6. Select the Capture (magnifying glass) icon from the toolbar (or select Capture from the Options menu or use Ctrl+E).

After FileMon starts displaying file activity, open Notepad or a word processor and start typing. Software keyloggers will hold keystrokes in a buffer before writing to the log file. Depending on the buffer size, you may need to type a fair amount of text to force the keylogger to write to a file.

If you see a series of writes associated with a particular file, and there is no system or other program activity, you probably discovered the log file for a keylogger.

Removing Visual Basic Runtimes

There are a number of freeware and commercial keyloggers that are written in Visual Basic and rely on the VB runtime files. If you aren't running any programs that need these files, removing them will stop any VB keyloggers. Runtime files, depending on the version of Visual Basic used, are named vbrun100.exe, vbrun200.exe, vbrun300.exe, vb4run.exe, MSVBVM50.EXE, and vbrun60sp5.exe. Search your hard drive to see whether any of these files exist. To prevent a Visual Basic program from using the runtime file, simply rename the runtime file and then reboot. Obviously, this technique doesn't apply to keyloggers written in other programming languages.

Searching for Strings

In a word processor, type a unique series of characters; then copy a part of the text string and use the Windows Find (Windows 9x/ME) or Search (Windows 2000, XP) command in the Start menu to locate a file that contains the string. This works only with keyloggers that don't encrypt the contents of the log file.

Using Personal Firewalls

On a networked computer, it's possible that a keylogger might not perform any writes to disk and immediately send the information over the Internet. If this is the case, FileMon won't discover the log file because no file calls are being made.

Installing a personal firewall (such as ZoneAlarm, which confirms whether to allow outgoing network connections from programs) would defeat such a keylogger.

If a spy had physical access to your computer, it's possible that he could change the firewall settings to grant permission to the keylogger to always access the Internet. It's worthwhile to periodically check the program settings of your firewall to ensure that there are no unknown programs that connect to the Internet without your permission.

Using File Integrity and Registry Checkers

When a spy installs a software keylogger, he obviously has to leave a trace of the program. Using a file integrity checker to search for new files added to a directory or a Registry monitor to track recent additions and changes to the Windows Registry can give you important clues about whether a keylogger has secretly been installed on your computer.

Tactics: Defeating Firewalls

One potential weakness of personal firewalls is if a trusted application is used to covertly send out information over the Internet. For example, most users trust that Internet Explorer isn't being malicious when it accesses the Internet, but if Internet Explorer could be exploited to somehow covertly send out data to a spy site, most personal firewalls wouldn't detect it.

Jason, of the German Rat Coding Team, developed a keylogger named God that takes advantage of this weakness. A spy first places a .php script on a Web server. He then installs the God keylogger on a target computer. As the keylogger collects data, it sends the keystrokes to the Web server running the .php script through Internet Explorer. Because most people set their personal firewalls to allow Internet Explorer to connect to the Internet without first asking for permission, the logged keystrokes escape detection.

See www.ratct.net for more information on God, but brush up on your German beforehand because the tutorial isn't written in English.

For a complete discussion of file integrity checkers and Registry monitors, see the "Countermeasures" section of Chapter 9.

Using Keylogger-Detection Software

Instead of going through the process of manually checking for covertly installed software keyloggers using some of the steps listed previously, there are a number of products on the market that can detect whether a keylogger has been installed. There are a couple of caveats to using automatic keylogger detectors instead of monitoring processes and file writes, however, as follows:

- ✓ The detection software typically works only on known keyloggers that the vendor has profiled; new or unknown keyloggers might not be detected.

- ✓ Just like antivirus software, vendors offer updated keylogger definition files. If you use one of these tools, keep it updated.

- ✓ Keylogger detectors may generate "false positives" (a keylogger is reported to be present, but it really isn't there). If a detector reports a keylogger based on the presence of a specifically named file, do a Web search to see if that file might belong to some other application you have installed that isn't a keylogger.

Some popular keylogger detectors are listed in the following sections.

SPYCOP

SpyCop claims to be able to detect more than 300 different keyloggers. When Spycop detects a keylogger, it offers the user the option of renaming files associated with a .spy extension (this usually prevents the keylogger from running, but may cause other problems). In addition to examining files for evidence of keyloggers, SpyCop currently has a beta feature that examines running processes for any suspected keyloggers. SpyCop has a free trial version that has been crippled and skips random files during a scan. The full version is available for $69.95 from www.spycop.com.

WHO'S WATCHING ME

Who's Watching Me is another dedicated keylogger detector. The program can be set to run at startup or at any point while the computer is running. Who's Watching Me reports if a keylogger is present and then presents information about it; however, the detector doesn't remove the spy tool. Who's Watching Me comes as a 90-day trial version ($24.95 to register) and is available from www.trapware.com.

PEST PATROL

PestPatrol is an all-purpose spyware detector that finds and removes keyloggers, Trojan horses, worms, and advertising spyware. The detector scans both files and processes and provides extensive information on discovered spy programs. PestPatrol is priced at $29.95; a limited function evaluation version is also available and can be downloaded from www.pestpatrol.com.

Countermeasures: Spy Wars — Keyloggers vs. Detection Software

In March 2002, the keylogger spy war heated up. MSNBC reported that commercial keylogger companies WinWhatWhere and Spectorsoft included code in their products to disable the popular keylogger countermeasure Who's Watching Me.

Richard Eaton, president of WinWhatWhere, was quoted as saying, "If someone's trying to make money trying to ruin my software, I have to take appropriate action."

Wes Austin, the developer of Who's Watching Me countered, "All we're doing now is telling people there is a monitoring program. So why break Who's Watching Me unless you are using the product illegally, trying to hide something . . . . They know what people are using it for."

What looked like an inevitable tit-for-tat code war, with the vendors coming up with countermeasures to use against each other's products, cooled down shortly after it hit the press. WinWhatWhere announced that it would no longer be modifying Who's Watching Me files that disabled the keylogger detection utility.

SPYBOT SEARCH & DESTROY
Spybot Search & Destroy is a popular freeware tool, written by Patrick Kolla, that detects and removes keyloggers, Trojan horses, advertising spy software, and other malicious code. Kolla's program has a large number of features, including online updating, removing program usage tracks, and a multilingual interface. SpyBot is available on the Web from `http://beam.to/spybotsd`.

Using Sniffers
If you suspect that a keylogger is covertly e-mailing information to a spy, use a packet sniffer such as Ethereal to monitor network traffic. Pay attention to mail protocols and remember that there's a good chance the data will be encrypted, so you won't be able to read the contents. (However, because many of the keyloggers use weak encryption, you can probably crack the encryption in a reasonable amount of time if you're even a little crypto-savvy.)

For more about sniffers, turn to Chapter 10.

Detecting Hardware Keyloggers
None of the tools or techniques designed to detect software keyloggers can detect hardware keyloggers. Depending on the type of hardware keylogger used, these surveillance devices can be very easy or very difficult to detect.

INLINE KEYLOGGERS
Detecting commercially available inline keyloggers is pretty easy. Look for something unusual plugged into the PC's keyboard port. Trace the cable from the keyboard directly to the back of your computer. If the cable connects to another cable or a plug, be very suspicious.

BUGGED KEYBOARDS
Detecting a keyboard that has been replaced with a bugged keyboard is much more difficult than discovering an inline keylogger. Some points to consider that may help with detection include the following:

✓ **The keyboard doesn't seem right.** If for some reason you think your keyboard looks different, be suspicious. Maybe the color is a little off, the grime patterns are slightly different, or the keys have a different feel.

✓ **Use reference keyboards.** In the old days of technical surveillance countermeasures (TSCM), reference telephones were kept to compare a suspected bugged phone against a "clean" one. The technician carefully examined the circuitry in the suspect phone to see if there were any differences between it and the clean phone. You could do the same by taking apart a suspected keyboard. The keylogging chips used by vendors are very obvious-looking.

✓ **Tampering marks.** One solution is to position the screw heads at different angles and record the angles by either sketching their positions or taking a digital photo. In the event that someone does plant a hardware-monitoring device in your keyboard, it's relatively unlikely that they will go to the extent of putting the screws back in the exact same position—unless you have an extremely sophisticated or anal adversary.

If you suspect that a bugged keyboard is being used, just go out and buy a new replacement keyboard. You can also use a virtual on-screen keyboard, designed for disabled computer users, to enter sensitive text. Because a hardware keylogger interacts directly with the keyboard, if you use some on-screen method of entering text, it will defeat the keylogger. This won't work with a software keylogger that captures screen images, though, and a clever spy may use both hardware and software keyloggers to ensure his chances of successfully eavesdropping on you. The old intelligence saying of "find one bug, look for others" holds true.

Remember that using a laptop or a USB keyboard greatly reduces the risk of you being bugged with a keylogger, unless you're up against a very sophisticated adversary.

Exploiting Keylogger Passwords

Most commercial hardware and software keyloggers use a password or key sequence for a spy to access the management features of a logger. If the spy makes the mistake of using the default setting, which is often listed on the vendor Web site, you too can access the keylogger.

An often-overlooked discovery technique is to write a brute-force script or program to reveal the presence of a keylogger. Most commercial keyloggers feature a default or user-specified key combination that displays the keylogger's control panel. A simple script could be written in Visual Basic, Perl, or another language to try all possible three-key combinations using Ctrl and two other keys.

Because hardware keyloggers use a password entered in a word processor to display a menu of commands, you could also write script to perform a brute-force attack on a hardware keylogger by sending all possible key combinations to a window and then recording if any output other than the tried password appears. Obviously, this could be very time-intensive if the password was more than seven characters.

Using Linux

Unlike the large number of Windows keyloggers available on the Internet, similar spy tools that eavesdrop on Linux users are currently few and far between. Although it's possible to create a keylogger for Linux by installing a modified kernel on a target computer, this level of technical

Countermeasures: Tamper Seals

If you're dealing with a deep-pockets adversary who wants to ensure that he avoids detection, there's always the threat of a keylogger that could be installed in your computer's case. This would be much more difficult to detect because it would require opening up the computer and then knowing what to exactly look for. A high-stakes government operation could even go to the extent of fabricating a keyboard controller chip that looked identical to a standard chip, but contained circuitry that functioned as a keylogger. (Please remember the discussion about risk analysis in Chapter 1 and whether this would be probable or possible in your case.)

One countermeasure to help discover whether spies are opening up your computer is to use tamper seals, which are pieces of tape that are placed over the area where the computer case comes apart. If the case is opened or if someone tries to remove the tape, the tape breaks and you have evidence that someone tried to tamper with your computer. A dedicated adversary can defeat tamper seals, but it makes his or her job more time-consuming and difficult.

If you're cheap, you can use a variation of an old tried-and-true spy trick. Open up your computer case, pull a hair out of your head (or borrow one from someone else if you don't have many to spare), and wedge it into the case as you close it so only a short portion sticks out. If an adversary adds an eavesdropping device to the inside of your machine, he won't notice the hair as it falls out when he opens the computer. If the hair is missing, be very cautious. (Techniques like this are best left for those who are justifiably paranoid, have too much time on their hands, or have watched too many reruns of the original *Mission Impossible* TV series.)

sophistication is beyond the average spy. However, the source code for at least two Linux keyloggers has recently been published, including one in the widely read *Phrack* e-zine. Both of these keyloggers are very simple and offer nowhere near the surveillance capabilities found in commercial Windows keyloggers. As with the recent appearance of Linux viruses, as the popularity of the operating system increases, particularly on the desktop, expect to see some of the same eavesdropping tools Windows users have to contend with start appearing with a Penguin flavor.

Watching for Unusual Crashes

Just like any other software, keyloggers crash and they'll often leave odd error messages when they do. Although it's sometimes easy to dismiss errors on Windows, many keyloggers aren't entirely reliable and can frequently cause system errors. If you think you may be the target of a keyboard monitoring, take the time to look at any system error messages after a crash to see if there might be something unusual happening.

Countermeasures: CompuSafe or Sorry?

Safe Technology Co. Ltd., a Korean company, makes a device called the CompuSafe. You plug the device into your keyboard port and then your keyboard cable into the device. The box has encryption hardware that communicates with a software driver. The result is supposed to be scrambled text that a software keylogger won't be able to read (at least those that don't have the capability to do screen captures).

The ExtremeTech Web site tested the device and found that keystrokes were still being recorded in the clear by WinWhatWhere's Investigator keylogger. The device did work against a no-name keylogger, but key entry was extremely sluggish when the device was running.

Although the idea has potential, the implementation seems to leave a little bit more to be desired. A complete review can be read at www.extremetech.com/article2/0,3973,472055,00.asp.

Removing Keyloggers

After you discover a keylogger and decide whether to start a disinformation campaign or not, you'll want to remove it. Commercial keyloggers can install a number of files on your hard drive, and it may be difficult to completely get rid of them all. Your best bet is to try to identify which type of keylogger has been installed. You can do this by using a Web search engine and entering evidence you've found, such as filenames or Registry values. If it's a commercial keylogger, check the company's Web site. Most vendors have instructions on how to remove the keylogger as well as other information that may be useful for helping you identify a particular type of logger.

If you can't uninstall the keylogger or are concerned that there may be other surveillance software present, back up your data files to fresh storage media, perform a low-level format of the hard drive, and then reinstall the operating system from a trusted distribution source (preferably the vendor's CD). This may be time-consuming, but it is the only practical and guaranteed way to defeat a software keylogger.

Summary

Keyloggers are some of the more common and insidious tools in a spy's bag of tricks. However, most commercial software and hardware keyloggers are relatively easy to detect and defeat after you're aware of the threat.

✓ If you don't have much technical experience, use a keylogger detection program and keep it updated.

✓ If you're more technically inclined, take some time to poke around and see what processes are running, what file activity is taking place, and what programs and drivers are being loaded on startup.

✓ Examine your PC and keyboard for any signs that a hardware keylogger has been installed.

Unless you're the target of a sophisticated espionage operation, these simple steps will mitigate most of the risks of being snooped on by a keylogger.

Chapter 9

Spying with Trojan Horses

"I ride into your town on a big black Trojan horse."
—The Cure, "Club America," *Wild Mood Swings*

SPYING IS OFTEN CALLED THE WORLD'S SECOND OLDEST PROFESSION, so before we discuss modern Trojan horses and computer espionage, a short refresher on Greek mythology is in order to set the stage for this chapter.

Way back in the 12th century B.C., Paris (the son of the king of Troy) made off with Helen, who was considered to be the most beautiful woman in the world and was the wife of King Menelaus of Sparta. Menelaus and his brother, the powerful Greek king Agamemnon, weren't too happy with Paris, so they launched an invasion of Troy. Unfortunately for Menelaus, the city of Troy was heavily fortified, they couldn't take Troy and retrieve Helen even after ten years of war.

After awhile, the Greeks finally realized they'd need to use deception to win the war, so they built a large wooden horse that was hollow, slipped a handful of men inside it, left it at the gates of Troy, and hopped into their ships to return to Greece.

The Trojans thought the horse was a peace offering, so they pulled it into the walled city and then proceeded to have a huge party celebrating their victory. As you might have guessed, this was obviously a big mistake because while everyone was drunk or sleeping, the Greeks snuck out of the horse, killed some guards, and let the rest of the Greek army (who had sailed back to Troy under the cover of darkness) into the city. The city fell, the Trojan army was slaughtered, and Helen was finally recovered.

The legacy of the Trojan horse continues today in the form of computer files and e-mail messages that aren't always what they seem. Trojan horse applications can remotely seize control of a computer through an Internet connection and allow a spy to pilfer files and eavesdrop on his intended victim. This chapter talks about how Trojans work, how they are installed on computers, which ones are suitable for espionage, and (probably most importantly) how they can be detected and defeated.

Spy Tactics

In this section, your spy role-playing assignment is to become an unethical reporter for a supermarket tabloid. You were once a rising star with a well-respected, major metropolitan newspaper, fresh out of Columbia University with your journalism degree. But in your zeal for a Pulitzer, you blurred fiction and nonfiction in a highly critically acclaimed exposé series, and were eventually found out and fired. Times were tough, and the only job you could find was digging up sordid details on celebrities. You're trying to scrape up enough cash to get a plane ticket to Afghanistan or the Middle East, where you figure you can redeem your reputation by doing some gritty war reporting as a stringer.

There's a certain diva-class singer that all the paparazzi have been trying to get the dirt on for years. There have been all sorts of scandalous whisperings about drugs, affairs, and violence, but no one has been able to get into her inner circle to get the real story. Your employer has a standing $50,000 offer open to anyone who can get enough on her to write an exclusive exposé. You've often thought that if you had the opportunity, that $50K could buy your plane ticket back to the world of credible journalism.

Your younger brother hangs out on IRC (Internet Relay Chat) a lot, downloads warez and MP3z, and has turned into a script kiddie (that means he downloads pirated software and music, and uses tools written by other people to break into computers). You've never been into the scene, but one day he starts telling you about Trojan horses and how he took over a bunch of Windoze (what script kiddies call Windows) computers to find files with credit card numbers and bank statements. All by sending the lamers (script-kiddie jargon for losers) an e-mail with a Trojan attachment. Something clicks as you remember that you managed to get a hold of a certain diva's private e-mail address a couple of months ago. You hung on to it, wondering what you'd use it for, but now you've got a pretty good idea. You start asking your little brother all sorts of questions about Trojans.

Exploiting the Vulnerabilities

Successful Trojan attacks are based on exploiting both computer security weaknesses and human weaknesses. First and foremost, to get a Trojan onto a computer you have to do some social engineering to convince the target (or "vic" for victim in the Trojan users' parlance) to do something that installs and runs the Trojan. You'll also need to deal with any electronic defenses that are in place, such as firewall, antivirus, or anti-Trojan software.

This may sound like a daunting task, but there are many approaches for exploiting different vulnerabilities to effectively use Trojans for spying. Trojan attacks against unsophisticated users are fairly easy to pull off and are even possible against security-conscious users with a bit of thought and planning.

AN INTRODUCTION TO TROJAN HORSES

For our purposes, a Trojan horse is an application that appears to be benign, but instead performs some type of malicious activity. A Trojan can be disguised as a game, an e-mail attachment, or even a Web page. After a target runs or opens the camouflaged application, the Trojan installs itself on the hard drive and then runs each time Windows is started.

Tactics: Trust No One?

Although Trojans have been around since the time of Helen, one of the first publicized examples of the dangers of the modern-day versions came in 1984, from Ken Thompson, one of the original developers of UNIX.

Thompson described an attack in which the source code of a C compiler was modified so that whenever code for the UNIX login command was compiled, the compiler would recognize the source code and then change it by adding a few lines that placed a back-door password into the binary output.

Whoever used the compiler to create the login command would unknowingly make a version that caused the system to be vulnerable to anyone who knew the backdoor password. The source code for login could be examined with a fine-tooth comb, and there would be no evidence of the Trojan.

Thompson suggested that by making the Trojan-ed binaries the default C compiler for UNIX distributions, the login backdoor would soon appear in many systems wherever someone had recompiled the operating system. Thompson's moral was, "You can't trust code that you did not totally create yourself." (The original paper, which was written for the Turing Award Lecture '84, is available at `www.acm.org/classics/sep95/`.)

Thompson's observation is still valid today; consider these events from the second half of 2002:

- ✓ In November, someone discovered the latest libpcap and tcpdump sources from tcpdump.org, and its mirrors contained a Trojan.

- ✓ Between September 28 and October 6, a Trojan was distributed in the source for Sendmail 8.12.6.

- ✓ In August, someone breached security at `ftp.openbsd.org` and installed a Trojan in the OpenSSH source package.

- ✓ In June, Dug Song's monkey.org security site was cracked; and someone replaced the sources for dsniff, fragroute, and fragrouter with Trojan-ed versions.

Although some Windows supporters might view this as a security indictment of open-source software, Trojans can also be added to Windows binaries by reverse-engineering and recompiling. (This topic is discussed further in Chapter 13.)

After the Trojan is running, it carries out whatever evil deeds that its creator designed it for. For example, with a Trojan that is networked-enabled, you can instruct the remote target to repeatedly open and close its CD drive bay, play sound files, change the background wallpaper, or perform other humorous activities that make its owner think it is possessed. But because this book isn't *Secrets of Computer Pranks*, let's look at some Trojan features that can be used exclusively for espionage purposes, including the following:

✓ Capturing microphone audio output

✓ Capturing Web cam output

✓ Editing the Registry

✓ Getting and modifying contents of startup files such as autoexec.bat and win.ini

✓ Modifying existing files

✓ Logging keystrokes

✓ Retrieving cached passwords

✓ Running applications

✓ Taking screenshots or viewing the desktop in real time

✓ Terminating running processes

✓ Uninstalling itself (removing evidence of the Trojan)

✓ Uploading and downloading files

As you can see, a Trojan offers some serious possibilities to a spy wanting to compromise data from a remote location. After the Trojan is covertly put in place and is running, all you need is an Internet connection and a utility to remotely control the Trojan, and you can access your target from anywhere in the world.

Trojans can generally be classified into three different types:

✓ **Local system access.** Some of the earliest computer Trojans were designed to gain access into protected systems. For example, a Unix system administrator might download a popular game, not knowing the game would first check to see if the user had root privileges, and if so, would secretly create another administrator account with a known password. Another example of this type of Trojan is a fake Windows logon screen that saves accounts and passwords to a text file before calling the real system logon routines.

✓ **Vandalism.** Some Trojans are expressly designed to cause damage; for example, erasing files, reformatting hard drives, or other acts of vandalism. About the only use these types of Trojans have in espionage is for destroying evidence.

✓ **Remote access.** Probably the most useful Trojans for spying are remote access Trojans, sometimes facetiously referred to as RATs (Remote Access Trojans, Remote Administration Tools, or switch the words around until they match the acronym). These applications allow an eavesdropper to remotely control and snoop on a target computer over a network.

It's important to note that unlike viruses, Trojans don't self-replicate. After the rogue application is installed on a system, it doesn't try to spread itself to other computers. If it does, then it is considered to be a virus or a worm. (However, many viruses are propagated by using what could be considered a Trojan horse approach, such as spreading the virus through an e-mail attachment to an unwitting user. Viruses that are suited for espionage work are discussed in Chapter 13.)

HOW TROJAN HORSES WORK

Your little brother explains to you that all Trojans generally work the same way. An unwitting user does something that causes the Trojan application to be saved onto his computer's hard drive. This action could be opening an e-mail attachment, viewing a Web page, or running a downloaded application. After the Trojan is installed, it either immediately executes or waits until the next time the computer reboots and then runs. The Registry or some other startup file is usually modified so the Trojan is executed whenever Windows runs.

For the majority of espionage operations, remote access Trojans hold considerable potential, so we'll focus mostly on how they work. Generally, a Trojan is composed of three components: a server, a client, and a server editor:

✓ **Server.** The server is the application that is installed on the remote target computer and does the actual eavesdropping. Different servers have different features, ranging from a several-hundred-kilobyte Trojan server that can do just about anything you can think of, to small Trojans called "uploaders." An uploader may be only 20K in size, which makes it much less suspicious than a 200K plus server when trying to sneak it on a target system. An uploader is used to get a foothold in a target computer; then, as its name suggests, it uploads a larger Trojan server with more snooping features. After any server is running, it opens up a port and listens for and then executes commands. Smaller is always better; for spying, at the minimum you can get by with a server that just downloads files from the target computer and perhaps monitors keystrokes.

✓ **Client.** The client application sends commands to the server and receives data from it. You enter the IP address of your target in the client, and if the server is running, a connection is initiated over the specified ports and then TCP or UDP packets are passed between the two applications. Many Trojans use some type of encryption with their protocols to obscure the contents of the client/server communications. Most clients have very user-friendly interfaces, so you don't need to be sending cryptic command strings to successfully communicate with the server.

✓ **Server editor.** The final component of a remote access Trojan is the server editor (an example is shown in Figure 9-1). This utility is used to set up the server before it is deployed. Most servers tend to be very configurable, and you can specify settings such as what filename you want to give the server, its connection port numbers, how the server will be started, and its password (so only you can access the server).

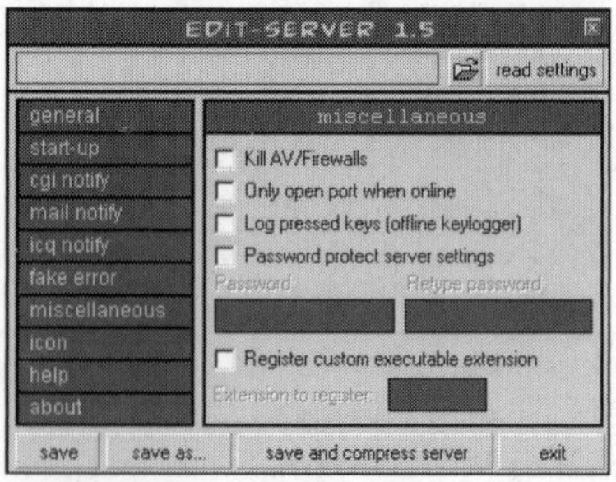

Figure 9-1: Server editor for the NetDevil Trojan, showing various configuration options.

Before you can send commands from the client to the server, you need to know the IP address of your target. When the server is executed, it listens on a specified port. You need the target's IP address so you can initiate a conversation with the server. (Some Trojans use default or fixed ports that make them easy to identify. During port scans, which are fully discussed in Chapter 10, crackers often scan for commonly used Trojan ports in an attempt to discover compromised systems (which saves them the work of having to install their own Trojans). For example, if a port scan reveals an active 27374 port, it's very likely the Sub7 Trojan, which uses that port by default, has been installed on the computer.)

Mikael Simovits maintains a comprehensive list of Trojans and the ports they use at `www.simovits.com/nyheter9902.html`.

There are different methods for finding out the target's IP address, and some servers get it for you when they run and use an e-mail message, ICQ notification message, or a Web-page CGI script to inform you of the target's address.

Servers can be written in virtually any programming language, and there are lots of sources available on the Internet if you want to code your own. Servers written in assembly and C/C++ are smaller and stealthier than a Trojan written in a higher-level language such as Visual Basic (however, Delphi is a very popular language among Trojan developers), but there are ways to shrink the size of the executable to make it less obvious.

Risk: International Trojans?

On February 2, 2000, the United States State Department sent out an urgent cable to 170 embassies around the world, asking that they remove a piece of budgeting software from all computers within five days.

After tightening security procedures several months earlier (following the arrest of a Russian diplomat who was suspected of spying on State headquarters), someone got nervous about a software package developed by a company called Synergy International Systems that was being used for budgeting and strategic planning.

The Diplomatic Security arm of the State Department learned that Synergy's employees, many of them former Soviet citizens, regularly visited department offices as part of the software-deployment process. State had granted a one-million-dollar, sole-source contract to the company to develop and install the software that processed unclassified but sensitive information.

Development of the application started in the mid-1990s at the U.S. Embassy in Moscow, and the staff was so pleased with the software that it was eventually adopted for use in all of the U.S. embassies throughout the world. This was a feather in the cap for Ashot Hovanesian, who is an Armenian and the original programmer who went on to found Synergy.

An internal State Department memo, dated February 1, 2000, stated that the goal of the investigation was to "help identify and eradicate any code that could execute a Trojan Horse, a computer virus or any other type of malicious code." The FBI and NSA conducted a counterintelligence probe and examined the application's million lines of code to ensure that there was nothing out of the ordinary. The inquiry never revealed any wrongdoing by Synergy, which still develops mission-critical database products.

The same thing happened again in December 2002, when the FBI investigated Ptech, Inc., a Massachusetts enterprise software-development company. The company got angel investment money from Saudi businessman, Yassin al-Qadi. It turned out that government intelligence agencies believed that al-Qadi had links to funding terrorists, specifically to Al Qaeda. The media reported that there was concern over whether software products that were in use by the government and Fortune 1000 corporations had "bin Laden Inside" Trojans.

The government gave Ptech a clean bill of health, but by mid-January 2003, the once-prosperous 65-employee company had been reduced to 10 people, with virtually no new business on the horizon.

HOW TROJANS AVOID DETECTION

For a Trojan server to successfully complete its spying mission, it has to avoid detection at two different levels: a user manually examining her system and automated utilities that are designed to uncover Trojans (specific discovery techniques and tools are described in the "Countermeasures" section of this chapter).

Some of the ways Trojans and the spies that send them avoid human detection include the following:

- ✓ **Exploiting trust.** If you get e-mail from someone you know, you're more likely to open it than a message that came from a stranger. Use this to your advantage and craft a message that appears to come from a trusted source that either has a Trojan attachment or points to a Web site link that installs a Trojan. (This could be just the ticket for getting a Trojan on a certain diva's computer.)

- ✓ **Camouflaging files.** Because many users are smart enough not to open an e-mail attachment with a .exe file extension, you should try to conceal the file type. One way to do this is by padding the file name with extra spaces, for example: sexypixs.jpg--.exe, in which each of the dashes is a space. By making the attachment's filename too long to be displayed by the e-mail application, the user won't see the .exe and assume that it is a harmless JPG image. The popular Microsoft Outlook and Outlook Express e-mail clients have experienced a number of vulnerabilities that makes it easy to potentially pass off a Trojan as a harmless file type.

- ✓ **Using a port not associated with any other Trojans.** Most Trojans use a default port for communications between the client and the server. There are widely distributed lists of these ports, and a savvy user can use the `netstat -a` command or a port-viewing utility to see whether there are any ports open that appear on the Trojan list. If you're using a Trojan that has a configurable port, select a unique number that doesn't appear on the list (high-numbered ports are less likely to interfere with standard services that tend to use lower-numbered ports).

- ✓ **Hiding in the Task List.** Most Trojans can hide their presence in the Task Manager List, just like the keyloggers that were discussed in Chapter 8. On Windows 2000/XP systems, this is more difficult, and you should give the server a name that makes it appear as part of the operating system. If a suspicious victim looks at a list of running processes in the Registry or in a startup folder, he might think the Trojan is a normal system service. An example would be to name the Trojan process Explorer.exe, which is close enough to the legitimate explorer.exe (in lower case) to escape detection by many people.

Defeating automated detection tools is a bit trickier and takes a few more technical skills. Some approaches include the following:

- ✓ **Developing a new server.** Many Trojan developers publish the source code to their creations, so it's relatively easy to build a variation of an existing Trojan or put together parts and pieces from different types to create your own if you have the programming skills. Unique Trojans stand a good chance of avoiding detection by antivirus and anti-Trojan utilities. Before you deploy your homemade Trojan, always test it against current versions of popular detection utilities.

✓ **Modify an existing server so it doesn't match an identification signature.** Antivirus and anti-Trojan utilities often look for certain byte sequences or checksum values in files that match Trojans. By using a hex editor to modify bytes that don't impact the operation of a Trojan with a hex editor, an altered server may not be detected.

✓ **Compressing the server.** By first running an executable compression utility on the server, it reduces its size and may make it harder for a virus or Trojan detection utility to identify the server by its file length or by a byte sequence.

✓ **Binding the server to another application.** There are utilities called .exe binders (executable binders) that can combine two or more applications into a single executable file. When the bound application is run, all the combined applications are also executed. With an .exe binder, you can easily bind a Trojan to a known trusted application.

Tools of the Trade: Compressors, Binders, and Droppers

If you start eavesdropping on the Internet Trojan community, you'll often hear three terms mentioned: compressors, binders, and droppers. They are very important tools in the Trojan user's arsenal that you should know about.

A compressor is a utility that takes an .exe file and shrinks it in size. Unlike the popular .Zip compression format, an application that's been shrunk by an executable compressor can be run without manually uncompressing it first. Compressors are very popular among Trojan users for reducing the size of servers as well as hiding servers from detection utilities that search for a fixed size or some other file signature. Although it wasn't designed for malicious purposes, one of the most popular compressors, called UPX (Ultimate Packager for Executables), is available at `http://upx.sourceforge.net`. However, popular compressors do have a unique file format that may be detected by anti-Trojan utilities.

A binder is an easy-to-use tool that allows you to bind one or more applications with another. When the bound application is executed, all the applications are run. A binder is useful for covertly associating a Trojan with a known application. One of the drawbacks to this technique is that most antivirus and anti-Trojan tools know about the headers that popular binders place in a bound file and will detect them. For a list of binders, go to `www.tlsecurity.net/exebinder.htm`.

A dropper is an application that contains code that covertly installs and executes a Trojan. A classic example of a dropper is the Whack-A-Mole game that spread around the Internet in 1998. Although the game appeared to be an entertaining exercise in bopping moles over the head with a mallet, it was actually a dropper for the NetBus Trojan. A variety of droppers and source code is available from `www.megasecurity.org/Droppers.html`.

COVERTLY INSTALLING TROJANS

Unless you can get your Trojan server on the target computer, it's a useless bunch of bytes. There are two options for deploying a server: either introducing it remotely over the network or installing it locally if you have physical access to the computer.

NETWORK INSTALLATION   As with most forms of computer espionage, if you do it right, there's less personal risk involved with a network versus a physical attack. However, because network attacks are fairly common, you may be faced with defensive measures designed to reduce the chances of you succeeding. The success or failure of deploying a Trojan over a network depends on how hard your target is (which you should have determined by now).

If you think your target may be vulnerable, there are several ways to use a network (typically the Internet) to covertly deploy a Trojan server, including the following:

- ✓ **E-mail attachments.** The most common way of delivering a server is with an e-mail attachment. When the user opens the attachment (or in some cases, simply views the e-mail message with Outlook or Outlook Express), the Trojan is installed. (Since you've got the diva's e-mail address, this option seems pretty appealing.)

- ✓ **Instant messaging (IM).** Trojans can be sent to a target during IM file exchanges. IM can also be a good way to find out the IP of a target computer. For example if you are chatting with someone over AOL's AIM, just enter `netstat -n` at the command line, and the address associated with port 5190 (the port AIM uses) is the IP address of the person you're chatting with.

- ✓ **Downloaded files.** This is the old-fashioned way of delivering servers, in which the target downloads an application or data file (that contains a hidden macro) without realizing that it is actually a Trojan horse.

- ✓ **Web pages.** Because of design flaws in older versions of Internet Explorer, it's possible to create a special Web page that covertly downloads a Trojan when the page is viewed. (Many of these same flaws can be exploited under Outlook/Outlook Express, which supports the ability to view HTML-formatted messages). Although Microsoft has provided security patches to address some of these vulnerabilities, this approach is still very effective against unpatched browsers or e-mail clients.

Much of your success in delivering a Trojan over a network depends on deception. Your goal is to somehow compel the target to open an e-mail attachment, visit a Web site, or perform some other activity that installs and then runs the Trojan server. The rapid spread of viruses seems to point out that this may not be as hard you might think. The "I Love You" and "Anna Kournikova" viruses both relied on computer users' curiosity to cause them to open an e-mail message. Other viruses that commandeer e-mail address books and then send spoofed e-mail out to friends, acquaintances, and business associates exploit trusted relationships. It's amazing that intelligent people who know about extensively publicized risks still fall victim to viruses spread in obviously suspicious e-mail messages written in broken English. Take the time to study some of the successful social-engineering approaches that have been used to spread viruses; they're also very applicable to launching Trojan espionage attacks (see a brief article on this topic at: `http:// searchsecurity.techtarget.com/originalContent/0,289142,sid14_gci537875,00.html`).

Tools of the Trade: HTAs

Microsoft's Internet Explorer supports something known as an HTA (HTML Application). An HTA is simply an HTML file with an .HTA file extension. The HTA can contain HTML, Cascading Style Sheets, and code written in various scripting languages. When Windows encounters an HTA, it treats it just like any executable file.

HTA could also stand for Heavy Trojan Action, and here's why. When Georgi Guninski, who is a walking, breathing Microsoft security hole finder, announced that a specially formatted Web page could covertly install an HTA on a remote computer if the page was viewed with Internet Explorer, Trojan writers soon started crafting tools to take advantage of the vulnerability. Utilities such as GodWill, Godmessage, and ExeToHTML allow you to insert a Trojan into the HTML source of a Web page as hexadecimal text. When the page is viewed, the Trojan is converted from the text in the HTML code to an HTA that's placed in the Startup folder. All this takes place without the user knowing it. The next time Windows starts up, the Trojan is executed. (The same exploit also works with Outlook/Outlook Express with an HTA embedded in an HTML-formatted e-mail.)

Most antivirus vendors quickly responded to this vulnerability and updated their products to detect secretly installed HTAs. Microsoft also released a series of security patches to address the problem. However, if the antivirus software can be covertly turned off and if the target computer doesn't have the latest security patches (which is all too common), this can still be a viable attack.

Microsoft has details about HTAs at `http://msdn.microsoft.com/workshop/author/hta/overview/htaoverview.asp`, whereas Guninski's Web site, at `www.guninski.com`, describes the Scriptlet.typelib ActiveX control vulnerability as well as other Microsoft holes that could be used for spying.

Because network attacks can be difficult to trace, consider using multiple avenues of attack. For example, instead of using a single e-mail attachment against your target, also try to get him to visit a Trojan Web page or download a Trojan posing as some useful utility. These types of attacks are known as "blended threats," and they're starting to become more common. Also, if your target is an organization, consider launching a number of stealthy attacks throughout the organization. Statistically, your odds will likely increase that someone in the organization will fall victim to the Trojan and give you a toehold inside.

Finally, don't launch an attack from an IP address that can be traced back to you. Use a public access Internet terminal, a "borrowed" wireless Internet connection, an open mail server relay, or some other method that prevents you from being associated with the attack.

LOCAL INSTALLATION   This one is simple. If you have physical access to the target computer, you just install the Trojan horse on the hard drive and then walk away (this isn't going to happen with the diva, since her mansion has more security than the White House). You can even get the IP address while you're there. If security measures prevent this, use your imagination and get creative. If you don't have access to the computer, consider having the target install the server for you. This involves some crafty deception and knowing that people are inherently less suspicious of things they receive in the mail versus over the Internet—especially when it involves something they are interested in or are familiar with.

Let's say your target is the CEO of a Fortune 500 company, who you know likes high-performance luxury cars. You visit a few manufacturer Web sites and download some luxury car PDF and Flash animation files. You then write a quick interface application that has links to all of the files and you burn everything (including a Trojan server carefully buried in an obscure folder) to a CD-ROM. You professionally label the CD with the logo of the popular magazine *Luxury Car Enthusiast Driver & Track* (which you know your target subscribes to). You then write a letter on some fake magazine letterhead you made, thanking your target for his subscription to the magazine and letting him know that the enclosed CD-ROM is filled with comparative information about a variety of high-performance cars.

The CD has an autorun.inf file that automatically runs the interface application, which installs the Trojan server before displaying the links to all the car information. If autorun.inf has been disabled on the target computer, the CEO will still likely run the "Our Top Picks.exe" application to check out the cars and unknowingly load the Trojan. You drop everything in the mail and wait for a few days before trying to connect to the server.

Trojan Horse Tools

You're getting a bit bored with your brother's lengthy discourse and finally in your best Jerry McGuire imitation say, "Show me the Trojans!" He explains there are thousands of Trojans available on the Internet. How you go about selecting one to use for spying depends mostly on your target and the security measures she might have in place. The more defensive the security measures, the stealthier the server and the deployment method have to be. (In some cases, you may want to use a variation of a publicly available Trojan because if it's discovered, it won't be clear whether the server was placed on the computer by a spy intent on espionage or a cracker being randomly malicious.)

Before you deploy a Trojan, you should always test it to make sure that it meets your needs. Be very careful because you may be playing with fire. If you don't have the source code and didn't build the Trojan yourself, you never know what the author might have put in the client, server, or server editor (surprisingly enough, there is a fair amount of honor among developers in the Trojan scene, in which reputation is extremely important within the social structure). With that in mind, follow these guidelines:

- ✓ Always test the type of Trojan you want to use on a computer that is configured similarly to your target.

- ✓ If you don't know what type of antivirus and anti-Trojan software may be running on the target computer, install popular versions and test against them all. After the server is installed and running, try some of the countermeasures listed at the end of this chapter to see if you can detect the Trojan.

✓ Perform your tests on a computer isolated from the rest of your network so you don't end up accidentally harming other computers. The computer you perform the test attack on should have enough security utilities in place to prevent the Trojan from turning around and biting you.

✓ Reformat the hard drive of the test computer when you've completed the test to ensure that there are no remnants of the Trojan code left.

Let's now take a look at some of the Trojans that can be used for espionage. They can be divided into three categories: classic Trojans that were some of the first on the scene several years ago (and were fairly widely publicized), the next generation of Trojans that are somewhat less-known, but more lethal and stealthy than their older cousins, and finally commercial products which are designed for network administration but can also be pressed into service as Trojans

CLASSIC TROJANS

The first Windows remote access Trojans appeared in the late 1990s, accompanied by a frenzy of media coverage and hype. Some of the first significant Trojans are described in the following sections.

NETBUS   NetBus, written by Carl-Fredrik Neikter and released in March 1998, was the first popular and easy-to-use Windows remote Trojan. The Trojan was in wide use by the time Back Orifice (see following) was released, but received nowhere near the amount of publicity. The first versions of NetBus were considerably larger than BO, but worked with Windows NT/2000. NetBus went through a series of updates and eventually evolved into the commercial Spector and eBlaster monitoring products, sold by SpectorSoft (`www.spectorsoft.com`). Original versions of NetBus are still available and can easily be found with a Google search.

BACK ORIFICE   During the summer of 1998, the hacking group Cult of the Dead Cow (cDc) released Back Orifice (BO), a remote access Trojan that worked with Windows 95/98 (see `www.cultdeadcow.com/tools/`). cDc masterfully promoted the launch and drew lots of media attention to the threat of remote access Trojans. A year later, cDc released a version of BO that worked under Windows 2000 (BO2K). BO2K was eventually turned into an open-source project as more of a legitimate system administration tool versus a Trojan, and development on it is still ongoing. For more information and to download the tool, go to `http://bo2k.sourceforge.net`.

SUB7   Written and released by MobMan at the end of 1999, Sub7 soon became the most popular and widely deployed Windows Trojan. Sub7 had a wide variety of features including being able to instruct a server to scan for other victims of the Trojan. There were a number of updated versions released, and the Trojan is still extensively used. All versions of Sub7, including the Defcon release, which has the reputation for being the most stable, are available from `www.megasecurity.org/trojans/subseven/Subseven_all.html`.

TROJANS: THE NEXT GENERATION

Although contemporary Trojans have many of the same basic features as their classic forbears, the current generation of Trojans is both more sophisticated and lethal. Trojan developers are engaged in an escalating battle with security software vendors coming up with new features such as the capability to disable firewalls and antivirus software, generating fake error messages to hide their activity, making the detection and removal more difficult, and broadcasting that the target's computer is running over IRC or email.

Some of the current Trojans of note that can be very useful for espionage are discussed in the following sections.

LANFILTRATOR   One of challenges facing a Trojan user is what if the target machine is behind a router; the internal LAN IP addresses aren't going to do much good in trying to connect to the server. LANfiltrator was one of the first Trojans to work in reverse; instead of the client attempting to contact the server, when the server becomes active, it contacts the client. Written by Read101, the Trojan is available at `www.digitalsin.net/cyn/HTML_/News.html`.

OPTIX   Developed by Evil Eye Software (EES), there are two versions of Optix: the small Optix Light and the full-featured Optix Pro (see Figure 9-2, which shows the Optix Pro client interface). The Light version is useful for getting a foothold into a system, and the Pro version contains just about every Trojan feature you can think of. The popular Optix family of Trojans is likely to become a serious challenger to Sub7 as the most widely distributed Trojans. The Trojans are free, but the EES developers will create an undetectable version of any of their Trojans for you for $300. Optix and other EES Trojans are available from `www.evileyesoftware.com`.

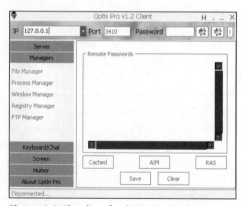

Figure 9-2: The client for the Optix Pro Trojan, showing commands that can be sent to a remote server, including extracting cached passwords.

NET-DEVIL   Net-Devil is a very popular, full-featured Trojan that can kill running firewall and anti-virus processes. It has a reputation for being very stable and working well on Windows XP systems. After many updates, its author Nilez stopped development in early 2003. Net-Devil is a good espionage tool and is available at `www.net-devil.com/main.html`.

Tactics: Inside the Mind of a Trojan Warrior

If you want to effectively use Trojans as part of your computer spy bag of tricks, take some time to learn about and understand the Trojan developer and user culture.

One of the more popular Web gathering places for Trojan coders and users is TrojanForge (`www.trojanforge.net`). This site features an online forum in which members exchange any and all information about Trojans and anti-Trojan utilities. There's even a new release section, in which Trojan authors can announce their latest creations and get feedback from other developers and users.

It goes without saying that a number of antivirus and anti-Trojan vendors regularly visit sites such as TrojanForge on a regular basis to see what their opposition is up to. It's also not too far a leap to assume that intelligence agencies and others interested in the use of Trojans for espionage purposes are also keeping tabs on these sites to learn about new techniques they can possibly use or defend themselves against. However, don't expect to see a post from the CIA in the new releases section announcing a new covert data-gathering Trojan that works on antiquated North Korean systems.

Just about any underground Web site will have information about Trojans along with at least several to download; however, there are some sites that tend to be more Trojan-focused than others, including the following:

✓ **Evil Eye Software:** Download site and forum for the Evil Eye Software Trojan writing crew (`www.evileyesoftware.com`).

✓ **Fearless:** Combination forum and download site for the Fearless Trojan writing team (`www.areyoufearless.com`).

✓ **SinRed:** News and files from the SinRed Trojan development crew (`www.sinred.com`).

✓ **MegaSecurity:** A general computer security site that specializes in Trojans (`www.megasecurity.org/Main.html`).

If you're planning on checking out Trojans for espionage purposes from any of these or other underground sites, make sure that you have strong security measures in place (such as firewalls, updated browser patches, and anti-Trojan and anti-virus software). If you're concerned that someone might be monitoring your Web browsing, you might also want to use some of the anonymity tools discussed in Chapter 10.

COMMERCIAL PRODUCTS

Throughout this book, you'll find examples of commercial products designed primarily for system administration, but which also can be used for more nefarious purposes. There are a number of products used for remotely administering computers that have the same capabilities as remote access Trojans (with the exception of such cute tricks as repeatedly opening and closing the CD drive bay). Because these are legitimate business applications, an antivirus or anti-Trojan utility may not detect them if they have been secretly installed on a computer.

Another point to consider with these remote administration applications is that they may already be installed on a target computer, which may make your job even easier (just use your own copy of the tool to access the remote computer). Like Trojans, commercial applications used fixed or default ports (see www.iana.org/assignments/port-numbers for a list of registered ports and the applications and protocols that use them); for example, an open TCP port 5631 indicates that the popular pcAnywhere is probably running. A number of vulnerabilities have been reported in different administration products, and if your target is running such a service, it's worth your time to research it. In addition, there are commonly available utilities that perform dictionary attacks on commercial applications that have password-protected connections.

Two widely used remote administration applications are the following:

✓ **pcAnywhere.** pcAnywhere from Symantec Inc. is a very popular corporate tool for remotely controlling computers over a network or through a dialup connection. The application has a number of security features that can thwart eavesdroppers, but if a spy has physical access to a computer and can install the application, it's just as good as a Trojan. Information about pcAnywhere is available at www.symantec.com/pcanywhere/.

✓ **VNC.** VNC (Virtual Network Computing) is a free, open-source, multiplatform client/ server software package that provides remote network access to graphical desktops. With VNC, you can access a computer from anywhere you have an Internet connection. VNC can be downloaded from the AT&T Laboratories Cambridge site at www.uk. research.att.com/vnc/. An enhanced version of VNC (also open-source), called TightVNC, is also available and favored by many system administrators because of increased performance and security. It can be downloaded at www.tightvnc.com/.

Now back to our story. After your little brother does a brain dump of everything he knows about Trojans, you decide that you will send the diva an e-mail with an Optix Lite attachment (from a spoofed e-mail address sent from a cybercafe, of course). Your plan is to use the small Trojan to get a foothold in her computer and then you'll upload Optix Pro to increase the surveillance of her activities. You use your honed writing skills to pen a personal e-mail from a friend you know she will open. You're confident that your electronic snooping will give you the dirt you need to write the big exposé that will bankroll your journalism comeback.

Countermeasures

Now go back to being a good guy who happens to be doing contract work for an executive protection service that a certain diva has hired to protect both herself and her interests. There's a team of ex-Secret Service and FBI agents who do the actual bodyguarding, and your job is to handle computer security issues, particularly tracking down electronic stalkers.

All the e-mail that comes to your client goes through a custom filter you wrote that examines e-mail attachments for viruses. Her personal e-mail address isn't publicized, but you still pick up an occasional message from strangers infected with the SirCam virus that must have come from her infected acquaintances address book. One day, you find something unusual when you check the logs. An e-mail whose From: header doesn't match its Received: header (which typically isn't displayed) clearly a spoofed message appearing to come from one of her friends (for more on spoofed e-mail and how to read e-mail headers see www.stopspam.org/email/headers/headers.html). Interestingly enough, there's an attachment that that doesn't contain a virus, but a small Trojan.

This e-mail message looks too sophisticated to be the work of script kiddies, and you're concerned that you have a serious cyberstalker on your hands. After telling your boss, you both decide to let the Trojan go active on a carefully controlled and monitored computer. If someone connects to it, you'll try to trace the origin point. A few days later, someone activates the Trojan, and you start logging all of the activity and determining the IP address of the incoming connection.

After a few days of the stalker eavesdropping on bogus e-mails and downloading fake files you planted on the computer, your boss decides that enough is enough and calls some friends in the Department of Justice (after all, this attack is violating a number of federal wiretap and computer crime statutes, and his client was a big supporter of the president during the last election). You hand over all the logs and information you've collected to a friendly FBI agent, and a week later you read an article in the newspaper about some obsessed fan being arrested in a cybercafe while downloading e-mail from a popular singer whose computer he had broken into. Crime just doesn't pay.

Although Trojans can be very stealthy and sneaky, there are actually a number of countermeasures you can apply to keep yourself relatively safe from being victimized by a spy. Some defensive measures to consider are covered in the following sections.

Network Defenses

There are several network-related countermeasures for discovering and defeating remote-access Trojans, including the following:

- ✓ **Viewing network connections.** The Trojan server has to use a port to communicate with the client. If you examine open ports and find one or more that aren't associated with Windows or a known application, you may have evidence of a Trojan.

- ✓ **Using firewalls.** A firewall that blocks outbound network connections can stop a Trojan in its tracks when it tries to connect to the Internet. Just be aware that newer Trojans have the capability to kill firewall processes (some firewall vendors have modified their products to make process killing much more difficult). You should periodically check that the firewall's icon is still present in the Windows Task Bar; although an extremely devious Trojan could simply add a fake firewall icon to the task bar after the process was killed, giving the illusion that the firewall was still running.

✓ **Monitoring network traffic.** By using a "sniffer" (network analyzer), you can monitor network traffic originating and arriving at your computer. Odd traffic, nonstandard ports, and unknown destination IP addresses are warning signs that a Trojan may be installed and running. Some Trojans encrypt their data, so if you encounter unusual data that seems scrambled or doesn't match a known protocol, this could also be a | warning sign.

These defenses, which work well for other types of network attacks, are fully discussed in the "Countermeasures" section of Chapter 10.

Using Registry Monitors and File-Integrity Checkers

In order to run each time Windows is started, Trojans typically modify the Registry, add a file to the Startup folder, or modify one of the standard Windows startup command files such as AUTOEXEC.BAT or WIN.INI on older systems.

These modifications can be detected with Registry monitors and file-integrity checkers. A Registry monitor informs you when any Registry keys are added or changed. A file-integrity checker works by traversing directories and calculating a hash (such as MD5) value for each file it encounters. Using this as baseline information, when the integrity tool is run again, it recalculates the hash values for files and compares them to the original values. If the two don't match, you know a file has been modified and if it's an application or system file, you might suspect that a Trojan could be involved. Using these tools can protect you against new Trojans that anti-Trojan utilities might not be able to detect.

Two popular free tools for detecting Registry and file changes are the following:

✓ **RegistryProt:** CSDiamond's Registry tool alerts you any time a Registry key value is changed or added. This utility is available from www.diamondcs.com.au/web/htm/regprot.htm.

✓ **GFI LANguard System Integrity Monitor:** This utility checks whether files have been changed, added, or deleted on Windows 2000/XP systems. You can download LANguard at www.gfi.com/lansim/index.html.

For more integrity checkers and other utilities that can stop Trojans, see the Wilders.org listing of free security tools at www.wilders.org/free_tools.htm.

Using Antivirus Software

Most antivirus software packages only include the most widely used Trojans in their signature databases. The vendors tend to mostly focus on viruses, and often Trojans are a secondary concern. The one antivirus product that Trojan developers and users respect is Kaspersky Anti-Virus (KAV), which has an excellent reputation for detecting both viruses and Trojans. For more information on KAV, go to www.kaspersky.com.

Using Trojan Detection Software

To fully protect yourself, in addition to running antivirus software, you should also use Trojan detection and removal software. Although not as widely known as antivirus products, anti-Trojan vendors concentrate specifically on Trojans and keep up on the latest releases and information from the underground. Trojan users often don't expect their victims to be running anti-Trojan software, which can throw a monkey wrench in their plans.

It's very important to understand that anti-Trojan software will detect only known Trojans that are listed in the product's signature database (just as with your antivirus software, be sure to keep your anti-Trojan tools frequently updated). A custom-built Trojan that isn't widely distributed may go entirely undetected. If you think you may be the potential target of a sophisticated espionage campaign, use a multilayer series of defenses to enhance your security.

There are a number of anti-Trojan products on the market, all claiming to seek out and destroy any Trojans that are present or attempt to be installed. Detection rates vary, depending on which reviews you read, but a handful of products that typically appear in most recommended lists include the following:

- ✓ **Trojan Defence Suite (TDS)**, $49, with a trial version available at http://tds.diamondcs.com.au/.

- ✓ **BOClean**, $39.95, available from www.nsclean.com/boclean.html.

- ✓ **Tauscan**, $29.95, with a trial version available (see Figure 9-3 for Tauscan in action) from www.agnitum.com/products/tauscan/.

- ✓ **Trojan Hunter**, $34.95, with an evaluation version downloadable from www.misec.net/trojanhunter/.

Mischel Internet Security, the developer of Trojan Hunter, recently released a free Trojan simulator utility that you can safely use to test your anti-Trojan and other security applications. It's available at www.misec.net/trojansimulator/.

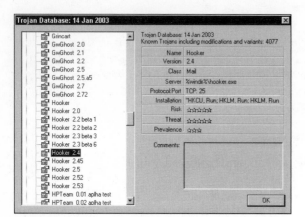

Figure 9-3: Tauscan scanning utility showing a discovered keylogger Trojan with a description of the identified malware (a generic term for Trojans, viruses, worms, and other malicious software).

Removing Trojan Horses

Although most anti-Trojan utilities automatically remove Trojans they discover, you should consider copying important data files onto a CD-ROM, reformatting the hard drive of the affected computer, and reinstalling Windows. Although this process may seem extreme, there's really no telling what the Trojan may have done to the system while it was running, and it's better to be safe than sorry. (Because data files may have been infected with a macro virus, be sure to have current antivirus software running before you restore the files to the clean system.)

There are several ways to manually remove a discovered Trojan from your system. First, you need to identify what you're dealing with, usually by tracing an open port back to a specific Trojan. Perform a Google search on the name of the Trojan to see what information is available about it. Many antivirus sites have descriptions of popular Trojans, along with instructions for removing them. If you can find a copy of the Trojan's client, and the server isn't password-protected, you may be able to remove the backdoor because many clients can uninstall and delete the server. Copy the client to the affected computer, and select 127.0.0.1 (localhost) as the IP address and attempt to connect to the server.

Using Non-Microsoft Software

Because of the history of security flaws in Microsoft Internet Explorer and Outlook/Outlook Express, consider replacing your browser and e-mail client with third-party applications if possible. Although Microsoft continues to patch its products when vulnerabilities are found, the high number of current vulnerabilities (and the potential for even more unreported holes) increases your exposure to a successful network attack.

Summary

Trojan horses can be a very effective tool in computer espionage operations, especially against unwary and unprepared targets. Network Trojan attacks using e-mail attachments, Web pages, or downloaded modified applications give a spy the opportunity to covertly place a backdoor in a computer and safely eavesdrop from thousands of miles away. If you have physical access to a computer, it's even easier to deploy a Trojan because you can often bypass security measures to install the backdoor.

As of yet, the Holy Grail of Trojan developers (the undetectable and impossible-to-remove Trojan) has yet to be written. Using the countermeasures described in this chapter, you should be able to detect and defeat any of the currently available crop of Trojans.

New Trojan technology is advancing rapidly, with Trojan developers and anti-Trojan vendors engaged in an arms race — each trying to keep up with the other side. Mainstream security sources often don't provide much coverage of new developments in the Trojan scene, and you should consider monitoring some of the underground Web sites to stay current with new threats.

And always remember: Beware of Greeks (or in this case, geeks) bearing gifts.

Chapter 10

Network Eavesdropping

"Saturday night I was downtown, workin' for the FBI . . ."
— The Hollies, "Long Cool Woman," *Distant Light*

Introduction to Network Spying

If you don't have physical access to a computer, you can always try to eavesdrop on it if it's connected to a network. The popularity of the Internet has made tens of millions of computers vulnerable to possible network attacks. When you say "network attack," the first thing most people think of is a malicious cracker trying to break into a computer. Network spying is a very close cousin to cracking because a spy uses many of the same tools and techniques as a cracker does in breaking into a system. The main difference is a professionally run espionage operation is going to be a whole lot harder to discover than your common, everyday "script kiddie" network attack, which often leaves behind many telltale signs.

This chapter provides a general overview of spying on wired networks (wireless network eavesdropping is discussed in Chapter 11), including the use of sniffers, vulnerability scanners, and other tools a spy often borrows from a cracker's black bag of tricks. A number of effective countermeasures that can blunt many of these attacks are also discussed.

Because entire books are devoted to networking attacks, the purpose of this chapter is to give you a basic working knowledge of the ins and outs of network eavesdropping. For those of you interested in developing and fine-tuning your network espionage skills, there are numerous references to Web sites and other resources that provide considerably more detail on specific vulnerabilities and exploits. Before launching into some of the particular tactics spies use in compromising networked computers, it's worthwhile to first explore some general network spying concepts.

Types of Network Attacks

Although there are thousands of possible network attacks based on different types of vulnerabilities, in general, data can be compromised two different ways.

✓ **Passive attack.** Passive attacks are attempts to compromise information by monitoring data packets that pass through a network and often involve using some type of a network monitor (sniffer) to eavesdrop on and view the data. Although it's theoretically possible to detect a sniffer, these types of attacks are very difficult to discover.

✓ **Active attack.** Active attacks directly compromise data on a hard drive or other storage media by taking advantage of operating-system and application vulnerabilities or poor security practices. An example is stealing documents from a system that has network file sharing enabled, but no password set to restrict access to the shared files. Another example is a Trojan horse application that covertly sends spy data out through a network connection. These types of attacks are discussed in Chapter 9.

In addition to passive and active attacks, there are also targeted and random attacks:

✓ **Targeted attack.** A targeted attack occurs when a specific computer or set of computers is selected for assault. Attacks can be launched remotely against known IP addresses or against the network itself by breaching physical security and installing a network-monitoring device. If an attack is launched from outside the network, valuable targeting information can come from DNS-related tools, such as whois, dig, or tracert. With these types of attacks, you're being specifically singled out for whatever reason. If this is the case, simple countermeasures may not be enough to stop a determined intruder.

✓ **Random attack.** In random attacks, which are much more common, the only reason you're being probed or attacked is because someone stumbled on your IP address during a scan for vulnerable systems. Random attacks are usually launched by crackers looking for a computer to break into to use as a relay point for other attacks, to store illegal files on, to launch distributed Denial of Service attacks from, to run IRC servers, or just to be generally malicious. These haphazard attacks are more the work of crackers or opportunistic criminals than spies; however, even if the intruder isn't specifically after your data, sensitive information still can be compromised if your system is breached.

Network Attack Origin Points

Unlike attacks that rely on physical access to a computer, network eavesdropping attempts can be launched from a number of different locations. This process gives the spy a number of advantages, including being harder to catch. If done correctly, trying to breach a system through a network is more difficult to detect and investigate than a black bag job, and is considerably less risky.

Some of the places a network attack can be initiated from include the following:

✓ **Network wall jack or cable.** This attack obviously requires physical access to the building where the network is in use. The spy connects to the network through an unused connection somewhere in a building (or taps into a cable). Laptops and PDAs are ideal for this type of attack because of their small size. Technical support staff will sometimes label an Ethernet cable or wall jack with its IP address, which then can be easily entered in the computer's network settings. If a server is running Dynamic Host Configuration Protocol (DHCP), an IP address will automatically be assigned to the spy's computer if it's configured to accept a dynamic address. That means Plug and Play network espionage. Some prior research may need to be done to reveal domain names and user accounts for targeted attacks.

✓ **Client computer in the network.** The spy relies on a computer already connected to the network. Although information on the hard drive is always a target, a larger goal may be to gain access to other computers on the network and compromise information that resides on them. This type of attack can be very damaging because most sites have defenses in place that protect a network against outside attack, but leave it open to attacks from within.

✓ **Server inside the network.** Physical access to a server presents a spy with many eavesdropping options. In addition to using the server as a launching point for compromising other computers, server logs can be read and monitored, a sniffer can be installed, and stored data can be compromised. Servers typically have more physical security measures in place to protect them, but they might not be sufficient to deter a serious spy.

✓ **Computer outside the network.** This is a classic cracker attack, in which the spy launches an attack on computers within the network (either clients or servers) from a computer outside the network. Most system administrators spend a lot of time and effort trying to prevent these types of break-ins. If a spy is smart, he will likely launch an attack through a series of compromised computers to hide his tracks. For example, instead of using his personal Internet account, he might visit a cybercafe across town and first telnet to a computer in Romania, Telnet from that computer to another in Japan, and then finally connect to a compromised university account in Mexico City to start his attack from. In the offhand chance that someone is able to follow his IP path across all of the international hops, they'll reach a dead end when they hit the cybercafe that the attack started from.

Information Compromised During Network Attacks

Instead of being vague and that saying "data" can be compromised during a network attack, let's get a bit more granular and look at exactly what type of data is vulnerable to network eavesdropping. In Chapter 5, you learned about some of the information and evidence that can be extracted from a hard drive if a spy has physical access to it. You should also know what types of information and evidence can be gathered during a networking attack.

If you're a spy, some of the data you can compromise — or if you're trying to protect your system, some of the data you need to secure — includes the following:

✓ **E-mail.** Who you send e-mail to, from whom you receive it, when you send and receive it, and what it says (including attachments) all passes through a network.

✓ **Passwords.** Any account names and passwords that are sent in the clear (unencrypted) over a network, including e-mail, FTP, and Telnet passwords and Web site logon information (if the site isn't using Secure Sockets Layer to encrypt the data) can easily be eavesdropped on.

✓ **Instant messaging/chat sessions.** Both sides of the conversation during instant messaging or chat sessions can be intercepted if they aren't encrypted.

✓ **Audio and video communications.** Any unencrypted audio (such as Voice over Internet or other protocols) or video communications can be monitored.

✓ **Web-surfing habits.** Profiles can be generated about you by examining the types of Web sites you visit and your activity within the Web site (when you visit, what you look at, and how often you visit).

✓ **File exchange transactions.** Any file uploading, downloading, or searching on peer-to-peer networks can be monitored.

✓ **Hard drive data.** A spy can launch an active attack against your computer over a network connection to gather information from shared folders or files. He can also use a Trojan horse attack, as described to Chapter 9, to have complete remote control of your computer.

Broadband Risks

The adoption of broadband Internet access through DSL and cable modems has increased the potential for computer espionage. Although corporate and government networks are often protected against network attacks, most home systems don't have the same level of protection. This lack can present a number of risks (or opportunities for a spy) if an employee is working on sensitive data at home.

Tactics: Traffic Analysis

Even if you encrypt your e-mail, an eavesdropper can still spy on you by using a technique called traffic analysis. *Traffic analysis* consists of recording and analyzing information, such as when messages are sent, to whom they are sent, and the size of the messages. This information can be compared with past or current events to make guesses about what the messages might relate to. When the government issues a terrorist alert based on "chatter," it's often because traffic analysis has detected an increase in message traffic from previously identified terrorist communication channels (whether it's e-mail, telephone, radio, or chat rooms). Increased communication may mean an attack is getting ready to happen as final instructions are given out (or it could also mean the terrorists are launching a disinformation campaign because they know traffic analysis is likely being performed on their communications networks).

A real world, noncomputer example of traffic analysis is the Pentagon Pizza Index. According to Frank Meeks, owner of a chain of Washington, D.C. Domino's Pizza parlors, late night pizza deliveries to the Pentagon and White House increased during the critical phase of an international crisis. Meeks says that during the invasions of Panama and Grenada, the start of the Gulf War, and other notable global incidents, pizza deliveries to the government skyrocketed. So you could count the number of pizza deliveries, and although you might not know the exact details of what was happening in planning and briefing rooms, you'd know it was something big. If you kept up on current events, you probably could make some pretty accurate guesses about possible outcomes.

Busted: John Deutch and the CIA

John Deutch headed the Central Intelligence Agency from May 1995 to December 1996. You don't get to be Director of Central Intelligence (DCI) by reading "Spy vs. Spy" in old issues of *Mad* magazine (see www.lambiek.net/prohias_antonio.htm), but sometimes you have to wonder.

Several days after Deutch's official departure as DCI, classified material was discovered on his government-owned computer, located at his Bethesda, Maryland residence. The computer was supposed to be for unclassified use only. If that wasn't bad enough, Deutch had used the computer to access the Internet, and at least two members of his family were also known to have regularly used it. (Deutch liked Macintoshes, and the five government-issued Macs he used all had PCMCIA card readers for 170MB Microtech microdrives that he swapped back and forth between office and home computers.)

Although he should have known better and was aware of the possible espionage risks, an investigation revealed that Deutch had a history of working with sensitive documents on unsecure computers. A CIA "technical exploitation team" (spook-speak for computer forensics team) recovered classified information from a number of Deutch's unclassified computers that included juicy tidbits about covert action, top-secret communications intelligence, and the National Reconnaissance Program budget. Investigators stated that it would be difficult to determine whether any classified information ever had been compromised, but noted that there definitely was potential for either a network or physical attack on the computers.

In 1999, Deutch was stripped of his security clearance by then-DCI George Tenet. Federal prosecutors continued to hound Deutch and offered him a deal, in which he would plead guilty to keeping government secrets on unsecured home computers, but not receive any prison time. On January 19, 2001, he signed a plea agreement, admitting to a misdemeanor and agreeing to pay a $5,000 fine. The next day, on his last day of office, President Bill Clinton surprised both the Justice Department and the CIA by giving Deutch a full presidential pardon.

John Deutch is currently a faculty member in the Department of Chemistry at MIT.

The complete unclassified CIA Deutch internal investigation report is available at www.fas.org/irp/cia/product/ig_deutch.html.

Some of the additional security concerns with broadband accounts include the following:

- ✓ **Fixed IP addresses.** Unlike a dial-up account, in which a different IP address is often assigned during each connection, broadband accounts usually provide a fixed IP address to a computer. If this address becomes known, you now have a static target.

- ✓ **Always on.** Because broadband accounts are always connected to the Internet, the computer is potentially vulnerable to attack whenever it's turned on.

✓ **Family access.** Even if the primary computer user takes adequate security measures to prevent attacks, other members of his or her family might not, which increases the chances of a successful compromise.

You shouldn't scrap broadband and return to a dial-up account though. Attack risks can be mitigated with some of the techniques discussed in the "Countermeasures" section of this chapter.

Spy Tactics

With some of the basic concepts of networking eavesdropping out of the way, it's time to get a bit more specific and explore vulnerabilities and exploits. In this section, your secret instructions are to place yourself in the shoes of an FBI Technically Trained Agent (TTA). You're investigating a suspected foreign terrorist in a large United States city. You've been granted a FISA wiretap court order (refer to Chapter 2 if you forgot what that is) and have full approval to use covert surveillance against the suspect. Your assignment is to monitor any computer network activity he might engage in. Normally, you'd rely on a DCS-1000 system (previously called Carnivore), but someone leaked the source code on the Internet a few weeks ago and a programmer in Russia discovered an obscure, packet-induced buffer overflow bug that crashes the system. Multiple platform exploit scripts were soon released, and the story appeared on Slashdot (slashdot.org). Now it seems that everyone is trying to crash real or imagined DCS-1000s that they suspect may be installed at their ISP. The Bureau has temporarily pulled in all of the units from the field to re-engineer them, so will have to do things the old-fashioned way. (For more information about the FBI's DCS-1000/Carnivore system, go to Chapter 13; the fictional buffer overflow is not described.)

Exploiting the Vulnerabilities

Before you perform your patriotic duty and start trying to crack the bad guy's computer over the Net, remember that computer espionage is about covertly gathering information without getting caught. Some common-sense tips to keep in mind before you fire up your tools and try to compromise network traffic or penetrate a system include the following:

✓ Don't scan or launch attacks from a computer whose IP address can be directly traced back to you.

✓ Always assume that the phone number you call a dial-up account from gets logged.

✓ Fully understand what traces of evidence you might leave on a computer if you successfully breach it.

✓ Have a thorough understanding of the way network intrusion detection systems (IDS) work.

✓ Assume that after you penetrated a system, your activities might be monitored.

✓ Don't spend a lot of time on a breached system.

✓ If you're with a law enforcement agency and are working with an ISP to monitor a criminal suspect, limit the number of ISP employees you have contact with, and reiterate the need for secrecy while the investigation is taking place.

✓ Depending on the target, it's possible to make an attack look like it was the work of crackers instead of spies. If you get burned, hopefully the target will think it was kids.

But because you're a highly trained TTA, you already know about operational security and all of this, so let's move forward and take a look at some approaches to compromising networked computers.

For more detailed accounts of specific network vulnerabilities and exploits, refer to *Hack Attacks Revealed,* by John Chirillo (Wiley, 2002). Information about the book is available at www.wiley.com/cda/product/0,,0471232823,00.html.

TARGET RESEARCH AND VULNERABILITY SCANNING

Just like any aspect of espionage, you need to do a bit of research before you start your operation. In this case, it will be on your target computer that's connected to a network (let's assume the Internet, but this could also be a corporate intranet). In general, this is a three-step process, including the following:

✓ **Target location.** Before you can perform a network attack on a computer, you need to know where it is. Unless you already know the IP address of the target, pinging and port scanning are generally used to discover a potential target.

✓ **Operating system identification.** After you locate a target, the next step is to determine what type of operating system and services it is running.

✓ **Vulnerability scanning.** After your target is located and identified, the next step is to check to see whether there are any vulnerabilities associated with it.

Let's look at each of these "ready, aim, fire" steps in a little more depth.

TARGET LOCATION   Just like you need to know the street address of a target to perform a black bag job, you also need to know the address (in this case, the IP address) of a target computer before you can attack it. You're in luck because your terrorist suspect has a DSL account with a fixed IP address, which his cooperative ISP already gave to you.

Target IP addresses are often discovered by using automated scanning utilities, specifically tools that perform ping scans and port scans.

✓ **Ping scan.** A ping scan involves sending packets of information to IP addresses to see whether a computer responds. This scan is performed with a ping utility that sends an ICMP Echo Request to a potential target. If the utility receives a reply, it logs the IP address. This method isn't entirely reliable because a computer may reject a ping request to avoid being detected.

✓ **Port scan.** A port scan is an attempt to locate a computer by determining whether services are running at a queried IP address. Different services have ports associated with them (for example, port 80 is associated with HTTP and Web servers, and port 23 is associated with Telnet). If a port-scanning tool discovers a port, it logs the IP address, and you know that you have a viable target. Port scanners are also very useful because an identified service might have a vulnerability that you can exploit to compromise a target computer.

Crackers tend to search for targets by scanning random blocks of IP addresses, looking for any potential targets. Spies are a bit more selective; they either target a single IP address discovered by other means (such as through social engineering or with a Trojan horse application) or a known block of IP addresses owned by a target corporation.

Keep in mind that a firewall can hide the presence of a computer (particularly if it's connected to the Internet and isn't running any services that support external connections), and a standard scan may report that there's no computer at an IP address, even though there really is. Additionally, a scan may reveal a corporate gateway that's protected by a firewall and blocks incoming network connections on various ports. Firewalls aren't impenetrable, though, and can be breached under certain circumstances.

Remember that unless you're using a port scanner that can perform stealth scans, your IP address will be revealed to the computer you're scanning and may be logged. A simple scan may go unnoticed, however, because there are so many Internet scans that occur on a daily basis launched by crackers all over the world looking for vulnerable systems.

For a complete list of commonly used ports and the services associated with them, go to the official Internet Assigned Numbers Authority list at `www.iana.org/assignments/port-numbers`. If you're using a port scanner, don't try to scan all the ports listed. Most port scans involve looking for only a handful of commonly used ports.

OPERATING SYSTEM IDENTIFICATION   After you identify a target's IP address and a list of services associated with it, the next step is to identify what type of operating system the computer is running. This is important so you know what type of vulnerabilities may be available to exploit. There are three ways to discover what kind of operating system a remote computer is running:

✓ **Unique ports.** The presence of certain ports may point to a specific operating system. For example, if you find an open 2869 TCP port, which is assigned for Universal Plug and Play, the computer at the other end is likely running Windows XP.

✓ **Banners.** Services often have an identification banner that's displayed when you connect to the service. For example, if you discover that a computer has an open port 25 (SMTP) after a port scan, you could use Telnet to connect to the port. Chances are, a banner with the name of the mail server and its version would be displayed (banners are usually not displayed by a client, for example your e-mail client doesn't display a banner when you connect to the mail server). This can be helpful in identifying the type of operating system being used.

✓ **TCP/IP fingerprinting.** Operating systems all have slight differences in TCP/IP stack implementations. By analyzing returned TCP packets, it's possible to identify a remote operating system. Utilities such as Nmap, described in the "Network-Information and - Eavesdropping Tools" section of this chapter, make operating system fingerprinting through TCP/IP fairly easy.

VULNERABILITY SCANNING   After you identify active ports and the operating system, the next step is to determine whether there are any vulnerabilities present that you can exploit to gain access to the computer. Vulnerability scans can either be performed manually or automatically. For example, the Unix Sendmail application was well-known for a number of security flaws. If you discover that a system is running a certain version of Sendmail (which the banner would display if you Telneted to port 25), you could use a specific version exploit to get root access.

Of course, manually checking for vulnerabilities is a very tedious and time-consuming process. A better approach is to use a commercial or free vulnerability scanner to probe a system. Just provide an IP address, and the tool consults a library of known vulnerabilities and then reports which ones are present. Then you locate an exploit that someone has already coded for the vulnerability (either a binary or the source code) and run it against the target to compromise the computer.

The Neohapsis archives are an excellent place to find information about vulnerabilities and exploits that have been published in a variety of security-related mailing lists. To visit the archives, go to `http://archives.neohapsis.com`.

WINDOWS FILE SHARING

Because this book focuses primarily on computer spying on Windows systems, it's important to discuss Windows file sharing, which is probably one of the largest potential networking vulnerabilities. (You might also hear references to Windows file sharing and NetBIOS, or Network Basic Input Output System. NetBIOS is an application-programming interface that supplements the BIOS by adding special functions for LANs. The terms *Windows file sharing* and *NetBIOS* are often used interchangeably.)

Starting with Windows 3.11 (Windows for Workgroups), Microsoft has provided all versions of Windows with the capability to share files or folders across a network with other Windows computers. The underlying mechanism of Windows file sharing is the Common Internet File System (CIFS) protocol, formerly known as Server Message Block (SMB). CIFS allows a computer to manipulate files on a networked remote Windows machine just as if they were local (CIFS also supports Unix-to-Windows connectivity).

Transparent file access is a very valuable feature, but network shares that are improperly configured can expose critical system files or sensitive data to attack. One of the ways the Sircam virus and Nimda worm spread so rapidly during the summer of 2001 was by discovering unprotected Windows network shares and copying themselves to the shares. Many computer users unknowingly open their systems up to eavesdroppers when they make their drives readable and writeable, so coworkers or family members can easily access files. Even when a system is configured securely, there are a number of tools and techniques for breaching protected shares.

Because of the vulnerabilities in Windows file sharing, it's long been a favorite target of crackers, and spies should find it just as exploitable. If active NetBIOS ports are discovered during a port scan, you know there's a Windows system present that might be sharing files. You can then target it with networking tools to get information about the shares, directly connect to them, or launch a brute-force attack to crack password-protected shares. If a system hasn't been hardened, you may be quite successful in compromising sensitive files.

However with our suspected terrorist, you tell your boss there's no real need to attempt a NetBIOS attack to access his files remotely. A team has already completed a black bag job on the suspect's apartment and has mirrored his hard drive. Also, because NetBIOS vulnerabilities are so widely known by crackers and virus writers, many ISPs, particularly broadband providers, block attempts to scan and access ports 137, 138, and 139 from the Internet. There are other investigative techniques you can use in this case that will be much more productive.

To learn more details about NetBIOS attacks, check out a cracker tutorial put together by "ethical hacker" Gaurav Kumar at www.mycgiserver.com/~ethicalhackers/netbios.html.

NETWORK MONITORING

Eavesdropping on data as it passes through a network can provide all sorts of interesting information for a spy. Any data that isn't encrypted is easily viewed, completely passively, and without a target ever knowing her data has been compromised.

With your terrorist investigation, you have two goals: collect possible evidence of criminal wrongdoing and gather intelligence that could prevent an upcoming terrorist incident in the process. Network monitoring is where you decide to concentrate your time and resources.

SNIFFERS   A sniffer (also called a packet sniffer, protocol analyzer, or network monitor) is a tool that eavesdrops on traffic in a computer network. If you monitor the raw packet traffic, all you see is a stream of bytes passing through the network a la the green phosphorescent characters in the movie *The Matrix*. That's not very useful, so to make sense out of the raw data in addition to capturing network traffic, sniffers decode the binary data and transform it into readable data based on the protocols that are associated with the connection. For example, a browser request to a Web server would be correctly decoded so you could easily read the HTTP conversation between the two computers.

On an Ethernet network, traffic passes through every network card, with the card ignoring any traffic that isn't meant for it. (If a packet frame has a different MAC address than the network card, the card won't accept that packet). However, network cards can be put into promiscuous mode, which allows the card to read all of the traffic passing over the network. A software-hosted sniffer puts a network card in promiscuous mode and then captures the data that passes through it.

Sniffers work great on a conventional Ethernet network that has routers and hubs, but when you start introducing switches into the network configuration, a software sniffer receives data only from the computer on which it's installed. Switches are designed to send network traffic only from one physical port to another. They typically don't transmit traffic to all computers in the network. To be able to sniff a switched network, you need to install a network tap device between the computer and its switch port. The tap echoes the data flow between the computer and the rest of the network. A sniffer can then be plugged into the tap to collect the data. You can also use a technique called ARP (Address Resolution Protocol) spoofing. Tom King wrote an excellent article about this approach, which is available at `www.sans.org/rr/netdevices/packet.php`.

Most sniffers can display data in real time as it's collected or save it for future viewing. Additionally, filters can be used to capture only certain types of traffic (for example, from a specific IP address). With your terrorism investigation, you could install a sniffer at the ISP and monitor only inbound and outbound network traffic related to your suspect, without violating the privacy rights of other customers. Networks generate a tremendous amount of noise with control packets, DNS requests, and other information that's probably not relevant to your spying activities. You can also use filters to display or save data related only to specific protocols, such as SMTP and POP for e-mail or HTTP for Web browsing.

Tools of the Trade: Commercial Carnivores

The FBI's DCS-1000/Carnivore program is fully discussed in Chapter 13, but because we're discussing sniffers, it's worth mentioning a few commercial products that perform the same type of network monitoring as DCS-1000 does. You don't need a badge to buy them, but hold on to your wallet. Some products of note include the following:

✓ **SilentRunner.** SilentRunner is a high-end networking and analysis tool produced by Raytheon (a longtime big government contractor). To learn more about the utility, see `www.silentrunner.com`.

✓ **NetIntercept.** NetIntercept is another network data-gathering and analysis tool developed by Sandstorm Enterprises. For more information, go to `www.sandstorm.net/products/netintercept/`.

✓ **DragNet.** DragNet, originally developed by Traxess Inc. (which was acquired by Network Associates in August 2002), combines keylogging and network-monitoring features. The product is supposed to be released in 2003, and information should be available upon its release at `www.nai.com`.

✓ **RetrievalWare.** It's one thing to collect gigabytes of data, it's another to wade through all of it and extract and analyze anything that's useful. Although not designed specifically for monitoring purposes, data mining applications, such as Convera's RetrievalWare, are in use by the FBI and various government intelligence agencies. For more information go to `www.convera.com`.

If you're on a budget and have networking and C experience, you can always snag a copy of Altivore, which was going to be an open-source version of Carnivore, but just barely got out of the starting blocks. Source code and information are available at `www.robertgraham.com/altivore/`.

Robert Graham, a computer industry veteran and developer of the BlackICE firewall product, has a comprehensive FAQ on sniffers at `www.robertgraham.com/pubs/sniffing-faq.html`.

SERVER LOGS   In addition to sniffing data from the wire, you can also gather information about network traffic that's logged by a server. Server logs typically provide transactional data, such as the source and destination IP addresses, the time a transaction took place, and information that's specific to a certain type of server (for example, a mail server will report the e-mail address of the sender and receiver, the time the message was sent or received, the size of the message, and other information). Anyone who has physical or remote access to a server, including legitimate system administrators, law enforcement officers with a court order, or spies who have breached security can get at this transactional data. (Also, don't forget about the logs generated by firewalls on home or small business computers.)

In the case of our hypothetical terrorist investigation, the suspect's ISP is very cooperative in letting you review server log entries related to the suspect. In order to protect the privacy rights of other customers, you request log entries associated only with the suspect's IP address. A helpful system administrator writes a quick Perl script that parses various logs and extracts entries related to the suspect. You quickly review the script and suggest that she add some code for generating an MD5 hash of the extracted data just for verification's sake. She sets up a chron job (commands or scripts that are automatically run at a specified time or date) so the script is run every day at 7:30 a.m.. The output is encrypted and then automatically e-mailed to a dummy Hotmail account you set up. (Sending it to your fbi.gov address would not be good tradecraft.)

Because server applications generate a considerable amount of data, log files are deleted on a regular basis to save disk space. During the investigation of Zacarias Moussaoui, the so-called 20th hijacker from the 9/11 terrorist attacks, deleted computer logs at Kinko's and Microsoft's Hotmail service prevented investigators from gathering possible evidence in the case. You request that various logs be archived for the duration of the investigation. In the event that your suspect is prosecuted, you know that the logs could play an important role as evidence, mostly to corroborate the hashed log entries you've been getting on a daily basis.

You thank everyone you had contact with at the ISP for their cooperation, stressing that this is a matter of national security and that secrecy about the investigation is crucial. After a few X-Files jokes, you tell the ISP manager that you'll stay in touch and let her know if you need anything else.

INSPECTING NETWORKING HARDWARE

Networking devices such as routers, switches, and firewalls (both hardware and software) can also provide information about a target's activities. This is especially true in home and small office networks, in which users often don't have enough of a technical background to understand the risks.

EXAMINING LOG FILES   These networking devices and applications keep logs of incoming and outgoing networking connections. The logs can be a valuable source of information for seeing what type of network activity someone has been engaged in. Log files typically contain the date and time, the source and destination IP addresses, and the port numbers (which will give you a general idea of what the target is doing; for example, activity on port 23 typically means an encrypted SSH connection).

Busted: Political Dirty Tricks

During the 2000 Minnesota state senate race, a series of e-mails were sent to Democratic Farmer Labor delegates, urging them not to support candidate Mike Ciresi at the party's state nominating convention. The e-mails attacked Ciresi, calling him anti-union and anti-environment. The e-mail came from a Hotmail account (kylomb@hotmail.com) and was from a "committed progressive" party member named Katie Stevens.

However, when Ciresi staffers started to investigate, they couldn't find a Katie Stevens. Evidence started to point toward Ciresi's rival, Republican incumbent Senator Rob Grams. Grams' campaign was being run by Christine Gunhus, who also happened to be his fiancée. As the e-mails were examined, a series of clues pointed authorities toward Gunhus and a dirty tricks campaign.

Some of the e-mails had Microsoft Word attachments, and the author in the document properties was listed as Christine Gunhus. (Word automatically inserts this information, based on the identity of the registered owner of the software.) Strike one.

Hotmail messages have an X-Originating-IP header that displays the originating IP address of the message. The first messages showed that they were sent from a pay-by-the-minute workstation at a Kinko's copy center. Later e-mail came from an AT&T WorldNet account, however. AT&T kept Caller ID records of all incoming calls to their modem pools. When authorities requested the records associated with the originating IP address in the timeframe the email was sent, they found one of the phone numbers used to access the dial-up service belonged to Christine Gunhus. Strike two.

Gunhus was using an older version of Word that inserted something called a Globally Unique Identifier (GUID). The GUID contained the Media Access Control (MAC) number of a network card if it was installed. Because MACs are supposed to be unique, the GUID could lead someone back to the computer that created the document (or at least its network card). When the police served a search warrant on Gunhus, they found that the MAC number on her computer's network card matched the GUID on the documents sent with the e-mail. Strike three, you're out!

Dirty tricks like the ones Gunhus pulled are a felony under Minnesota's Fair Campaign Practices Act, which prohibits campaigns from disseminating anonymous information. In June 2001, Gunhus pleaded no contest to the offense and was fined; prosecutors decided not to press for jail time. Ciresi lost the primary for his party (not from Gunhus's e-mail, but due to a strong ad campaign by opponent Mike Dayton), and Grams ultimately lost the general election and failed to regain his Senate seat.

Log data is stored in the device's memory and then is accessed with a software application that interfaces to the hardware device. Data in memory is then transferred to a log file that resides on the user's hard drive. By default, a number of software firewalls keep a text file log or logs of network connections. Many users don't realize this, so they neglect to deal with router and firewall logs that list the sites they were visiting and when they were accessed when they clean up traces of their Web-surfing activities at the browser level.

EXPLOITING DEFAULT PASSWORDS   Most networking devices have a password to restrict access to management features of the device, and in many instances, the user or system administrator never changes the default password. This is especially risky because lists of default passwords are widely available on the Internet. If you can identify what type of networking device is being used and then remotely or locally access the device with a default password, you can change security settings or access information stored in the hardware.

For an extensive and frequently updated list of default passwords for a number of different hardware devices, go to `www.phenoelit.de/dpl/index.html`.

OTHER NETWORK-RELATED ATTACKS

Aside from breaking into a computer over a network, using sniffers, or examining server logs, there are other network-related attacks you can perform to compromise data, including the following:

MALICIOUS APPLICATIONS   Another approach to network monitoring is to install some type of malicious application on a target computer that gathers information (whether it's from network traffic or not) and have the application send the data to you. There are commercial keyloggers, discussed in Chapter 8, that can do this, as well as Trojan horse applications, covered in Chapter 9.

Malicious applications can either be installed during a black bag job or remotely in the same manner in which a virus or worm is spread, such as with an e-mail attachment. In our suspect terrorist case, a black bag job might be appropriate; for example, the one the FBI performed on Nicodermo Scarfo. (The keylogger they used may or may not have had the capability to remotely send data. We'll never know because details about the keylogger were never revealed, unless a leak or Freedom of Information Act request provides more clues sometime in the future.)

These types of malicious applications are especially useful on computers with broadband connections because they are always connected to the Internet and can readily send data at any time, such as when the target is sleeping and doesn't notice network activity occurring. The main drawback of this kind of attack is that a computer-security-savvy target will likely be using firewalls and other countermeasures that could easily detect and defeat the application after it was installed.

A classic example of a malicious application that uses a network connection is a tool called the Stealth Email Redirector (SER). After SER is installed, it automatically sends a copy of all outgoing mail that passes through port 25 (SMTP) to a specified e-mail address (be sure to use a hard-to-trace dummy account). Information about this product is available at `www.softsecurity.com/products/ser/`.

MALICIOUS WEB SITES   Related to malicious code directly installed on a computer is malicious code that runs when the target visits a Web site. Internet Explorer is currently the most widely used Web browser, and unfortunately it has a very checkered reputation for having a number of security flaws. Malicious ActiveX controls, Active Scripting vulnerabilities, Java virtual machine holes, and stack overflows are just some of the techniques a spy could use in a Web page that was crafted to steal information off of a hard drive after the page was opened. The Web site code could be very selective and only execute against a known IP address or other pieces of user information extracted from the browser. Getting the target to visit the Web page is a matter of social engineering, either through e-mail or over the phone.

These attacks can be very effective because

✓ Unlike viruses, must users aren't aware of the dangers of malevolent Web pages.

✓ If executed correctly, the attack is very hard to detect.

✓ Most people don't use security patches to address vulnerabilities.

For a comprehensive list of recently patched and unpatched security flaws in Internet Explorer that could possibly be used by a spy, go to pivx.com/larholm/unpatched/.

PUBLIC ACCESS INTERNET TERMINALS AND NETWORKS   Another network-related vulnerability you could exploit for espionage purposes revolves around the growing popularity of cybercafes, libraries, hotels, Kinkos', and Internet kiosks that offer a cheap and easy way to connect to the Internet. These convenient public access sources provide a way for busy people to check e-mail and access the Net while on the road. Some of the techniques you can use to compromise sensitive data include the following:

✓ **Shoulder surfing.** "Shoulder surfing" is cracker jargon for watching someone as he types in his account and password on a keyboard. Any public access Internet terminal provides an opportunity (you shouldn't be blatant when you do this, of course). Even if the keyboard can't be fully seen, a good shoulder-surfer can narrow down possibilities by watching the finger position as keys are entered and by counting the number of keystrokes. This skill is useful in any setting when someone is logging on to a computer.

✓ **Keyloggers.** Hardware or software keyloggers can easily be installed on public access computers to record data entered by a user. For more about keyloggers, refer to Chapter 8.

✓ **Server and network access.** Court orders, bribery, social engineering, cracking, or just plain employee nosiness can give someone access to a network. There have been reports that some hotels in Europe monitor business traveler Internet traffic on hotel-provided computers or network connections for economic espionage purposes at the behest of their government. In the United States, the FBI has actively sought information from public-access Internet providers for its investigations.

Network-Information and -Eavesdropping Tools

Now that you have a basic understanding of some of the vulnerabilities and associated attacks you can launch against networked computers, it's time to look at some of the specific tools you can use to make your eavesdropping job easier. Most are free and publicly available, and you don't need to flash a badge to download them.

SAMSPADE

SamSpade is a freeware network information and discovery tool (shown in Figure 10-1). It includes a number of network tools such as whois, tracert, ping, and dig that are useful for finding out information about networked computers. This is an invaluable tool for researching specific targets. SamSpade can be downloaded from www.samspade.org. The same Web site also offers online versions of the software tools, just in case you're somewhere with a Net connection and don't have your trusty tools with you.

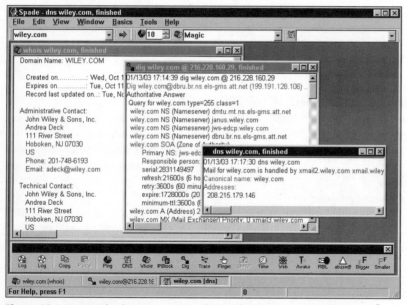

Figure 10-1: SamSpade, showing a variety of data relating to a targeted company's network. Information like this can be very useful in planning a network attack.

NMAP

There are many port scanners available on the Internet, but the top choice for security professionals and spies is Nmap. Nmap, which stands for Network Mapper, which is a free, open-source utility written by Fyodor, can locate target computers, query what services they are running, and identify operating systems running on the targets.

What sets Nmap apart from other port scanners is its capability to use a number of different methods for discovering information about a target computer. Some of the scan techniques are incredibly stealthy and difficult to detect, even when target computers are running intrusion detection systems (IDS). One technique called Idlescan allows an attacker to probe a computer without revealing his IP address by bouncing packets off some unwitting host.

Nmap originally was a command-line tool that ran only under Unix systems, but recently a Window version has been developed. The original Unix version of Nmap can be downloaded from www.insecure.org/nmap/, and the Windows version can be downloaded from www.nmapwin.org.

SUPERSCAN

If you don't care about stealth (which as a spy you should), but are looking for a fast, easy-to-use TCP port scanner, check out SuperScan (see Figure 10-2) from Foundstone. The utility is free and can be downloaded from www.foundstone.com/knowledge/proddesc/superscan.html.

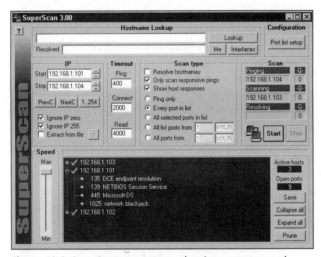

Figure 10-2: SuperScan port scanner, showing computers and open ports on a LAN behind a router.

NESSUS

Nessus is an open-source security scanner written by Renaud Deraison that's been around since 1998. Nessus has a server component that carries out the security checks and a client component that acts as the user interface. The utility has an extensive library of vulnerabilities to check for. In January 2003, there were more than 1,100 "plug-ins" available that you could download to see whether security weaknesses were present in a number of different devices and operating systems. New plug-in scripts are constantly added as new vulnerabilities are discovered.

After you configure the client and server components, just enter a target IP address (Nessus can work with Nmap to perform stealthy port scans), select which security tests you want to run, and Nessus will probe the target for vulnerabilities. When it finishes the scan, the utility generates a complete report, listing discovered vulnerabilities, external references, and solutions to fix the problem.

The downside for Windows users is that the server component is available only for Unix-compatible systems. However, this is a valuable enough tool to persuade you to install Linux just so you can use it. To get more information or to download the free utility, go to www.nessus.org. (If you absolutely need to have a Windows-hosted vulnerability scanner, you'll need to turn to relatively expensive commercial products such as Internet Security Systems' Internet Scanner, which you can learn more about at www.iss.net.)

NETBIOS TOOLS

There are a number of tools available for compromising computers using Windows file sharing. Two popular NetBIOS attack utilities include the following:

✓ NAT (NetBIOS Auditing Tool) is a command-line tool that can identify NetBIOS shares and launch brute-force password attacks against them. The utility is free and can be downloaded from http://online.securityfocus.com/tools/543.

✓ Legion is similar in function to NAT, but is written in Visual Basic and sports a Windows user interface. The now-defunct Rhino9 security group wrote the tool, and it was shareware at the time of its release in 1997. Although showing its age, the tool still works with current versions of Windows and is available at packetstormsecurity.org/groups/rhino9/legionv21.zip.

ETHEREAL

One of the most popular sniffers for both Windows and Unix systems is a free tool called Ethereal (see Figure 10-3). Originally written by Gerald Combs, the utility has turned into an open-source project with many contributors, and is widely used by network administrators as well as spies and crackers all over the world.

Ethereal can interactively capture traffic from Ethernet, Token-Ring, and other networks, as well as read capture files from other sniffers (the protocol analysis routines can reconstruct data from more than 340 different protocols). This is handy if you want to install a small simple packet sniffer, such as WinDump (available from windump.polito.it), for unattended network monitoring and then come back later to examine the captured data. Ethereal has extensive filtering capabilities and a "Follow TCP Stream" option for reviewing a session's complete protocol data stream.

Ethereal is a must-have tool for any spy interested in network eavesdropping. You can learn more about the tool and download it at www.ethereal.com.

Many Windows-hosted sniffers such as Ethereal require WinPcap, a Win32 port of Unix's libpcap (a widely used network programming API for capturing and sending network packets). Researchers at the Politecnico di Torino in Italy developed the free WinPcap and companion applications. If you're using Windows XP, be sure you're running WinPcap version 2.3 or higher. For more information about WinPcap and to download it, go to http://winpcap.polito.it.

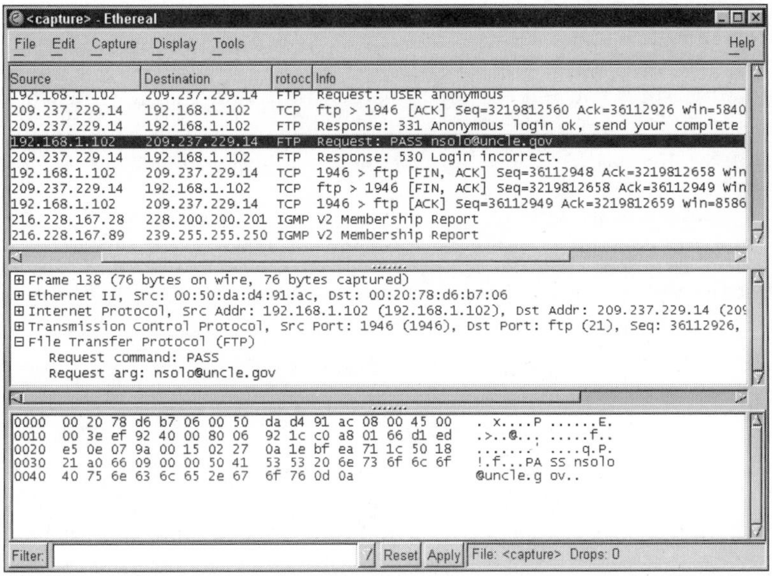

Figure 10-3: Ethereal, capturing network traffic from a sniffed FTP session including the user account and password.

OTHER SNIFFERS

Although Ethereal and other commercial packet sniffers are well-suited to both spying and legitimate system administration purposes, there are a few other sniffers out there that seem to have been designed expressly for espionage, including the following:

✓ **Dsniff.** Dsniff is a password sniffer written by Dug Song that was originally designed to run under Unix. Instead of capturing and displaying all network traffic, Dsniff just shows accounts and passwords sniffed from any FTP, Telnet, HTTP, POP, NNTP, IMAP, IRC, AIM, Microsoft SMB, and a variety of other protocol authentication sequences. Mike Davis ported a version that runs under Windows, and it's available from www.datanerds.net/~mike/dsniff.html.

✓ **Ettercap.** Ettercap is a multiple platform sniffer, developed by Alberto Ornaghi and Marco Valleri, that's designed to capture data on switched networks by using ARP spoofing. It can scan for information on a network and collect passwords used by a number of protocols. Ettercap is free and available from http://ettercap.sourceforge.net.

✓ **Cain & Abel.** Cain & Abel is an amazing Swiss Army knife tool that's capable of sniffing data on switched networks and cracking a number of encrypted passwords that it encounters. The utility, which was written by Massimiliano Montoro, is available at www.oxid.it.

Countermeasures

There are a variety of countermeasures you can employ to harden your system against network spies. These defenses also help protect you from network attacks launched by crackers, who are probably more of a viable threat due to their sheer numbers and the large number of cracking tools readily available on the Internet.

For detailed information on various countermeasures, refer to *Hack Attacks Denied,* by John Chirillo (Wiley, 2002). Information about the book is available at `www.wiley.com/cda/product/` `0,,0471232831,00.html`.

Some of the defensive measures include using the same offensive tools a spy might use against you (kind of like fighting fire with fire), so you'll have a better understanding of your system weaknesses. The following section outlines the key countermeasures to consider in your fight against network eavesdroppers.

Applying Operating System and Application Updates

Make sure that Windows, Internet Explorer, Outlook, Microsoft Office products, and any software that connects to the Internet all have current security patches installed. (Chapter 4 lists several ways to stay up-to-date with Windows and other Microsoft software security-related patches.)

Because of the many security flaws in Outlook, Outlook Express, and Internet Explorer, consider replacing your Microsoft e-mail client and Web browser with third-party applications if you're serious about security. There are many free and low-cost alternatives to these Microsoft products. (Some third-party, non-Microsoft products may invoke code in Internet Explorer and Outlook when they run, which subjects them to the same browser and e-mail vulnerabilities. Either do some research to ensure the application doesn't depend on potentially insecure code or if it does, be sure to apply Internet Explorer and Outlook security patches even if you're not using the Microsoft products.) Also, you might consider trying a desktop-oriented version of Linux because the operating system is becoming friendly enough for the average user to install. In addition, products such as Open Office (available for both Linux and Windows) offer a free alternative to Microsoft's Office suite. (This isn't to say that Linux and Linux applications aren't vulnerable to attacks. As Linux increases in popularity, expect more security flaws to be discovered in the operating system and its associated applications. There is a positive correlation between popularity and discovered vulnerabilities.)

Using Intrusion Detection Systems

An intrusion detection system (IDS) is a software utility that looks for signs that your network is being probed or attacked. A network IDS listens to network traffic and analyzes it for patterns that might indicate that an attack is taking place. A host-based IDS examines server logs looking for attack patterns and may also incorporate file integrity options to detect covertly modified system files. After an attack pattern is recognized from a series of rule sets, the IDS alerts an administrator that an attack is taking place.

Some commercial and free Windows-hosted IDS products to consider include the following:

✓ **Snort.** Snort is a very popular, free, open-source intrusion detection tool. Originally developed for Unix-type operating systems, a version was ported to Windows. Snort performs real-time traffic analysis and packet logging on networks and can detect a number of different attacks and probes, such as buffer overflows, stealth port scans, CGI attacks, SMB probes, and OS fingerprinting attempts. Snort is a bit complicated to set up and install for a nontechnical user, but there are some decent tutorials for installing it under Windows. The tool is available at www.snort.org.

✓ **BlackIce PC Protection.** Although some security experts argue whether BlackIce (formerly called BlackIce Defender) is primarily an IDS or a firewall, this pioneer security product offers a number of powerful features for the moderate to advanced user. A single license PC version is $39.95, with the server version priced at $299.95. For more information about BlackIce or to download a trial version of the product, go to www.iss.net.

✓ **Securepoint Intrusion Detection.** Securepoint Intrusion Detection is a relatively new freeware Windows IDS that shows some promise. The product was developed by the German security company Securepoint and can be downloaded at www.securepoint.cc/en/products-sids.html.

Robert Graham has an excellent FAQ on intrusion detection systems at www.robertgraham.com/pubs/network-intrusion-detection.html.

Using Firewalls

Firewalls offer protection from intruders by serving as a barrier between a computer system and the outside world (usually the Internet). Firewalls work by preventing certain data packets from reaching the computer while allowing other types of data in. Think of a firewall as a guard for all TCP/IP traffic on your network, constantly challenging packets to identify themselves as friend or foe, based on a set of rules you've provided the firewall with.

There are both hardware and software firewalls, and sometimes the two are used together. In general, firewalls use three types of filtering mechanisms to restrict network traffic, including the following:

✓ **Application filtering.** Usually found in personal software firewalls, this type of filtering allows outbound network connections from trusted applications and blocks or alerts the user when an untrusted application tries to establish an outbound connection. This is useful for stopping Trojan horses and other spyware that try to covertly send data over the Internet.

✓ **Packet filtering.** Packet filtering is simply allowing or blocking packets based on their packet header information. You establish a set of rules for accepting or denying packets based on attributes, such as the source or destination IP address, the source or destination ports, or the network protocol.

✓ **Stateful packet inspection (SPI).** The firewall looks at the source and destination IP addresses, the source and destination ports, and the sequence numbers to decide whether the packet belongs to a current open connection. This ensures that all communications are initiated by the computer the firewall is running on and take place only with remote computers that are known and trusted from previous interactions. SPI firewalls also close off ports until a connection to the specific port is requested, which helps defeat port scanning.

One very important point to consider is that firewalls aren't magic and don't provide an impenetrable layer of defense for your system. There are a number of ways in which firewalls can be breached, many based on architecture or unpatched product vulnerabilities. (For example, go to www.paoloiorio.it/fw.htm and check out Paolo Iorio's FIREWAR, which can remotely disable many popular personal firewalls.) Be sure that you know the capabilities and limitations of your firewall before you stake your security on it.

 There are a number of free Web-hosted services that perform probes and port scans against a computer at a specified IP address in order to test its firewall (or lack of one). Steve Gibson's Shield's Up site is a very popular, trusted site that can be accessed at www.grc.com/x/ne.dll?bh0bkyd2. Sygate offers a more thorough port scan service at http://scan.sygatech.com.

HARDWARE FIREWALLS

Firewall functionality is usually built into network routers and switches that serve as a gateway from a LAN to a WAN such as the Internet. Inbound and inbound traffic are controlled by a set of user-defined rules. You specify the rules and set up the firewall by using Telnet or a browser to connect to the device and then configure it.

Many routers feature Dynamic Host Configuration Protocol (DHCP) and Network Address Translation (NAT). DHCP automatically assigns IP addresses to computers connected to the router. This feature is popular with home and small business users who set up networks to share a single broadband connection. NAT hides the IP addresses of the computers behind the router, so all outgoing traffic appears to come from a single address. Some manufacturers call products with NAT firewalls, but they really aren't.

It's important to understand that all hardware firewall products aren't created equal. An under-$100 Linksys router designed for home or small business use will not have the features found in a Cisco router designed for enterprise use. Enterprise firewalls have more sophisticated packet filtering and logging capabilities and are better equipped to handle higher network traffic volumes.

SOFTWARE FIREWALLS

With the advent of home and small business broadband connections, software firewalls have dramatically increased in popularity over the past several years. There are really two types of software firewalls:

Countermeasures: Watching the Walls

If you're serious about your security, you should regularly check your firewall logs. Information in the logs can provide clues about whether someone is interested in breaking into your system.

Many popular lower-end hardware firewalls have limited logging capabilities and don't do a great job of capturing information about probes and attack attempts. There are software applications that interface with the hardware to offer better data on network activity, including probes and attacks. Two popular utilities include the following:

✓ **WallWatcher,** a free logging tool for Linksys products available from `www.wallwatcher.com`.

✓ **Kiwi Syslog Daemon,** a tool that works with firewalls that generate standard syslog output with free and commercial versions available from `www.kiwisyslog.com`.

These tools can provide you with detailed statistics of your network traffic, including hostile connections.

✓ **Gateway.** A gateway firewall is a computer that sits between the Internet and a LAN exclusively running firewall or router software. Old 486 and Pentium computers running Linux and free security software are popular in this role. (If you're interested in this topic, check out `www.linux-firewall-tools.com/linux/`.)

✓ **Personal.** A personal firewall is installed on an individual computer and acts as a watchdog for incoming and outgoing network traffic. Popular Windows firewalls include Kerio, Norton, Sygate, and ZoneAlarm.

Personal firewalls tend to be fairly easy to use and don't require much skill to install. They can be used alone or in conjunction with a hardware firewall as an insurance policy in case one or the other is breached.

Another reason for using a personal firewall is they support something hardware firewalls don't: filtered outbound connections. The firewall can be a useful feature if a Trojan horse has been covertly installed on your computer because it alerts you that an application is trying to make an outbound connection to the Internet to send data. You can select applications you know are trustworthy, such as a Web browser, so you aren't alerted each time a trusted application connects to the Internet. (The Windows XP Internet Connection Firewall (ICF) doesn't provide outbound filtering. Because of this lack, consider using a free or commercial third-party firewall to maximize your security.)

It's possible for a skilled spy to compromise Internet Explorer to use it to covertly send data under the radar screen of a personal firewall. If you're serious about security, you may want to consider using a different Web browser, such as Mozilla, Phoenix, or Opera.

Most commercial personal firewall vendors have free versions of their products available that are only for personal use and have a reduced set of features (they are usually perfectly adequate for protecting a home computer against a network attack).

For a list of firewall vendors, mainly enterprise-oriented, check the Computerworld Buyer's Guide at `www.computerworld.com/services/buyersguide/subcat/0,4846,KEY73_ SUB16,00.html`. For more detailed information on SOHO (Small Office Home Office) firewall products, including specifications and reviews, go to `www.firewallguide.com`.

Running a Virtual Private Network

A virtual private network (VPN) is a private network that uses the public Internet instead of dedicated leased network lines. With a VPN you can access your home or office network transparently from anywhere you have an Internet connection.

VPNs work by using special protocols, such as IPSec, L2TP, or PPTP, between two computers or networks connected to the Internet. This process is known as *tunneling*. Each IP packet is encrypted and then wrapped inside another packet with header information that allows it to travel from point to point. When the packet reaches its destination, the VPN software removes the header, decrypts the packet, and routes it to its intended destination. VPNs offer a secure way of networking over the Internet without exposing your data to spies armed with sniffers.

Countermeasures: Knowing the Enemy

One way to determine whether attacks on your system are specifically targeted against you or are part of a larger scale series of probes and attacks, is to install software that parses your firewall log and sends it to a central server that collects and analyzes the data.

There are several free services that process firewall log data and report any cracking attempts to the ISP the attack originated from. If the ISP replies back, you can learn whether any actions have been taken against the suspected attacker. You can also look up information about the IP address and see whether it has been used to scan or crack other computers (or whether you're the exclusive target).

The two most popular clients, MyNetWatchman and Dshield, are both free. For more information or to download them, go to their companion Web sites at

✓ `www.mynetwatchman.com`

✓ `www.dshield.org`

The service providers who developed these tools and run these sites believe that if more people use the clients, casual cracking attempts will decrease because the attackers are held accountable for their actions by ISPs.

Windows 2000 and XP both have built-in support for setting up VPN connections and acting as clients. There is also a variety of free and commercial software packages as well as hardware available for setting up VPNs. (One popular, free, open-source application is called Stunnel, which uses Secure Sockets Layer to set up secure communications between a server and client. For more information, visit www.stunnel.org.)

VPN Labs is an excellent Web resource for learning more about VPNs. To visit it, go to www.vpnlabs.com.

Monitoring Network Connections

Sometimes you might not need all the information provided by a sniffer. Perhaps you're only curious about the possible presence of some spyware that's covertly transmitting information from your computer out over the Internet. There are several tools you can use to monitor which ports on your computer are listening for and receiving data.

The easiest way to get a list of the ports that are currently open is to type the following at the command line: netstat -a.

The only problem with the netstat command is it won't tell you which program is using a port. Fortunately, there are other more user-friendly Windows utilities that provide you with more detailed port information, including the following:

✓ **Inzider.** Lists the processes and which ports are currently listening. It is free and available from ntsecurity.nu/toolbox/inzider/.

✓ **TCPView.** Displays processes that currently are listening or have a network connection established. It is free and available from www.sysinternals.com.

✓ **TDImon.** Another Sysinternals.com tool that displays real-time TCP and UDP information, including the process that's connected to the Internet, source and destination ports and IP addresses, and other networking information.

Using Sniffers

Put on your trenchcoat and play spy by running a sniffer such as Ethereal or Ettercap on your own network to see what kind of data an eavesdropper could possibly be compromising. The results might surprise you. The more you know about network protocols, the better off you'll be in interpreting the data that you see, but you don't need to be a networking guru to look for passwords that are sent in the clear, e-mail contents that are easily read, or other bits of sensitive data that come across the wire.

Busted: Russell Filler and NASA

In November 2002, 47-year old NASA contractor Russell Filler hopped into a single-engine Cessna with a flight instructor to renew his pilot's license. As the plane leveled off to 9,000 feet and the instructor glanced away, Filler unfastened his seat belt and stepped out of the plane. His body was found two days later.

Details began to emerge about the case, including the fact that Filler was going to be charged with the theft of a NASA laptop that had disappeared from a Johnson Space Center facility at the end of October. The media was all over the story, breathlessly reporting that a tracking device in the laptop had led authorities to Filler's home.

Prior to his apparent suicide, Filler told investigators that he saw an ad posted in a supermarket with a laptop for sale for $500. He told them he knew it had to have been stolen, but was too good a deal to pass up. The investigators didn't buy his story, and charges against him were being drawn up before his death.

Authorities said there was no sensitive information on the computer, but they never mentioned just what it was in the laptop that brought the police to Filler's door. Had it been a GPS tracking device, a special network card that "phoned home" over the Internet, or maybe a radio transmitter that authorities homed in on? Possibly, but not likely.

There's some evidence to suggest that the NASA employee who was previously issued the laptop simply saved his account name and password with the settings for a dial-up connection to one of NASA's servers. Filler probably found the saved dial-up connection, hooked the laptop into a phone line, and clicked Connect. The laptop dialed into the server, and the server more than likely recorded his originating home phone number. The authorities then back-traced the number to Filler. Although it's possible that NASA could have secret homing devices in its laptops, it's more probable that Filler made a mistake that triggered a series of events that cost him his life.

Using Port and Vulnerability Scanners

Related to using a sniffer against your own network is to port scan computers in your network as well as run vulnerability scanners against them. (Please get the necessary permission to do this beforehand, so you don't get busted as a spy and end up in jail.) Hopefully, this exercise will put you a step ahead of a spy, so you can plug any security holes before they are exploited. This process also helps you better identify what the probe and attack signatures look like by examining your intrusion detection system and system logs after you've run a test scan. Security scans should be performed from both inside and outside the firewall because attacks can be launched from either side. Scans should be done on a regular basis to detect new computers in the network, software changes on existing computers, or newly discovered vulnerabilities (be sure to update your vulnerability scanner as often as you update your antivirus software).

Encrypting Your E-Mail

You can prevent spies from eavesdropping on your e-mail by encrypting your messages before you send them and by having people you communicate with do the same. PGP (Pretty Good Privacy) is the de facto utility for securing e-mail due to its popularity and strong encryption.

For more on PGP, go to Chapter 5.

One problem with encryption is that if someone is monitoring you, encrypted data may draw attention to your activities. Even if encryption is legal, as it currently is in the United States, there may be occasions when you don't want people to be suspicious about your correspondence. (Obviously, if you're using encryption, you have something to hide, right?). One way to avoid extra scrutiny is to use steganography, which is concealing messages in some other form of data such as a digital picture or MP3 file. The "Countermeasures" section of Chapter 4 has more information about this technique, and it lists some utilities designed for hiding messages. (With the ubiquity of SPAM, an effective covert communications method is to use some prearranged code words in an unsolicited advertising e-mail that promises to make you rich, improve your sex life, or sell you online prescription drugs. The recipient would recognize the e-mail was really a secret message and not SPAM, and decode the prearranged code words. Done correctly, it's very unlikely that someone monitoring e-mail would detect this.)

Encrypting Your Instant Messages

Instant messaging (IM) has become extremely popular for business and personal use. Up until recently, IM conversations could easily be monitored with sniffers because their protocols all transmitted conversations in the clear. However, a number of IM add-ons have become available that use strong encryption to protect IM sessions from eavesdroppers. If you're in a corporate environment and use IM as part of your business operations, you should definitely consider using encryption for sensitive communications.

Some examples of free or low-cost IM encryption utilities include the following:

✓ **Trillian.** A unified IM product that supports all the major IM protocols in one user interface. Free and commercial versions ($25) both support strong encryption of AIM and ICQ conversations. For more information, go to `www.trillian.cc`.

✓ **SpyShield.** A free PGP encryption plug-in for MSN Messenger and Windows Messenger that is available from `www.commandcode.com`.

✓ **IIP.** The Invisible IRC Project offers a free proxy application that provides anonymous encrypted access to Internet Relay Chat (IRC). The proxy works with a standard IRC client (such as mIRC or X-Chat) and then connects to special IIP IRC servers to provide secure communications. For more information about IIP, go to `www.invisiblenet.net/iip/index.php`.

Using Secure Protocols

Any time you have an opportunity to use a secure protocol, use it. For example, instead of using Telnet, use SSH (Secure Shell). Instead of using FTP, use SSH or SCP (Secure Copy). If a server at the other end of your connection supports these protocols, which many do, your entire transaction (including logon account and password) will be encrypted and won't be able to be monitored. There are free and commercial versions of SSH clients and servers available. If you're using SSH, make sure that you have the latest updated versions, especially the server, because vulnerabilities have been found in different implementations.

John Fitzgibbon has a comprehensive Web page devoted to using free Windows SSH and SCP utilities to secure network traffic. To visit his site, go to `www.jfitz.com/tips/ssh_for_windows.html`.

Don't Trust "Strange" Computers and Networks

This doesn't mean that you should *never* use a Macintosh or AppleTalk. It does mean that you should be careful with any computer you connect to a network that you don't implicitly trust or know for certain what type of security has been implemented on that computer. For example, public access computers could have keyloggers running on them or the network traffic monitored. If you need to use a public access computer, consider changing your password on any accounts you accessed with the untrusted computer as soon as you get to a computer you trust. Public access networks are somewhat safer if you're using a laptop that you know is secure, and rely on secure protocols for any network communications.

Hardening Windows File Sharing

When it comes to Windows file sharing, there are simple steps you can take to strengthen your defenses against NetBIOS attacks. Practical measures include the following:

- ✓ If you're not using file or printer sharing, be sure that it's turned off.

- ✓ Disable the TCP/IP protocol for file or printer sharing and use IPX/SPX instead. This makes it more difficult for outside intruders to gain unauthorized access to the shared resources through the Internet.

- ✓ Always use strong passwords to restrict access to shared data.

- ✓ Limit sharing to single folders that contain only files you need to share. Never share the root directory.

- ✓ Set sharing permissions on folders to the minimum levels required (such as read-only). Never permit write access unless absolutely necessary.

✓ Consider restricting shared access to specific IP addresses because DNS names can be spoofed.

✓ Block the NetBIOS ports commonly used by Windows shares at your network perimeter by using either an external router or a perimeter firewall. The ports that should be blocked are 137–139 TCP, 137–139 UDP, and 445 TCP and UDP.

Using Secure Web E-Mail

Popular Web-based e-mail systems such as Microsoft Hotmail or YahooMail offer minimal protection from eavesdroppers. Messages can be intercepted with a sniffer or viewed at the server by a system administrator working for the mail service. Additionally, many law enforcement agencies have agreements in place with major ISPs and Web mail providers to access e-mail. Prior to 9/11, court orders were typically required, but now many service providers have become increasingly cooperative with law enforcement in complying with information requests.

Another potential security issue with public e-mail services is system reliability. For example, in August 1999, a flaw in Hotmail was discovered. By entering a known user's name in an HTML script, the user's Hotmail inbox was completely exposed, and messages could be viewed, forwarded, or deleted. The exploit was widely publicized before it was fixed, and it's difficult to estimate how many mailboxes were compromised.

If you use Web-hosted e-mail, consider a more secure alternative such as Hushmail. Hushmail uses a number of different encryption techniques to prevent spies from snooping on your messages. You start by using a Secure Socket Layer (SLL) connection to the mail service Web site, which prevents anyone from monitoring data between your computer and the Web server. You then enter a password to access your mail account. Hushmail features a 2,048-bit public key encryption system based on the OpenPGP standard for account holders to send and receive encrypted e-mail. (Only Hushmail users can send secure messages back and forth to each other.)

The HushMail system is architected so a user's public and private keys are stored on a server and then encrypted with a user-supplied passphrase. In the event HushMail was subpoenaed to turn over a copy of the keys or transmitted e-mail, it could give a law enforcement agency only the encrypted versions because the company has no way to decrypt user keys and e-mail.

You can sign up for a free basic account or a subscription-based, enhanced account at www.hushmail.com.

Using Anonymous Remailers

An *anonymous remailer* is a server that anonymously forwards an e-mail message to someone. Unlike forged e-mail, which will leave a telltale IP origin address and timestamp in the message header, anonymous remailers strip off any header information that identifies the sender.

To use an anonymous remailer, you send a specially formatted e-mail message to a remailer server, with the message encrypted with the remailer's PGP key. When the remailer receives the message, it automatically decrypts the message; then, based on the message formatting, it forwards the message on to the recipient. Only message headers from the remailer are present, and there are no telltale signs about who sent the message. If a spy were monitoring your e-mail, all she would know was that you sent a message to someone through an anonymous remailer, but not who the person was. If someone were eavesdropping on the recipient, he would see that an e-mail message came from a remailer, but he would not know whom it was from.

Anonymous remailers have all sorts of advanced security features you can use, depending on your level of paranoia. For example, if you wanted to securely communicate with Natasha, you'd encrypt the message with her PGP before sending it through a remailer. Next, you'd put time-delay instructions in the formatting, so the remailer would wait a certain number of minutes after the message was received before forwarding it. (If someone were monitoring the remailer, he might assume that an outgoing message was associated with the last incoming message, but a delay in sending it would confuse attempts to track the message.) Finally, it's possible to "chain" remailers. This means you can send a message through a series of remailers. Each "hop" is encrypted with the respective remailer's PGP key. After your message is correctly formatted and encrypted, you'd send it to the first remailer, which would decrypt the message and then forward it to the next remailer in the chain, and so on, until the message finally reached the recipient.

All of this sounds rather complex, and it was fairly painful to correctly encrypt and format messages to go through remailers in the early days of remailers. However, utilities are available that make the process considerably easier.

Anonymous remailers are typically free and are usually run by privacy advocates using open-source code for their mail servers. There are two types of remailers: Cypherpunk Type I and the more secure Mixmaster Type II, which uses enhanced techniques to provide even more security against traffic analysis. At the start of 2003, there were about 50 active remailers throughout the world.

For more information on anonymous remailers, see the following resources:

✓ `www.sendfakemail.com/~raph/remailer-list.html`. Lots of information about the different types of remailers. Some of the resources and links are dated, but it is a good site for general information.

✓ `www.chez.com/frogadmin/`. A French Web site with up-to-date remailer statistics and client downloads.

x-ref

I wrote one of the first, easy-to-use Windows-based anonymous remailer and PGP tools called Private Idaho (PI) in 1995. It's a bit long-in-the-tooth now, but it still is used by a number of people. The tool was eventually released as open-source, and more up-to-date versions by other developers are available. For more information about Private Idaho and anonymous remailers in general, go to `www.eskimo.com/~joelm/pi.html`.

Using Web Proxies

A proxy server sits between a client computer and another server and processes all requests sent between the client and the other server. Proxy Web servers are frequently set up to improve network performance by caching commonly accessed pages and saving bandwidth by delivering cached local content versus content delivered over the Internet. Proxies can also be set up to filter requests. For example, in a corporate LAN, when an employee accesses a Web page, the request would first go through a proxy server, which might block certain sites.

Aside from these conventional uses for proxies, there are also proxy servers designed specifically for privacy. Normally, when a browser accesses a Web site, the Web server logs the client's IP address and other information about the client. If you connected through a proxy server, the destination Web server would log information about the proxy and not you.

Web page contents are also sent to a browser in the clear, and anyone monitoring the connection can view the contents. This isn't possible when accessing sites that use the Secure Sockets Layer (SSL) protocol, though, because all the data is encrypted. Some privacy proxies encrypt visited Web sites with SSL, whether the Web site you're visiting supports it or not. For example, if you visited the cia.gov site, the proxy would encrypt requested pages with SSL and send it to your browser where they would be decrypted for viewing. Anyone monitoring your network connection would only know that you were connected to a proxy server and were receiving encrypted data. They wouldn't know you were checking up on the CIA, and as a bonus, the CIA Web server wouldn't log your IP address as a visitor.

In your browser settings, specify to use a proxy and then provide the server's IP address and port number. The next time you visit a Web site, your browser will route the request through the proxy first. There are also even simpler-to-use proxies where you can go to a Web site, enter the URL of a Web page you want to visit, and the page will be anonymously served to you.

If you decide to use a Web proxy to secure your Web surfing, consider the following points:

✓ Ultimately, you have to trust whoever is running the proxy because they can monitor and log all connections.

✓ Use proxies that support HTTPS (Hypertext Transfer Protocol Secure). This is simply an implementation of HTTP that uses SSL to encrypt data.

✓ Although the content may be encrypted, the Uniform Resource Locators (URLs) that appear in your browser's history won't be. Some proxies scramble the URL so a snoop won't be able to see the list of site addresses you've been visiting.

✓ Browsing may be considerably slower, depending on the proxy server load.

✓ Traffic analysis can still be performed based on the amount of information that is being served; for example, a large amount of network activity could suggest that large files, such as MP3s or pirated software, were being downloaded.

There are a number of free and commercial Web proxy servers that can help conceal your browsing activities from snoops. Check Google's directory of free proxies for more information and lists of current services and servers. It's available at `http://directory.google.com/Top/Computers/Internet/Proxies/Free/`.

Summary

A network connection can provide a spy with a number of ways to compromise data. The espionage techniques described in this chapter only begin to scratch the surface when it comes to possible network attacks. A determined and skilled spy will use (pardon the pun) a host of sophisticated methods and tools to take advantage of a network connection to achieve his goals.

If you're dealing with sensitive data, don't take network security lightly. It's critical that either you or someone in your organization learn as much about network vulnerabilities as possible and stay current with new vulnerabilities, exploits, and security patches that seem to appear on a daily basis.

Chapter 11

802.11b Wireless Network Eavesdropping

"We got computers, we're tapping phone lines. I know that ain't allowed."
— Talking Heads, "Life During Wartime," *Fear of Music*

An Introduction to Wireless Networks

The popularity of 802.11b wireless local area networks (WLANs) is exploding. WLANs are appearing in corporations, homes, airports, hotels, restaurants, and coffee shops. According to Gartner Dataquest, sales of wireless network devices are expected to exceed 26 million units in 2003, up from more than 15 million units in 2002. The market is expected to continue growing until 2007. Gartner expects that almost 50 percent of business laptop users will be wireless-enabled by the end of 2003.

WLANs are cheap and easy to install (when you see *WLAN* in this chapter, it refers to an 802.11b network). They also make life easy for a computer eavesdropper. When you mix weak protocol security, insecure default hardware settings, and poorly informed users with inexpensive interception hardware and easy-to-use snooping software, you've got the perfect recipe for spying.

Before talking about how a spy can compromise a WLAN, let's do a quick and simple overview of some wireless network fundamentals. If you're already up to speed on 802.11b, you can skip this section and get right into the espionage tactics.

History of the Wireless Network

In 1997, the IEEE (Institute of Electrical and Electronics Engineers) 802.11 standard was established, laying the groundwork for today's wireless networks. 802.11b, one of the variations of the standard, is also known as Wi-Fi, or Wireless Ethernet. Since the first 802.11b products were released in 1999, 802.11b has become the most popular and widely used wireless network standard.

In an 802.11b network, data is transferred via radio waves at speeds of up to 11 Mbps. Network devices communicate with each other using a 2.4 GHz frequency range with 15 channels (the first 11 are used in the United States based on the FCC's radio spectrum frequency allocation). A computer in the WLAN has a wireless Network Interface Card (NIC) that contains a transmitter/receiver. The NIC can be a laptop PC Card, a conventional expansion card in a desktop PC, or a device that connects through a USB port.

In addition to NICs, most WLANs have a device called an access point (AP), or base station, which is a transmitter/receiver that connects directly to the Internet or to a network hub or router. The AP acts as a bridge between the wired network and the computers with wireless NICs. As WLAN popularity has increased, manufacturers have also started to offer wireless routers.

Both NICs and APs have built-in antennas to transmit and receive the radio waves. The indoor range of wireless devices is advertised between 50 to 150 feet, but some have external antennas for extending their coverage.

A key advantage to a WLAN is that it can quickly and easily be set up without extensive cabling or networking knowledge. A small network can easily be built for several hundred dollars, simply by plugging in various pieces of hardware.

However, unless a WLAN is properly secured, it can easily be spied on without the network administrator or owner even knowing it. An eavesdropper can be sitting in his car at the burger joint, munching on fries, and secretly capturing data packets from a business's WLAN across the street.

Spy Tactics

It's time to start thinking like a spy again. In this case you're a Technical Surveillance Countermeasures (TSCM) specialist, also known as a "sweeper." You make your living by discovering audio and video surveillance devices (bugs) for your clients; who include politicians, business executives, and other people who think their privacy may be electronically compromised. It's good money, but you need to expand your services to stay competitive. You figure computer security is a logical direction, and since you've been dealing with wireless bugs for years, you decide to come up to speed on wireless networks first. A good way to do that is to look at wireless networks from the potential spy's point of view.

The first question to ask yourself then is why a spy would want to penetrate a WLAN. Think about it for a minute or two, and see whether your answers match some of the following:

- ✓ To access files and information stored somewhere on the network
- ✓ To find user accounts and passwords
- ✓ To covertly install Trojans or other software on computers in the network
- ✓ To use the WLAN as a launching point for attacks on other targets

Although the underlying technology behind a WLAN is fairly complex, the methods involved in compromising networks are quite simple. In most cases, you don't need to have a lot of networking experience or certification credentials to locate and access wireless networks. Consider that somewhere in the world a teenager in a beat-up old Toyota is probably doing it right now.

Wireless technology is fairly immature, and most users aren't clued in to the espionage risks they face when they set up a WLAN. So let's examine some of the vulnerabilities you — pretending to be a would-be spy — can exploit and the spy tools you'll use.

Exploiting the Vulnerabilities

To start with, it's important to understand that 802.11b was never designed to provide industrial-level security. There are a number of inherent weaknesses in the protocol that a spy can take advantage of.

SSIDS

802.11b uses SSIDs (service set identifiers) as part of its security, and an SSID is the name of a particular wireless network. It's a lot like a workgroup name in a Microsoft network. For a wireless computer to associate with the network, the NIC must be set to the same SSID as the AP (access point). There are a number of design and implementation weaknesses in this scheme that a spy can exploit.

The first vulnerability is that manufacturers use default SSIDs for their APs. For example, if you buy a Cisco AP, its default SSID is set as *tsunami*. A list of default SSIDs by manufacturer is shown in Table 11-1.

TABLE 11-1 Default SSIDs for Common APs

Manufacturer	SSID
Cisco	Tsunami, WaveLan Network
3Com	101, comcomcom
Dlink	WLAN
Bay	Default SSID
Addtron	WLAN
Intel	101, 195, intel, xlan
Linksys	Linksys, Wireless
Netgear	Wireless
SMC	WLAN, BRIDGE
Lucent/Cabletron	RoamAbout Default Network Name
Compaq	Compaq

If your NIC matches the AP's SSID and no other security measures are in place, your computer will associate with the target network. After you've associated with a network, you can use all your favorite network-cracking and assessment tools to breach security even further.

Entering default SSIDs by trial-and-error can be tedious, and what happens if an administrator has changed the default name?

An AP is constantly broadcasting its SSID several times per minute in what's known as the beacon frame. All a spy needs is a laptop with a wireless NIC and the right software, and he can pluck a WLAN SSID out of the air and then specify it in the setup program for his NIC and try to associate with the network.

WEP

As a sweeper you've encountered a couple of high-tech bugs that you know had to have been planted by the government. Instead of transmitting an analog radio signal, they transmitted a digital signal that appeared to be encrypted. You've heard that WLANs can support encryption, so is a network safe from eavesdropping if encryption is enabled?

A somewhat more difficult 802.11b security hurdle to overcome is Wired Equivalent Privacy, commonly referred to as WEP. The designers of 802.11b knew that radio signals could easily be intercepted and eavesdropped on, so WEP's goal was to come close to the security of conventional wired networks through the use of encryption.

WEP uses a 64-bit RC4 stream cipher to encrypt data. The cipher's key is generated from a seed value that combines a user-specified, 40-bit WEP key and a 24-bit initialization vector (IV) value. The reason why the WEP key is so small is that 40 bits was the longest key length allowed by U.S. cryptographic export regulations at the time. The WEP key is a ten-character hexadecimal string or a five-character ASCII text string.

Because such a small key, RC4 cipher can be readily brute-force attacked in the span of a few days, many 802.11b manufacturers also support 128-bit RC4 encryption. Although not part of the protocol specification, this stronger level of encryption has become common, and the same 24-bit initialization vector is used with a 104-bit WEP key. In this case, the key consists of a 26-character hexadecimal string or a 13-character ASCII string.

There is also an optional authentication scheme in the protocol that makes use of WEP's encryption mechanism. Shared key authentication is a fairly primitive, automated, encrypted challenge/response system in which data is generated and sent to the client; the client encrypts the data and sends it back; then the response is decrypted and verified to confirm that it was the original data sent.

When WEP is used in a wireless network, APs and NICs all must use the same WEP keys. This process allows data to be successfully encrypted and decrypted as well as authenticating clients to associate with the network. Up to four 40-bit keys (or one 104-bit key) can be used concurrently.

There are a number of vulnerabilities associated with WEP. The first one, although not a fault of the protocol, is that most vendors don't have WEP enabled by default in their products. When WEP isn't being used, the data packets can easily be viewed in clear text with sniffer software (which is covered in the section titled "Wireless-Network-Eavesdropping Tools").

The second weakness is that even when WEP is enabled, only the data packets are being encrypted. Separate packets containing management information, such as the destination and source addresses, SSID, and MAC address, are all sent in clear text. Even if you can't read the encrypted data packets with your sniffer, you still can discover a significant amount of information about the network through the management packets.

The final and most glaring WEP weakness has to do with the implementation of the encryption. When a computer-related technology starts to become popular, its security begins to receive more scrutiny, and WEP was no exception. During the first half of 2001, a series of research studies popped the bubble of perceived 802.11b network security. Theoretical vulnerability research soon gave birth to a series of software tools that could compromise WEP-enabled networks.

Tactics: WEP Attacks

Spies love the academic part of the computer world: the bright, curious people always looking to poke a hole in someone's supposedly well-designed security system. 802.11b went through the security test wringer in 2001 and didn't come out looking very pretty.

January 2001 — The Internet Security, Applications, Authentication and Cryptography (ISAAC) group at the University of California released a paper that described weaknesses in the IV and RC4 checksum. The 802.11 subcommittee already knew about the shortcomings, and changes were being slated for future implementations. The potential attacks were dismissed as not much of a threat because they required a considerable amount of computing horsepower.

March 2001 — Researchers at the University of Maryland released a paper that explored weaknesses in sending unencrypted management data and vulnerabilities in Shared Key authentication (which is briefly discussed following).

July 2001 — Researchers Fluhrer, Mantin, and Shamir revealed that by knowing the unencrypted IV value and how the first data bytes are decrypted, the value of a WEP key could be determined. A month later, a team from Rice University and AT&T successfully demonstrated a practical attack based on the paper and they revealed WEP keys in a matter of hours using off-the-shelf equipment.

Although the Rice and AT&T researchers never publicly published their attack code, the cat was out of the bag. Within months, a series of tools were distributed on the Internet that gave anyone the power to compromise a wireless network. Simply crack a WEP key, use the revealed key with your wireless NIC, and you can sniff the data or (barring any other security procedures) associate with the network.

Always pay attention to current research. The more vulnerabilities and exploits in your bag of tricks, the better.

Almost overnight, someone without too much technical ability could crack WEP by using inexpensive, off-the-shelf hardware and freely available software.

MEDIA ACCESS CONTROLLER (MAC) ACCESS LISTS

All wireless NICs and APs have a Media Access Controller (MAC) address. This is a unique, hard-coded number that's assigned to devices that are nodes of a network. The MAC address, which is in the firmware of the device, is printed somewhere on the outside of the product. The first six digits of the MAC address identify the manufacturer, and the remaining six digits are its unique identifier.

Similar to Internet Protocol (IP) addresses, the source and destination MAC addresses are passed back and forth between devices communicating with each other.

Another security feature of 802.11b networks is a MAC address access list, which is a list of authorized devices that can access the network through an AP. If a laptop with a wireless NIC tries to associate with the network, and the MAC address of the NIC isn't on the AP's authorized list, the laptop will be prevented from joining the network.

Although MAC address filtering seems like a reasonable security measure, there are several weaknesses to it:

✓ First, if you have physical access to the computer or even just the NIC, the AP automatically permits you to associate with the network.

✓ Second, even if you don't have physical access, you can always masquerade as the authorized client because MAC addresses can easily be spoofed. Although the factory-set MAC address is broadcast from the hardware, this value can be overridden through the operating system or with other software.

Looking at this from the spy's perspective, let's say you're sniffing an unencrypted network and know which MAC addresses and SSIDs are being used. You set the target's SSID on your NIC, but you still can't associate with the network. Your next step would be to try changing your MAC address to one of the known MAC values that's being used on the network.

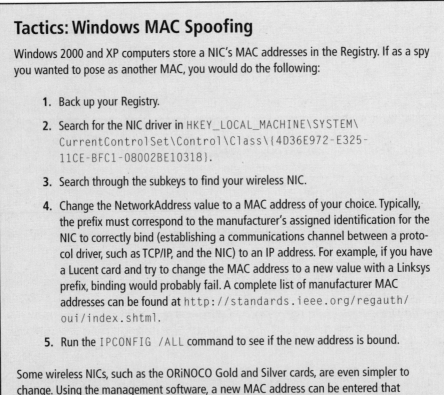

Tactics: Windows MAC Spoofing

Windows 2000 and XP computers store a NIC's MAC addresses in the Registry. If as a spy you wanted to pose as another MAC, you would do the following:

1. Back up your Registry.

2. Search for the NIC driver in `HKEY_LOCAL_MACHINE\SYSTEM\CurrentControlSet\Control\Class\{4D36E972-E325-11CE-BFC1-08002BE10318}`.

3. Search through the subkeys to find your wireless NIC.

4. Change the NetworkAddress value to a MAC address of your choice. Typically, the prefix must correspond to the manufacturer's assigned identification for the NIC to correctly bind (establishing a communications channel between a protocol driver, such as TCP/IP, and the NIC) to an IP address. For example, if you have a Lucent card and try to change the MAC address to a new value with a Linksys prefix, binding would probably fail. A complete list of manufacturer MAC addresses can be found at `http://standards.ieee.org/regauth/oui/index.shtml`.

5. Run the `IPCONFIG /ALL` command to see if the new address is bound.

Some wireless NICs, such as the ORiNOCO Gold and Silver cards, are even simpler to change. Using the management software, a new MAC address can be entered that overrides the one that comes with the NIC. There are some legitimate network management reasons for this feature, such as some network operating systems require that each device be identified by a Local MAC Address; it's not just meant for spies. If that's too complicated, a wireless hacker named BlackWave developed a command-line tool called BWMACHAK that can quickly change a MAC address.

RADIO WAVES

You've found a number of bugs in your career that transmit in the 398- to 399.5-MHz range. A lot of "spy shops" sell these low-end bugs, and they're easy to find. Moving up the radio spectrum around 2.4 GHz, you run into 802.11b networks. This is a fairly crowded part of the radio spectrum, shared with microwave ovens, medical devices, compact florescent light bulbs, and even certain types of cordless phones, all of which can degrade wireless network performance with their stray signals.

Because a WLAN depends on radio signal propagation, it becomes vulnerable to a "jamming" Denial of Service (DoS) attack. Jamming is just what it sounds like: overpowering the radio waves with a more powerful source to disrupt data from being transferred. Although conventional packet-based attacks such as those used against wired networks are also possible, with a WLAN a spy could use a high-powered 2.4-GHz transmitter to disrupt a network by transmitting on the known 802.11b frequencies. Maximum radiated power on wireless devices is limited to a maximum of 4 watts, so it wouldn't be that difficult for someone with an amateur radio or electronics background to modify an AP to drown out a target network. This is not going to make the jammer very popular with the FCC, but because he's already probably breaking a series of laws, why not add another one to his potential rap sheet?

How could a DoS attack be used for espionage purposes? It could give you a pretext to gain access to a facility. Consider the following.

With the network having problems all morning and no one having a clue as to what's happening, a smiling man in a blue uniform with an ID badge pinned to his shirt shows up at the receptionist's desk. "Hi, I'm John Smith from the telephone company. We got a report that you were having network problems today, and we think the shielding on one of the trunk lines is generating a bunch of radio interference. I think I can fix it, though. Can you show me where your routers are?" The friendly repairman in the fake telephone company uniform used a 2.4-GHz transmitter to jam the WLAN, so he could get inside the building to steal information.

PROBLEMS WITH DEFAULT CONFIGURATIONS

You might think that with all of the vulnerabilities in 802.11b, things couldn't get any worse in terms of security or, in a spy's case, any better. As anyone who has ever been exposed to security issues knows, there's always a trade-off between ease-of-use and security. This trade-off applies to wireless products as well. Vendors typically configure their APs and NICs to be as fast and as easy to install as possible, right out of the box. This is usually at the expense of security.

War drivers (whom you learn about in the next section) report that anywhere from 50 percent to 80 percent of the APs they find have default SSIDs set and WEP that isn't enabled. Users and administrators like instant gratification — plug it in and it simply works — and vendors cater to this ease-of-use to sell more products. Some implementation issues you can easily exploit include the following:

- ✓ **WEP not enabled by default.** The impact is obvious. A spy can eavesdrop on all the packets that pass by with a sniffer.

- ✓ **Known default WEP keys.** Even if WEP is enabled, some vendors have default WEP keys that a lazy or unknowing user might not change. These keys are widely known, and if an AP or NIC type is identified by a MAC address or default SSID, a spy can try one of the default WEP keys to see if it works.

✓ **Remote administration weaknesses.** APs typically have remote management options that allow an administrator to configure network settings. Protocols used include the Simple Network Management Protocol (SNMP), Telnet, and HTTP for Web browser access. The problem with all of these protocols is that unencrypted information is sent over the network. Anyone sniffing the network at the time an administrator is logging into the management software now has access to password information that's being entered. If that's not bad enough, in some cases it can be ridiculously simple to access the Web-based configuration features of the AP. After you've associated with a wireless network, if you know the IP address of an AP (which a sniffer can reveal), just point your browser to the IP address to run the configuration manager. Default management passwords for APs are widely known, so you'll have complete control over AP settings if the password hasn't been changed.

For more on sniffers, turn to Chapter 9.

Even though wireless security issues have gotten a tremendous amount of coverage in both the popular and trade press during the past year, users and administrators still continue to use the default settings. A target's ignorance or attitude that no one would ever eavesdrop on his or her network makes a spy's job easy.

Wireless-Network-Eavesdropping Tools

With a general knowledge of the vulnerabilities of an 802.11b network, it's time to examine some of the tools that can be used by a spy to compromise WLANs. A large selection of software can be paired up with inexpensive hardware to successfully discover and exploit wireless networks. Many of the tools and techniques for wireless espionage have come from an Internet subculture called "war drivers." It's important to understand how some of these tools evolved and to learn a bit about the people that develop them.

AN INTRODUCTION TO WAR DRIVING

In corporate computer security terms, "war driving" is performing a mobile audit of wireless networks. More simply put, it's driving around in a car with a laptop and wireless NIC looking for WLANs to eavesdrop on. (The van you have for performing occasional surveillance work when you're not sweeping for bugs is perfect for this. Ironically, to test the security of a wireless network, you will use the exact same methods a spy would to break into the network.)

War driving gets its name from the 1980s cracker practice of "war dialing." Back before it was easy to identify potential target computers with Internet port scans, crackers used modems and programs, such as THC-Scan or ToneLoc, to dial through blocks of phone numbers. The program would sequentially dial a range of numbers, checking if another modem answered. If it did, that meant a computer was on the other side of the phone number, the number would be logged, and the cracker would attempt to log on to the system at some later time.

Tactics: Wireless Networks, I See You

802.11b isn't just for browsing the Web or general network access. It's starting to become popular for use in wireless surveillance cameras, and spies can exploit the same vulnerabilities in new ways.

In August of 2002, a report surfaced about the Department of Defense Information Systems Agency (DISA). The Arlington, Virginia–based agency is responsible for the security of the DoD's networks and command and control systems. A consultant using NetStumbler discovered the security cameras at the agency headquarters were part of an 802.11b network. WEP wasn't enabled, and NetStumbler reported an AP SSID named "AP-BLDG 12," which gave away its physical location because it corresponded to a facility clearly marked on the outside, BLDG 12. A spy could have easily eavesdropped on the video transmissions (knowing where they originated from due to the SSID name) and with a bit more effort could have taken control of the system or even injected spoofed images to fool guards at the monitors. This is rather disturbing considering the agency involved and the fact it happened post-9/11.

Even toys can be enlisted as spies. Sony's high-end toy, AIBO the robot dog, features an 802.11b option that you can use to remotely control the dog from a laptop or desktop PC. Using AIBO Navigator software, the robot transmits images and sounds back to the controlling PC. The eavesdropping options are endless because an AIBO could be hijacked and then moved around an unoccupied room, looking for interesting information. If you're using NetStumbler and find an SSID named AIBONET, there's a wireless dog at the other end. Its default WEP key is AIBO2.

Another popular product that is very susceptible to spying is the X-10 wireless camera. For awhile, it seemed as if X-10 pop-up ads were appearing on every Web site you visited, hyping a small, golf-ball-sized video camera. The camera broadcasts on a 2.4 GHz frequency to a remote wireless receiver, which then displays images on a TV, VCR, or PC. Its range is up to 100 feet. A small detail that X-10 neglects to mention is there are no security features that prevent someone else with an X-10 receiver from eavesdropping on the video transmissions. Snoops have driven around viewing video from bedrooms, baby cribs, and home security systems. Other wireless cameras on the market broadcast in the 900 MHz frequency range and can also be spied on with enhanced radio scanners. The Icom R-3 scanner not only receives audio transmissions, but also can display wireless video transmissions. Although it burns through batteries quickly and has a limited range, it's an option for eavesdropping on wireless surveillance systems.

In the fall of 2000, California computer security consultant Pete Shipley took a laptop equipped with a wireless card, some basic WLAN discovery software, and a Global Positioning Satellite (GPS) device, and started driving the streets of the Bay Area. After 18 months, Shipley had discovered more than 9,000 APs. About 85 percent of the networks weren't using WEP and could easily be compromised. Shipley publicized his study and dubbed wireless network auditing as "war driving." The term caught on in the media as well as the security and computer underground communities.

By 2001, a very active population of war drivers had evolved mostly due to the release of a Windows WLAN detection tool called NetStumbler and a considerable amount of information sharing over the Internet. With NetStumbler, you just plugged a wireless NIC into your laptop, ran the program, and started driving around. When the program located a network, it would display the SSID, whether WEP was enabled, and other information about the network. If you had a GPS device attached to your laptop, NetStumbler would even record the location of the network.

Because NetStumbler is so easy to use, war driving has become extremely popular all over the world. Databases collect information about networks discovered, maps are published showing AP locations, and there are active public discussions on what is the best hardware and software to use to discover WLANs.

There are two sides to war driving. On the light and happy side, many people view driving around looking for WLANs as a pretty harmless activity. The war drivers aren't trying to break into the networks they find; they're only locating the networks. They think of it as a hobby along the lines of a high-tech, electronic treasure hunt, with bragging rights based on the number of networks they discover. Then there's the dark side. After a WLAN is found and especially when WEP isn't enabled on that WLAN, it can be very tempting to go after easy-to-grasp forbidden fruit. A little voice says, "Just a little look around the network or maybe mooch a free Internet connection to do some Web browsing for a bit. No one will know." And at that point, the legal boundary gets crossed, and by most statutes, the war driver becomes a computer criminal.

Busted: The Empire Strikes Back

Legal and criminal actions against wireless eavesdroppers were virtually nonexistent up until July of 2002, when Stefan Puffer was federally indicted by a Grand Jury on two counts of fraud. Puffer is a 33-year old computer security consultant in Houston, Texas. On March 18, 2002, he demonstrated to a Harris County IT department head and *Houston Chronicle* newspaper reporter that a County District Clerk's office WLAN was unsecured. He'd been war driving for networks earlier in the month, found the county's network, and decided to be a good citizen (Puffer had done computer work for the county in the past).

The county stated that they were forced to shut the wireless network down, which caused damages of at least $5,000 (the typical threshold amount for federal involvement), and the FBI investigated. It's interesting to note that the county stated that no files were compromised and officials never did give a reason why the network was shut down instead of secured. In September of 2002, the county suspended its own investigation of Puffer and said it wouldn't issue a final report or press charges.

In February 2003, after 15 minutes of deliberations, a jury decided that Puffer had not planned to cause harm to the county's system, and he was acquitted. If Puffer had been convicted, he would have faced a maximum penalty of up to 5 years in prison and a fine of $250,000 on each count in the indictment.

It's likely this case was an initial effort by the Department of Justice to send a message to war drivers that it's serious about vigorous prosecution. Spies and crackers that actually break into wireless networks take note.

What does all of this history and background have to do with spying? Simple. War drivers have paved the ground for you as a neophyte wireless spy. The tools, techniques, and informal support groups are all in place to make it easy for anyone interested to successfully eavesdrop on a WLAN.

HARDWARE

Unlike other forms of high-tech spying, discovering and eavesdropping on WLANs don't require sophisticated or expensive hardware. In fact, you probably already have the primary hardware components and can easily purchase the remaining equipment for only a few hundred dollars.

LAPTOPS   Although it's certainly possible to eavesdrop on a wireless network with a desktop PC, laptops are a bit more convenient. Just put a suitably equipped laptop on the passenger seat of your car, stash it on the car floor, or covertly tuck in it a backpack and you're ready to go.

You don't even need a state-of-the-art laptop. An older model with enough memory and processor speed to run Windows 98 or Linux works just as well as a new Pentium IV machine. The laptop needs a free PC Card slot as well as a serial port in case you want to attach a GPS unit to record network locations.

The only other major consideration is screen readability. Bright sunlight makes it difficult to see what's being displayed on the screen, so you'll want a laptop that works well outdoors. You can compensate for screen readability somewhat by changing the operating system's color themes, for example using an easier to view, monochrome black-and-white color scheme.

Although any laptop will work, subnotebooks (smaller and lighter than typical laptops) are favored because of their smaller size and weight. They are more versatile because they can be used in a car, as well as tossed in a backpack or briefcase for close-in monitoring—just power-up the laptop and run the scanning software as you walk around.

Laptop batteries limit spying activities to between two and four hours, so if you plan on doing any extended surveillance, bring spare batteries or use an external power source that plugs into your car's cigarette lighter.

POCKET PCS   For the ultimate in stealthy wireless spying, you can't beat a Pocket PC. Compaq iPAQs are favored because of their small size, compatibility with wireless network cards and GPS units, and the capability to run both popular Windows and Linux wireless discovery tools.

An iPAQ is perfect for covertly locating WLANs inside buildings and out—on-foot scanning is known as "war walking." There are even sniffers available for the Pocket PC so you can eavesdrop on packets after you find a network.

For more on war chalking and new proposed symbols, see www.warchalking.org.

NETWORKING CARDS   Before you can start eavesdropping on a WLAN, you need a wireless NIC for your laptop. Wireless NICs slide into the PC Card slot with the antenna housing protruding about an inch outside of the slot (a few models, such as 3Com's OfficeConnect, come with a retractable antenna). With the popularity of 802.11b, wireless NICs have dramatically dropped in price with even high-end cards retailing for well under $100.

Tactics: War Chalking

Using a hidden Pocket PC or small laptop for war walking, has even given rise to a new recreational activity called "war chalking." During the Depression, hobos came up with a series of symbols to help keep their fellow travelers informed about local conditions. A certain mark scratched on a fence might mean a friendly person who'd share some food or to watch out for a dangerous dog. In the summer of 2002, Internet designer Matt Jones breathed new life into the idea of "hobo signs" with something he called "war chalking." Jones publicized a series of standardized symbols relating to wireless networks that could be chalked on buildings or sidewalks when a WLAN was discovered (see Figure 11-1). If a passerby with a laptop and wireless card saw a certain symbol outside an office building, he'd know he could access a free Internet connection from somewhere nearby. Some security consultants took the symbols as more of a tongue-in-cheek parody. However, the FBI thought it was very serious and advised businesses to be on the lookout for strange symbols chalked outside their buildings.

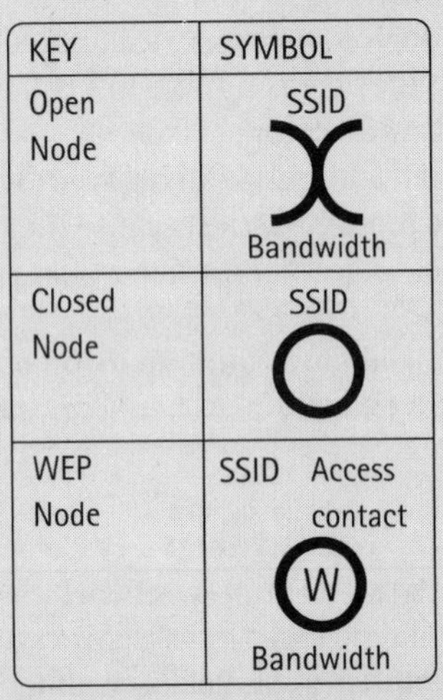

KEY	SYMBOL
Open Node	SSID)(Bandwidth
Closed Node	SSID ◯
WEP Node	SSID Access contact Ⓦ Bandwidth

Figure 11-1: War chalking symbols. The actual SSID and bandwidth values of a discovered wireless network would appear next to the symbol. The access contact area would contain known contact information, such as an e-mail address or phone number, for gaining access to a wireless network that's protected with WEP.

Because you're a savvy spy, you'd never chalk your target to reveal it to others, but now that you know what the symbols are, they could make your job that much easier if you come across them.

Newer model laptops are starting to come equipped with built-in wireless cards. Instead of having the antenna visibly stick out of the PC Card slot like add-on cards, the antenna is built into the laptop's case. If you're sitting on a park bench across the street from a target office, this type of design makes it difficult to tell if you have a wireless-enabled laptop.

There are three chipsets available for 802.11b devices: Hermes, Prism-2, and Aironet.

✓ **Hermes** products come under the name of Lucent, Wavelan, ORiNOCO (see the following sidebar), Avaya, RoamAbout, and BuffaloTechnology. They have better reception than the Prism cards and feature an external antenna connector.

✓ **Prism** cards are manufactured by SMC, D-Link, Linksys, Microsoft, and other vendors. They are the most popular mass-market chipset, tend to be inexpensive, and have a shorter range than the Hermes cards. Their main advantage is they can easily be put into promiscuous mode to sniff raw 802.11b packets, and a large number of software tools have been written to support them.

✓ **Aironet** cards are top-of-the-line, high-performance, wireless NICs manufactured by Cisco. They aren't as common as Hermes and Prism-2 cards, and have fewer wireless tools written for them.

Each of the chipsets has its own developer kits, so a software tool written for a Hermes chipset card doesn't work on a Prism card. A classic example is the popular NetStumbler, which is designed to work only with Hermes cards, although a new version does work with some Prism cards if you are using Windows XP.

Wireless NICs are cheap enough that it makes sense to buy both Hermes and Prism cards to take advantage of the numerous available software tools. At present, there is no one definitive wireless eavesdropping tool for a particular chipset, and you'll want the versatility of being able to use different software depending on the need. The ORiNOCO Gold (Hermes) and Proxim RangeLAN-DS (Prism 2) cards both are recommended.

ANTENNAS All wireless NICs have small, built-in antennas that are designed to have an adequate range for office and home networks. Relying on a standard antenna's range limits you in discovering and compromising WLANs. If you use an external antenna, you'll be able to find more networks and remain further away from a target to help you avoid being detected.

For mobile monitoring, it's important to select a wireless NIC that supports an external antenna. These aren't easy to find, and although there are plans to modify cards to accept antennas, it's simpler to just purchase one out of the box. Both the ORiNOCO Gold and the Proxim RangeLAN DS have jacks to connect an external antenna. Most commercial antennas have a cable that terminates with an N-type connector (a large metal screw connector typically used with amateur and commercial radio products). You need a pigtail adaptor cable to connect the card to the antenna cable, but the pigtails are somewhat fragile, so it's important not to bend or kink them.

War drivers originally used small antennas designed specifically to extend the range of WLANs. As the popularity of war driving increased, more choices somewhat more covert in nature have become available.

Tools of the Trade: Scanning for Gold

If you start looking at war-driving Web sites and read some of the discussion forums, you'll no doubt hear about the ORiNOCO Gold card (see Figure 11-2). Manufactured by ORiNOCO Wireless, which was acquired by Proxim in August 2002, the Lucent-designed card consistently receives high marks for performance. It also has a small jack for an external antenna that can dramatically extend range.

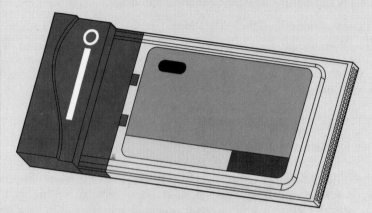

**Figure 11-2: The ORiNOCO Gold wireless card.
The antenna housing is on the left of the card.**

The ORiNOCO Client Manager software that comes with the NIC supports scanning for WLANs right out of the box. To scan for WLANs:

1. Run the Client Manager application.

2. Select Add/Edit Configuration Profile from the Actions menu.

3. Create a profile with the SSID set to "ANY" or null. This instructs the NIC to search for any nearby WLANs.

4. Set the new profile as the current configuration profile.

5. Select Site Monitor from the Advanced menu.

Although the Client Manager software doesn't give as much information on discovered WLANs as NetStumbler or other tools, it's a good basic reconnaissance utility.

Antennas must be designed for working with 2.4 GHz frequencies. Any old antenna won't necessarily work. For example, trying to use a television antenna wouldn't be effective for wireless eavesdropping because a TV antenna is optimized to receive signals in the 50- to 220-MHz frequency range.

When looking at an antenna's specifications, you'll see a number followed by "dBi," which refers to antenna gain — how much signal an antenna can pick up compared to another antenna. The larger the gain number, the better the antenna is able to receive weak signals. Smaller antennas may have a rating of 5 dBi, although larger antennas are over 10.

Not all antennas designed to receive (and transmit) at 2.4 GHz work the same. There are two general types of antennas, omni-directional and directional, and each has a different purpose (see Figure 11-3).

✓ **Omni-directional antennas.** An omni-directional antenna sends out and receives radio signals in all directions. These antennas are ideal for discovering wireless networks. Some models come with magnetic bases for low-profile mounting on car roofs. Omni-directional antennas suited for wireless spying typically cost between $50 and $100.

✓ **Directional antennas.** A directional antenna is designed so it concentrates signal strength in the direction it's pointed in and reduces the strength of signals coming from other directions. These antennas are perfect for targeting a known WLAN. You can point it at a building to pick up a signal from a distance or if you're closer, receive weaker signals from deep within a building that an omni-directional antenna might not be able to receive. Directional antennas tend to be larger than omni-directional antennas. You can use them yourself by hand in a car, but if you're pointing the antenna from a fixed location at a distance, use a camera tripod or something else to steady the antenna. Directional antennas that are suitable for wireless espionage are priced under $200.

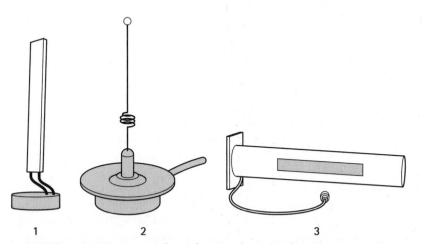

1   2   3

Figure 11-3: Three 2.4 GHz antennas, from left to right (note that these images are not to scale): (1) Lucent range extender, popular with early war drivers, (2) magnetic mount, omni-directional antenna commonly used for war driving, and (3) an enclosed Yagi directional antenna good for finding WLANs at a distance.

Perhaps you've seen TV news accounts of war drivers out with their laptops, pointing Pringles chips cans at buildings. Pringles cans?

If you're on a budget, there are a number of instructional resources on the Internet for building 2.4 GHz directional antennas out of everyday materials, found in the kitchen, such as coffee, chili, and Pringles cans (see Figure 11-4). For about $5 in parts, not counting the price of whatever was in the can, some of these homemade designs actually outperform commercial antennas. These antennas are perfect for the socially conscious spy who believes in recycling.

An excellent review of different homebrew antennas can be found at `www.turnpoint.net/wireless/has.html`.

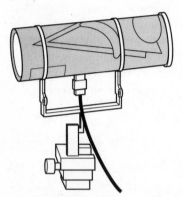

Figure 11-4: Stealth antenna: A Pringles can housing a homemade directional antenna.

Homebrew directional antennas are fairly quick and easy to build and don't require much technical knowledge. Omni-directional antennas on the other hand take a bit more knowledge and work. Unless you've got a ham radio or electronics background, you're probably better off buying a commercial omni-directional antenna.

MOUNTING ANTENNAS   After you have your antenna, where should you mount it? If you're in a vehicle, you want to limit shielding from the car body and any electromagnetic interference. You also want the antenna to be fairly discreet without it being permanently mounted just in case you need to quickly get rid of the evidence. War drivers typically use a magnetically mounted antenna and run the coax cable out through an open window or sunroof. Routing through the back of the car and out through the trunk is another option because the thicker weather-stripping seal isn't as likely to cause as much damage to the cable. Just be careful not to pinch the antenna cable, such as by shutting a door on it or rolling the window up tight against it. If a cable is damaged, it can decrease signal strength, sometimes making it almost as bad as having no antenna at all.

GPS UNITS   NetStumbler and other WLAN discovery tools interface with Global Positioning Satellite (GPS) units. A GPS unit is a small electronic device a little smaller than a TV remote control that displays your current latitude and longitude, and it uses an ASCII-based protocol called NMEA 0183 to transfer information to a computer or other device (see Figure 11-5). Boaters were the original wide-scale users of GPS, and the National Marine Electronics Association developed the standard to work with autopilots and other navigation equipment.

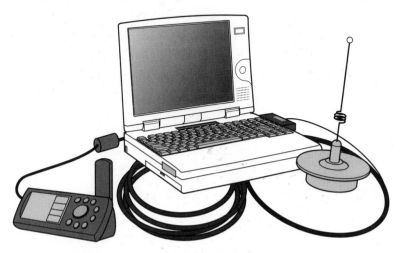

Figure 11-5: Garmin III+ GPS connected to Toshiba Libretto laptop ready for wireless discovery

A proprietary cable, which varies by manufacturer, connects the GPS to the laptop's serial port. USB is slowly outdating serial devices, and some newer laptops don't have serial ports. GPS manufacturers have yet to start moving toward USB interfaces, so if you don't have a legacy serial port, you'll need a USB-to-serial adaptor.

If the laptop has a GPS unit connected to it, and NetStumbler or a similar tool is running, a network's location is recorded and logged when it's discovered. This information can then be imported into electronic mapping programs to visually show all of the discovered WLANs. Wireless networks are displayed with different icons that indicate whether WEP is enabled or not. This makes it very easy for you to quickly identify possible targets.

The two largest manufacturers of GPS units are Garmin and Magellan. Both companies offer basic GPS models that retail in the $100 price range. Wireless eavesdroppers especially favor the Garmin eTrex series because of their small size.

An even stealthier GPS unit is the Sapphire GPS Mouse. This product was designed to exclusively interface with a laptop or PDA. It's not as versatile as a GPS designed for land or water navigation because it doesn't have a display or control buttons, but with a 5-centimeter diameter, it is perfect for concealment applications.

APS   Although most of the preceding tools are suited for mobile eavesdropping, a sophisticated spy can also use a standard AP for espionage purposes (see Figure 11-6). There are a couple of possibilities.

If you have physical access to a building, you could covertly place your own AP on a target network, giving you remote access to the network. For example, a spy could secretly plug an AP into some out-of-the-way Ethernet network tap near a window. Then after he left the building, he could point a directional antenna at the AP's location and start eavesdropping on the bugged corporate network with a sniffer.

Another AP-based attack is to place your own similarly configured AP somewhere in the WLAN and monitor traffic that comes through it. For example, an insider spy could place his own AP between a client PC and the real AP. Because the rogue AP is closer to the real AP, the client will attempt to associate with the bogus AP. The spy would be running a sniffer to monitor and record all traffic from the client passing through the "man-in-the-middle" AP. Another variation of a man-in-the-middle-attack is to launch a denial of service attack against an AP, and then use your own AP to handle the wireless traffic. (Tools for WLAN DoS attacks are starting to appear. At Black Hat 2002 in Las Vegas, a collection of Linux-based utilities called Air-Jack was released.)

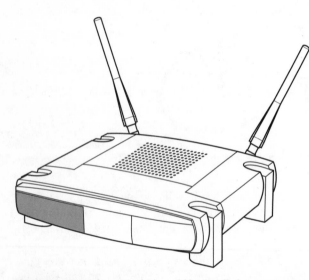

Figure 11-6: A Linksys AP, which could be installed as a covert tap to a network or be used in a man-in-the-middle attack

PLANES, TRAINS, AND AUTOMOBILES   Unless you're on foot, you'll need a place to run your eavesdropping operation from. When you're engaged in wireless espionage, you'll either be doing mobile reconnaissance or setting up a fixed listening station.

Mobile reconnaissance is simply war driving. You're out looking for WLANs. You may have a specific target in mind and are interested in whether a WLAN is being used at a building, or perhaps you're opportunistic, searching for an unsecured WLAN to launch an attack from.

As with any type of spying, the key word is inconspicuous. Both you and whatever vehicle you're driving should blend in with the surroundings. Although a civil libertarian war driver would love nothing more than to argue the legalities of scanning for WLANs to a suspicious cop who just pulled him over, your success depends on blending in. You and your car shouldn't draw any unwarranted attention.

For mobile reconnaissance, you may be by yourself or have a partner. If alone, your laptop will be on the passenger seat or on the floor. A sheet of non-skid rubber, kitchen cupboard material on the seat will keep the laptop from sliding around too much. War drivers like to immediately see information about the WLANs they just discovered. As much a temptation as this is, it's better for you to have the laptop case closed after you confirm the discovery software is running. You should look at the results of your reconnaissance after it's completed. Being distracted by a laptop although driving could make a police officer or onlooker suspicious, or at the very least increase the chances of you getting into an accident by not watching the road.

An exception to this would be to use a partner: He or she will be responsible for running the laptop and passing information on to you. If you're a male, take a hint from professional surveillance teams and use a partner of the opposite sex. Couples don't draw as much attention as two males, and the ultimate inconspicuous surveillance team is a female with a child. During the reconnaissance, the passenger should take notes about any possible targets, either written or with a tape recorder.

Before heading out to perform a mobile reconnaissance, take some time looking at maps and drive the route ahead of time to familiarize yourself with any issues that could impact the reconnaissance. You shouldn't randomly drive around; use a predetermined travel route.

When's the best time of day to do your reconnaissance? That depends on the target. APs may be powered down at night after 5:00 p.m. and won't be found by discovery software after office hours. On the other hand, if the target has decent security, during the day someone may be actively monitoring for scans from tools such as NetStumbler. Although a lot of war drivers like to drive around at night, a laptop screen illuminates the interior of a car and makes you very conspicuous in the dark.

A basic rule of surveillance is to always make sure your vehicle is in legal working order (for example, no burned-out taillights) and always obey traffic laws. The police like to use traffic infractions as a chance to investigate suspicious activity more thoroughly. What if you're pulled over by a police officer during a reconnaissance? The vast majority of law enforcement officers aren't computer-savvy, and most have never even heard about war driving. Be courteous and cooperate, but have a cover story established ahead of time. Explain that you're doing a survey of radio station signal strength for a school project or that it's a consulting job, which isn't that far from the truth. Show him the laptop screen and GPS, and start talking about antenna gain, microwave oven radio frequency interference, signal-to-noise ratios, and other technical issues guaranteed to put the average person to sleep. Saying that you're a computer security consultant doing a wireless network audit for a client probably isn't the best response. A cop will hear the word "security" and suddenly start to get more interested, especially in these post-9/11 times of heightened awareness.

The second type of wireless spying involves using a fixed listening station. This could be in an office building overlooking the target or using your car as an unoccupied listening post. After a target WLAN has been identified, you'll want to use a sniffer to either gather unencrypted packets for later examination or encrypted packets to reveal a WEP key. In the case of using a car for a listening station, sitting in it for hours on end reading a newspaper isn't too smart. In the cop-and-spy parlance, you'll get burned. It makes more sense to arrange your surveillance equipment so you can park your car near a target and then walk away for a while.

There are three main considerations in setting up an unoccupied listening post:

✓ The vehicle must be inconspicuous and fit in with other cars in the area. (That means no "War Driver" bumper stickers.)

✓ The monitoring equipment shouldn't be in plain view; this means the laptop. This is as much to avoid detection as to prevent having the hardware stolen. A couple of solutions are to either place the laptop in the trunk or perform the monitoring from a van. A van or a camper with curtains is ideal, as a directional antenna on a tripod can be pointed at an office building through one of the windows.

✓ There needs to be enough electricity to power the laptop for an extended period of time while the vehicle isn't running. Two alternatives are to use lead-acid batteries with the same voltage as the laptop or some type of solar charging system.

For long-distance listening stations, rain, snow, and fog can diminish the signal strength of 802.11b networks. For targets that are a considerable distance away, pick a day with good weather to monitor the target network.

Don't limit yourself to cars, trucks, and vans. Realistically, any vehicle can be used for wireless eavesdropping. There have been reports of "war-boating" on canals, rivers, lakes, and next to port cities. In Europe, trains have been used, as have bicycles.

War driving, or more appropriately war flying, is even taking to the air. Within days of each other in August 2002, two accounts of using an airplane to discover WLANs in Australia and the United States were publicized on the Internet. The Australian crew reported locating more than 95 networks while flying over Perth at 1,500 feet. The Americans spent 1.5 hours flying over the San Diego area and detected 437 APs while speeding along over populated areas a little under 140 miles an hour, between 1,500 and 2,500 feet above the ground. The statistics they collected are telling. Sixty percent of the APs still had their default SSIDs set and only 23 percent of the WLANs had WEP enabled.

SOFTWARE

Normally you use a spectrum analyzer as one of your bug-finding tools, and everything is built in to the hardware. But what about wireless networks? You've got a laptop with a wireless card, an antenna you built, and a GPS, but you need the software to tie it all together to discover wireless networks and to see if they're vulnerable to attack (of course you'd never engage in any illegal eavesdropping). You're in luck because a number of skilled programmers who also happen to be wireless fans have created a veritable arsenal of tools for detecting and eavesdropping on WLANs. There's software that runs on Windows, Linux, BSD, Mac, and Pocket PC operating systems. In general, the tools fall into three categories:

✓ **Discovery tools** simply tell you that a WLAN is present.

✓ **Sniffers** capture actual wireless traffic, allowing you to examine packets.

✓ **Mapping tools** visually display the locations of WLANs.

Some of the tools are very complex, but even if you're a spy with limited technical skills, you should be able to find a program that works for you. You don't even need an NSA budget because the majority of the tools are free.

The following are brief descriptions of some of the more popular software tools of the trade. A more complete listing of wireless tools is available at this book's Web site.

NETSTUMBLER   Network Stumbler, popularly called NetStumbler (see Figure 11-7), is a Windows program that's responsible for the popularity of war driving. Written by Marius Milner, an employee of wireless networking company Avaya, NetStumbler seeks out APs. First released in May 2001, NetStumbler has evolved into a sophisticated and incredibly easy-to-use WLAN discovery tool.

NetStumbler works by sending out a broadcast probe about once per second. This is important to remember because NetStumbler doesn't work passively and it leaves a signature when it probes. If an AP responds, NetStumbler will get the AP's SSID and other information. NetStumbler isn't a sniffer because it doesn't save or analyze the full range of 802.11b packets that travel over a wireless network.

When an AP is located, you're informed with a cheery, metallic "boing" sound, and the discovered AP shows up on a list. A small circle appears to the left of the AP's MAC address and SSID; its color indicates signal strength. If a padlock appears in the circle, it means that WEP is enabled. If a GPS is attached to the laptop, the location is also recorded. This isn't the precise location of the AP, but the spot you were when NetStumbler first encountered the AP.

NetStumbler is designed to work with Hermes chipset NICs such as ORiNOCO, Avaya, and Toshiba Wireless LAN Card. When using Windows XP, users have reported being able to use Cisco and some Prism-2 cards, although they aren't officially supported.

In addition to the Windows version of NetStumbler, Milner also has a version of the program that works on Pocket PCs such as the Compaq iPAQ.

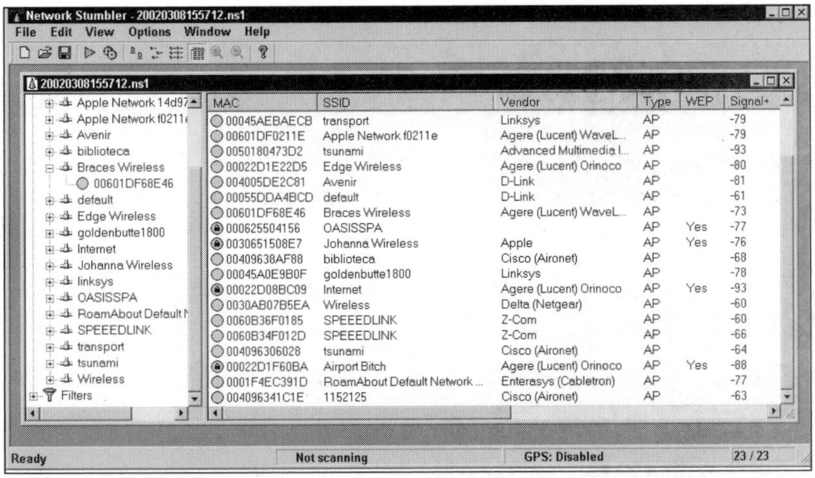

Figure 11-7: NetStumbler screen showing identified APs and signal strength

The popularity of NetStumbler has grown an entire subculture on the Internet. Web sites provide discussion forums, latest software releases, and a user-contributed database of more than 25,000 WLANs that have been discovered. The software has even come up with an alternative to the term war driving. "Stumbling," also means to go out looking for WLANs.

You can download the latest version of NetStumbler as well as access discussion forums at `www.netstumbler.com`. Marius Milner also maintains his own site at `www.stumbler.net`.

NetStumbler is a side project of Milner's, and he works on it whenever he has the time. He considers the tool to be "BeggarWare" and encourages satisfied users to contribute to his PayPal account.

KISMET   For those who prefer Linux to Windows, Kismet is the tool of choice for discovering WLANs (see Figure 11-8). Although NetStumbler is more popular and widely known, the free, open-source Kismet is actually a more effective wireless discovery utility.

Unlike NetStumbler, which works by sending out a broadcast probe, Kismet passively listens for 802.11b packets and collects information about them. Essentially, Kismet is a sniffer. Because it's passive, it's undetectable, and unlike NetStumbler, it can locate APs that have the SSID broadcast option turned off.

```
dragorn@gir.lan.nerv-un.net:/home/dragorn                              O O O
 Networks--(Autofit)----------------------------------------------  Info----
 |        Name             T W Ch Packts Flags                   |  |        |
 | +      St Francis       G N 07   324          0.0.0.0         |  | Ntwrks |
 |        VBHWOUND         A Y 11    48          0.0.0.0         |  |     22 |
 | +      Cenhud-POK       G N 06   339          0.0.0.0         |  | Pckets |
 |        <no ssid>        A N 01  1508 U3       10.132.112.0    |  |   6148 |
 |        cvsretail        A N 11  1091          0.0.0.0         |  | Cryptd |
 | +      IBM-POK          G Y 00   432          0.0.0.0         |  |    386 |
 |        pserwap003       A Y 07    56          0.0.0.0         |  |   Weak |
 |        linksys          A Y 06   155          0.0.0.0         |  |      0 |
 |        <no ssid>        A Y 11   175          0.0.0.0         |  |  Noise |
 |        tsunamisgt3624t  A N 06     4          0.0.0.0         |  |      0 |
 |        <no ssid>        A Y 06    58          0.0.0.0         |  | Discrd |
 |        default          A N 11   284          0.0.0.0         |  |   1448 |
 |        arlington        A N 06    15          0.0.0.0         |  |        |
 |        linksys          A Y 06    91          0.0.0.0         |  |        |
 |        LuoHomeNet       A Y 06  1107          0.0.0.0         |  |        |
 | .      linksys          A N 02   107          0.0.0.0         |  |        |
 | !      CPT_Wireless     A N 01   170          0.0.0.0         |  |        |
 | !      WLAN             A N 11    22          0.0.0.0         |  |        |
 |                                                               |  |        |
 |                                                               |  | Elapsd |
 |_____|  |_000203_|
 Status------------------------------------------------------------------------
 | Detected new network "WaveLAN Network" bssid 00:02:2D:22:86:C1 WEP N Ch 10 @  |
 | Detected new network "WLAN" bssid 00:90:D1:00:D9:57 WEP N Ch 11 @ 11.00 mbit  |
 | Detected new network "CPT_Wireless" bssid 00:02:2D:0D:D4:C0 WEP N Ch 1 @ 11.  |
 | Detected new network "linksys" bssid 00:04:5A:DD:56:0F WEP N Ch 2 @ 11.00 mb  |
```

Figure 11-8: Kismet screen showing discovered APs. Kismet has a text-based interface, and although not as pretty as NetStumbler, it is much more powerful.

Kismet also has a number of powerful and useful features such as capturing packets for later viewing in Ethereal or tcpdump, AirSnort-compatible logging, output to mapping programs, and identification of IP ranges used by the WLAN. Versions of Kismet are even available for iPAQ and Zaurus handhelds that run Linux. Originally, Kismet was designed to run with Prism-2 cards, but there are patches available for Hermes and Aironet cards.

You can download the latest version of Kismet and get extensive information about its features and how to install it at www.kismetwireless.net.

If Kismet is so powerful, why isn't it as popular as NetStumbler? NetStumbler is a snap to install under Windows. Kismet takes a fair amount of work because it first must be compiled and then linked with a number of packages that aren't part of most default Linux distributions. You need a much higher level of technical proficiency to get Kismet up and running.

Despite the amount of work, if you're serious about wireless spying, it's definitely worth the effort because of its increased sensitivity and enhanced options.

COMMERCIAL AND FREE WIRELESS SNIFFERS   A "sniffer" is another name for a protocol or network analyzer whose purpose is to capture packets as they move through the network. Sniffers were originally designed to help administrators and technicians troubleshoot performance issues on networks because a sniffer can individually examine packets to look for a number of different problems.

For espionage purposes, you can use a sniffer to discover accounts, passwords, and sensitive information that is passed over the network. After capturing some amount of data of your choice, you can examine the packets to see if there is anything of interest.

Sniffers take a moderate amount of technical skill to use effectively. They aren't as simple or intuitive as NetStumbler, and you need to be familiar with various protocols to understand the contents of packets. If you will be doing a lot of wireless eavesdropping, it's well worth your time to become a skilled sniffer user because of the power of the toll in compromising information.

There are a number of both commercial and free wireless sniffers available. Let's take a look at some of the commercial sniffers first:

✓ **AiroPeek NX** is a Windows-based wireless sniffer from WildPackets. It can capture and decode packets simultaneously and offers on-the-fly decryption of WEP keys (AiroPeek doesn't crack WEP; you must supply the valid keys). You can learn more about AiroPeek at www.wildpackets.com/products/airopeek_nx.

✓ **Sniffer Wireless** is another Windows sniffer from Network Associates. Although it doesn't decode packets on the fly (you need to stop sniffing first), it can decode an amazingly large number of protocols. It also has security-related features such as the ability to spot rogue APs. The Sniffer product family has been around for quite some time and is often found in enterprise settings. Visit www.sniffer.com for more information on the Sniffer product family.

Tools of the Trade: Are Sniffers a Real Threat?

Are sniffers a viable or theoretical threat? Because sniffing is passive, it's very difficult to tell how much is happening. Businesses that are being eavesdropped on may not know it, or if they do discover an intrusion, they may choose not to disclose it because of negative publicity.

In the spring of 2002, electronics retailer Best Buy and home improvement outlet Home Depot were in the news after wireless data was sniffed at store locations. War drivers equipped with sniffers eavesdropped on wireless cash register transactions and databases. The corporations quickly announced that they had plugged any wireless security holes, and that no customer data was ever exposed. This contradicted various war driver reports that credit card information could easily be plucked out of thin air.

It's important to understand that wireless sniffers don't magically display accounts, passwords, credit card numbers, and other information of value. All network traffic is being collected, and although filtering can be applied, the spy will have to manually sift through a large number of extraneous packets to find any nuggets worth keeping.

Sniffers are a threat, but to be effectively used for spying they need to capture a large amount of traffic (because statistically, valuable information only accounts for a small percentage of total traffic). The spy must also be patient enough to tediously examine all of the collected data to see if there is anything worthwhile.

Commercial sniffing tools are marketed toward corporate administrators who need to troubleshoot their wireless networks. The programs have a number of features that go beyond the needs of a typical spy who looks only for useful information, and their cost reflects this. Expect to pay anywhere from $4,000 to $20,000 for a commercial sniffer software package.

In most cases, commercial sniffers are probably overkill for espionage purposes, and you're better off looking at free programs that you can download from the Internet.

Linux users have a number of open-source options including Kismet; Ethereal (discussed in Chapter 10), which can capture and display raw 802.11b packets; MogNet (http://chocobospore.org/mognet), which is written in Java; AirTraf (http://airtraf.sourceforge.net); and Wellenreiter (www.remote-exploit.org).

For more information about available Linux wireless sniffers and other tools, see www.personaltelco.net/index.cgi/WirelessSniffer.

Unfortunately, if you're a Windows user, there aren't really any decent open-source wireless sniffers available at this time. You have to use Linux or spring for a commercial product.

AIRSNORT   AirSnort is a Linux tool that passively monitors encrypted wireless transmissions in an effort to discover WEP keys. AirSnort needs a sample of between 5 to 10 million encrypted packets (roughly 100MB to 1GB of data) before it can successfully reveal a key. Depending on the amount of network traffic, this could take days to weeks. As with Kismet, binaries aren't available, and the sources must be compiled — this is not for the spy who uses Windows and doesn't have much technical experience with Linux. More information about AirSnort is available at http://airsnort.shmoo.com.

MAPPOINT   Although it's not a wireless tool, Microsoft MapPoint (see Figure 11-9) and other mapping software are popular because they can visually show where discovered wireless networks are located. Location data collected from a GPS unit is imported into MapPoint from NetStumbler and other tools to create a map.

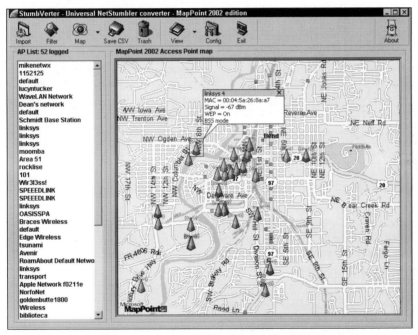

Figure 11-9: NetStumbler output to MapPoint 2002 using StumbVerter

A free, standalone application called StumbVerter (available from www.sonar-security.com) readily imports NetStumbler's summary files into MapPoint. Discovered APs are displayed with green icons when WEP isn't enabled, and red icons are displayed when it is. Clicking on an icon displays a balloon with more information about the AP, including its SSID, MAC address, and signal strength.

WINDOWS XP   Although some critics have complained that Windows XP has built-in spyware, it also has built-in functionality for spying on wireless networks. By default, whenever a Windows XP system encounters an SSID broadcast, the operating system will automatically set the NIC to the same SSID in an attempt to associate with the newly discovered network. This is a nice feature for the nontechnical spy who encounters an unsecured WLAN. Where do you want to snoop today?

Countermeasures

When you're sweeping for bugs, it's easy. You find them and then you get rid of them (or at least let your client know that they're there in case they want to mount a disinformation campaign against whoever is spying). But these wireless networks are a bit more complicated, because once you show a client his network is vulnerable, he'll want to know how to secure it. After learning about all of the 802.11b vulnerabilities and tools to exploit them, you're probably wondering if getting into the computer security business was such a good idea after all.

Take heart. Despite the many WLAN security weaknesses, you can still shore up a network to prevent eavesdroppers from snooping over the airwaves. There's no one single magic solution that will plug up all of the holes, though. You need to take a multilayered approach with your countermeasures, building one on top of the other.

Audit Your Own Network

Get a copy of NetStumbler or Kismet and see what a spy will see when he comes nosing around your client's building. Go for a walk or a drive with your laptop and a decent antenna and see what shows up. Because of the ease of installation and low price, network administrators are literally stumbling on to internal wireless networks that employees have set up without authorization. Don't just rely on NetStumbler; it's limited to only finding APs that are broadcasting SSIDs. Kismet or a sniffer will find those less-than-obvious APs that NetStumbler won't, and those are the ones you should be most worried about.

Position Antennas Correctly

AP antennas should be positioned to reduce the chance of radio waves leaking out of buildings. APs that are close to windows or exterior walls are susceptible to snooping with directional antennas pointed in their direction. In Shipley's war driving study, he reported standing on a hillside with a directional antenna and locating networks more than ten miles away. Optimize the placement of APs and range extending antennas to maximize network coverage within a facility, while limiting the chance of stray signals reaching the spy who may be lurking outside.

Countermeasures: AirMagnet

AirMagnet is a WLAN-management device that runs on a Pocket PC. It comes bundled with a special wireless card. Some of its features include rogue AP and client detection, wireless Denial of Service detection, AP impersonation detection, unconfigured AP detection, and real-time packet capture and decode. AirMagnet is priced at $2,495 plus the cost of a Pocket PC. In addition to legitimate management audits, AirMagnet can also be used for stealthy espionage purposes. See www.airmagnet.com for more information.

Countermeasures: Honey, It's for You

In June of 2002, government contractor Science Applications International Corporation (SAIC) began a wireless honeypot project. *Honeypots* are computer networks designed to lure crackers to attack them and then record their methods. The Wireless Information Security Experiment, or WISE, is housed in a secret location in Washington, D.C. It has five Cisco APs and a series of networked computers, all having known vulnerabilities. Omni-directional antennas even extend the range of the WLAN to draw in intruders from a distance. Intrusion-detection system and logging software tracks any attempts to access the network.

Consultant KPMG has a similar wireless honeypot running outside its London headquarters to better understand how much war driving is taking place and the frequency of network intrusion attempts.

Comparable honeypots could easily be set up in a corporate environment that has a high risk of espionage to see if there are any active penetration attempts. With the growing interest in WLAN security, commercial and open-source wireless honeypot packages will likely start appearing in the near future.

With all of this "war trapping" going on, the war-chalking community will probably come up with a Winnie the Pooh symbol for suspected honeypot locations.

Detect Wireless Discovery Tools

Because of the popularity of 802.11b, Intrusion Detection System (IDS) packages are starting to incorporate features that detect wireless probes and attacks. An IDS system won't be able to detect a sniffer, but it will detect more active attacks in which the spy has actually entered your network.

As previously mentioned, NetStumbler isn't a passive discovery tool, and tools such as the Windows-based NSSpyglass are emerging that notify you if a spy with NetStumbler has probed your network. More information about NSSpyglass is available at `http://home.attbi.com/~digitalmatrix/nsspyglass/`.

A start-up company called AirDefense offers another hybrid hardware/software approach. The AirDefense system consists of distributed radio-based sensors that sniff for unauthorized access points, read wireless packets, and assess access point vulnerabilities. These sensors use algorithms and a database of WLAN information to detect and analyze any changes to a network and then notify administrators of any risks or attacks. See `www.airdefense.net` for more information.

Fool Discovery Tools

A classic military electronic countermeasure is to confuse the enemy by making it appear that there are hundreds of targets on a radar screen instead of one or two. The Black Alchemy group did the same thing with a free tool called Fake AP. Fake AP broadcasts false information to NetStumbler and similar programs, deceiving them into thinking that there are thousands of APs in the vicinity. This can make it much more difficult for a spy to isolate which is the real AP.

Fake AP runs on Linux platforms and can be downloaded from `www.blackalchemy.to`.

Countermeasures: To WEP or Not to WEP

Between August 31 and September 7, 2002, war drivers all over the world participated in the First WorldWide WarDrive. NetStumbler log files were sent to a central location for analysis. In North America, 9,102 WLANs were discovered. Nearly 70 percent didn't have WEP enabled. This generally corresponds to other surveys that have shown that anywhere from 60 percent to 80 percent of discovered WLANs aren't using WEP.

If you care about your security, use WEP.

Enable WEP

Although we've seen that WEP isn't secure, it does provide a basic level of protection for WLANs and should be a layer of your countermeasures. Keep in mind that WEP somewhat degrades network performance due to the data packets being encrypted and decrypted. The slower speed is a trade-off for better security.

Change WEP Keys Regularly

You should also change the default key on your AP after you enable WEP. Just like default SSIDs and passwords, default keys are commonly known. In addition, you should regularly change the key values. Although WEP can be cracked, tools such as AirSnort need to capture a fairly substantial amount of data to successfully compromise a WEP key. If your network generates a large amount of traffic, you should perhaps consider changing the key on a weekly basis. If you have a low amount of packet traffic, you might be able to get away with changing the key once a month. This can be a time-consuming administrative task in a large organization because all the keys on the client computers must also be changed. As with any countermeasure, always weigh the potential threat against the cost of the effort.

Authenticate MAC Addresses

Most APs support association with a list of authorized MAC addresses. For example, if the MAC address of a NIC isn't on the list, the AP will prevent that client from joining the network. In theory, this sounds like an excellent countermeasure. However, wireless sniffers readily reveal the MAC addresses of both clients and APs, and after a MAC address is known, it is fairly easy to spoof. In addition, if the spy has physical access to a laptop or even its NIC (such as stealing the card from an unattended laptop), MAC authentication becomes useless. Finally, this countermeasure works in a small network, but it is a management nightmare in a large enterprise due to the constant need of ensuring that the authenticated MAC address list is kept up-to-date.

Rename the SSID

Some administrators immediately rename the default SSID of their AP, which doesn't do much in terms of security because tools such as NetStumbler easily reveal a broadcast SSID as well as the type of AP. If you rename the SSID, use something that isn't going to sound interesting to a spy. For example, an SSID named RD_LAB has target written all over it.

You might think that renaming the AP's SSID with another manufacturer's default SSID may confuse a spy. The eavesdropper might try to exploit some known Cisco AP vulnerability because the SSID is "tsunami," but in reality, it's a D-Link AP. Although clever deceptive practices are good countermeasures, this one won't work. Tools such as NetStumbler examine the broadcast MAC address of the AP to determine the device manufacturer. Parts of the MAC identify the manufacturer and the device. For example, on a MAC with an address of 00055D-A6F60C, 00055D is the prefix for devices made by D-Link Systems. Even though it's named "tsunami," the 00055D gives it away as a D-Link.

Even if broadcast SSID is not turned on, a sniffer will still reveal the SSID, and if WEP isn't enabled, a spy can use the SSID to try to associate with the network. Max Moser, the author of the Linux Wellenreiter wireless tool offers this bit of advice. SSIDs can have up to 34 characters and support nonprintable characters; such as an ASCII 7 (BEL) or 9 (Tab). If you use nonprintable characters for your SSID, sniffers and scanners may not be able to correctly display the name.

Disable Broadcast SSID

Most APs have an option to turn off the broadcast of the SSID. If the SSID isn't being broadcast, NetStumbler won't discover and display the SSID. Additionally, a Windows XP system won't automatically configure itself in an attempt to join the network.

This isn't an entirely foolproof countermeasure. Whenever a computer boots or (in the case of a laptop) moves within the coverage area of the wireless network, an association frame is sent. These frames always contain the SSID and are readily viewable by a spy using a wireless sniffer.

Change the Default AP Password

If a spy sees a default SSID, there's a good chance he may try to access the AP with the default management password. If he's successful, he can reconfigure your WLAN, creating even more security holes. Unless absolutely required, remote administration should be disabled.

Use Static IP Addresses versus DHCP

Before a client can access resources on the network, it needs to have an IP address. Dynamic Host Protocol Hosting (DHCP) automatically assigns an IP address to a client as it becomes active. DHCP is frequently used to make life easy for an administrator. Unfortunately, it also makes it easy for a wireless spy, who just has to associate with the WLAN to have access to it because his laptop will automatically be assigned an IP address with DHCP. Static IP addresses should be assigned to clients in a wireless network, with DHCP disabled. This still isn't entirely foolproof because an IP address can possibly be sniffed and then used by the spy.

Locate APs Outside Firewalls

Because of the numerous vulnerabilities in 802.11b, wireless networks should always be considered untrusted and should never be installed behind a firewall. With this strategy, if an AP is compromised, the rest of the network is still protected by the firewall.

Use VPNs

A virtual private network (VPN) is a way to connect to a private network, such as an office LAN, from a public network such as the Internet. VPNs encrypt all data on the network with encryption that's much more robust than WEP. Using a VPN is probably one of the most effective single countermeasures to use for beefing up your WLAN's security.

For more on VPNs, turn to Chapter 10.

Don't Rely on Distance as Security

Many administrators think that the advertised limited range of 802.11b networks is a security measure in itself, that it's easy to keep an eye out for strange cars with antennas in corporate parking lots. It's worth pointing out that Pete Shipley was able to connect to a network in western San Francisco from the hills above the University of California at Berkeley some 15 miles away.

Turn Off the AP

Consider turning off the AP when it's not in use. If your wireless network is used only during the day, power it down at night. If you have set office hours, you can even hook the AP up to an electric security timer so it turns on in the morning and off at night. Sometimes, simple countermeasures are remarkably powerful.

Summary

The threat of wireless network eavesdropping is very realistic. Over the past several years, war drivers have demonstrated that the majority of WLANs are unprotected and vulnerable to attack. Despite a considerable amount of media coverage on security issues, users and administrators still are using vendor default settings and leaving their networks open to spies.

Although the human behavior side of security will always remain a challenge, from a technology standpoint, the future should bring enhanced security to wireless networks. The current weaknesses in 802.11b have been recognized, and revised standards are emerging to address the deficiencies.

The 802.11i standard, which is currently under final review, is the planned successor to WEP. The Wi-Fi Alliance industry trade group (www.wi-fi.org) introduced an interim security specification as a step toward 802.11i called WPA (Wi-Fi Protected Access). This standard addresses many of the flaws in WEP, and certification specifications are expected by May 2003, with products incorporating WPA available by the third quarter of the year.

The 802.1x Network Port Authentication standard is designed to improve authentication in large enterprises by using a Remote Authentication Dial-in User Service (RADIUS) server.

In closing, it's worthwhile to remember that wireless is a fairly immature technology and is going through the same security teething stage that all technologies go through. It's a given that new vulnerabilities will be discovered and new tools will be developed to exploit them. If you administer or support a wireless network, it is critical to stay current with up-and-coming security issues over the next few years.

Chapter 12

Spying on Electronic Devices

"I know you're working for the CIA . . ."
— War, "Why Can't We Be Friends?" *Why Can't We Be Friends?*

HIGH-TECH SPYING ISN'T JUST LIMITED TO PERSONAL COMPUTERS. Information from business and personal electronic devices can also be gathered and analyzed. Although many people focus on beefing up their computer security, they neglect looking at other threats that could compromise sensitive data. This chapter discusses the types of information that can be extracted from common office, communication, and consumer electronic devices and offers some practical counter-measures for reducing the chances of being victimized by a spy. You can take a break from pretending you're a spy as in previous chapters, and just sit back, relax, and learn about spying on electronic devices.

Office Devices

In the old days when life was much simpler, spies commonly relied on discarded sheets of carbon paper or typewriter ribbons to get information about what their target was up to. Today's sophisticated office equipment can be just as much at risk as the lowly typewriter was when it comes to compromising sensitive data. Any device that processes important or confidential information should be reviewed for possible weaknesses a spy could exploit. Two commonly used office devices that should jump to the top of your vulnerabilities list are fax machines and shredders.

Fax Machines

In the days before e-mail, fax machines were the primary way of quickly sending documents over a long distance. Although e-mail, image scanners, and FTP all have somewhat diminished the use of faxes, they're still widely used in homes, business, and government. Because sensitive information is often sent over a facsimile machine, faxes can be a primary espionage target.

Generally, there are four security concerns when it comes to faxes, including the following:

✓ **Interception.** Fax machines use a low baud rate and a well-documented, unencrypted protocol to transfer data. Because of this, fax transmissions are fairly easy to intercept and monitor. Commercial fax interception and monitoring devices have been available to law enforcement and government agencies for a number of years (see Figure 12-1 for an example). If an eavesdropper doesn't have access to one of these devices, which typically are a restricted sales item in the U.S., he can always tap the fax phone line and digitally record the actual transmission on a Digital Audio Tape (DAT). He can then play it back with another fax machine, spoofing the fax device into believing that it is actually receiving a fax from another machine.

✓ **Film rolls.** Many plain-paper fax machines use a carbon film for printing documents (this is the same type of film used in electric typewriter cartridges). The carbon film roll retains an exact image of what was printed. If a discarded roll is fished out of a dumpster or replaced by a spy posing as a maintenance technician, a negative image of the contents of all of the faxes you've received is clearly visible. (This same type of attack can be used against typewriter and dot matrix printer ribbons.)

✓ **Fax logs.** Most fax machines keep a log of incoming and outgoing fax transmissions with dates, times, number of pages, and phone numbers. If a spy has physical access to the device, this information can be useful for establishing patterns and relationships.

✓ **Incoming and outgoing transmissions.** An obvious risk is when incoming faxes sit in the tray in full view of everyone until the recipient picks them up. For outgoing transmissions, there have been a number of instances in which sensitive information has accidentally been sent to someone other than its intended recipient because of a misdialed phone number. Aside from an accident, a spy could change the fax machine settings or modify the hardware to covertly send a copy of all outgoing documents to a certain phone number whenever any fax was sent.

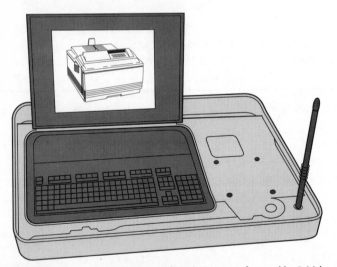

Figure 12-1: A portable fax-monitoring device manufactured by British surveillance company Eskan Electronics (www.eskan.com)

There are several countermeasures you can use to protect yourself from eavesdroppers when you use a fax machine:

✓ **Use a fax encryption device.** This is a piece of hardware that connects between the fax machine and the phone line and then encrypts the transmission. You must have at least two devices: one on the sending fax machine and the other on the receiving fax machine (besides thwarting eavesdroppers, an added bonus to these devices is that the scrambled transmission won't connect to an erroneously dialed fax machine that doesn't have a fax encryption device installed). For the highest levels of security, select a device that uses a nonproprietary, strong cryptographic algorithm.

✓ **Don't use carbon film fax machines.** Ink jet or toner fax machines don't leave exact duplicates of your received faxes like a carbon roll will. If your fax does use carbon film, limit access to it by unauthorized people and consider burning a used roll to dispose of it.

✓ **Don't fax sensitive documents.** Overnight delivery may cost a bit more but generally is a more secure way of sending a document. Alternatively, you can use an application, such as Symantec's WinFax Pro, to scan a series of documents, save the fax file to your hard drive, encrypt the file with PGP or a similar utility, and then e-mail it to the recipient.

Tactics: Copier Caper

A 1996 issue of *Popular Science* had an interesting article about how the CIA had been using bugged copy machines to spy on people since the early 1960s. The article, which was independently verified by several sources, detailed how the government intelligence agency had approached Xerox to design a miniature camera that could be planted in a photocopier. Their target was the Soviet Union's embassy in Washington, D.C.

A team of Xerox engineers modified a home movie camera with a special photocell that activated the camera whenever a copy was made. The camera was then stealthily concealed in normal-looking copy machine parts. A Xerox technician installed the camera during a regular maintenance visit to the Soviet embassy in 1963. During subsequent service calls, the camera's film was retrieved and replaced. There are indications that the operation was so successful that similar cameras were installed in photocopiers all over the world.

There's no reason to think that the same type of surveillance couldn't be used today, not only with photocopiers, but also with bugged faxes, scanners, and shredders. With a digital camera and wireless networking, the smiling Xerox man might not even need to make a regular visit after a covertly modified device was in place.

Shredders

A favorite practice of both spies and crackers is rooting through discarded documents that have been hauled out to the trash. "Dumpster diving" can produce all sorts of sensitive information that careless or clueless people throw away. A key defense against this type of attack is to use a shredder: a mechanical device that renders paper documents unreadable. (With the increasing popularity of CDs and DVDs for backing up data, special media shredders have come on the market in the past few years that are available as stand-alone units or integrated with paper shredders.)

Shredders and secure document disposal services are big business, and it's estimated that corporate and government shredders in the United States generate an estimated five million tons of paper residue each year. The sales of personal home shredders are growing rapidly as the public becomes worried that pilfered paper fished out of a trash bin could be used for identity theft.

There are all sorts of ways paper documents can be destroyed, including cutting, grinding, rip-shearing, pulverizing, and disintegrating, but the two commonly used ways to destroy documents in an office setting are the following:

✓ **Stripping.** Low-end shredders use this method, which cuts paper into strips (depending on the shredder, strips can range from 1/2-inch wide to a 5/32-inch wide). Strip shredders shouldn't be used for destroying sensitive data because documents can be easily reconstructed by piecing the strips together. A classic example of this was when the U.S. Embassy in Iran was seized in 1979. Hundreds of classified documents were painstakingly reconstructed and published in a 23-volume collection called "Documents from the Den of Spies" (see www.gwu.edu/~nsarchiv/NSAEBB/NSAEBB21/ for an example). To the Embassy and CIA employees' credit, they thought they'd have enough time to burn the shredded documents per protocol, but the Embassy fell faster than they expected. Another drawback to strip shredders is they create more waste volume because of the air volume between the strips. One cubic foot of paper will be transformed into roughly ten cubic feet of paper after it has been shredded.

✓ **Crosscutting.** Crosscut shredders are more secure than strip shredders because they cut paper in one direction and then another, producing harder-to-reconstruct confetti-like pieces of paper. Typically, the more expensive the crosscut shredder, the faster it works and the smaller the paper pieces end up. Typical shredded paper size can range from 5/32 × 2 9/16 inches to 1/32 × 1/2 inch.

The general rule of thumb with shredders is the smaller the pieces of paper a document is shredded to, the more secure you are. The U.S. Department of Defense requires that destroyed CONFIDENTAIL, SECRET or TOP SECRET documents be reduced to shred sizes no larger than 1/32 inch wide × 1/2 inch long (for more details on classified document destruction refer to the Department of the Army Information Security Program document AR 380-5, Appendix K at http://ia.gordon.army.mil/iaso/Army/AR%20380-5/AppendixI-K.htm; shredders meeting the newer NSA/CSS specification #02-01 are appearing on the market that can shred in the 1mm wide by 4mm long range. For a low-end shredder that meets government standards, figure on spending at least $800 and up. (You really didn't expect that embassies are using a $20 shredder from the office supply store around the corner, did you?) Some of the manufacturers that produce shredders that meet government standards include Dahle (see Figure 12-2), Intimus, Olympia, and Security Engineered Machinery.

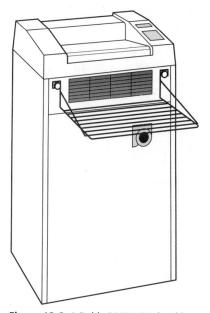

Figure 12-2: A Dahle 20634 EC shredder that meets NSA standards and can reduce paper documents into 4mm × 1mm pieces

Do you really need a DoD- or NSA-certified shredder? You need to consider the probable threat and who may be interested in compromising your data (as discussed in Chapter 1). You should definitely get a crosscut model; beyond that consider how much paper you'll be shredding on a daily basis, the number of sheets of paper that can be fed at once, and the size of the shredder.

If you really want to ensure there's no possible information left in your shredded documents, shred, burn, and then flush (as in down the toilet). This is likely overkill for most people, but for those who are dealing with extremely sensitive information (or have delusions and think they are), this is a common and effective method.

Tools of the Trade: Document Reconstruction Software

Although manually reconstructing shredded documents takes a considerable amount of time and patience, there's speculation that intelligence and law enforcement agencies may use automated processes to recover shredded information.

In the late 1990s, a company called Wakefield Integrated Technologies was advertising a software application called the Unshredder, which worked by using a scanner to scan the shredded pieces of paper. After all the recovered strips were scanned, the application used pattern recognition algorithms to reassemble the destroyed documents.

Wakefield had a Web site at unshredder.com that advertised the product, but both it and the company seemed to disappear several years ago. It's unknown whether the technology was immature, the site was a hoax, or if some government "alphabet agency" ended up acquiring the product and technology.

(Kevin Murray, of Murray and Associates, a respected name in the counterespionage business, has a copy of some old Unshredder marketing literature on his informative Spybusters Web site at `www.spybusters.com/pdf/UNshredder.pdf`.)

Communication Devices

Information from communication devices (such as telephones, cellular phones, pagers, and voice-mail) can all be compromised either remotely (by eavesdropping) or locally if a spy has physical access to the device. Communication devices are traditionally one of the weakest links in most security systems (people just love to talk), and they can be readily exploited by a spy with the right technical equipment. On the other hand, if you believe that someone is or may be attempting to eavesdrop on your conversations, there are a number of electronic countermeasures you can use to secure your communications.

Telephones

Eavesdropping on telephone conversations has been going on since telephones started to become popular in the late 19th century. Spies, cops, PIs, and jealous significant others have used everything from picking up an extension phone to sophisticated bugs to covertly monitor conversations. Up until the 1960s, phone and room bugs were available from mail-order sources to just about anyone. Federal laws clamped down on the use and manufacture of audio bugging devices and restricted their availability to the government or law enforcement agencies with a court order that authorized their use. However, laws don't do much to stop a dedicated and motivated spy, especially when they are difficult to enforce, and illegal telephone eavesdropping is still a viable threat. (It's beyond the scope of this book to get into the details of telephone bugging, audio surveillance techniques, or the countermeasures that can be applied against them. If you're interested in learning more about this side of espionage, a good place to start is Marty Kaiser's Web site at www.martykaiser.com. Kaiser is a legend in the surveillance business and has developed all sorts of interesting devices for government TLA (Three-Letter-Acronym) agencies since the 1960s. In general, telephones can be compromised for surveillance purposes in two different ways:

✓ **Taps.** Tapping a telephone is placing some type of monitoring device on a phone line. The biggest advantage to tapping is you don't need physical access to the phone (no risky black bag jobs are involved), and the tap can be placed miles away from the target. Most court-approved wiretaps will take place at a phone company's central office switching facility, which makes them extremely hard to detect. ("Spy shops" sell relatively low-cost telephone bug detectors, but they work only against the most basic eavesdropping devices and techniques and are useless against an opponent using sophisticated equipment.)

✓ **Bugs.** If a spy has physical access to a telephone, he might install a monitoring device inside of it. These bugs not only eavesdrop on phone conversations, but also on any sounds or conversations taking place in the room while the phone is on the hook. (A brief warning for office managers: Some speakerphones, fresh out of the box with no modifications, can transmit radio frequency energy that can be intercepted up to several hundred feet away.)

Although there are high-tech countermeasures for defeating telephone eavesdropping (discussed following), the most effective defense is simply to keep your mouth shut and limit discussing sensitive topics on the phone.

x-ref

Commercial telephone bugs and other equipment designed specifically for covert audio surveillance is illegal in the U.S. and available only to government and law enforcement agencies. (However, there are companies such as Ramsey Electronics, www.ramseykits.com, that manufacture legal kits for devices that could be used for surveillance, and Winston Arrington's book *Now Hear This*, available from www.covertbug.com, is filled with do-it-yourself bug designs). To get an idea of some of the products legally available to law enforcement or illegally available to others, check out U.K. surveillance manufacturer Lorraine Electronics' Web site at www.lorraine.co.uk.

SECURE PHONES

One way to defeat telephone eavesdropping is to use a secure phone. Voice encryption devices have been around since the 1960s, and the most widely used secure phone is something the government calls a Secure Telephone Unit or STU. STUs, or as they're more commonly called "stew phones," first came into use in 1970, and are currently in their third generation (the STU-III). A STU-III looks like an ordinary desk phone (see Figure 12-3) and works like an ordinary desk phone, but also supports having a secure conversation with someone else who's using a STU-III.

Figure 12-3: Government security poster showing a typical STU-III phone and an enlarged version of the KSD-64A Crypto Ignition Key (CIK) used to initiate a secure conversation

It works like this. You call another STU-III user over a normal telephone line and then tell her to "go secure." This involves inserting a special key (known as a Crypto Ignition Key, or CIK) into the phone. After the key is inserted and both parties press the Secure Voice button, their conversation is encrypted. If a phone line is tapped, the spy hears nothing but strongly encrypted noise; for the conversation parties, with some secure phones there can be Donald Duck–like voice distortion that may sound like the other person has been breathing helium. When the keys are removed, the conversation returns to normal unencrypted talk. (Whenever a CIK is inserted into the STU-III, the phone becomes classified and can be used only by people cleared and authorized to use a STU-III. When the CIK is removed, the phone becomes yet another unclassified, although expensive, piece of government property; STU-III phones are in the $3,000 and up price range.)

Defectors from foreign intelligence services report that the STU-IIIs are very effective for preventing eavesdropping. However, a fair amount of intelligence can still be gathered from conversation tidbits before the phones go secure.

 For more about STU-IIIs, check out a user's handbook that the Department of Defense publishes for defense contractors at http://koeln.ccc.de/archiv/doku/stu3.pdf. For detailed descriptions of STU-IIIs (including photos) and other secure government communication devices, go to www.tscm.com/stu.html.

You can't just go down to your local Radio Shack and buy a STU-III, although there are versions available to the public with weaker encryption. However, if you're an average citizen interested in protecting your privacy, you have a couple of options for making secure telephone calls.

Many spy shops sell devices that scramble a telephone conversation to prevent someone from successfully eavesdropping on it. You need two of these devices: one on the sending side and the other on the receiving side. The cheaper scramblers use frequency inversion to distort speech (frequency inversion is easily defeated using inexpensive hardware devices that restore the scrambled audio to recognizable speech). The more expensive devices, targeted to corporations and individuals with a need for higher security, start in the $1,500 range and use a strong encryption algorithm to secure a conversation.

In 1999, a company called Starium, Inc. announced that it would be bringing secure encrypted telephone hardware to the masses. Co-developed by noted cryptographer Eric Blossom, the handheld device would retail for around $100, connect to any phone, and provide a high level of security through strong encryption (see www.starium.com/pics.htm). The product was never released, and the company was in limbo at the end of 2002, with some talk of making another effort to get the product to market.

There are also secure Voice over Internet Protocol (VoIP) applications that provide an alternative to making easily compromised POTS (Plain Old Telephone Service) phone calls. Most Internet voice applications are insecure and can be easily eavesdropped on, but there are two applications that encrypt conversations, defeating attempts to snoop on your conversation.

- ✓ **Speak Freely** is a free open-source utility developed by Brian C. Wiles and John Walker that runs on Windows and Unix systems. It can be downloaded from www.speakfreely.org.

- ✓ **PGPfone** was originally written for the Apple Macintosh and then ported to Windows. Written by Phil Zimmermann and Will Price, the utility became a commercial product when Network Associates (NAI) acquired PGP Inc. in 1997. NAI really didn't do much with the product, and Zimmermann eventually released the source code. PGPfone is available at www.pgpi.org/products/pgpfone/.

Tools of the Trade: DTMF Decoders

An indispensable tool for a spy eavesdropping on telephones is a DTMF decoder. DTMF stands for Dual Tone Multi-Frequency. Whenever you press one of the numeric keys on a telephone, it generates a unique tone. A DTMF decoder analyzes a tone and translates it back to the number of the key that was used to generate it.

If you have a recording of phone keys being pressed, you can input the sound into a DTMF decoder, and the keys that were pressed will be displayed. This is extremely useful for discovering dialed phone numbers and voice-mail passwords.

There are a number of inexpensive, commercial hardware and software DTMF decoding products available on the Internet. To find out more, do a Google search for "dtmf decoder."

PHONE FORENSICS

Eavesdropping on phone conversations isn't the only way you can get information from a telephone. If you have physical access to a phone, you can also get useful information from the following:

- ✓ **Caller ID.** Caller ID is great for screening calls: The phone rings, and the name and phone number of whomever is at the other end of the line appears. Stand-alone Caller ID boxes, or those built directly into phones, are handy because they also keep a log of incoming phone calls (answered or not). If you don't delete the numbers stored by the Caller ID device, anyone who has access to the phone can get insights to who's been calling you. (From a spy's standpoint, there are a number of ways to defeat Caller ID and avoid having your incoming call identified. See www.artofhacking.com for a considerable amount of information on bypassing and spoofing Caller ID.)

- ✓ **Last number redial.** Many telephones have a last number redial feature, in which pressing a single button dials the last number dialed once again. This is convenient for trying to reach a busy phone number without having to manually redial it each time, but if a spy has physical access to the telephone, it's also a way for him to find out whom you last called. As the call is made, the tones can be decoded with a DTMF device held next to the phone's handset speaker.

- ✓ **Speed dial.** Preprogrammed speed-dial telephone numbers are useful for calling people you frequently talk with. The labels on the phone and the phone numbers associated with them can also let a spy know whom you frequently talk with.

Cellular Phones

Cellular phones can be an even higher security risk that a landline telephone. Because cell phones are just radio transceivers, with the right equipment, you can pluck conversations out of the air without even tapping into a phone line or performing a black bag job to bug the phone. This type of passive eavesdropping can be very difficult to detect and prevent.

Before discussing how cellular phones can be compromised for espionage purposes, it's important to have a very general understanding of how cellular phone technology works.

CELLULAR PHONE TECHNOLOGY

Cellular phone networks are named for a series of interconnecting cells. Each cell has a base station (a building with radio equipment and an antenna) that provides coverage over an approximate ten-square-mile area.

A cellular carrier in a city operates one central office called the Mobile Telephone Switching Office (MTSO). This office handles all the phone connections to the land-based phone systems and controls all the base stations in the region.

Each cellular phone (or handset) has an Electronic Serial Number (ESN) and a Mobile Identification Number (MIN) that uniquely identify the phone. If your phone is turned on, this information as well as other authentication, validation, and routing data are passed back and forth between your phone, the base station of the cell you currently are in, and the MTSO. If you're having a conversation and move toward the edge of a cell, the base station recognizes that your signal strength is dropping while the adjacent base station sees your signal strength is increasing; and through the MTSO, the weaker base station transparently hands off the conversation to the stronger base station.

Most people tend to think that a cell phone is a cell phone, but different cellular systems and phones use different technologies and protocols, which, depending on the type, may make it easier for a spy to eavesdrop on you. Current popular cellular technologies include the following:

✓ **AMPS.** Older "Advanced Mobile Phone System" systems, which the first cell phones in the U.S. were a part of, use analog signals that are easy to eavesdrop on with a police-type scanner. During the 1990s, the government stopped U.S. manufacturers from producing scanners that could receive transmissions in the frequencies allocated to cell phones, but there are numerous sources on the Internet with information on how to modify scanners to receive the blocked frequencies. It's important to understand that although analog AMPS conversations can be easily eavesdropped on with consumer-grade scanners, conversations using newer digital cellular technologies cannot.

✓ **TDMA (IS-136).** Time Division Multiple Access systems use a digital signal that thwarts snoopy radio hobbyists; however, by using commercial TDMA phone test equipment, you can eavesdrop on cell conversations that use this technology.

✓ **GSM.** Just like TDMA phones, digital Global System for Mobile Communication cell phones also require specific test equipment to monitor a conversation. GSM phones also add an extra layer of security by encrypting conversations with an algorithm called A5.

✓ **CDMA (IS-95 or 1xRTT).** Code Division Multiple Access phones use digital spread-spectrum frequencies, making it extremely difficult to monitor calls. Phones such as Qualcomm's NSA-approved QSec-800 enhance security even more by using built-in strong encryption, TEMPEST shielding, and tamper-resistant seals (see `www.qualcomm.com/govsys/pdf/qsec800datasheet.pdf`).

For more on TEMPEST and electromagnetic eavesdropping, turn to Chapter 13.

The take-home message is that for all of these different cellular technologies, there are ways to eavesdrop on conversations. Cell calls can be intercepted in real time by monitoring known frequencies, plucking signals out of the air, and then demodulating the transmissions. If you work for a law enforcement agency and have a court order, you can simply install monitoring equipment at the MTSO.

If your threat model leads you to believe that someone may expend considerable resources against you, you should never consider cell phone conversations secure. If you're using an analog cell phone, it's almost certain that your conversations will be overheard by any number of scanner enthusiasts. Using a digital cell phone eliminates the scanner threat, but your conversations are still vulnerable to government and law agencies or to someone with the right training and technical equipment.

In terms of countermeasures, the government and military have some slick secure wireless technology and products that you can learn more about from the Military Information Technology Online site at `www.mit-kmi.com/features/7_1_Art2.cfm`. If you don't work for the government and use a GSM cellular system, you could consider the German TopSec phone that uses strong encryption and is based on the popular Siemens model S35i handset. Don't expect to get one free by signing up for a new cellular plan, though. The phone costs a bit under $3,000, and you'll need at least two of them to carry on a secure conversation.

Although they're not cellular phones, cordless phones are also vulnerable to eavesdropping. Many models transmit an analog signal that can be received by a radio scanner. Frequencies used for cordless phones (and baby monitors) have not been blocked out of U.S. manufactured scanners as cellular phone frequencies have; it's still illegal to monitor these frequencies though. A 2.4 GHz, spread-spectrum cordless phone offers considerably more security than standard cordless phones.

Tactics: Cellular Eavesdropping and Encryption

The cellular phone industry likes to say that digital phones can't easily be eavesdropped on. Compared to older analog phones this is true, but it doesn't take resources bankrolled by a government or a court order giving you access to a cellular switch to monitor cell-phone conversations.

Let's say that your target is using a GSM phone, and you want to eavesdrop on him (and you're not a government law enforcement agency that has access to commercial monitoring devices). The first thing you need is a "Digital Radio Test Set." This is diagnostic and test equipment, manufactured by companies such as Agilent and Racal Instruments, that's specifically designed for troubleshooting cellular phones and networks. These devices can monitor both voice and SMS traffic and can be purchased for under $10,000.

But even if you can monitor the digital signals, what about the encryption used to protect the traffic? Unfortunately, the "A" series of encryption algorithms used to protect GSM conversations have turned out to be pretty weak, and numerous vulnerabilities and exploits have been reported since the late 1990s, including the following:

- ✓ **A5/1.** If you can capture data associated with the first two minutes of a conversation, the A5/1 key can be discovered in less than a second by using a common desktop PC.

- ✓ **A5/2.** A5/2 is the weaker of the two A5 voice-encryption algorithms and can easily be cracked in real time.

- ✓ **A3 and A8.** A3, the authentication algorithm used to prevent phone cloning, and A8, the voice-privacy key-generation algorithm, can both be compromised in roughly eight hours' time.

In July 2002, a new GSM encryption algorithm called A5/3 was introduced. Only time will tell whether this encryption scheme adds more security to cellular phone conversations.

There's some speculation that government intelligence agencies on both sides of the Atlantic and Pacific have purposely kept cell-phone encryption just strong enough to prevent most people from being able to eavesdrop on calls, but weak enough that conversations can still be compromised by a government.

DETERMINING YOUR LOCATION

If eavesdropping on your conversations isn't bad enough, how about being able to track where you are? It's possible to determine the location of a cellular phone that's turned on by measuring the time it takes for the signal to reach surrounding base stations or by determining the direction the signal is coming from and then triangulating the phone's position. These techniques have been used on several occasions to find and rescue lost and stranded motorists during winter storms. Law enforcement also uses location-detecting technology in criminal investigations. In 1995, the FBI used a device called Triggerfish, made by Harris Communications, to track down most-wanted cracker Kevin Mitnick who was making a cell call in his Raleigh, North Carolina apartment at the time.

Tracking cell phones will soon be even easier for government and law enforcement agencies. Whenever you have an emergency and call 911 on a landline phone, the dispatcher sees the address you're calling from. The Federal Communications Commission is mandating a similar system called Enhanced 911 (E-911), which will be in place for cellular phones by 2005. New cellular phones will have GPS units built into them, or existing cellular systems will use sophisticated triangulation techniques to be able to pinpoint the location of a phone. For network-based systems using triangulation, the revised FCC rules call for carriers to achieve 100-meter accuracy for 67 percent of mobile emergency calls and 300-meter accuracy for 95 percent of all of these calls. Carriers that install GPS in handsets, which is more accurate and reliable, must have an accuracy of 50 meters for 67 percent of its emergency calls and 150 meters for 95% of those calls.

CELLULAR PHONE EVIDENCE

If you have physical access to a cell phone, it can contain all sorts of potentially useful information and evidence. (If you're in law enforcement and have seized a cell phone, be careful to not let it sit in an evidence property room too long before you examine it. The batteries on some models will fully discharge, and you'll lose any phone numbers or other data stored in the phone.)

Any cell phone owner who is even a little bit security-savvy will lock his phone with a security code. Depending on the phone model, this defense can be just a minor speed bump to a knowledgeable spy. Programming and unlock codes are widely available on the Internet for most popular phones, and all a spy needs to do is press a correct sequence of backdoor numbers to unlock a phone (to learn how simple this is, check out www.cellphonehacks.com).

Once the phone is unlocked, some of the information that can be retrieved includes the following:

✓ **Phonebooks.** Most cellular phones have built-in memory for storing phone numbers. This is handy for quickly dialing up friends, family members, and business associates and eliminates the need to carry an address book around with you. Law enforcement officers love cell phonebooks because if they have a court order, they can examine the contents and put together a list of known associates of a suspect. This can be a powerful tool for establishing linkages in criminal investigations.

✓ **Call logs.** Many cell phones have call logs that list calls sent and received from a phone, including the phone number and time and date of the call.

✓ **Internet-related.** Over the past several years, cell phones have started to incorporate features such as e-mail and Web browsing. The same type of evidence extracted from a PC can often be gathered from an Internet-enabled cell phone. E-mail or SMS (Short Message Service) text messages stored on a phone can be especially valuable.

✓ **PDA-related.** There is a trend for cell phones to incorporate many of the features found on Personal Digital Assistants (PDAs). Built-in calendars, to-do lists, and address books all can provide sensitive information to a spy.

Answering Machines and Voice-Mail

Answering machines and voice-mail have become an essential part of day-to-day business and personal life. These convenient devices and services can also be a spy's top ten list to attack because of the information they contain and the fact they are frequently overlooked as a possible security vulnerability.

Virtually all voice-mail systems and answering machines allow a user to check and access messages from a remote location. If an eavesdropper can compromise a user's password from a telephone anywhere in the world, he can remotely listen to and erase any messages that have been left for the target.

Voice-mail systems and answering machines can be compromised several different ways:

✓ **Brute-force attacks.** This attack consists of trying every possible numeric combination that a password could consist of. A consumer answering machine with a three-number password has a maximum of only 1,000 possible password variations. Commercial voice-mail systems tend to have longer maximum passwords (up to 15). Obviously, a brute-force attack can take a lot of time; however, there are tools and scripts available that automate the process so you don't wear your finger out pressing phone keys.

✓ **Dictionary attacks.** A dictionary attack relies on a pre-selected series of numbers to try as passwords. These can be default passwords, frequently used passwords (common sequences such 12345, numbers that follow a pattern such as in the shape of a "Z" or "U," or the same number as the mail box), or passwords based on personal information (birthdays, anniversaries, or social security numbers).

✓ **Social engineering.** With a social engineering attack, a spy can compromise a password simply by asking for it (obviously with a convincing cover story).

✓ **Physical access.** If a spy has access to a phone or answering machine, the password may be printed on a label or written down somewhere near the device.

ANSWERING MACHINES

Consumer answering machines used in homes and small businesses are an easy target for a spy because most have passwords that are only two or three numbers, which make them extremely insecure. A two-digit password can be brute-forced in about five minutes. After a spy has access to an answering machine, he can check and erase messages, and on some models turn on the microphone to monitor conversations and sounds in the room. A number of these answering machines look only for a correct sequence of numbers, not a distinct password. For example, on a machine like this with a two-digit password, you could spoof the device's password by entering one of the following sequences:

```
00112233445566778899135790246803692581471593704948382726160517395062840852963007419753186420987654321012345678987654321357924686429731474193366994488552277539596372582838491817161511026203040506070809001
```

VOICE-MAIL

Corporate and telephone company voice-mail services are just as vulnerable to attack as answering machines are. Although voice-mail systems have a few more security features, such as longer passwords and login lockouts if a password is not correctly entered after a certain number of tries, some features present a spy with even greater opportunities for compromising information. Central phone numbers that a user can remotely access e-mail from without dialing their extension gives a spy a single phone number from which to launch attacks on multiple mailboxes. Additionally, corporate voice-mail systems often work in conjunction with a company's PBX (Private Branch Exchange) phone system, and if a spy can penetrate that, she can use the PBX to hide her tracks for carrying out a number of different types of attacks.

Voice-mail products typically have unique characteristics (such as the greeting) that can clue a spy into the type of system she is dealing with so she can exploit vulnerabilities associated with the system (commands and default passwords for a number of commonly used voice-mail products are readily available on the Internet).

From a countermeasures standpoint, there are several simple steps you can take to reduce the chances of information being compromised through a voice-mail system or answering machine:

- ✓ Select a numeric password that can't be easily guessed and is as long as the machine or service allows.

- ✓ If the voice-mail system supports it, configure the system so it prevents logins after a certain number of unsuccessful password tries.

- ✓ Never, ever leave sensitive information on a voice-mail system or answering machine. That means you should never leave a message with sensitive information on voice-mail, and if you receive a message with important information, you should never keep it stored on the system.

Stephan Barnes (a.k.a. "M4phr1k") of the security consultancy Foundstone has a large amount of information on breaching and shoring up PBX and voice-mail security on his Web site at www.m4phr1k.com. @Stake also has two very useful papers on voice-mail security written by Joe Grand (a.k.a. "Kingpin"): "Security Advisory on Telephone Answering Machines" (www.atstake.com/research/advisories/1998/ansmach.txt) and "Compromising Voice Mail Systems" (www.atstake.com/research/reports/acrobat/ompromising_voice_messaging.pdf).

Pagers

Although pagers are slowly going the way of the dinosaur and are increasingly being replaced by cell phones that support e-mail and short message service (SMS), they are still commonly used and can be both a source of evidence and information.

Traditional pagers only receive messages, whereas newer devices such as the Research in Motion (RIM) BlackBerry offer two-way capabilities. As with any other communications device, pagers can be compromised by intercepting message traffic or by physically gathering information from the device.

Law enforcement agencies can always get court orders for a pager company to reveal which messages have been sent to a particular pager, but a spy can also eavesdrop on pager traffic by using inexpensive hardware and software. (Unauthorized eavesdropping on pagers is illegal under a number of federal and state statutes, but as with illegally monitoring cell and cordless phones, its passive nature makes it difficult to detect.)

A pager is simply a radio receiver, and the messages it receives are sent from the vendor as analog radio signals using protocols, such as POCSAG (Post Office Code Standardization Advisory Group) or Motorola's Flex. Each pager has a unique identifier called a "cap code," which is typically a seven- to eight-digit number that's the electronic identification number (EIN) for the pager. The pager is constantly monitoring a stream of messages, and when it identifies a message that has its associated cap code, it decodes the data into numeric or alphanumeric format and displays the message on a small LCD screen.

Pager traffic is not encrypted, so if you can decode the protocol, you can read the message (devices such as the RIM BlackBerry are an exception; BlackBerry uses a digital protocol that incorporates Triple DES, which provides end-to-end security). To eavesdrop on conventional pager messages, you need four things:

✓ **PC.** A computer running Windows.

✓ **Scanner.** A radio scanner is used to intercept signals in the frequency range allocated to pagers. This doesn't have to be anything fancy and can be a cheap, basic handheld police scanner. Scanners use a discriminator chip to filter the audio to make it suitable for listening through a speaker or earphone. Unfortunately, the filtered audio isn't suitable as a source for decoding pager messages. You need to modify the scanner by tapping the discriminator chip so the raw data can be sent to an interface device. (There are plans to do this for most types of scanners as well as companies that perform the modification if you're not good with a soldering iron.)

✓ **FSK interface.** The analog audio signals from the pager need to be converted into a digital format so the message text can be displayed. This is done with a hardware interface that supports Frequency Shift Keying (FSK). Input from the scanner's discriminator chip is sent to the FSK interface, which demodulates the audio signals into a digital format. (Some software can perform limited decoding of messages without the use of a separate interface by using your soundcard, but an interface device is a must if you're serious about monitoring traffic.)

✓ **Software.** The software receives the data sent from the FSK interface and displays it on the computer. Some of the freeware and shareware tools are quite sophisticated and incorporate features such as only intercepting messages sent to a specific pager, date and time logging, and outputting all messages to a text file. Two popular pager utilities that are commonly available on the Internet include PDW and WinFlex.

With the right programming equipment, it's also possible to create a "clone pager" that receives all the messages a targeted pager receives. Pager companies provide such pagers to law enforcement agencies with a court order to monitor a suspect's messages. (Commercial pager eavesdropping products similar to the homemade versions are available for law enforcement use when a court order has been issued.)

Keep in mind that a pager message can also be compromised at the sending end. If the telephone that the message is sent from is being tapped, a pen register is installed on the pager number; or if a message is sent from a Web site or with an e-mail message, the origin point of a page can be discovered.

The best countermeasure against pager eavesdropping is to simply be aware that any messages sent to a pager can potentially be compromised. It's possible, though, to beat pager eavesdropping by using codes (drug dealers do this all the time). However, substitution ciphers can easily be cracked, and numeric codes can usually be defeated with traffic analysis if there is enough message traffic. Probably the best way to secure alphanumeric pager communications is to use a personal digital assistant (PDA) running a utility that uses a strong cryptographic algorithm, such as IDEA, 3DES, or AES, and encrypting a message before sending. When the pager message arrives, the recipient enters the encrypted message in his PDA and then decrypts it with a prearranged password. Although a bit time-consuming and not seamless, this is an effective approach if a strong password is used.

x-ref

There is a wealth of information on the Internet about decoding pager messages. Just do a Google search for "POCSAG decoder," and a number of links show up. For starters, you might want to try Mike ZL3TMB's POCSAG site that lists a number of different software utilities for decoding pager messages (http://homepages.ihug.co.nz/~Sbarnes/pocsag/software.html), or if you're electronically inclined, Libor Ulcak's site has hardware schematics for building a pager decoder (www.applet.cz/~ulcak/4_level_fsk_interface.htm).

Aside from monitoring a pager, if you have physical access to the device, you can also extract useful information, including the following:

✓ Undeleted and stored alphanumeric messages

✓ When and how (e-mail, Web site, and phone) alphanumeric pages were sent

✓ Numeric information (phone numbers and codes)

Newer two-way pagers, such as RIM's BlackBerry (which is really a cross between a pager and a wireless PDA), are much more complicated devices to examine. Michael Burnette wrote an excellent paper called "Forensic Examination of a RIM (BlackBerry) Wireless Device" (available at www.rh-law.com/ediscovery/Blackberry.pdf), which discusses some of the challenges and techniques of gathering evidence from a BlackBerry.

Consumer Electronics

Computer spying and forensics used to be pretty straightforward; you'd look for information or evidence on a computer's hard drive, floppy disks, or any other storage media that might be lying around. However, the popularity of consumer electronic devices has made searching for information more complicated. Personal Digital Assistants (PDAs) are incredibly popular and require a different approach in seeking out data. In addition, data can now be hidden in all sorts of different electronic devices, including consumer products primarily designed for taking pictures, playing music, or recording television shows. Technically savvy users might conceal information on some of these devices, which may go completely undetected during a search. This provides a number of challenges to law enforcement and forensic examiners, who are faced with expanding their technical knowledge outside of traditional computers as well as developing new tools and ways of forensically processing digital evidence found in consumer electronics products.

PDAs

Personal Digital Assistants, or PDAs, are incredibly popular. Their success comes from the devices' capability to store contact information, appointments, financial records, spreadsheets, and text documents in a handheld, go-anywhere platform. It is estimated that more than 20 million Personal Digital Assistants (PDAs) have been sold in the last five years.

As you might expect, PDAs are a favorite target of snoops interested in the information they contain. Because of their small size, PDAs are easy to misplace and steal. In a Gartner Group report released in January 2002, the company projected that 250,000 PDAs and cell phones will disappear in airports each year. Anderson Consulting research released at the end of 2001 estimated that 10 to 15 percent of all cell phones and PDAs will eventually become lost or stolen. You might think that a piece of hardware worth only a couple of hundred dollars isn't a big deal, but the same report stated that the estimated value of the information on a PDA ranged between $10,000 and $20,000. (If you own a PDA, think about the value of all of the names, addresses, phone numbers, appointments, e-mail messages, and other files in the device.)

Let's focus on situations in which someone ends up being more interested in what's stored on the PDA versus the device itself. Some of the ways information on a PDA can be compromised include the following:

✓ **Poor user security practices.** Most PDAs have some form of password authentication to protect data, but many users don't use this feature, which makes it a snap for a spy who has physical access to the device to peruse all the stored information.

✓ **Weak encryption.** Even when a manufacturer's authentication system is used, it still can be notoriously weak. For example, the scheme used to protect Palm OS documents marked "Private" was found to be a simple XOR algorithm that could be easily cracked in seconds (see www.atstake.com/research/advisories/2000/a092600-1.txt).

✓ **Synching vulnerabilities.** Synching is the process of exchanging data between a desktop PC and PDA: Data is transferred between the two devices with a cable or docking cradle attached to the PC's serial or USB port. When synching takes place, information on the PDA is typically backed up on the PC's hard drive. Anyone with access to the PC can examine these files (including recovering the PDA's password) or mirror the backed-up PDA by uploading the files to a similar PDA model. PDAs can also be attacked remotely through infrared synching. @Stake released a tool that runs on a Palm called NotSync (www.atstake.com/research/advisories/2000/notsync.zip) that establishes an infrared conversation with another Palm and spoofs it into thinking that it's synching with a PC. The tool then grabs the targeted Palm's password and decodes it.

✓ **Dumping memory to a file.** If you have physical access to a PDA, it's relatively trivial to dump the entire contents of memory to a PC's hard drive, in which the data can be examined and searched. Palm OS PDAs are especially easy to dump memory with tools such as pdd (www.mindspring.com/~jgrand/pdd/).

x-ref

At the end of 2002, Palm OS PDAs held a commanding 65 percent market share in the United States, and although Microsoft's competing Pocket PC is catching up, if you encounter a PDA, it will probably be some type of a Palm system. For spies and forensic examiners that need to tease information out of a Palm, a good place to start is to read "pdd: Memory Imaging and Forensic Analysis of Palm OS Devices" by Joe Grand (www.mindspring.com/~jgrand/pdd/pdd-palm-forensics.pdf). You should also check out Paraben's PDA Seizure product, a software utility for acquiring and examining the contents of both Palm OS and Pocket PCs. The tool is priced at $199 (the company also sells a complete kit with cables and adaptors for gathering evidence from 30 different models of PDAs); you can get information at www.paraben-forensics.com/pda.html.

The first countermeasure against PDA espionage is awareness. Understand the value of the information that's stored on your PDA and take measures to physically protect it from being lost or stolen. Standard security features that come with a PDA are inadequate for providing a decent level of protection against spies. Your best bet is to use a third-party encryption application to better secure your PDA. Some possible options include the following:

✓ **PDA Defense.** For both Palms and Pocket PCs, priced at $29.95 and available from `www.pdadefense.com`.

✓ **Sentry 2020.** Available for the Pocket PC, $49.95 with more information at `www.softwinter.com/sentry_ce.html`.

✓ **OnlyMe.** A Palm security application from `www.tranzoa.com`, priced at $9.95.

✓ **TealLock.** A Palm-compatible security application with personal ($16.95) and corporate ($21.95) editions, available at `www.tealpoint.com/softlock.htm`.

Digital Cameras

There's more to looking for information associated with digital cameras than just examining any photos that have been snapped. Some other considerations when examining digital cameras for evidence include the following:

✓ The JPEG format supports attaching small amounts of text (as comments) or sound to an image, and some cameras support annotating a photo after you take it. This information could be valuable (particularly as evidence) and can sometimes be overlooked.

✓ Time- and date-stamping may be turned on, with the information overlaid on an image when the photo was taken. Time and date can also be determined from the file-creation date of the image (if the clock was set correctly on the camera or if the date hasn't been changed on purpose).

✓ By default, digital cameras use a sequential naming format for stored images. If files have not been renamed, this format can be useful for determining how many photos have been taken as well as the order they were taken in.

✓ Digital cameras store images on flash memory cards, and they should always be checked because these cards can also store other forms of data.

GPS Units

GPS (Global Positioning System) devices use information from satellites to tell you exactly where you're located. Originally used for navigation by pilots, ship captains, and hikers, the location systems are now showing up in cars, PDAs, laptops, and other devices. (They're also quite handy for spies to identify secret meeting and information exchange points. Convicted spy Patrick Regan had a Garmin III+ GPS unit with him when he was arrested.)

Tactics: GPS Stalking

Connie Adams, a resident of Kenosha, Wisconsin, couldn't figure it out. No matter where she went, it seemed her ex-boyfriend showed up. She'd look in her rearview mirror and see him following her to work or while she was running errands. He even unexpectedly showed up at a bar she'd never been to before while she was on a date.

When police investigated, they found that Adam's former boyfriend, Paul Seidler, had installed a GPS tracking device between the radiator and grille of her car. The device remotely transmitted her location to Seidler, who was able to follow her movements. In January 2003, Seidler pleaded innocent to felony counts of stalking, burglary, recklessly endangering safety, and a misdemeanor count of disorderly conduct.

Seidler used a commercial system from a company named L.A.S. Systems (www. landairsea.com). The $695 piece of hardware transmits the location of a vehicle through a cellular phone network. You can watch a car move in real time on a street map displayed on your PC's monitor or have the location sent to your cell phone in the form of a short text message. Products like this (called AVL or Automatic Vehicle Location) have been used for years to legitimately track trucks and vehicle fleets, but decreasing prices and increasing availability are putting them into the hands of spies, snoops, and stalkers.

Commercial AVL units are pretty obvious if you know what you're looking for; however, if you're concerned about a really small and stealthy device you might not be able to find, you can always take a hint from the military and employ electronic countermeasures (ECM). In December 2002, *Phrack* (the seminal hacker and cracker electronic magazine) published an article on how to construct a do-it-yourself GPS jammer to defeat tracking devices. Plans and information are available at www.phrack.com/phrack/60/ p60-0x0d.txt.

If you own a GPS device, waypoints and track files can be retrieved and examined to provide a snoop with information about where you've been and when you were there. GPS chipsets have become smaller, cheaper, and more power-efficient within the past several years; and "location-aware" features will become more common in wireless, consumer electronic, automotive, and mobile computing products. Any time location information is stored or transmitted, it's vulnerable to someone who has physical access to the unit or can eavesdrop on the transmission.

Video Game Consoles

The latest generation of video game consoles, such as Microsoft's Xbox and Sony's PlayStation 2, have come a long way since the days of Pong and the Atari 2600. In addition to realistic graphics and sound, modern game consoles feature internal hard drives and Internet connectivity. The

PlayStation 2 even has an add-on kit consisting of a keyboard, software, and hard drive that allow you to turn the game console into a Linux desktop computer. With enhanced features and software, a console might not be all fun and games and could covertly store files and data you might not even know were there. (Also see www.securityfocus.com/news/558 for an interesting article on using a game console for network eavesdropping.)

MP3 Players

Just like a game console, a portable MP3 player can be a secret data repository. Sporting megabytes to gigabytes of storage, a flash memory card or internal hard disk can store music as well as other types of data. Be careful not to dismiss what looks like a normal personal radio or CD player. If the device plays MP3s, it could have much more data on it than tunes ripped from a CD.

Television Digital Recorders

Hardware devices and services, such as TiVo, have made television watching a much more pleasant experience by digitally recording hours of TV programming onto a hard drive. You can record an entire season's worth of your favorite TV episodes without worrying about tapes or timers (plus fast-forwarding through commercials in the blink of an eye). The TiVo Digital Video Recorder hardware uses Linux as an operating system, and it's possible to perform all sorts of hacks to enhance features, including copying files from a PC to the TiVo box (see the "Hacking the TiVo" FAQ at www.tivofaq.com/hack/faq.html). Because the box looks like a VCR or satellite decoder, someone looking for digital evidence could easily overlook it as a storage device.

Summary

Computers aren't the only devices that a spy might target to extract data from. Anything that transfers or stores information (especially if it's in a digital form) can be vulnerable to attack. You can increase your security by going through a simple set of steps:

1. Make a list of all of devices or services you use on a regular basis that either store or transfer information.

2. Now, pare down the list to include only devices or services that deal with information you think is sensitive.

3. Analyze this list and understand how the data is stored or transferred, how it's protected, and how someone could remotely or locally access the information.

4. After you've identified potential vulnerabilities, come up with ways to harden the data from attack. (Remember the differences between probable and possible attacks, and try not to venture too far into tinfoil hat paranoia.)

As new technology increasingly finds its way into consumer and business electronic devices ("IP everywhere," "location-aware" products, radio frequency identification tags, inter-networked consumer products), the potential for eavesdropping rises. If you're an early adopter of new technology that stores or transfers information, remember that security features (if they're even present) invariably will never have the kinks worked out with the first releases, and there may be a spy lurking in the shadows just waiting to exploit a newly discovered vulnerability.

Chapter 13

Advanced Computer Espionage

"They've given you a number and taken away your name."
— Johnny Rivers, "Secret Agent Man"

THIS CHAPTER EXAMINES SOME ADVANCED AND EXOTIC WAYS of conducting computer spying, typically used by the government, military, and those engaged in high-level economic espionage (of course, because all of these entities thrive on secrecy, sometimes you need to make educated guesses at what they might be up to). Also discussed are some techniques that could be used in a sophisticated intelligence-gathering operation and that you don't necessarily need to be a well-financed government intelligence or law enforcement agent to use. Looking at it from the target's point of view, unless you've done something or have something that's made you a target of a powerful and well-financed organization, most of these methods should be fairly low on your list of possible threats.

TEMPEST — Electromagnetic Eavesdropping

TEMPEST is a U.S. government code word that refers to a classified set of standards for limiting electromagnetic radiation emanations from electronic equipment (lots of things give off emissions that can compromise data, and the military and spooks use the term "Emissions Security" or EMSEC to describe protective measures). Microchips, monitors, printers, and all electronic devices emit radiation in the air or through conductors such as wiring or water pipes. For example, if you use a kitchen appliance while watching television, the static on your TV screen is emanation-caused interference from the appliance.

There have been a number of attempts to turn TEMPEST into a meaningful acronym, such as Transient ElectroMagnetic Pulse Emanation STandard. The official government line states that TEMPEST is a code word given to the standards, and it doesn't have any particular meaning.

During the 1950s, the government became concerned that emanations could be captured and then reconstructed. Obviously, the emanations from a blender aren't important, but emanations from an electric encryption device would be. If the emanations were recorded, interpreted, and then played back on a similar device, it would be extremely easy to reveal the content of an encrypted message. Research showed that it was possible to capture emanations from a distance, so the TEMPEST program was started in response.

The purpose of the program was to introduce standards that would reduce the chances of electromagnetic emanations "leaking out" from devices used to process, transmit, or store sensitive information. Government agencies and contractors use TEMPEST computers and peripherals (printers, scanners, tape drives, mice, and so on) to protect data from being snooped-on through emanation monitoring. This protection is typically accomplished by shielding the device (or sometimes a room or entire building) with copper or other conductive materials.

In the United States, TEMPEST consulting, testing, and manufacturing is a big business, estimated at more than one billion dollars a year. (Economics have caught up with TEMPEST though. Purchasing TEMPEST-rated hardware is not cheap, so a less-strict security standard called ZONE has been implemented. ZONE doesn't offer the level of protection of TEMPEST hardware, but it is quite a bit cheaper and is used in situations in which data isn't as sensitive.)

The United States (particularly the NSA) and its allies have doggedly kept TEMPEST standards classified so that unfriendly nations remain at a disadvantage when it comes to shielding their own systems, theoretically making it easier for the "good guys" to spy on them. However, after TEMPEST became publicly known during its first mention in a nonclassified briefing in 1965, the cat was out of the bag, and any foreign power that even had the slightest clue about emanation eavesdropping could use a series of basic countermeasures against a monitoring attack.

One big issue with the TEMPEST "security through obscurity" approach was that only government agencies and government contractors (usually in the defense industry) benefited from the standards. Any American corporation without a security clearance didn't have much of a chance to protect sensitive information from emanation monitoring attacks. Granted, this was during the Cold War period, when there wasn't much of an emphasis on economic espionage, but because TEMPEST was so closely guarded, it left large corporations vulnerable to attacks by foreign intelligence agencies.

Although TEMPEST was once shrouded in mystery and secrecy, it is less so now. By sifting through public source material, including a number of documents that were released through the Freedom of Information Act, an astute person can piece together most of the puzzle of what TEMPEST is all about. Despite this publicly available information, the nearly 50-year old standard still remains classified.

Emanation Monitoring: Fact or Fiction?

If TEMPEST is about preventing someone from intercepting emanations, just how realistic a threat is eavesdropping through emanation monitoring? If you've done any reading on computer security or have watched TV or the movies, the following scene is probably familiar.

Across the darkened street, a windowless van is parked. Inside, an antenna is pointed out through a fiberglass panel. It's aimed at an office window on the third floor. As the CEO works on a word-processing document, outlining his strategy for a hostile take-over of a competitor, he never knows that what appears on his monitor is being captured, displayed, and recorded in the van below.

That's pretty cool from a spy's perspective: passive, undetectable eavesdropping, but before we discuss whether it's real or not, some background is in order. Because most people don't have security clearances, you need to look at publicly available information to come to educated conclusions about how much of a threat emanation monitoring actually is.

A BRIEF PUBLIC HISTORY

The first public indications that emanation monitoring might be a viable eavesdropping tool came during the mid-1980s. In 1985, Wim van Eck, a Dutch engineer, published "Electromagnetic Radiation from Video Display Units: An Eavesdropping Risk?" The paper described how you could eavesdrop on video display terminals (VDTs), the precursors of modern computer monitors, from up to a kilometer away and by using relatively inexpensive components. (The paper was purposely incomplete on several points, and modifications were required to actually build a working device based on his plans. Figure 13-1 shows what his device looked like.)

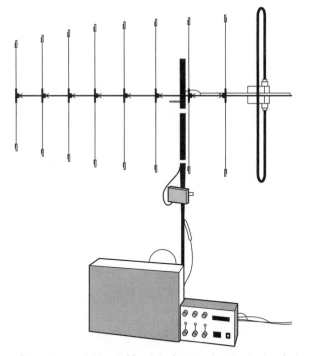

Figure 13-1: Wim van Eck's original emanation monitoring device that (under the right conditions) could eavesdrop on a Video Display Terminal (VDT) up to a kilometer away.

Shortly after the paper was published, a series of British television exposés had reporters driving around London with van Eck–type monitoring devices, having great fun snooping on lawyers, banks, and New Scotland Yard. People in the security industry started to get a little edgy over the prospects of a spy secretly accessing their data without even setting foot inside a building.

The NSA also got edgy that this technology had now found its way out into the public realm. Wang Research Laboratories (a large producer of TEMPEST equipment) was scheduled to give a demonstration of eavesdropping equipment to computer security professionals, but the NSA stopped it by classifying the presentation. At the Interface '87 conference, a prominent Washington, D.C. company was slated to give a presentation on "How Computer Security Can Be Compromised," with a demonstration of emanation eavesdropping techniques, but cancelled it at the last minute at the request of the NSA. (This contrasts with the Swedish government's approach in the 1980s, which included informing businesses about the possible criminal threat of emanation monitoring and publishing a booklet called "Läckande Datorer" (Leaking Computers), which described the threat in detail and included countermeasures.)

In the United States during the late 1980s, a number of "van Eck Phreaking" products and plans became commercially available, many of dubious design and effectiveness. These products continued into the '90s, with several rigged television demonstrations of supposed "TEMPEST monitoring" devices and sales of fraudulent hardware. (It seems when it comes to TEMPEST and emanation monitoring, the media for some reason gets all starry-eyed and doesn't do a good job of due diligence.)

The hype and hoopla surrounding emanation monitoring gave way to all sorts of erroneous information about TEMPEST, including the idea that anyone could easily build an eavesdropping device with a trip to Radio Shack and a $100 bill (perhaps a device that could intercept signals from an old VDT, but certainly not with a modern computer monitor). Although there have been a variety of papers published that demonstrate eavesdropping in lab settings, the reality is that there are no monitoring devices that are effective for field espionage use and are readily available to the public.

Considering the interest in TEMPEST, the number of bright individuals with electronics backgrounds, and the popularity of the Internet for disseminating information, no one has yet posted plans for an inexpensive, easy-to-use monitoring device. Emanation monitoring is definitely not as easy as plucking 802.11b wireless data out of the air, as described in Chapter 11.

An excellent chronology of key events in the history of TEMPEST can be found at `http://cryptome.org/tempest-time.htm`.

THE GOVERNMENT PERSPECTIVE

So we know that emanation monitoring won't be much of a threat from the general public, but what about the government? Here's where things start to get a little murky because of secrecy associated with TEMPEST and the need to protect espionage "sources and methods."

There are no public government records that give an idea of how much emanation monitoring is taking place or has taken place. There are isolated anecdotal accounts of monitoring being used for political, military, and industrial espionage, but not much in the way of publicly accessible information to back up the claims. For example, an FBI agent participating in a 1999 MIT panel discussion stated that emanation monitoring could be used as a possible investigative technique. Was his statement true, misinformed, or a deliberate attempt at disinformation?

One of the main difficulties in tracking instances of emanation monitoring is that because of its passive nature and because it's conducted at a distance from the target, it's hard to discover unless you catch the perpetrator red-handed (a bad Cold War pun). Even if a spy were to be caught, more than likely the event wouldn't be publicized, especially if it were economic espionage. Both government and private industry have a long history of concealing security breaches from the public.

There are a few data points that can lead one to believe that there is a risk from emanation monitoring, though — at least from foreign intelligence services. The TEMPEST industry is a more-than-a-billion-dollar-a-year business, which indicates that there's a viable threat to justify all the required protective hardware (or else it's one big scam that's making a number of people quite wealthy).

Then there are all sorts of government and military references to the threat, such as this quote from a Navy manual that discusses "compromising emanations" (CE): "Foreign governments continually engage in attacks against U.S. secure communications and information processing facilities for the sole purpose of exploiting CE."

So if the threat is out there, just how real is it? A reduced picture of the threat was painted in the 1990s by a series of intelligence agency and military reports and directives, including the following points:

✓ In 1991, a CIA Inspector General report called for an Intelligence Community review of domestic TEMPEST requirements based on the potential threat. The outcome suggested that hundreds of millions of dollars had been spent to protect a vulnerability that had a very low probability of exploitation. This report galvanized the Intelligence Community to review and reduce domestic TEMPEST requirements.

✓ In 1992, the National Reconnaissance Office (NRO), the secret agency in charge of U.S. surveillance satellites, eliminated the need for domestic TEMPEST requirements.

✓ In 1994, the Joint Security Commission issued a report called "Redefining Security" to the Secretary of Defense and the Director of Central Intelligence. The Commission recognized the need for an active overseas TEMPEST program, but believed that the domestic threat was minimal, suggesting that TEMPEST countermeasures be employed domestically only in response to specific threat data.

In the government's Cold War zeal, after the emanation monitoring vulnerability was discovered, the intelligence agencies and the military probably severely overestimated the potential for it to be exploited. After the TEMPEST standard requirements ball got rolling, however, it was very difficult to stop it.

CONCLUSIONS

So, is emanation monitoring a viable security threat? Based on the information at hand, we can make the following conclusions:

✓ van Eck's research was successful in intercepting emanations from fairly primitive VDTs. Being able to reconstruct the contents of a modern, sophisticated computer monitor at a distance is much more of a challenge, especially because now there are considerably more electronic devices happily generating electromagnetic radiation that can interfere with locking on to the monitor on which you want to eavesdrop.

✓ The government doesn't believe that emanation monitoring is a significant threat by foreign powers within the United States. Outside the United States, however, such as at an embassy or a U.S. military installation, things change because the foreign intelligence service is now on its own home playing field.

✓ Emanation monitoring is definitely not a make-believe TV-show espionage method; it is much more challenging than many people may think. Unless your adversary is extremely well-funded and has access to sophisticated electronic equipment and the trained personnel to operate it, emanation monitoring should be pretty low on your threat list.

EMSEC Countermeasures

When looking at any type of attack, you really need to weigh the costs and benefits of it being executed as well as being defended against. From your opponent's standpoint, is it cheaper and more efficient to have a spy pass himself off as a janitor to obtain information or to launch a fairly technical and sophisticated monitoring attack to get the same data? Although some "hard" targets may justify a technical approach such as emanation monitoring, traditional human-intelligence (HUMINT) gathering techniques will be used more often, without a doubt.

Because there are cheaper and more effective ways to compromise data, most people don't need to worry about emanation attacks. However, if you have a reason to be concerned about the threat and don't happen to have a government security clearance, there are a number of countermeasures you can employ, including the following:

✓ **Purchasing TEMPEST certified equipment.** This is the logical choice if you're a government agency or defense contractor. However, TEMPEST-certified computers and peripherals aren't cheap, and most vendors won't sell them to the general public. However, surplus TEMPEST hardware does come on the market every now and then and is often inexpensive.

✓ **Employing architectural design.** An even more expensive alternative to shielding individual hardware is to shield a room or entire building with copper mesh and special windows that block emanations. Check out the Army's "Engineering and Design — Electromagnetic Pulse (EMP) and Tempest Protection for Facilities" document at www.usace.army.mil/inet/usace-docs/eng-pamphlets/ep1110-3-2/toc.htm.

✓ **Using standard Radio Frequency (RF) and Electromagnetic Interference (EMI) shielding techniques.** Although somewhat dated, Grady Ward's description of shielding methods is still applicable and offers some viable, cheap solutions for the do-it-yourselfer. It's available at www.eff.org/Privacy/Security/tempest_monitoring.article.

✓ **Using special fonts.** Ross Anderson and Markus Kuhn discovered that it was possible to defeat emanation monitoring by using specially designed fonts. Their paper is available at www.cl.cam.ac.uk/~mgk25/ih98-tempest.pdf. The German company Steganos GMbH (www.steganos.com) incorporates the countermeasure fonts in some of their products, including a freeware Windows notepad–type application.

For more public source information on TEMPEST that's been gathered over the past six years, see the author's comprehensive "Complete, Unofficial TEMPEST Information" page at `www.eskimo.com/~joelm/tempest.html`.

Optical TEMPEST — LEDs and Reflected Light

In March 2002, Joe Loughry released a fascinating paper on what he called "Optical TEMPEST." To quote the paper's introduction, "A previously unknown form of compromising emanations has been discovered. LED status indicators on data communication equipment, under certain conditions, are shown to carry a modulated optical signal that is significantly correlated with information being processed by the device. Physical access is not required; the attacker gains access to all data going through the device, including plaintext in the case of data encryption systems. Experiments show that it is possible to intercept data under realistic conditions at a considerable distance. Many different sorts of devices, including modems and Internet Protocol routers, were found to be vulnerable."

Later the same day, Markus Kuhn released a paper entitled "Optical Time-Domain Eavesdropping Risks of CRT Displays." Essentially, it's possible to view the contents of a computer monitor from the light it reflects on a wall. In the conclusion, Kuhn stated, "The information displayed on a modern cathode-ray tube computer monitor can be reconstructed by an eavesdropper from its distorted or even diffusely reflected light using easily available components such as a photo-multiplier tube and a computer with a suitably fast analog-to-digital converter."

Whether government intelligence agencies previously knew about these vulnerabilities is unknown. In both cases, the attacks would require some rather sophisticated equipment and could be easily and cheaply defeated by placing black electrician's tape over any exposed LEDs and simply keeping the curtains or blinds shut when working with sensitive information (a good practice in any case).

For more details on these two types of attacks, Loughry's paper can be downloaded from `http://applied-math.org/optical_tempest.pdf` and Kuhn's paper is available at `www.cl.cam.ac.uk/~mgk25/ieee02-optical.pdf`.

HIJACK and NONSTOP

Somewhat related to TEMPEST is another pair of classified standards that are codenamed HIJACK and NONSTOP. HIJACK and NONSTOP refer to the compromise of cryptographic devices through nearby radio transmitters (such as a cell phone, handheld radio, or intercom). At this point in time, there isn't much public information available about these two standards, and they are considerably more secret than TEMPEST. However, by putting together a few scattered pieces of non-classified information, we can get a general idea of what the code words refer to.

HIJACK appears to relate to a form of compromising emanations involving digital versus electromagnetic signals. Compromising data is similar in nature to an attack against hardware that isn't TEMPEST-shielded, in which the spy doesn't need to be close to the device that's being eavesdropped on. The attack does require access to communication lines (these can be wire or wireless). A spy uses antennas, receivers, a display device, a recording device, and one additional piece of equipment (a special detection system that is supposedly very sensitive, very expensive, and very rare). Also, the technician operating this special equipment supposedly requires a great deal of training and experience.

NONSTOP apparently relates to a form of compromising emanations, but involves signals transmitted from radio frequency devices (handheld radios, cell phones, pagers, alarm systems, cordless phones, or wireless networks; AM/FM commercial broadcast receivers are excluded) in proximity to a device containing secure information. There are specific guidelines for either turning the RF device off or keeping it a certain distance away from the secure device, such as a computer or printer.

ECHELON — Global Surveillance

So far, the surveillance methods we've discussed are used mostly for targeting an individual computer or network, but there's a much more powerful tool in the government's arsenal of eavesdropping technologies that's codenamed ECHELON.

ECHELON is an extensive government surveillance program that can intercept different types of communications anywhere in the world. It's jointly operated by the United States, the United Kingdom, Canada, Australia, and New Zealand. Although ECHELON officially started up in the early 1970s, its roots go back to 1948, when the five participants in the collective signed intelligence-sharing agreements.

It's been suggested that ECHELON is capable of intercepting up to three billion communications a day, including e-mail messages, faxes, Internet file transfers, satellite transmissions, telephone calls, and telexes. Some sources believe that ECHELON may examine up to 90 percent of all traffic that passes over the Internet. (The term *ECHELON* is thought to technically refer only to intercepting satellite communications, but it is also widely used to refer to the entire intercept system.)

ECHELON has been a closely guarded secret for many years, and the United States government won't even comment on it or acknowledge its existence (when it comes to programs that are supposed to be secret, sometimes the government adopts an ostrich "head-in-the-sand" position, believing that saying nothing will make the problem go away; sometimes this is valid operational security or "OPSEC," and other times it's rather a joke). What we know about ECHELON comes mostly from whistleblowers, the admissions of the Australian and New Zealand governments, and European government–sponsored reports on the surveillance system. It's likely what we do know about ECHELON is only a small part of the scope and scale of the program.

The United States National Security Agency (NSA) takes the lead in ECHELON activities, followed by its foreign counterparts, the United Kingdom's Government Communications Head Quarters (GCHQ), the Australian Defense Signals Directorate (DSD), the Canadian Communications Security Establishment (CSE), and New Zealand's Government Communications Security Bureau (GCSB). Data gathered by ECHELON is also often selectively shared with friendly governments.

ECHELON isn't the only surveillance program of its type (it's by far the largest and most sophisticated, though). Other countries, such as China, India, Israel, France, Germany, Pakistan, and Russia, have the resources and intelligence agencies to maintain their own communications (especially Internet) interception projects.

How ECHELON Works

ECHELON acts like a giant vacuum cleaner, automatically sucking up all sorts of information. It then analyzes the data by using a series of powerful, computerized artificial intelligence applications. Keywords are searched for in either audio or text intercepts. (For example, if "Kim Jong Il" ~ ~~ on a search list, any communications mentioning the North Korean president would be ~~~ld view the contents.) Keywords can be names, addresses, telephone num- ~ a voice pattern; in some cases, ECHELON can supposedly match ~uter systems that analyze all the collected data are thought to be

~d that ECHELON is both a specific piece of hardware and an intelli- ~. Each of the countries participating in the ECHELON program has ~e sy ~ s and methods. Information collected from these different systems is ~C~~N members, with each intelligence agency possessing a copy of the ~h words. For example, while automatically scanning intercepted com- ~ian DSD surveillance station encountered words related to the North ~hat were on an NSA search list, the data would be automatically sent to ~work. ~ is collected in a number of different ways. For the interception of commercial satellite communications, the system has a series of large antennas located throughout the world. In addition to intercepting satellite transmissions, the program also has its own intelligence satellites in orbit designed to intercept wireless communications from major cities back on earth. The spy satellites beam the collected data to processing centers in the United States, Great Britain, Australia, and Germany.

For surface communications, such as phone calls and faxes, an ECHELON member may have a confidential agreement in place with a telecommunications company to route communications through a sophisticated, high-speed monitoring device. It's also known that cooperative projects between the military and intelligence agencies have succeeded in tapping underwater communications cables.

But because this book is about computer espionage, let's go back to that statement about 90 percent of the Internet traffic being eavesdropped on. According to Wayne Madsen, an investigative journalist and former NSA employee, and reported in the European "Interception Capabilities 2000" document (see www.nrc.nl/W2/Lab/Echelon/ic2kreport.htm), the NSA had installed traffic collection software on nine major Internet exchange points by 1995 (see Table 13-1). An Internet Exchange Point is a physical network infrastructure whose purpose is to facilitate the exchange of Internet traffic between ISPs. If you monitor all the exchange points, you could essentially monitor all of the Internet traffic. (For a current list of Internet Exchanges, go to www.ep.net/ep-main.html.)

TABLE 13-1 Alleged NSA-Monitored Internet Exchange Points (1995)

Internet site	Location	Operator	Designation
FIX East	College Park, Maryland	U.S. government	Federal Information Exchange
FIX West	Mountain View, California	U.S. government	Federal Information Exchange
MAE East	Washington, D.C.	MCI	Metropolitan Area Ethernet
New York NAP	Pennsauken, New Jersey	Sprintlink	Network Access Point
SWAB	Washington, D.C.	PSInet/Bell Atlantic	SMDS Washington Area Bypass
Chicago NAP	Chicago, Illinois	Ameritech/Bellcorp	Network Access Point
San Francisco NAP	San Francisco, California	Pacific Bell	Network Access Point
MAE West	San Jose, California	MCI	Metropolitan Area Ethernet
CIX	Santa Clara, California	CIX	Commercial Internet Exchange

The more paranoid (or perhaps security-conscious) computer users have long thought that the Internet was being monitored. Dating back to the 1980s, some people included words such as NSA, CIA, KGB, plutonium, and Mossad at the end of innocent e-mail and USENET newsgroup messages as "spook bait." This half-serious, half-joking practice reached a new height on October 21, 1999 with "Jam Echelon Day," an organized attempt to get as many people as possible to encrypt their Internet communications and include "trigger words" in e-mail. The goal was supposedly to overwhelm ECHELON with data, bringing it to a standstill. Although it's very doubtful the effort succeeded, it was repeated again in 2001, and at the least raised awareness about the surveillance system.

ECHELON also allegedly actively seeks out Internet data instead of passively sniffing it. For a four-year period, a "bot" (a robot application designed to automatically gather information from a Web site) visited John Young's Cryptome.org site on a daily basis, downloading any updated material. The bot was anything but stealthy, with its origin IP address easily tracked back to the NSA. It doesn't seem too much of a leap to believe that it was shoveling the data into ECHELON.

ECHELON Controversy and Countermeasures

If it weren't for the numerous sources that corroborate the existence of ECHELON, you'd think it was the delusional product of some obsessed conspiracy theorist. This isn't the case, and although ECHELON serves a purpose in helping to track down terrorists and provide evidence of weapons of mass destruction possessed by rogue states, the secrecy and sheer power of such a surveillance program concerns many people. Some of the key issues that worry privacy advocates and countries that aren't part of the ECHELON club include the following:

✓ Although ECHELON was originally developed to eavesdrop on Cold War political and military communications, there are reports that it is now being used for economic espionage. There are several cases in which American corporations have supposedly beaten out European competitors for lucrative contracts based on ECHELON data.

✓ The United States and many other countries have privacy laws in place, which prevent government intelligence agencies from spying on their own citizens. However, there are suspicions that ECHELON has been used to circumvent these restrictions. For example, although the NSA might not be able to legally spy on a U.S. citizen, if GCHQ had ECHELON data related to that individual, it could pass the information over to its American NSA counterparts who were interested in the subject. Wink, wink, nudge, nudge.

✓ There are no known checks and balances or oversight in place to prevent abuses within the ECHELON program. The *Washington Post* reported in December 1998 that the NSA admitted that it had files on Diana, Princess of Wales, some of the information based on intercepted phone calls. No explanation was given about why an American intelligence agency had information about a former member of the British royal family.

We won't get into the debate of "I don't have anything to hide, so why should I be concerned about ECHELON?" Let's say you're a privacy advocate or you do indeed have something to hide. The odds are that your downloading of MP3s won't trigger ECHELON to record your downloading habits (although the Recording Industry Association of America might like it to). ECHELON is collecting and parsing so much data that unless you're up to something pretty evil, the odds are that you will be lost in the crowd.

Also, consider that ECHELON is simply a surveillance technology, although a sophisticated and powerful one, and like any eavesdropping method, it can be defeated. Some of the countermeasures that can be used against ECHELON include the following:

✓ **Encryption.** It's pretty obvious that if you encrypt any data you send over the Internet with a strong cryptographic algorithm, it will be hard for someone to compromise the information. Keep in mind, though, that ECHELON is probably tagging any encrypted communications it encounters just because it's encrypted (someone must have something to hide). If you do end up as a government target, various attempts may be made to crack the encryption. If it can't be cracked, it's likely that it will be stored with millions of other encrypted messages for possible cryptanalysis at some point in the future (using some factoring breakthrough, a quantum computer, alien technology, or whatever).

✓ **Covert channels.** Instead of using encryption that can draw attention to yourself, you can use a covert channel to hide your communications, which could be disguising a message as SPAM or embedding a message in a Web page. Accused spy Patrick Regan advised the Iraqis to change their UN Web site to indicate whether they would be interested in buying American military and intelligence secrets from him.

✓ **Low-tech.** If you're really paranoid about ECHELON and have something to hide, you can always resort to low-tech communications methods that don't use computers, telephones, or radios. After Al Qaeda members had an understanding of the surveillance capabilities of the United States during the invasion of Afghanistan, they stopped using satellite phones and radios and started relying on couriers to pass messages.

Tactics: U.S. vs. Regan

Brian Patrick Regan worked for the National Reconnaissance Office (NRO), the agency responsible for the United States surveillance satellites. He first worked for the NRO as a Master Sergeant in the Air Force, in which he had access to TOP SECRET and even more secret sensitive compartmented information (SCI). When Regan retired from the military in 2000, he continued with the NRO as a contractor for TRW Inc., which was later acquired by Northrop Grumman.

Regan was arrested on August 23, 2001 on charges of attempting to sell classified information, including satellite photos, to Iraq, Libya, and China. When he was detained at Dulles International Airport before boarding a plane headed for Zurich, FBI agents found that he was carrying coded coordinates of missile sites in Iraq and China, information on the types of missiles, and the dates the missiles were first spotted. The information allegedly came from U.S. spy satellite photos.

On a laptop seized from his home, the FBI recovered letters to Iraq and Libya, offering to provide classified information for $13 million. The letters began with the statement, "I am willing to commit espionage against the United States."

Regan was worried about FBI countersurveillance (he should have been worried because the FBI ultimately followed him to a public library and watched him surf the Web looking for the addresses and phone numbers of foreign embassies), so he decided to use a covert channel as part of his communications with the Iraqis.

In his indictment, a copy of the letter Regan drafted to Saddam Hussein is included. Part of the letter reads (typos and grammatical errors left intact), "The first thing I need you to do is make a minor change to your UN homepage to prove to me that you are not the FBI seting [sic] a trap for me. I have a print out of your UN page . . . . If you make some minor changes to this page (switch one word or another, add a comma, or change some numbers) this will let me know that you have received both letters and are planing on proceedding [sic] with the plan." A nearly identical letter was drafted and sent to Libyan leader Muammar Qadhafi.

In early 2003, Regan's espionage trial started. This was the first public trial of an American accused of espionage in more than 50 years. Walker, Pollard, Hanssen, Ames, and other notable spies all had made plea bargain deals with the government and never went to trial. Regan claimed he never provided classified information to a foreign power, and all of the information he possessed was publicly available. He was found guilty and in March 2003 was sentenced to life in prison.

For more information on ECHELON, see the ACLU's ECHELON Watch Web site at `www.echelonwatch.org` and Cryptome's collection of ECHELON documents at `http://cryptome.org/cryptout.htm#Echelon`.

Carnivore/DCS-1000

Carnivore (currently known as DCS-1000, as in Digital Collection System) is the FBI's computer-based system for conducting wiretaps of Internet communications. Unlike ECHELON's vacuum cleaner approach, Carnivore eavesdrops only on data associated with a targeted individual.

Carnivore is essentially an enhanced packet sniffer designed specifically for law enforcement use. It's installed at a suspect's Internet service provider (ISP) after a court order has been granted. (The FBI maintains that Carnivore is used only when an ISP cannot or will not comply with a court order seeking certain information.) The "investigative tool" sifts through incoming and outgoing traffic, recording data associated with the target of the wiretap order. Carnivore can operate as either a "content wiretap" or a "trap and trace/pen register" device, as follows:

- ✓ **Content wiretap.** Captures all e-mail or network traffic directed to and from a specific IP address or user. There are typically more stringent court order requirements for these types of wiretaps.

- ✓ **Trap and trace/pen register.** Captures only transactional information, not content. Examples are e-mail headers (with the exception of the subject) or visited Web sites and FTP servers. These wiretaps are usually easier to get than content wiretaps.

Carnivore first came to light in the summer of 2000, and what we know about it comes from around 600 pages of FBI documents released under the Freedom of Information Act to the Electronic Privacy Information Center (many of these pages were heavily redacted) and information provided from an independent review of Carnivore conducted by the Illinois Institute of Technology.

An Overview of Carnivore

Carnivore is part of a collection of FBI investigative tools known as the DragonWare Suite. In addition to Carnivore, there's CoolMiner and Packeteer. Packeteer processes Carnivore's raw output and reconstructs protocols (such as SMTP and HTTP) from IP packets. CoolMiner creates statistical summaries and formats pen register or content information so it can be viewed with a Web browser. (The DragonWare utilities consist of DLLs written in C++ and GUI front ends developed in Visual Basic.)

A third-party contractor developed Carnivore. All references to the identity of this contractor were redacted in the Freedom of Information Act (FOIA) documents, but there have been unsubstantiated rumors that the large defense and intelligence consulting and engineering firm Booz, Allen & Hamilton played a role in developing Carnivore and other FBI computer surveillance applications.

The FBI maintains that there was nothing sinister about choosing the name Carnivore for the utility. Depending on with whom you talked about the origin of the name in the Bureau, you'll get replies such as the system "get(s) to the meat of an investigation," or "Carnivore chews all the data on the network, but it only actually eats the information authorized by a court order." Even when Carnivore was renamed to DCS-1000, the FBI was insistent that the name change had nothing to do with the negative public reaction to the name Carnivore.

Carnivore debuted in 1999, but there were at least two other monitoring tools before it. Omnivore was its predecessor and ran on a Sun Solaris system. It was designed to monitor incoming and outgoing e-mail, print the contents in real time, and store data on 8mm tapes. Omnivore, which was first used in October 1997, replaced an earlier tool whose name hasn't been disclosed; the utility is still a classified secret.

The FBI didn't like the Solaris-based system and wanted something simpler, so they started a development project codenamed "Phiple Troenix." (There's a palm tree that goes by the name of Triple Phoenix, but who knows what the FBI or their contractor was thinking when they named the project). Phiple Troenix, which would eventually become Carnivore, was designed to run on a Microsoft Windows NT–based computer. $800,000 was budgeted to the project to port Omnivore over to the new platform and provide training on its use.

The first versions of Carnivore were buggy and prompted the "Enhanced Carnivore" project in November 1999. According to the FOIA documents, versions 2.0 and 3.0 were planned with new features, such as being able to wiretap Voice over Internet Protocol communications.

Carnivore was installed on a Windows NT, Pentium III class computer with a 10Mbps/100Mbps Ethernet card and an Iomega Jaz drive for storing captured data (the drive had a physical lock on it to prevent unauthorized access to the Jaz disk). The Carnivore machine was connected to the ISP's network with a Shomiti network tap. In addition to the operating system and the surveillance software, a copy of pcAnywhere was also installed to allow an agent to remotely control the computer through a phone line.

An FBI Technically Trained Agent (TTA) was in charge of the Carnivore installation and would configure the software with the suspect's IP address or e-mail address (other filtering rules could also be applied). Carnivore would then sniff network traffic, copying packets only to and from a particular location or suspect. Any other packets passing through the network would be ignored.

All of the data would be saved to the 2GB Jaz disk. An agent would retrieve the disk on a regular basis and place it in a dated and sealed container to maintain the evidence's chain of custody (which is discussed in Chapter 5). The evidence would then be examined with the other DragonWare tools to see whether there was sufficient evidence to be used in a case against the suspect.

After the surveillance was completed (typically, the courts grant an initial 30-day period for wiretaps), the hardware would be removed from the ISP's network.

Carnivore Controversy and Countermeasures

The biggest concern raised by privacy advocates about Carnivore is the fact that the system accesses and processes all incoming and outgoing network traffic, including that of users not targeted for surveillance and not named in a court order.

When word leaked out about Carnivore in 2000, there was a large public outcry against the tool based on possible violations of civil liberties. (The FBI was probably surprised by all the fuss because they had only 20 Carnivore boxes that had been used the previous year a couple of dozen times.)

Because of the controversy, the FBI allowed an independent review of Carnivore and selected the Illinois Institute of Technology Research Institute to conduct it. (Privacy advocates weren't happy about this because the review was to be completed in six weeks, and the review team consisted of a number of government insiders, including people with Justice Department, NSA, and Department of Defense backgrounds.)

The final release of the report in December 2000 took much of the technical mystery out of Carnivore, and the controversy slowly waned (the report can be viewed at www.cdt.org/ security/carnivore/001214carniv_final.pdf). However, Carnivore bared its teeth once again during the spring of 2002, when it was revealed that the capture utility had collected e-mails from individuals who weren't on the wiretap order during a terrorism investigation. Internal FBI memos stated that Carnivore had the tendency to cause "the improper capture of data," noted that "[s]uch unauthorized interceptions not only can violate a citizen's privacy but also can seriously contaminate ongoing investigations," and stated that such interceptions are unlawful.

With the war on terrorism, FBI use of Carnivore will continue, probably at an expanded rate, and although hopefully the data "over-collection" bugs will be fixed, there is still the potential of abuse. All of the standard countermeasures used to prevent other forms of computer eavesdropping can be used to limit the effectiveness of Carnivore. These countermeasures include using strong encryption, anonymous remailers, and anonymizing Web proxies.

(For those readers who work for law enforcement agencies, these countermeasures are by no means new or revolutionary, and mentioning them isn't meant to give bad guys a way to circumvent the law. The reality is that criminals and terrorists will increasingly use a number of technologies to thwart your efforts. Even if legislation bans certain privacy tools, it won't stop people who are already breaking the law from using them. You need to be aware of this sooner rather than later, and you should realize that you may need to alter your investigative techniques when dealing with a technically savvy suspect.)

For more information on Carnivore, see the Electronic Privacy Information Center collection of resources at www.epic.org/privacy/carnivore/.

Magic Lantern

The FBI has clearly seen the future of digital communications and is trying to keep its investigative techniques in step with advancing technology. At the end of 2001, information surfaced about yet another FBI surveillance project, this one named Magic Lantern. According to the FBI, Magic Lantern was a "workbench project" (prototype) that had yet to be deployed. From the sketchy descriptions, it appeared to be a Trojan horse application that an agent could install on a suspect's computer that would log keystrokes and gather evidence. The difference between this keylogger and the one used in the Scarfo case was that agents wouldn't need to gain physical access to a suspect's computer; they could remotely install the Trojan with an e-mail attachment or some type of a Windows operating system exploit.

Tactics: Magic Lantern and Sexual Predators?

Patrick Naughton was a dot-com wunderkind. In 1988, he started work at Sun Microsystems and was part of the team that developed Java. Catching the start of the Internet craze, he worked for Starwave, a Web development company, serving as president and Chief Technology Officer. He then joined Infoseek, which was subsequently acquired by Disney, and he was riding high during the dot-com gold rush as an executive vice president responsible for Disney's Go Network at 34 years old.

Naughton's world came crashing down in September 1999 when FBI agents arrested him on federal charges of crossing state lines to solicit sex from a minor. Naughton had been chatting online with what he thought was a 13-year-old girl for several months and had made arrangements to meet her at the Santa Monica Pier. Instead of ending up in the nearby hotel room he had reserved, he ended up behind bars as part of an FBI sting. During the investigation, agents also discovered a handful of child porn images on one of Naughton's computers.

Patrick Naughton pleaded guilty and was sentenced to five years of probation and nine months of home detention, and he had to register as a sex offender anywhere he lived or worked. The story would have ended there, but a document released by a Los Angeles federal court in August 2000 contained some interesting revelations.

As part of a reduced-sentence deal, Naughton was to provide the government with five software applications. He ended up spending more than 1,000 hours working for the FBI in exchange for no jail time.

Although the details of the work that Naughton performed for the FBI were sealed, a request by the *San Jose Mercury News* did shed light on the five applications he was tasked with developing for the government. They included a utility for matching images, a tool for tracing a server used to send e-mail or host a Web page, a utility for logging chat sessions, and another tool for detecting the use of steganography.

All these tools would be useful in child pornography and sexual predator investigations, but the fifth one was the most intriguing. Naughton created a "framework" for an application that would allow the FBI to remotely access and search a computer.

Whether this had anything to do with the Magic Lantern project isn't publicly known. A Department of Justice spokesperson stated the following to a *Mercury News* reporter: "The details of the software are under seal, therefore, secret. And second, the disclosure of details about the use of these applications may compromise law enforcement's use of these programs."

All sorts of rumors started swirling about Magic Lantern, including one that a company named Codex Data Systems was the primary developer, and the software was based on a product of theirs called Data Interception by Remote Transmission (D.I.R.T.). Frank Jones, Codex's CEO, had been trying to hawk D.I.R.T. to a variety of law enforcement agencies. Unfortunately, a number of federal agencies (and foreign governments) didn't perform enough due diligence to learn that Jones was a fired New York City cop and convicted felon, currently on probation for illegal possession of surveillance devices, who had a rather long history of selling security products regarded by many experts as snake oil. (Jones, who used the name SpyKing, ducked jail time on his conviction, claiming that a mental condition caused him to engage in illegal acts, which he seemed to continue after his sentencing. In 2001, Jones's probation officer received a severe reprimand for overlooking multiple probation violations that Jones committed.) It's rather doubtful that the FBI would use D.I.R.T., but stranger things have happened when it comes to the Bureau's dealings with high-tech felons.

As with Carnivore, the revelations about Magic Lantern created considerable public controversy. Representatives from popular antivirus vendors Symantec (Norton AntiVirus) and McAfee initially said their products wouldn't detect the government Trojan (they later retracted these statements), whereas other antivirus vendors said they'd definitely let users know if government spyware was on their systems. (The reality is that Magic Lantern would likely be used so infrequently that an antivirus company would never get its hands on a "live" copy to add to its virus and Trojan signature database.)

Since the initial news about Magic Lantern, not much new information has leaked out about the Trojan or other FBI computer surveillance projects. Although few people outside of the government have access to Magic Lantern and similar surveillance Trojans, aside from using a commercial scanning product, most of the other countermeasures discussed in Chapter 9 should prove effective in detecting and defeating these types of eavesdropping applications.

John Young's Cryptome Web site has a considerable amount of information on D.I.R.T. and Magic Lantern (including a leaked copy of the D.I.R.T. executable, which appears to be based on Back Orifice). See `http://cryptome.org/dirt-guide.htm`, `cryptome.org/dirty-lantern.htm` and `cryptome.org/dirty-secrets2.htm`.

Modified Applications and Operating System Components

Another relatively sophisticated way of compromising sensitive data is to replace an application or operating system component (such as a library) with a modified version that either leaks information or makes secure information vulnerable to attack. A modified executable could perform espionage-related activities, such as the following:

✓ Weakening cryptographic software (introducing algorithm weaknesses or additional keys that would make decryption easier)

✓ Allowing unauthorized network activity (such as a modified version of a firewall that covertly permits certain connections)

✓ Secretly recording data (logging keystrokes)

Modified executables and libraries are often called Trojans or backdoors, but there's an important distinction between modified executables and the Trojans discussed in Chapter 9. Most simple Trojans modify the operating system in memory by "hooking" Windows API calls. This means additional code is executed either before or after a Windows API call is made. Hooking is fairly simple, but an application must first be run for an API call to be altered.

A more sophisticated approach involves modifying a copy of an executable prior to an attack and then swapping the original executable for the modified version, either by gaining physical access to the computer or by exploiting a network vulnerability.

There are two ways to modify an application or operating system component:

✓ **Recompile the source.** This involves making changes to the source code and then recompiling the executable or library. (Even if you don't have the original source code, it's still possible to make a modified version of the original.)

✓ **Patch the executable.** This involves using an editor to modify the executable by changing the hexadecimal representations of various assembly language instructions. The executable is first examined with a disassembler (a tool that converts an application into human readable assembly language) to determine what instructions to modify.

Some people believe that proprietary software such as the Windows operating system, in which distribution of the source code is restricted, is inherently more secure than open-source software such as Linux. The argument goes that because someone doesn't have access to the source code, he can't add code to do malicious things and then recompile and distribute the executable or library to an unsuspecting victim.

Although having the source code certainly does make it easier to modify an operating system or application for espionage purposes, not having it won't stop a determined and skilled opponent. All it takes is a knowledge of assembly language, a disassembler, and a compiler; and you can take apart an existing piece of software, alter it, recompile it, and replace the original file with your changed copy. (In addition to disassemblers, which output code in assembly language, there are also decompilers, which can analyze a file and generate code in a higher-level language such as C.)

Although this sounds like an extremely technical undertaking, it really isn't. Reverse-engineering dates back to the early days of personal computing when programmers cracked software copy-protection schemes on games and applications. There are numerous reverse-engineering tools available on the Internet, as well as a large support infrastructure in place for anyone interested in taking apart an executable and putting it back together again. Although there are some brilliant reverse-engineers, brilliance is not generally required to be effective.

(If you're still not convinced that Windows is vulnerable to these types of attacks, pay a visit to www.rootkit.com for some practical information and real-world code examples. You may be very surprised.)

x-ref

For five years, a European known as Fravia ran a Web site that provided a remarkable amount of information on reverse-engineering. The site contained tutorials and essays by a number of skilled "reversers" on disassembling applications and then modifying them. Since 2000, Fjalar Ravia has turned his energies to mastering the nuances of locating information on the Internet. His www.fravia.com site is required reading for any spy wanting to go beyond simple Google searches. Mirrors of the original Fravia reverse-engineering site are still around, including one at http://tsehp.cjb.net/. (Remember that the U.S. Digital Millennium Copyright Act takes a dim view of reverse-engineering.)

Tactics: Patriotic Duty?

Every now and then, a rumor surfaces about a technology company cooperating with the government to make it easier to eavesdrop on its customers. After all, it's the patriotic thing to do (especially in these post-9/11 days).

Intelligence agencies have a history of stepping outside the law to spy on American citizens, sometimes with the willing cooperation of a U.S. corporation.

In 1945, the predecessor of the NSA established a partnership with RCA, ITT, and Western Union to obtain copies of all telegraph messages entering and leaving the United States. Dubbed Operation Shamrock, upwards of 150,000 messages per month were handed over to intelligence agencies for analysis. The illegal eavesdropping continued until 1975, when the operation was revealed during congressional testimony.

Does this kind of thing still go on? Only the government knows for sure, but here are a couple of interesting, fairly recent news accounts.

In 1997, a Swedish news article reported that the encryption in Lotus Notes was vulnerable to eavesdropping by the American government. At the time, cryptographic products shipped outside the United States were subject to a number of restrictions. Although the 64-bit encryption that Lotus Notes implemented could be used in the United States, it was export-restricted outside of the U.S. Lotus had apparently made a deal with the government to be able to sell the product with 64-bit encryption to other countries. Eileen Rudden, a Lotus vice president, was quoted as saying, "The difference between the American Notes version and the export version lies in degrees of encryption. We deliver 64-bit keys to all customers, but 24-bits of those in the version that we deliver outside of the United States are deposited with the American government. That's how it works today." The Swedes didn't know about this and weren't too happy. The U.S. government agency to whom the keys were delivered was not identified.

In September 1999, a security researcher discovered that the Microsoft Cryptographic API had an undocumented key labeled "NSAKEY." Accusations started flying that Microsoft had placed trapdoors in its operating systems to allow the NSA and other government agencies to circumvent security. The software company denied the allegations, saying that the key was labeled NSA because the NSA acted as the review body for the export of encryption technology and that the key was only there to comply with U.S. export laws. Microsoft said the NSA-labeled key was simply a "backup" for the one used by the company to allow it to update cryptography components, that the key's name was poorly chosen, and that the accusations were ironic because Microsoft was against proposed government key escrow policies. (For what it's worth, though, according to journalist Wayne Madsen, during a 2001 Interagency Technical Forum at the National Institute of Standards and Technology (NIST), Microsoft's director of Mobile Code Security revealed that the company maintained a full-time office at NSA headquarters with a security cleared staff.)

It's interesting to note that in the June 1995 issue of *Computer Fraud & Security Bulletin*, Madsen, a former NSA employee, wrote that both Microsoft and Lotus had just concluded agreements with the NSA concerning privacy-related features in their products.

Your basic line of defense against these types of attacks is to use an MD5 hash utility to generate hash values for the freshly installed executables and libraries immediately after you have installed software from a trusted source. Periodically check these baseline hash values against current ones. If a value is different for no apparent reason, you may have a file that's been modified for espionage purposes.

It's also important to encrypt the list of hashed values or store it in a remote, secure location. If a spy is planting a modified file on a system, he may first search the hard drive for a file containing hashes and then change the hash value of the file replaced by the modified version. When the user verifies the hashes, he'll probably never know one or more files have been swapped for modified versions.

Intelligence-Gathering Viruses and Worms

With the widespread use of the Internet, espionage opportunities exist that weren't present five or ten years ago. Viruses and worms offer remarkable potential for compromising sensitive information.

There are several differences between these types of attacks and the more common everyday instances of viruses and worms that you encounter and read about on a regular basis:

✓ Intelligence-gathering code is designed to covertly gather information. The code's only purpose is to steal information and remain undetected; the developer wants his creation to avoid publicity. Unlike many viruses and worms, the code is sophisticated and well-tested. It may make use of a number of exploits instead of only one to ensure its success. It will probably attempt to disable any security software that could stop it from completing its mission.

✓ The code may target only certain individuals or organizations. Unlike conventional malicious code, which is opportunistic in nature, intelligence-gathering code can be more selective, kind of like a laser-guided missile. Before attacking, there are a number of Windows Registry entries the code can check to see whether a computer matches its target profile. A targeted attack also means there's less chance of detection because an attack on a limited number of computers that goes undetected won't register on the radar of commercial antivirus vendors. (This concept of targeted attacks could also be applied to non-espionage components of information warfare. Consider code that checked the Registry for which localized version of Windows was running and only attacked computers running Arabic versions.)

Although we have yet to see any confirmed accounts of intelligence-gathering code being deployed by a government or organization involved in high-level economic espionage, the potential goes beyond theory. Real live examples, in varying degrees of sophistication, have already widely hit the Internet on a number of occasions. It's not too much of a leap to assume that espionage attacks similar in nature, although smaller and more targeted, have already taken place.

Viruses and Worms

A virus is an application that carries out some specific act and replicates by infecting other programs or files. A worm is similar, but doesn't replicate by infecting other files. The problem is that sometimes even antivirus vendors and security experts have difficulties clearly making distinctions between these two different types of malevolent code. For the purposes of discussion, let's just lump them together and say they're both applications that replicate and perform some action without the user knowing it.

The purpose of an intelligence-gathering worm or virus is to spread itself, collect information from infected computers, and send the message back to its creator (this could be through e-mail, FTP, a USENET newsgroup post, a fax, a network printer connection, or any method of electronically sending data). The applications could be broadly deployed so they would work against anyone they encountered or be selectively used against only certain targets. For example, if you were conducting corporate espionage against IBM, you might employ a virus that would steal documents after first checking a Microsoft Office Registry value to determine which organization or business the software was registered to. If the organization value were some variation of IBM, the virus would copy the documents and send them to a remote location. If the value didn't match the target, the virus might delete itself before replicating to destroy evidence of its presence (or perhaps not even replicate and end the propagation cycle there).

The Internet has actually seen several intelligence-gathering viruses and worms deployed over the years, including those discussed in the following sections.

CALIGULA

In 1997, I wrote a paper about possible practical attacks that could be launched against PGP (see www.privacy.com.au/pgpatk.html). One of the options I briefly mentioned was an "espionage-enabled" virus that was designed to collect or steal information. I raised the possibility of a virus that spread and functioned only on computers running PGP. Little did I know that a few years later someone would take the general concept and turn it into a live virus, crediting me in the process.

In February 1999, the media picked up on a story about a new virus dubbed Caligula, written by Opic of the now defunct CodeBreakers virus-writing group. Caligula was one of the first publicly known intelligence-gathering viruses, and it was targeted at PGP users. The Word macro virus would search for the presence of PGP on a users' hard drive. If the encryption utility were found, the virus would make an FTP connection to a remote site and upload a copy of the user's private key ring. Conceivably, a dictionary attack could be launched against the file to determine if a weak password was being used. If a weak password was present, encrypted e-mail from that user could be compromised.

In interviews, Opic stated that the virus was meant only to be a proof-of-concept, designed to show how PGP could be exploited. It's not known how many PGP key rings were copied or if any successful attacks were launched against them. (An archived version of Opic's now long-gone home page with the original information about the virus can be viewed at http://web.archive.org/web/19990221015817/http://members.tripod.com/opiccb/index.htm.)

MARKER

A few months after Caligula was released, another virus written by the CodeBreakers group appeared. This one was called Marker (because of text at the beginning of the code that read "this is a marker") and it retrieved the name of the registered Microsoft Word owner and logged when the virus infected the target. On the first of each month, it would attempt to connect to the CodeBreakers FTP site and upload the information it collected. Again, this appeared to be more of a proof-of-concept virus designed to track infection rate and spread. The author of the Marker, a 17-year-old known only as Spooky, supposedly gave up virus writing when he found out that the virus infected organizations such as Blue Cross. "There have to be limits, and I think I have found mine," he explained on his Web site at the time.

SIRCAM

In July 2001, the SirCam worm was running rampant over the Internet. Lots of people unwittingly opened an attachment associated with an e-mail message that read, "Hi! How are you? I send you this file in order to have your advice. See you later. Thanks." (Sure, the worm pulled e-mail addresses out of the Windows address book so it looked like the message came from someone you knew, but honestly, how many of your friends, acquaintances, or business associates write e-mails worded like that? This is an excellent example of social engineering in action.)

When the attachment was opened, the worm would copy a randomly selected document (.DOC, .XLS, or .ZIP format) from the infected computer, attach the document to an e-mail message, and then try to replicate itself by automatically sending the worm with the attachment to people in the address book.

For several months, SirCam clogged the Internet, sending infected e-mail containing personal and business documents to strangers. Among the victims was the FBI's National Infrastructure Protection Center, where several private documents were sent to people outside the Bureau. The FBI maintained that no classified or sensitive documents were compromised.

Tactics: The Dalai Lama Virus

In September 2002, the manager of the Tibetan Computer Resource Center in Dharmsala, India accused the Chinese government of designing and deploying a virus designed to steal information. Other activist groups around the world were e-mailed the virus, which appeared to have originated from the Resource Center. According to the manager, the virus was designed to send data back to six e-mail addresses in China, including universities and government institutions. Supposedly, the perpetrators sent the virus-infected e-mail on two separate occasions.

The Chinese government denied involvement, saying that the government always opposes the activities of hackers. Copies of the virus haven't surfaced on the Internet to independently confirm whether the virus was espionage-enabled or not. From the description, it's possible that the virus could have been a generic SirCam-type virus; that wasn't specifically directed at organizations supporting the Dalai Lama. However, knowing the antipathy the Chinese have against the Free Tibet movement and the government's interest in information warfare techniques, a targeted attack virus could have been possible.

BADTRANS.B

In November 2001, another intelligence-gathering worm victimized Internet users. This worm was named Badtrans.B (a variant of Badtrans, which came out earlier in April), and people who opened the infected e-mail attachment were exposed to some heavy-duty spying. After the worm was executed, it replicated by sending copies of itself to e-mail addresses in Outlook's address book. It also installed a keylogger designed to steal e-mail, FTP, Telnet, and Web account passwords. In addition to the passwords, anything else the user was typing was recorded.

After Badtrans collected the purloined data, it would send it out to one of between 17 and 22 different e-mail addresses; all free Web e-mail-type accounts. One of the dummy addresses the data was sent to was s*#!_my_p$#*%@ijustgotfired.com. The account began getting e-mails from compromised computers the afternoon of November 24. The volume soon exceeded the mailbox quota, and the account was disabled. The next day, when the system administrator checked the logs to try to see why the server was so sluggish, he found that the account was receiving more than 100 e-mails per minute. Further examination revealed that Badtrans had sent confidential information to the account from more than 100,000 compromised computers during the first day alone.

MonkeyBrains.net, the ISP that hosted the ijustgotfired.com domain, soon figured out what was happening and started collecting the e-mail. Rudy Rucker, Jr., the company's owner, built a database with a Web page front end, in which you could look at the compromised data. News about the site soon spread, and Rucker disabled some of the "full-disclosure" data-viewing options.

The FBI also heard about Rucker and asked him for a copy of the several gigabytes of compromised data that MonkeyBrains had received; including more than 1.5 million account/password pairs, nearly 6 million keylogged sessions, and more than 300,000 e-mail addresses of people who had been infected. Without having a warrant, Rucker declined, concerned about the personal privacy of the hundreds of thousands of people who were already victimized.

The Badtrans.B worm is a classic example of the speed in which an e-mail attachment virus or worm can spread and its power when it was specifically designed to gather information. A distilled version of Rucker's database is still online at `http://badtrans.monkeybrains.net/` and makes interesting reading.

THE FUTURE

It goes without saying that as new Windows vulnerabilities are discovered, virus and worm writers will take advantage of them. Beyond this, there are two developing technologies that can provide even more opportunities for intelligence-gathering code attacks.

- ✓ **Mobile devices.** As of yet, virus writers haven't targeted mobile devices such as cell phones, but it's a matter of time before this happens. As PDA functionality is built into an increasing number of cell phones, the prospects for an espionage-enabled virus that could steal phonebooks, calendars, and other information becomes quite real.

- ✓ **"IP everywhere."** Although currently just crystal ball gazing, the prospects of having all sorts of IP-enabled products networked together in a home or business offers incredible espionage potential. Not only could information from each of the devices possibly be compromised, but also that a vulnerability in one device could put the entire network at risk. Considering that security measures in new technologies always seem to have some weaknesses, when ubiquitous computing and IP everywhere devices do start to become available, you should exercise some prudent caution.

Countermeasures

Although antivirus and anti-Trojan utilities and firewalls are an obvious first-line defense against intelligence-gathering viruses and worms, a sophisticated opponent will undoubtedly craft a custom piece of code designed to escape detection from commercial security products.

You can reduce the chances of falling victim to these types of attacks by having a strong security policy in place (especially when it comes to dealing with e-mail) and using utilities that track network connections, Registry entries, and file writes. (These policies and utilities are discussed in the "Countermeasures" sections of Chapters 8 and 9.)

Another way to minimize the risks of these attacks is to not keep sensitive information on computers with network connections that could provide a conduit for a hostile attack. To accomplish this, the military and intelligence agencies use a concept called "Red/Black." Red computers and networks are considered secure (they may have TEMPEST-shielding, encrypted VPNs, and other protective measures). Black computers and networks are deemed to be insecure, so information on them could potentially be exposed to a threat. The red and black systems are separated to avoid any classified information on the red systems from leaking over to the unsecure black systems.

You don't need to work at the Ft. Meade NSA headquarters to implement this type of security measure. A simple red/black system consists of a single black computer that's connected to a network (such as the Internet) and a red computer that isn't connected to any network. Any encrypted messages received on the unsecure black computer are manually transferred by disk, flash card, or USB pocket hard drive to the secure red computer.

The red computer is used for encrypting and decrypting e-mail messages and working with sensitive data (only data files, preferably in a format that doesn't support macro viruses, should be passed from the black computer to red computer). Using this computer eliminates any possible network threats from compromising information on the secure computer. Both computers should obviously be running a complement of antivirus, anti-Trojan, firewall, and other security software. (Although this approach certainly isn't as convenient as using a single computer, it can defeat most remote attacks in a high-threat environment.)

Surveillance Cameras

If you have physical access to a target, one way of compromising information (including passwords) is to use a surveillance camera. The FBI has used concealed video cameras in a number of its espionage investigations to monitor what a suspected spy was doing on his computer. Just select a hidden location (such as overhead in a drop ceiling), point the camera at the computer monitor and keyboard, and wait as the camera records what your target is up to.

You'll probably be using some type of device that incorporates a "camera on a chip," so let's briefly discuss the technology. Video and digital cameras use sensors that convert light into electrical charges. There are two types of sensors: charge coupled device (CCD) and complementary metal oxide semiconductor (CMOS).

- ✓ A CCD sensor is a collection of tiny diodes that convert photons (light) into electrons (electrical charges). There can be several hundred thousand diodes on a single chip.

Countermeasures: TSCM

Technical Surveillance Countermeasures (TSCM) is the art and science of detecting and defeating surveillance devices. Traditionally, this term has meant audio eavesdropping, but it now applies to just about any type of surveillance technology, including video. (Consider that audio bugs can also be used against computers. In Operation ENGULF during the 1950s and '60s, the British compromised encrypted French and Egyptian communications by detecting the noises made by setting the cipher machines used to encode messages. Attacks of this nature have been alleged to occur against dot matrix printers and keyboards.)

An excellent Web resource to access to learn more about surveillance countermeasure tools and techniques is the Granite Island Group's TSCM site at `www.tscm.com`. Hosted by James Atkinson, a respected TSCM professional, the site contains an amazing amount of detailed information about eavesdropping and countereavesdropping.

✓ CMOS sensors generally work the same way as their CCD cousins, but they are currently about ten times less sensitive and can't capture images at as high a resolution. Their primary advantages are that they cost less to manufacture and consume considerably less power.

Unlike audio bugs, which transmit a Radio Frequency (RF) signal and, depending on the device, may be easy to detect with a spectrum analyzer or specialized debugging gear, hidden wired video (sometimes called CCTV for Closed Circuit Television) surveillance equipment doesn't give off detectable RF signals. One way of detecting hidden cameras, without tearing a room apart, is to use a portable, handheld thermal imager. Both the camera and the power source register a visible heat signature on the imager's display screen, even if it's hidden behind or in some object. (All bets are off if you're the target of a government intelligence agency, which may use custom video surveillance equipment that can defeat standard detection methods.)

Webcams

Although WebCams (small cameras designed to broadcast live video over the Internet) really aren't an advanced spy technology, they definitely can be used for surveillance or countersurveillance. In Chapter 9, you learned how Trojan horse applications could hijack the output of a WebCam and send the video feed back to an eavesdropper. In Chapter 11, you saw that a spy with the right type of hardware could eavesdrop on wireless video cameras. If you're using a WebCam or a similar type of camera, always remember that it could be used against you.

In addition to remotely monitoring the video signal from an unsuspecting user's camera, you can also use a WebCam to conduct local surveillance. There are a number of software applications available that can turn your WebCam into a surveillance system that monitors your home or office. These applications use motion detection algorithms to capture images whenever someone

Tools of the Trade: Public Surveillance Cameras

Video surveillance cameras are appearing in increasing numbers on street poles and building exteriors across the United States. The video output is frequently used by law enforcement to respond to crimes before they are reported by citizens, serve as evidence, and to develop leads in criminal cases.

The surveillance cameras may either be unmonitored (such as at an ATM at a bank, where the video is stored on tape) or actively monitored by a person. Monitored cameras can be moved by remote control, so a security employee can change the camera angle or zoom in to focus on an individual or activity.

Surveillance cameras have become an integral part of the social fabric of England (the leading country when it comes to public video surveillance). Non-profit groups estimate that there are between 1.5 million and 2 million closed-circuit television cameras in Britain. The London-based watchdog group Privacy International estimates up to $9 billion in government money has been spent on surveillance over the past 15 years.

To give you an idea of the prevalence of these monitoring devices in the United States, The New York City Surveillance Camera Project has been identifying and recording the locations of surveillance cameras in public places around the Big Apple. So far, more than 2,300 surveillance cameras have been identified on the streets of New York, all catching unknowing pedestrians and motorists as they go by. (This number includes only outdoor cameras, and doesn't account for cameras installed in buildings.) You can get maps and more information about known video cameras in New York from the project's Web site at www.mediaeater.com/cameras/.

Although surveillance proponents say cameras help reduce and solve crime, privacy advocates aren't so sure and see the cameras as yet another step in the erosion of personal privacy. For more on the privacy implications of surveillance cameras in public places, see www.epic.org/privacy/surveillance/.

or something moves within the camera's view (the camera could be pointed inside a room or outside through a window). When the camera detects motion, the software can optionally notify you by e-mail, and you can even view the images in real time from a remote location over the Internet with some applications.

Several popular WebCam surveillance software products include the following:

✓ **Digi-watcher**, a $39 package with extensive logging functions, available at www.digi-watcher.com.

✓ **InetShepard** records both video and audio and can be controlled over a telephone; a single camera version is $35 and can be downloaded from http://inetshepherd.com.

For information about a number of other WebCam surveillance products, see www.webattack.com/shareware/webpublish/swwebcam.shtml.

Although the image quality of a WebCam certainly doesn't match the resolution of broadcast television, it may be sufficient for different types of espionage activities. However, if you need a stealthy hidden camera or one capable of outputting high-resolution images, you should consider a camera designed specifically for surveillance.

Commercial Surveillance Cameras

Although WebCams can be pressed into service for eavesdropping, it's often better to use a camera that's been manufactured primarily for surveillance purposes. These commercial products are often smaller than a WebCam (see Figure 13-2), have better image resolution, and can have enhanced features such as capturing images in the dark. Small surveillance cameras can be hidden in drop ceilings, clocks, thermostats, radios, sprinkler heads, speakers, or just about any place you can think of.

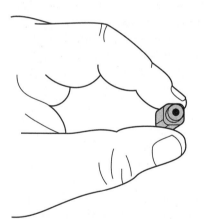

Figure 13-2: SuperCircuits miniature black-and-white video camera. At only .375 by .625 square inches, the camera can be concealed virtually anywhere and produces a standard NTSC video signal. Priced at $99, it's even affordable by spies on a tight budget.

Most of these cameras are designed to use an external battery power source and output a video signal to a VCR type-recording device. Small wireless cameras are also available that eliminate the need to wire a camera directly to a recorder.

A popular source of video surveillance for law enforcement agencies and the security industry is a company called SuperCircuits. The vendor provides cameras, recorders, and just about everything you need to conduct video surveillance. An online catalog is available at www.supercircuits.com.

Although various federal laws have restricted the sale and use of audio eavesdropping devices, there are currently few restrictions on the manufacture and sale of video surveillance gear. Sophisticated cameras and video recording devices are readily available to most anyone at fairly reasonable prices. (Keep in mind that there may be state privacy laws in effect that prohibit covertly video taping certain activities.)

Summary

Barring some cataclysmic event that fries the circuitry of all electronic devices, there will always be computer espionage going on around us. As we become increasingly dependent on computers and they mesh fully into our everyday lives, the potential for abuse by spies and eavesdroppers increases.

That's not to say you should start wearing foil on your head, use a voice scrambler for your telephone calls, and start shopping for surplus TEMPEST equipment on eBay. For the most part, unless you're the target of federal law enforcement, a government intelligence agency, or some other organization with a large bankroll, you shouldn't need to worry about some of these advanced espionage techniques.

Although well-funded entities (the NSA's budget is classified but estimated to be more than $13 billion per year) have the resources to be between 5 to 20 years ahead of the civilian world in some types of security technology and have all sorts of interesting toys we don't know about, economics dictates that these assets can't be used effectively against a large number of people on a daily basis. (Take ECHELON, for example: at the end of all of the intercepted communications, a human analyst is still needed to examine the intercept and see whether it's a piece of a larger puzzle.)

Also, consider that well-funded organizations chartered with surveillance and intelligence gathering are not the all-powerful, infallible machines that the media and entertainment industries like to portray them as. Just think about the government's inability to discover and prevent the September 11 terrorist attacks, the fact that as of yet no arrests have been made in the anthrax mailings that shortly followed, or the relatively limited successes (depending on your perspective) on the war against international terrorism despite a massive commitment of money and resources.

When thinking about whether advanced computer espionage might be levied against you, always apply common sense to your security measures (remember the differences between probable and possible threats), but never underestimate your opponent.

Appendix A

What's on the Web Site

YOU CAN FIND A WEB SITE WITH LINKS LEADING you to many of the tools and information sources discussed in this book at `www.wiley.com/compbooks/mcnamara`. This appendix provides you with information on the contents of that Web site. Specifically, this appendix covers the following:

- ✓ System Requirements
- ✓ Links on the Web Site
- ✓ Troubleshooting

System Requirements

Because this book focuses on elements of computer espionage that impact systems running Microsoft Windows, many of the tools referenced (surprisingly enough) run on Windows. (There are also a few good Linux utilities thrown in for the nonconformists and to hopefully spark a bit of curiosity for those of you who never have played with the operating system before.)

Because Microsoft has released a whole bunch of different versions of Windows over the years, there are tools listed in the book and on the Web site that might work only with Windows 3.x, 9x/ME, NT, or 2000/XP. The version of Windows that a tool is appropriate for is clearly stated in the associated chapter of the book. Please read about the tool first before you take the time to do something such as download a .PWL password tool and think you can crack SAM passwords on a Windows XP computer.

In terms of hardware requirements, it will completely depend on the operating system you're using. The general bare bones, minimum, ridiculously slow, and outdated requirements for many of these tools are as follows:

- ✓ Intel architecture PC with a Pentium (or similar) chip running at 120 MHz or faster
- ✓ At least 32MB of total RAM installed on your computer
- ✓ Modem with a speed of at least 28.8 Kbps or some type of a broadband connection
- ✓ Internet access

In general, the more memory you have and the faster your processor is (up to a point), the happier you'll be.

Links on the Web Site

The Web site is organized by chapter headings from this book. Under each heading, you'll find links to Web resources mentioned under that chapter's heading, along with a brief description of the resource.

There are a lot of Web resources referenced in this book, and instead of adding another dozen or so pages listing them all, read a chapter and then visit the Web site, or just go to the Web site and browse through some of the resources. The organization of the Web site and the descriptions should steer you in the right direction for what you're looking for.

Web sites come and go like spies in the night, so if a link appears to be dead, do some intelligence work of your own and hit up Google or your favorite search engine and see if you can find what you're looking for. There's a tremendous amount of duplicate content on the Net that is either mirrored or cached, and the odds are there is enough information on the Web site to help you put together a successful search query.

Troubleshooting

I doubt that you'll have too many problems with the Web site because it's written in plain vanilla HTML and doesn't require Flash or any other plug-ins. Internet Explorer, Opera, and Mozilla all display the Web site quite nicely.

However, if you have trouble with the Web site, please call the Wiley Customer Care phone number: 1-800-762-2974. Outside the United States, call 317-572-3994. You can also contact Wiley Customer Service by e-mail at techsupdum@wiley.com. Wiley Publishing, Inc. will provide technical support only for general quality-control items; for technical support on the tools themselves, consult the utility's vendor or developer. (And if a link doesn't work for some reason, reread the "Links on the Web Site" section in this appendix before you make a phone call.)

Index

A

Abi-Coder file-encryption utility, 126
Above the Law, David Burnham, 52
AccessData
  Distributed Network Attack (DNA), 148
  Forensic Toolkit (FTK), 119
  Password Recovery Toolkit, 148
ACT (Association for Competitive Technology), 10
Address Resolution Protocol (ARP) spoofing, 237
ADS (Alternate Data Stream), 106–108
Advanced Encryption Standard (AES), 148
Advanced NT Security Explorer, 86
Agee, Phillip, *Inside the Company: CIA Diary,* 177
AIBO robot dog, 267
AirDefense utility, 285
Air-Jack utility, 276
AirMagnet utility, 284
AiroPeek NX sniffer, 281
AirSnort utility, 283
Alert Standard Format (ASF) technology, 73
Alibris Internet bookseller, 42
Al-Qaeda, 87, 129, 211
Alternate Data Stream (ADS), 106–108
Altivore utility, 237
AMA (American Management Association), 6
Amazon, 42
Amecisco
  Hardware KeyLogger, 189–190
  Invisible KeyLogger Stealth (IKS), 187
American Civil Liberties Union, 35
American Library Association, 37
American Management Association (AMA), 6
American Megatrends, Inc. (AMI), 71
American Society for Industrial Security, 4, 14
anonymous remailers, 255–256
answering machines, 303–304

anti-Trojan software, 223–224
antivirus software, 223
Apple iPod, 171
ARP (Address Resolution Protocol) spoofing, 237
Arrington, Winston, *Now Hear This,* 295
ASF (Alert Standard Format) technology, 73
Association for Competitive Technology (ACT), 10
Automatic Vehicle Location (AVL), 310
Award BIOS passwords, 71

B

Back Orifice Trojan, 217
backdoor BIOS passwords, 70–72
Badtrans.B worm, 335
bag jobs. *See* black bag jobs
banners, 234
Baseline Security Advisor tool, 90
Basic Input/Output System. *See* BIOS
BestCrypt utility, 126
binders (Trojan horses), 213
Biometric Consortium, 159
biometrics, 157–160
BIOS (Basic Input/Output System)
  boot sequence, 69
  chassis intrusion detection option, 73
  CMOS, 73–75
  hard drive, 73
  laptops, 75–76
  manufacturer, 68
  passwords, 68–76, 90
  reference, 68
  security settings, 89–90
  version, 68
  vulnerabilities, 68–76
BIOS password crackers, 83–84

black bag jobs
  cleaning up, 62
  command team, 51
  computer espionage, 48
  countermeasures, 62–66
  court orders, 52
  defined, 47
  documenting the scene, 60–61
  gaining entry, 57–60
  gathering information, 61
  getting away, 62
  inside team, 51
  legality of, 47, 52–53
  network attacks, 48–49
  observation team, 51
  opportunistic, 50
  physical attacks, 48
  pickup team, 51
  planned, 49–50, 53–55
  six T's, 55–56
  surveillance team, 51
  trial runs, 54–55
  vulnerabilities, 55–56
  Watergate, 49
BlackBerry, 305, 307
BlackIce PC Protection, 247
Blowfish Advanced CS file-encryption utility, 125
BND (Bundesnachrichtendienst), 13
BO (Back Orifice) Trojan, 217
BOClean utility, 223
boot sequence, 69
breaking and entering, 59–60
Brown, Stephen Paul (eavesdropper), 18
browsers
  autocomplete, 112
  caches, 111
  cookies, 113
  CyberScrub, 131
  favorites list, 112
  history list, 112
  Index.dat files, 113
  malicious Web sites, 240–241
  proxy Web servers, 256–257
  security, 248
  Window Washer, 131
brute-force password attacks, 143–145
bugs
  keyboards, 199–200
  telephones, 295
BugTraq e-mail list, 80
Bundesnachrichtendienst (BND), 13
Burnham, David, *Above the Law,* 52
Business Engine (software company), 5
business intelligence, 4
business spies, 4–6
BWMACHAK utility, 264

C

Cain & Abel utility, 245
CALEA (Communications Assistance for Law Enforcement Act), 29
Cali Cartel, 15
Caligula virus, 333
Caller ID, 298
Carnivore/DCS-1000 program, 237, 325–327
cDc (Cult of the Dead Cow) hacking group, 217
CD-R/CD-RW, 166–167
cellular phone eavesdropping, 299–303
Center for Democracy and Technology, 35
Central Intelligence Agency (CIA), 12–13
CERT (Computer Emergency Response Team), 80
certification programs, 97
CF (CompactFlash), 169–170
CFAA (Computer Fraud and Abuse Act), 32–33, 37–38
chain of possession, 100
changing passwords, 156
Chevron, 7
Chirillo, John, *Hack Attacks Revealed,* 233
Chntpw (Change NT password) utility, 88
Church Commission, 12–13
CIA (Central Intelligence Agency), 12–13
CIA Commander utility, 87
Ciresi, Mike (politician), 239
civil court, 41–42

classified standards
    HIJACK, 319–320
    NONSTOP, 319–320
    TEMPEST, 313–319
ClearLogs utility, 88
Cmospwd utility, 74, 83–84
CodeBreakers group, 333–334
color codes (awareness and preparedness), 19
Communications Assistance for Law Enforcement Act
    (CALEA), 29
CompactFlash (CF), 169–170
Compaq iPAQ, 269
compartmentalized passwords, 155
competitive intelligence, 4
compression tools, 164
compressors (Trojan horses), 213
CompuSafe device, 202
computer case tamper seals, 201
computer cops
    certification, 97
    chain of possession, 100
    challenges, 98
    defined, 95
    demand for, 98
    evidence characteristics, 120
    forensic duplication, 100–101
    forensic examination, 101–117
    jobs, 95, 97
    law enforcement investigations, 7–9
    seizure of computers and related equipment,
        98–100
    skills, 96–97
    training, 97
Computer Emergency Response Team (CERT), 80
computer forensic examiners
    challenges, 98
    defined, 95
    demand for, 98
    jobs, 95
    skills, 96
computer forensics, 8, 11
Computer Fraud and Abuse Act (CFAA), 32–33, 37–38

consultants, 9, 11
consumer electronics, 307–311
Content Scrambling System (CSS), 136–137
Convera RetrievalWare, 237
CoolMiner, 325
Cooper, Colonel Jeff (color code developer), 19
copying data
    available resources, 164
    CD-R/CD-RW, 166–167
    compression tools, 164
    digital cameras, 175
    DVDs, 168–169
    floppy disks, 166
    guidelines, 163–165
    hard drive, 171–173
    memory storage devices, 169–170
    Microdrives, 174
    tape backup systems, 174
    transfer rate, 164–165
    transferring over a network, 174–175
    USB hard drive, 173
    Zip disks, 169
cordless phone eavesdropping, 300
corporate spies, 4–6
Corporate Systems Portable Pro Drive, 172
Counterfeit Access Device and Computer Fraud and
    Abuse Act, 32–33, 37–38
countermeasures
    BIOS vulnerabilities, 89–90
    black bag jobs, 62–66
    DCS-1000/Carnivore program, 326–327
    defined, 20
    eavesdropping, 246–257
    ECHELON data surveillance system, 322–323
    emanation monitoring, 318
    keyloggers, 191–196
    network attacks, 246–257
    password vulnerabilities, 93
    Trojan horses, 221–224
    viruses, 336
    Windows operating system vulnerabilities, 89–93
    worms, 336

crackers, 14
Creative Labs
    Cardcam digital camera, 175
    Nomad Jukebox Zen, 171
criminal court, 41–42
criminal spies, 14–15
Crucial ADS utility, 108
Crucial Security, 108
cryptanalysis, 145–146
Cryptcat utility, 175
cryptography
    defined, 122
    history of, 122–123
    resources, 122
cryptome.org Web site, 16
cryptosystem cracking, 152–153
CSDiamond RegistryProt, 222
CSS (Content Scrambling System), 136–137
Cult of the Dead Cow (cDc) hacking group, 217
custom keyloggers, 190–191
CyberScrub utility, 131
Cypherpunk Type I anonymous remailer, 256

D

data copying
    available resources, 164
    CD-R/CD-RW, 166–167
    compression tools, 164
    digital cameras, 175
    DVDs, 168–169
    floppy disks, 166
    guidelines, 163–165
    hard drive, 171–173
    memory storage devices, 169–170
    Microdrives, 174
    tape backup systems, 174
    transfer rate, 164–165
    transferring over a network, 174–175
    USB hard drive, 173
    Zip disks, 169
data dumper (dd) utility, 118
Data Encryption Standard (DES), 122, 144

Data Interception by Remote Transmission (D.I.R.T.),
    328
data recovery businesses, 116
data recovery tools, 121
DCFL (Department of Defense Computer Forensics
    Laboratory), 116
DCS-1000/Carnivore program, 237, 325–327
DeCSS, 137
default passwords, 240
Déjà Vu recognition system, 160–161
Deloitte & Touche (accounting firm), 11
Department of Defense Computer Forensics Laboratory
    (DCFL), 116
Department of Defense Information Systems Agency
    (DISA), 267
Department of Justice
    *Electronic Crime Scene Investigation: A Guide for
    First Responders* manual, 97
    views on Title III and computer investigations, 27
DES (Data Encryption Standard), 122, 144
DESCHALL project, 144
detecting
    keyloggers, 180, 191–202
    Trojan horses, 212–213, 221–224
Deutch, John (former CIA director), 231
Dialpwd utility, 152
Dial-Up Networking (DUN), 152
DIBS USA, 101
dictionary attacks, 142–143
digital cameras, 175, 309, 336–340
Digital Intelligence, 101
Digi-watcher WebCam surveillance software, 338
D.I.R.T. (Data Interception by Remote Transmission),
    328
DISA (Department of Defense Information Systems
    Agency), 267
disk editor, 120–121
Distributed Network Attack (DNA), 148
Dow Chemical, 7
DragNet utility, 237
DragonWare Suite, 325
DriveCrypt utility, 126

DriveSavers Data Recovery, 116
droppers (Trojan horses), 213
Dshield utility, 250
Dsniff utility, 245
DTMF (Dual Tone Multi-Frequency) decoder, 298
DUN (Dial-Up Networking), 152
DVDs, 168–169

E

EasyRecovery Professional utility, 121
eavesdropping
    answering machines, 303–304
    broadband risks, 230–232
    cellular phones, 299–303
    compromised information, 229–230
    cordless phones, 300
    countermeasures, 246–257
    default passwords, 240
    ECHELON data surveillance system, 3, 320–323,
        325
    electromagnetic eavesdropping, 313–318
    fax machines, 289–291
    GPS units, 309–310
    keyloggers, 177
    LED status indicators, 319
    log files, 238–239
    malicious applications, 240
    malicious Web sites, 240–241
    MP3 players, 311
    NetBIOS, 235–236, 254–255
    operating system identification, 234–235
    origin points, 228–229
    pagers, 305–307
    PDAs, 307–309
    ping scan, 233
    port scan, 234
    public access computers, 241, 254
    reflected light (computer monitors), 319
    server logs, 238
    sniffers, 236–237
    target location, 233–234
    telephones, 294–298

TiVo, 311
traffic analysis, 230
typewriters, 177
U.S. government's partnerships with technology
    companies, 331
video game consoles, 310–311
voice-mail systems, 303–305
vulnerability scanning, 235
Windows file sharing, 235–236, 254–255
wireless networks, 268–272, 276–279
eavesdropping tools
    Ethereal, 244–245
    Kismet, 280–281
    Legion, 244
    Nessus, 243–244
    NetBIOS Auditing Tool (NAT), 244
    NetStumbler, 279–280
    Nmap, 242–243
    SamSpade, 242
    SuperScan, 243
eBlaster keylogger program, 18
ECHELON data surveillance system, 3, 320–323, 325
economic espionage, 4–6, 13–14
Economic Espionage Act (EEA), 34
ECPA (Electronic Communications Privacy Act),
    29–32, 42
EES (Evil Eye Software), 218
EFS (Encrypting File System), 87, 93, 127
802.11b wireless networks. *See* wireless networks
ElcomSoft, 149
electromagnetic eavesdropping, 313–318
Electronic Communications Privacy Act (ECPA),
    29–32, 42
*Electronic Crime Scene Investigation: A Guide for First
    Responders,* Department of Justice, 97
Electronic Frontier Foundation, 35
Electronic Privacy Information Center, 35
elicitation, 58
e-mail
    anonymous remailers, 255
    clients, 114

continued

e-mail *continued*
    copying data, 174
    encryption, 124–125, 253
    forensic examination, 113–114
    passwords, 114
    Stealth Email Redirector (SER), 240
    vulnerabilities, 114
    Web e-mail, 255
emanation monitoring, 314–318
employee monitoring
    Electronic Communications Privacy Act, 42
    e-mail signatures, 43
    express consent, 43
    implied consent, 43
    National Labor Relations Act, 43
    public employees, 42–43
    statistics, 6
    typical monitoring programs, 6–7
    union employees, 43
EnCase utility, 118–119
Encrypting File System (EFS), 87, 93, 127
encryption
    Abi-Coder file-encryption utility, 126
    Advanced Encryption Standard (AES), 148
    Blowfish Advanced CS file-encryption utility, 125
    cellular phones, 301
    cryptanalysis, 145–146
    Data Encryption Standard (DES), 122, 144
    defined, 122
    EFS (Encrypting File System), 127
    e-mail, 124–125, 253
    Encrypting File System (EFS), 93
    fax machines, 291
    files, 125–126
    GnuPG (Gnu Privacy Guard), 124–125
    guidelines for using, 123
    instant messaging (IM), 253
    Microsoft products, 150–151
    on-the-fly (OTF) encryption, 126
    PDAs, 308–309
    Pretty Good Privacy (PGP), 31, 124
    steganography, 127–130
    strong encryption, 153
    weak encryption, 136–137
    wiretaps, 31
ERD Commander, 87
Ethereal utility, 244–245
Ettercap utility, 245
evidence characteristics, 120
Evil Eye Software (EES), 218
eye scanners, 159–160

F

Fake AP utility, 285
FakeGINA, 86
fax machines, 289–291
FBI
    DCS-1000/Carnivore program, 237, 325–327
    investigations, 9, 40
    Key Logger System (KLS), 182–183
    Magic Lantern project, 190, 327–329
    Regional Computer Forensics Laboratory (RCFL), 96
    reporting cyber-crime, 40
    Special Operations Groups (SOG), 52
    Surreptitious Entry Program, 52
    Technically Trained Agents (TTA), 52
FBI Secrets: An Agent's Exposé, Wes Swearingen, 51
federal laws
    Communications Assistance for Law Enforcement Act, 29
    Counterfeit Access Device and Computer Fraud and Abuse Act, 32–33, 37–38
    Economic Espionage Act, 34
    Electronic Communications Privacy Act, 29–32, 42
    enforcement, 39–41
    Foreign Intelligence Surveillance Act, 27–28, 36–38
    limitations, 45
    National Labor Relations Act, 43
    Stored Communications Act, 30, 32, 36
    Title III Wiretap Act, 26–27, 36, 44
    USA Patriot Act, 8, 35–39, 53
File Monitor utility, 195–196
File Viewer utility, 120
file wipers, 130–131

file-integrity checkers
    keyloggers, 196–197
    Trojan horses, 222
files
    Alternate Data Stream (ADS), 106–108
    changed extensions, 105
    Clipboard, 111
    clusters, 108
    deleted files, 105–106
    encryption, 125–126
    hidden files, 104
    INFO file, 107
    MAC times, 103
    Most Recently Used (MRU) file list, 110
    page file, 108–109
    print spooler files, 106
    Recycle Bin, 107
    Registry, 110–111
    Scan Disk temporary files, 106–107
    shortcuts, 103
    slack space, 108
    swap file, 108–109
    temporary files, 104
    unallocated space, 108
    Windows file sharing, 235–236, 254–255
Filler, Russell (NASA contractor), 252
fingerprint scanners, 158–159
firewalls
    application filtering, 247
    gateway firewalls, 249
    hardware firewalls, 249
    log files, 249
    packet filtering, 247
    personal firewalls, 196–197, 221–222, 248–250
    processing log data, 250
    software firewalls, 248–249
    stateful packet inspection (SPI), 248
    testing, 248
    vendors, 250
    vulnerabilities, 248
FIREWAR utility, 248
flash drives, 169–170

FlashGo! Card reader and writer, 170
floppy disks, 116, 131, 166
Foreign Intelligence Surveillance Act (FISA), 27–28,
    36–38
Foreign Intelligence Surveillance Court (FISC), 28
Foreign Intelligence Surveillance Court of Appeals, 28
forensic duplication, 100–101, 171–173
forensic duplication tools, 117–118
forensic examination (of computers)
    automated evidence-gathering and analysis
        software, 102, 118–119
    e-mail, 113
    files, 103–111
    floppy disks, 116
    hard drives, 115–116
    instant messaging (IM), 114–115
    manual examination, 102
    memory, 117
    primary tasks, 101
    Web browser evidence, 111–113
    Windows Registry, 109–111
Forensic Toolkit (FTK), 119
Forensics Computers, 101

G

gateway firewalls, 249
General Motors, 5
GFI LANguard System Integrity Monitor utility, 222
Ghost, 117
GINA (Graphical Identification and Authorization), 86
Glide utility, 150–151
Global Positioning System (GPS) units, 275, 309–310
GnuPG (Gnu Privacy Guard), 124–125
God keylogger, 197
government intelligence agencies, 11–14
GPS units, 275, 309–310
Grams, Rob (politician), 239
Graphical Identification and Authorization (GINA), 86
guessing passwords, 73, 78–79, 141
Gunhus, Christine (political campaign staffer), 239

H

Hack Attacks Revealed, John Chirillo, 233

Hanssen, Robert (former FBI agent and spy), 58, 167

hard drive
file wipers, 130–131
forensic duplication, 117–118, 171–173
forensic examination, 115–116
passwords, 75
unallocated space, 108
USB hard drive, 173

hardware firewalls, 248

Hardware KeyLogger, 189–190

hardware keyloggers, 183–186, 188–190

Hawaiian Airlines, 33

hex editor, 105, 120–121

hidden files, 104

High Technology Crime Investigative Association (HTCIA), 97

HIJACK, 319–320

honeypots, 285

Hotfix Checker utility, 90

Hotmail, 255

HTML Application (HTA), 215

HushMail, 255

I

IACIS (International Association of Computer Investigative Specialists), 97

IDS (intrusion detection system), 246–247, 285

IEEE 1394, 168

IETF Site Security Task Force, 66

IGI (Investigative Group International), 10

IIP utility, 253

IKS (Invisible KeyLogger Stealth), 187

ILook utility, 119

IM (instant messaging), 114–115, 253

Imation FlashGo! Card reader and writer, 170

Independent Institute, 10

industrial espionage, 4–6

InetShepard WebCam surveillance software, 338

Inside the CIA — Revealing the Secrets of the World's Most Powerful Spy Agency, Ronald Kessler, 13

Inside the Company: CIA Diary, Phillip Agee, 177

instant messaging (IM), 114–115, 253

intelligence agencies, 11–14

Intelligent Computer Solutions Image Masster Solo-2, 173

Interface Security, 189

Interloc, Inc., 42

International Association of Computer Investigative Specialists (IACIS), 97

Internet Assigned Numbers Authority, 234

Internet Engineering Task Force (IETF) Site Security Task Force, 66

Internet Explorer, 241

intrusion detection system (IDS), 246–247, 285

Investigative Group International (IGI), 10

Investigator keylogger, 188

Invisible KeyLogger Stealth (IKS), 187

Inzider utility, 251

iOpus Password Recovery XP, 152

"IP everywhere," 335

iPAQ (Compaq), 269

iPod (Apple), 171

J

Jasc Quick View Plus, 121

John the Ripper utility, 89

K

Kaspersky Anti-Virus (KAV), 223

Kessler, Ronald, *Inside the CIA — Revealing the Secrets of the World's Most Powerful Spy Agency,* 13

Key Logger System (KLS), 182–183

KeyDisk utility, 76

KeyGhost utility, 189

KeyKatcher utility, 189

keylogger detectors
PestPatrol, 198
Spybot Search & Destroy, 199

SpyCop, 180, 198
    using, 197
    Who's Watching Me, 198
keyloggers
    bugged keyboards, 199–200
    cost, 186
    countermeasures, 191–196
    custom keyloggers, 190–191
    defined, 177
    deploying, 178
    detecting, 180, 191–196, 199–202
    disinformation campaigns, 192
    eBlaster, 18
    error messages, 201
    features, 181
    file-integrity checkers, 196–197
    God, 197
    Hardware KeyLogger, 189–190
    hardware keyloggers, 183–186, 188–190
    hiding, 180
    Investigator, 188
    Invisible KeyLogger Stealth (IKS), 187
    KeyGhost, 189
    KeyKatcher, 189
    Key Logger System (KLS), 182–183
    Linux, 200–201
    Magic Lantern project, 190
    monitoring file writes, 195–196
    passwords, 200
    personal firewalls, 196
    Registry monitors, 196–197
    removing, 202
    reviews of, 187
    sniffers, 199
    software keyloggers, 179–181, 183, 187–188
    Spector Professional Edition, 187
    string search, 196
    Title III Wiretap Act violations, 44
    VB runtime files, 196
    Web cams, 181
    WinWhatWhere Investigator, 188

Kismet utility, 280–281
Kiwi Syslog Daemon, 249
KLS (Key Logger System), 182–183
Konop, Robert (Hawaii Airlines pilot), 33
Kopp, James (anti-abortion activist), 115
Kroll, Inc., 116

L

LANfiltrator Trojan, 218
laptops
    BIOS passwords, 75–76
    theft, 76
    war driving, 269
L.A.S. Systems, 310
last number redial (telephones), 298
laws
    Communications Assistance for Law Enforcement Act, 29
    Counterfeit Access Device and Computer Fraud and Abuse Act, 32–33, 37–38
    Economic Espionage Act, 34
    Electronic Communications Privacy Act, 29–32, 42
    enforcement, 39–41
    Foreign Intelligence Surveillance Act, 27–28, 36–38
    limitations, 45
    National Labor Relations Act, 43
    state laws, 34–35, 39
    Stored Communications Act, 30, 32, 36
    Title III Wiretap Act, 26–27, 36, 44
    USA Patriot Act, 8, 35–39, 53
LC utility, 84–85
LED status indicators, 319
Legion utility, 244
listening to network connections, 251
Locks, Safes, and Security, Marc Tobias, 59
locksmithing, 59
log cleaners, 88
log files
    firewalls, 248
    network attacks, 238–239
Logicube SF-5000 hard drive duplicator, 172

Logon.scr file, 89
Lopez, Jose Ignacio (business spy), 5
Lotus Notes, 331
L0phtCrack utility, 84–85

M

MAC spoofing, 264
MAC times, 103
Magic Lantern project, 190, 327–329
malicious applications, 240
malicious Web sites, 240–241
Manley, Martin (president of Alibris), 42
MapPoint, 283
Mares, Dan (computer forensics expert), 117
Marker virus, 334
memory storage devices, 169–170
MemoryStick, 169
MICE (Money, Ideology, Compromise, and Ego), 57
Microdrives, 174
Microsoft
    accusations about use of trapdoors in operating
        systems, 331
    Baseline Security Advisor, 90
    encryption schemes, 150–151
    Hotfix Checker utility, 90
    Hotmail, 255
    MapPoint, 283
    security bulletins, 80, 90
    vulnerabilities in software, 224
minimization, 28, 38
Minox subminiature digital camera, 175
Mischel Internet Security, 223
Mixmaster Type II anonymous remailer, 256
mobile devices, 335
modified executables, 329–330, 332
Money, Ideology, Compromise, and Ego (MICE), 57
monitoring network connections, 251
Montes, Ana Belen (Defense Intelligence Agency
        employee), 131
MP3 players, 171, 311
MSinfo32 utility, 194–195

Mueller, Robert (FBI Director), 40
Multimedia Memory Card (MMC), 169
MyNetWatchman utility, 250

N

NAT (NetBIOS Auditing Tool), 244
National Center for Education Statistics, 66
National Conference of State Legislatures, 35
National Consortium for Justice Information and
        Statistics, 187
National Counterintelligence Executive, 65
National Industrial Security Program Operating
        Manual (NISPOM), 66
National Infrastructure Protection Center (NIPC), 80
National Labor Relations Act (NLRA), 43
National Security Agency (NSA), 12–13, 92
National Security Agency Security Manual, 66
National Security Institute, 35
National White Collar Crime Center (NWCC), 97
Naughton, Patrick (sexual predator), 328
Nessus utility, 243–244
NetBIOS, 235–236, 254–255
NetBIOS attack utilities, 244
NetBIOS Auditing Tool (NAT), 244
NetBus Trojan, 213, 217
NetCat utility, 175
Net-Devil Trojan, 219
NetIntercept utility, 237
netstat command, 251
NetStumbler utility, 268, 279–280
Network Associates, 190, 237, 281
network attacks
    active, 228
    black bag jobs, 48–49
    broadband risks, 230–232
    compromised information, 229–230
    countermeasures, 246–257
    default passwords, 240
    log files, 238–239
    malicious applications, 240
    malicious Web sites, 240–241
    NetBIOS, 235–236, 254–255

operating system identification, 234–235

origin points, 228–229

passive, 227

ping scan, 233

port scan, 234

public access computers, 241, 254

random, 228

server logs, 238

sniffers, 236–237

target location, 233–234

targeted, 228

traffic analysis, 230

vulnerability scanning, 235

Windows file sharing, 235–236, 254–255

network connections, 251

network monitors. *See* packet sniffers

New Technologies Inc. (NTI), 97

New York City Surveillance Camera Project, 338

Nicholson, Harold (CIA agent), 48

Niku Corporation (software company), 5

NIPC (National Infrastructure Protection Center), 80

NISPOM (National Industrial Security Program Operating Manual), 66

NLRA (National Labor Relations Act), 43

Nmap utility, 242–243

Nomad Jukebox Zen, 171

NONSTOP, 319–320

Nortek Computers, Ltd., 77

Norton Ghost, 117

Norton Utilities, 121

Now Hear This, Arrington, Winston, 295

NSA (National Security Agency), 12–13, 92

NSSpyglass utility, 285

NTBugTraq e-mail list, 80

NTFSDOS utility, 88

NTI (New Technologies Inc.), 97

NWCCC (National White Collar Crime Center), 97

O

office equipment

fax machines, 289–291

shredders, 292–294

Omnibus Crime Control and Safe Streets Act, 26–27

OnlyMe utility, 309

on-the-fly (OTF) encryption, 126

Ontrack Data International, 116

OnTrack EasyRecovery Professional, 121

operating system

modified operating system components, 329–330, 332

passwords, 75–79, 81–82

version, 68

Operation CHAOS, 12

Optical TEMPEST, 319

Optix Trojan, 218

Oracle, 10

organized crime, 14–15

ORiNOCO Gold card, 272

OTF (on-the-fly) encryption, 126

P

packet sniffers

AiroPeek NX, 281

Altivore, 237

Cain & Abel, 245

DragNet, 237

Dsniff, 245

eavesdropping, 236–237

Ethereal, 244–245

Ettercap, 245

keyloggers, 199

NetIntercept, 237

RetrievalWare, 237

running on your own network, 251

SilentRunner, 237

Sniffer Wireless, 281

threats, 282

Trojan horses, 222

wireless sniffers, 281–282

Packeteer, 325

Packetstorm Security Web site, 149

page file, 108–109

pagers, 305–307

Passware Kit, 149–150

password crackers
  Advanced NT Security Explorer, 86
  application passwords, 146–147
  BIOS, 83–84
  Chntpw (Change NT password), 88
  CIA Commander, 87
  ClearLogs, 88
  Dialpwd, 152
  Distributed Network Attack (DNA), 148
  ElcomSoft, 149
  ERD Commander, 87
  FakeGINA, 86
  Glide, 150–151
  iOpus Password Recovery XP, 152
  John the Ripper, 89
  L0phtCrack, 84–85
  NTFSDOS, 88
  Passware Kit, 149–150
  Password Recovery Toolkit, 148
  PasswordSpy, 151–152
  PhoneBook Viewer v1.01c, 152
  Pwdump, 86–87
  PWLHack, 151
  PWLTool, 151
  PWLView, 151
  Ratware Win9x Screen Saver Buster, 84
  resources, 149
  Revelation, 151–152
  Scrsavpw, 84
  Snitch, 151–152
  WinZapper, 88
  WS_FTP, 151
Password Crackers, Inc., 76
password manager applications, 156
password policies, 154
Password Recovery Toolkit, 148
passwords
  alternatives to, 157–158, 160
  BIOS, 68–76, 90
  brute-force attacks, 143–145
  changing, 156
  compartmentalized passwords, 155
  default passwords, 240
  Dial-Up Networking (DUN), 152
  dictionary attacks, 142–143
  e-mail, 114
  guessing, 73, 78–79, 141
  hard drive, 75
  instant messaging (IM) accounts, 115
  keeping a list of, 156
  keyloggers, 177, 200
  LAN Manager password hashes, 93
  length of, 93
  logon dialog box, 77
  randomly generated, 154–155
  recovering, 73
  screensavers, 77–78
  selecting, 93, 138–139
  shoulder surfing, 151, 241
  social engineering, 155
  strong passwords, 154
  supervisor, 69
  user, 69
  weak passwords, 137–140
  Windows operating system, 76–79, 81–82, 93
PasswordSpy, 151–152
PC Magazine, 187
pcAnywhere, 220
PDA Defense utility, 309
PDAs, 307–309
pen registers, 27, 37
personal digital assistants (PDAs), 307–309
personal firewalls
  benefits of using, 249–250
  keyloggers, 196
  Trojan horses, 221–222
  vulnerabilities, 197
PestPatrol keylogger-detector, 198
PGP (Pretty Good Privacy) utility, 31, 124, 253
PGPfone utility, 297
Phoenix Technologies BIOS passwords, 72
PhoneBook Viewer v1.01c, 152
physical attacks (black bag jobs), 48
physical security, 63–64

ping scan, 233
PI (Private Idaho) utility, 256
Pocket PCs, 269–270
Pockey DataStor, 173
port scan, 234
port scan services, 248
port scanners, 252
Pretty Good Privacy (PGP) utility, 31, 124, 253
PricewaterhouseCoopers, 4
Private Idaho (PI) utility, 256
private investigators, 9–11
privilege escalation attacks, 82–83
Process Explorer utility, 193–194
Project RAHAB, 13
protocol analyzers. See packet sniffers
proxy Web servers, 256–257
Ptech, Inc., 211
public access computers, 241, 254
Pwdump, 86–87
PWL cracking tools, 151
PWLHack utility, 151
PWLTool utility, 151
PWLView utility, 151

Q
Quick View Plus utility, 121

R
RAHAB, 13
Ramsey Electronics, 295
randomly generated passwords, 154–155
Ratware Win9x Screen Saver Buster, 84
Raytheon SilentRunner, 237
RCFL (Regional Computer Forensics Laboratory), 96
recovering
    data from a hard drive, 116
    deleted files, 105–106
    passwords, 73
Recycle Bin, 107
reflected light (computer monitors), 319
Regan, Brian Patrick (spy), 324

RegEdit utility, 110–111
Regional Computer Forensics Laboratory (RCFL), 96
Registry, 109–111
Registry monitors
    keyloggers, 196–197
    Trojan horses, 222
RegistryProt utility, 222
remote access
    Trojan horses, 209
    wireless networks, 266
removing
    keyloggers, 202
    Trojan horses, 224
RetrievalWare utility, 237
Revelation utility, 151–152
reverse-engineering, 330
RIM BlackBerry, 305, 307

S
Safe Technology Co. Ltd., 202
SafeBack forensic duplication tool, 117
SAM (Security Accounts Manager), 81–82
SamSpade utility, 242
Sandstorm Enterprises NetIntercept, 237
Scarfo, Nicodermo, Jr. (mobster), 182–183
SCP (Secure Copy), 254
screensaver passwords, 77–78
script-kiddies, 14
Scrsavpw utility, 84
Secure Copy (SCP), 254
Secure Digital memory card, 169
secure protocols, 254
Secure Shell (SSH), 254
secure telephones, 295–297
Securepoint Intrusion Detection, 247
security
    access point (AP), 287–288
    Web browsers, 249
    wireless networks, 266, 284–288
Security Accounts Manager (SAM), 81–82
security policies, 64–66

security settings
    BIOS, 89–90
    Windows operating system, 89–92
Sentry 2020 utility, 309
September 11 terrorist attacks, 35
SER (Stealth Email Redirector), 240
server logs, 238
shortcuts, 103
shoulder surfing, 241
shredders, 292–294
SilentRunner utility, 237
SiPix StyleCam Snap digital camera, 175
SirCam worm, 334
Site Security Handbook (RFC2196), IETF Site Security
    Task Force, 66
slack space, 108
smart cards, 160
SmartMedia, 169
Sniffer Wireless, 281
sniffers
    AiroPeek NX, 281
    Altivore, 237
    Cain & Abel, 245
    DragNet, 237
    Dsniff, 245
    eavesdropping, 236–237
    Ethereal, 244–245
    Ettercap, 245
    keyloggers, 199
    NetIntercept, 237
    RetrievalWare, 237
    running on your own network, 251
    SilentRunner, 237
    Sniffer Wireless, 281
    threats, 282
    Trojan horses, 222
    wireless sniffers, 281–282
Snitch utility, 151–152
Snort intrusion detection utility, 247
social engineering, 58, 155
Society of Competitive Intelligence Professionals
    Web site, 4

software firewalls, 249
software keyloggers, 179–181, 183, 187–188
Sony AIBO robot dog, 267
SpamMimic Web site, 128
Speak Freely utility, 297
Spector Professional Edition keylogger, 187
speed dial (telephones), 298
spies
    amateurs, 1
    bosses, 6–7
    business spies, 4–6
    consultants, 9, 11
    crackers, 14
    criminal spies, 14–15
    family and friends, 16–18
    government intelligence agencies, 11–14
    motivations, 2–3
    police, 7–9
    private investigators, 9–11
    professionals, 1
    protections against, 18–19
    risk analysis, 20–23
    spooks, 11–14
    whistleblowers, 15–16
spoofing
    Address Resolution Protocol (ARP) spoofing, 237
    MAC spoofing, 264
spooks, 11–14
Spybot Search & Destroy keylogger-detector, 198
SpyCop keylogger-detector, 180, 198
SpyShield utility, 253
SSH (Secure Shell), 254
stalking, 310
Starium, Inc. (retailer of secure telephones), 297
state laws, 34–35, 39
statistics
    employee monitoring, 6
    laptop thefts, 76
    wiretaps, 31
Stealth Email Redirector (SER), 240
steganography, 127–130

Steganos
    fonts, 318
    Security Suite, 126
Stegdetect utility, 130
S-Tools utility, 130
Stored Communications Act, 30, 32, 36
strong encryption, 153
strong passwords, 154
STU-IIIs (secure telephones), 295–297
StumbVerter utility, 283
Stunnel utility, 251
Sub7 Trojan, 217
Suchyta, Nicholas J. (eavesdropper), 17
SuperCircuits miniature video camera, 339–340
SuperScan utility, 243
supervisor password, 69
SurfSecret Privacy Protector, 133
Surreptitious Entry Program (FBI), 52
surveillance cameras, 336–340
surveillance devices
    ECHELON, 3, 320–323, 325
    pen registers, 27, 37
    trap-and-trace devices, 27, 37
    WebCams, 337–339
swap file, 108–109
Swearingen, Wes, *FBI Secrets: An Agent's Exposé,* 51
Symantec
    Norton Utilities, 121
    pcAnywhere, 220
symbol recognition, 160–161
Synergy International Systems, 211
Sysinternals
    FileMon, 195–196
    Process Explorer, 193–194
    TCPView, 251
    TDImon, 251
system requirements for utilities, 341

T

tamper seals, 201
tape backup systems, 174
Task Manager, 193

Tauscan utility, 223–224
TCP/IP fingerprinting, 235
TCPView utility, 251
TDImon utility, 251
TDS (Trojan Defense Suite), 223
TealLock utility, 309
technical consultants, 9, 11
technical support (for the Web site), 342
Technical Surveillance Countermeasures (TSCM), 337
telephone eavesdropping, 294–298
TEMPEST, 313–314, 316–319
testing
    firewalls, 248
    Trojan horses, 216–217
theft of laptops, 76
TightVNC, 220
Title III Wiretap Act, 26–27, 36, 44
TiVo, 311
Tobias, Marc, *Locks, Safes, and Security,* 59
traffic analysis, 230
trap-and-trace devices, 27, 37
traveling abroad, information-protection tips, 65
Treason 101 Web site, 57
Trillian utility, 253
TriWest Healthcare Alliance Corp., 165
Trojan Defense Suite (TDS), 223
Trojan horses
    anti-Trojan software, 223–224
    antivirus software, 223
    Back Orifice, 217
    binders, 213
    client, 209
    compressors, 213
    countermeasures, 221–224
    culture of developers and users, 219
    defined, 205–206
    deploying, 216–217
    detecting, 212–213, 221–224
    droppers, 213
    features, 208
    file-integrity checkers, 222

continued

Trojan horses *continued*
  how they work, 206, 208–210
  HTAs, 215
  installing, 214–216
  LANfiltrator, 218
  local system access, 208
  NetBus, 213, 217
  Net-Devil, 219
  Optix, 218
  pcAnywhere, 220
  personal firewalls, 221–222
  ports, 210, 220
  Registry monitors, 222
  remote access, 209
  removing, 224
  self-replication, 209
  server, 209
  server editor, 210
  sniffers, 222
  source code, 207
  Sub7, 217
  testing, 216–217
  vandalism, 208
  VNC (Virtual Network Computing), 220
  Web cams, 208
Trojan Hunter utility, 223
TrojanForge Web site, 219
TSCM (Technical Surveillance Countermeasures), 337
tunneling, 250
typewriter eavesdropping, 177

U

Ultimate Packager for Executables (UPX), 213
unallocated space (hard drive), 108
Universal Serial Bus (USB), 168
Unshredder application, 294
U.S. Chamber of Commerce, 4
USA Patriot Act (USAPA)
  analysis, 36
  Computer Fraud and Abuse Act, 37–38
  concerns about, 53
  Foreign Intelligence Surveillance Act, 36–38

  impact on state laws, 39
  implications, 8, 35–36
  provisions, 39
  Stored Communications Act, 36
  Title III Wiretap Act, 36
USA Today, 129
USB Flash Drive, 170
USB (Universal Serial Bus), 168
user password, 69
utilities
  Abi-Coder, 126
  Advanced NT Security Explorer, 86
  AirDefense, 285
  Air-Jack, 276
  AirMagnet, 284
  AiroPeek NX, 281
  AirSnort, 283
  Altivore, 237
  anonymous remailers, 255–256
  Baseline Security Advisor, 90
  BestCrypt, 126
  BlackIce PC Protection, 247
  Blowfish Advanced CS, 125
  BOClean, 223
  BWMACHAK, 264
  Cain & Abel, 245
  Chntpw (Change NT password), 88
  CIA Commander, 87
  ClearLogs, 88
  Cmospwd, 74, 83–84
  Crucial ADS, 108
  Cryptcat, 175
  CyberScrub, 131
  dd (data dumper), 118
  Dialpwd, 152
  disk editor, 120–121
  Distributed Network Attack (DNA), 148
  DragNet, 237
  DragonWare Suite, 325
  DriveCrypt, 126
  Dshield, 250
  Dsniff, 245

EasyRecovery Professional, 121
ElcomSoft, 149
EnCase, 118–119
ERD Commander, 87
Ethereal, 244–245
Ettercap, 245
Fake AP, 285
FakeGINA, 86
File Monitor, 195–196
File Viewer, 120
FIREWAR, 248
Forensic Toolkit (FTK), 119
GFI LANguard System Integrity Monitor, 222
Glide, 150–151
hex editor, 105, 120–121
Hotfix Checker, 90
IIP, 253
ILook utility, 119
intrusion detection system (IDS), 246–247
Inzider, 251
iOpus Password Recovery XP, 151–152
John the Ripper, 89
KeyDisk, 76
Kismet, 280–281
Kiwi Syslog Daemon, 249
Legion, 244
log cleaners, 88
L0phtCrack, 84–85
MapPoint, 283
MSinfo32, 194–195
MyNetWatchman, 250
Nessus, 243–244
NetCat, 175
NetIntercept, 237
NetStumbler, 267–268, 279–280
Nmap, 242–243
Norton Ghost, 117
Norton Utilities, 121
NSSpyglass, 285
NTFSDOS, 88
OnlyMe, 309
Passware Kit, 149–150

Password Recovery Toolkit, 148
PasswordSpy, 151–152
PDA Defense, 309
PestPatrol keylogger-detector, 198
PGPfone, 297
PhoneBook Viewer v1.01c, 152
Pretty Good Privacy (PGP), 31, 124, 253
Private Idaho (PI), 256
Process Explorer, 193–194
Pwdump, 86–87
PWLHack, 151
PWLTool, 151
PWLView, 151
Quick View Plus, 121
Ratware Win9x Screen Saver Buster, 84
RegEdit, 110–111
RegistryProt, 222
RetrievalWare, 237
Revelation, 151–152
SafeBack, 117
SamSpade, 242
Scrsavpw, 84
Securepoint Intrusion Detection, 247
Sentry 2020, 309
SilentRunner, 237
Sniffer Wireless, 281
Snitch, 151–152
Snort, 247
Speak Freely, 297
Spybot Search & Destroy keylogger-detector, 199
SpyCop keylogger-detector, 180, 198
SpyShield, 253
Stealth Email Redirector (SER), 240
Steganos Security Suite, 126
Stegdetect, 130
S-Tools, 130
StumbVerter, 283
Stunnel, 251
SuperScan, 243
SurfSecret Privacy Protector, 131
system requirements, 341

continued

utilities *continued*
    Tauscan, 223–224
    TCPView, 251
    TDImon, 251
    TealLock, 309
    Trillian, 253
    Trojan Defense Suite (TDS), 223
    Trojan Hunter, 223
    WallWatcher, 249
    wbStego4, 130
    Who's Watching Me keylogger-detector, 198
    Window Washer, 131
    WinHex, 120–121
    WinZapper, 88
    WS_FTP, 151

V

van Eck, Wim (engineer), 315
vandalism, 208
video cameras, 336–340
video game consoles, 310–311
Vidstrom, Arne (computer programmer), 86
Virtual Network Computing (VNC), 220
virtual private network (VPN), 250–251, 287–288
viruses
    Caligula, 333
    countermeasures, 336
    defined, 333
    intelligence gathering, 332–334
    Marker, 334
Voice over Internet Protocol (VoIP), 297
voice scanners, 159
voice-mail systems, 303–305
VoIP (Voice over Internet Protocol), 297
Volkswagen, 5
VPN Labs Web site, 251
VPN (virtual private network), 250–51, 287–288
vulnerabilities
    BIOS, 68–77
    black bag jobs, 55–56
    defined, 20
    eavesdropping, 235

    e-mail, 114
    fingerprint scanners, 159
    firewalls, 248–250
    Internet Explorer, 241
    Microsoft software, 224
    personal firewalls, 197
    Windows operating system, 68, 77–83
    wireless networks, 260–266

W

Wakefield Integrated Technologies, 294
The Wall Street Journal, 87
WallWatcher utility, 249
Wang Research Laboratories, 316
war chalking, 270
war driving, 266–269, 276–279
Watergate, 49
wbStego4 utility, 130
weak encryption, 136–137
weak passwords, 137–140
Web browsers
    autocomplete, 112
    caches, 111
    cookies, 113
    CyberScrub, 131
    favorites list, 112
    history list, 112
    Index.dat files, 113
    malicious Web sites, 240–241
    proxy Web servers, 256–257
    security, 249
    Window Washer, 131
Web e-mail, 255
Web proxies, 256–257
Web sites
    companion Web site for this book, 341–342
    Crucial Security, 108
    cryptome.org, 16
    National Conference of State Legislatures, 35
    National Security Institute, 35
    Nortek Computers, Ltd., 77

Packetstorm Security, 149
Password Crackers, Inc., 76
Society of Competitive Intelligence Professionals, 4
SpamMimic, 128
Treason 101, 57
TrojanForge, 219
VPN Labs, 251
Webcams
    keyloggers, 181
    surveillance, 337–339
    Trojan horses, 208
Whack-A-Mole game, 213
whistleblowers, 15–16
Who's Watching Me keylogger-detector, 198
Wiley Customer Care, 342
Window Washer utility, 131
Windows file sharing, 235–236, 254–255
Windows operating system
    automatic updates, 90
    Encrypting File System (EFS), 87, 93, 127
    Graphical Identification and Authorization
        (GINA), 86
    Logon.scr file, 89
    page file, 108–109
    passwords, 75–79, 81–82, 93
    privilege escalation attacks, 82–83
    Recycle Bin, 107
    Registry, 109–111
    Security Accounts Manager (SAM), 81–82
    security settings, 89–92
    slack space, 108
    swap file, 108–109
    versions, 68
    vulnerabilities, 68, 77–83
    wireless networks, 283
WinHex utility, 120–121
WinPcap, 244
WinWhatWhere Investigator keylogger, 188
WinZapper utility, 88
Wireless Information Security Experiment (WISE), 285

wireless networks
    access point (AP), 260, 275–276
    antennas, 271–274, 284
    base station, 260
    default configurations, 265–266
    denial of service attacks, 265
    eavesdropping, 268–272, 276–279
    GPS units, 275
    history, 259–260
    honeypots, 285
    intrusion detection system (IDS), 285
    laptops, 269
    Media Access Controller (MAC) access lists,
        263–264, 286
    networking cards, 269, 271–272
    ORiNOCO Gold card, 272
    Pocket PCs, 269
    popularity of, 259
    radio waves, 265
    remote access, 266
    security, 266, 284–288
    SSIDs (service set identifiers), 261–262, 286–287
    virtual private network (VPN), 287–288
    vulnerabilities, 260–266
    war chalking, 270
    war driving, 266–269, 276–279
    Windows operating system, 283
    Wired Equivalent Privacy (WEP), 262–263, 286
wireless sniffers, 281–282
Wiretap Act, 26–27, 36, 44
wiretaps
    Communications Assistance for Law Enforcement
        Act, 29
    encryption, 31
    family and domestic matters, 43–44
    statistics, 31
    telephones, 295
WISE (Wireless Information Security Experiment), 285
WLANs (wireless local area networks). See wireless
    networks

worms
    Badtrans.B, 335
    countermeasures, **336**
    defined, 333
    intelligence gathering, **332–335**
    SirCam, 334
WS_FTP utility, 151

X
X-10 wireless camera, **267**
Xerox
    copy machine cameras, **291**
    employee monitoring, 7

Y
YahooMail, 255
Young, John (whistleblower), 16

Z
Zip disks, 169